Teach Yourself®
Microsoft®
Access 2000

Teach Yourself®
Microsoft®
Access 2000

Charles Siegel

IDG Books Worldwide, Inc.
An International Data Group Company

Foster City, CA • Chicago, IL • Indianapolis, IN • New York, NY

Teach Yourself® Microsoft® Access 2000

Published by
IDG Books Worldwide, Inc.
An International Data Group Company
919 E. Hillsdale Blvd., Suite 400
Foster City, CA 94404
www.idgbooks.com (IDG Books Worldwide Web site)

ISBN: 0-7645-3282-0

Printed in the United States of America

10 9 8 7 6 5 4 3 2 1

1P/TQ/QU/ZZ/IN

Distributed in the United States by IDG Books Worldwide, Inc.

Distributed by CDG Books Canada Inc. for Canada; by Transworld Publishers Limited in the United Kingdom; by IDG Norge Books for Norway; by IDG Sweden Books for Sweden; by IDG Books Australia Publishing Corporation Pty. Ltd. for Australia and New Zealand; by TransQuest Publishers Pte Ltd. for Singapore, Malaysia, Thailand, Indonesia, and Hong Kong; by Gotop Information Inc. for Taiwan; by ICG Muse, Inc. for Japan; by Norma Comunicaciones S.A. for Colombia; by Intersoft for South Africa; by Le Monde en Tique for France; by International Thomson Publishing for Germany, Austria and Switzerland; by Distribuidora Cuspide for Argentina; by Livraria Cultura for Brazil; by Ediciones ZETA S.C.R. Ltda. for Peru; by WS Computer Publishing Corporation, Inc., for the Philippines; by Contemporanea de Ediciones for Venezuela; by Express Computer Distributors for the Caribbean and West Indies; by Micronesia Media Distributor, Inc. for Micronesia; by Grupo Editorial Norma S.A. for Guatemala; by Chips Computadoras S.A. de C.V. for Mexico; by Editorial Norma de Panama S.A. for Panama; by American Bookshops for Finland. Authorized Sales Agent: Anthony Rudkin Associates for the Middle East and North Africa.

For general information on IDG Books Worldwide's books in the U.S., please call our Consumer Customer Service department at 800-762-2974. For reseller information, including discounts and premium sales, please call our Reseller Customer Service department at 800-434-3422.

For information on where to purchase IDG Books Worldwide's books outside the U.S., please contact our International Sales department at 317-596-5530 or fax 317-596-5692.

For consumer information on foreign language translations, please contact our Customer Service department at 800-434-3422, fax 317-596-5692, or e-mail rights@idgbooks.com.

For information on licensing foreign or domestic rights, please phone +1-650-655-3109.

For sales inquiries and special prices for bulk quantities, please contact our Sales department at 650-655-3200 or write to the address above.

For information on using IDG Books Worldwide's books in the classroom or for ordering examination copies, please contact our Educational Sales department at 800-434-2086 or fax 317-596-5499.

For press review copies, author interviews, or other publicity information, please contact our Public Relations department at 650-655-3000 or fax 650-655-3299.

For authorization to photocopy items for corporate, personal, or educational use, please contact Copyright Clearance Center, 222 Rosewood Drive, Danvers, MA 01923, or fax 978-750-4470.

Library of Congress Cataloging-in-Publication Data
Siegel, Charles.
   Teach Yourself Micrososft Access 2000 / Charles Siegel.
      p.   cm.
   ISBN 0-7645-3228-0 (alk. paper)
   1. Microsoft Access.   2. Database management.   I. Title.
QA76.9.D3S56355   1999
005.75 ' 65--dc21   99–10961
                                                                CIP

ABOUT IDG BOOKS WORLDWIDE

Welcome to the world of IDG Books Worldwide.

IDG Books Worldwide, Inc., is a subsidiary of International Data Group, the world's largest publisher of computer-related information and the leading global provider of information services on information technology. IDG was founded more than 30 years ago by Patrick J. McGovern and now employs more than 9,000 people worldwide. IDG publishes more than 290 computer publications in over 75 countries. More than 90 million people read one or more IDG publications each month.

Launched in 1990, IDG Books Worldwide is today the #1 publisher of best-selling computer books in the United States. We are proud to have received eight awards from the Computer Press Association in recognition of editorial excellence and three from Computer Currents' First Annual Readers' Choice Awards. Our best-selling *...For Dummies®* series has more than 50 million copies in print with translations in 31 languages. IDG Books Worldwide, through a joint venture with IDG's Hi-Tech Beijing, became the first U.S. publisher to publish a computer book in the People's Republic of China. In record time, IDG Books Worldwide has become the first choice for millions of readers around the world who want to learn how to better manage their businesses.

Our mission is simple: Every one of our books is designed to bring extra value and skill-building instructions to the reader. Our books are written by experts who understand and care about our readers. The knowledge base of our editorial staff comes from years of experience in publishing, education, and journalism — experience we use to produce books to carry us into the new millennium. In short, we care about books, so we attract the best people. We devote special attention to details such as audience, interior design, use of icons, and illustrations. And because we use an efficient process of authoring, editing, and desktop publishing our books electronically, we can spend more time ensuring superior content and less time on the technicalities of making books.

You can count on our commitment to deliver high-quality books at competitive prices on topics you want to read about. At IDG Books Worldwide, we continue in the IDG tradition of delivering quality for more than 30 years. You'll find no better book on a subject than one from IDG Books Worldwide.

John Kilcullen
Chairman and CEO
IDG Books Worldwide, Inc.

Steven Berkowitz
President and Publisher
IDG Books Worldwide, Inc.

*Eighth Annual
Computer Press
Awards ≥1992*

*Ninth Annual
Computer Press
Awards ≥1993*

*Tenth Annual
Computer Press
Awards ≥ 1994*

*Eleventh Annual
Computer Press
Awards ≥1995*

IDG is the world's leading IT media, research and exposition company. Founded in 1964, IDG had 1997 revenues of $2.05 billion and has more than 9,000 employees worldwide. IDG offers the widest range of media options that reach IT buyers in 75 countries representing 95% of worldwide IT spending. IDG's diverse product and services portfolio spans six key areas including print publishing, online publishing, expositions and conferences, market research, education and training, and global marketing services. More than 90 million people read one or more of IDG's 290 magazines and newspapers, including IDG's leading global brands — Computerworld, PC World, Network World, Macworld and the Channel World family of publications. IDG Books Worldwide is one of the fastest-growing computer book publishers in the world, with more than 700 titles in 36 languages. The "...For Dummies®" series alone has more than 50 million copies in print. IDG offers online users the largest network of technology-specific Web sites around the world through IDG.net (http://www.idg.net), which comprises more than 225 targeted Web sites in 55 countries worldwide. International Data Corporation (IDC) is the world's largest provider of information technology data, analysis and consulting, with research centers in over 41 countries and more than 400 research analysts worldwide. IDG World Expo is a leading producer of more than 168 globally branded conferences and expositions in 35 countries including E3 (Electronic Entertainment Expo), Macworld Expo, ComNet, Windows World Expo, ICE (Internet Commerce Expo), Agenda, DEMO, and Spotlight. IDG's training subsidiary, ExecuTrain, is the world's largest computer training company, with more than 230 locations worldwide and 785 training courses. IDG Marketing Services helps industry-leading IT companies build international brand recognition by developing global integrated marketing programs via IDG's print, online and exposition products worldwide. Further information about the company can be found at www.idg.com. 1/24/99

Credits

Acquisitions Editor
Debra Williams Cauley

Development Editors
Grace Wong
Philip Wescott

Technical Editor
Eileen Steele

Copy Editor
Tim Borek

Book Designers
Daniel Ziegler Design, Cátálin Dulfu,
Kurt Krames

Production
Indianapolis Production Department

Proofreading and Indexing
York Production Services

About the Author

Charles Siegel is a computer consultant and writer who specializes in training business users and in writing custom database applications. In addition to authoring books on FoxPro and Paradox, Charles has authored several successful titles for MIS:Press, including *Teach Yourself Access for Windows 95, Teach Yourself dBase IV for Windows, Practical Approach 3.0 for Windows,* and *Teach Yourself C.*

To my son, Beni

Welcome to
Teach Yourself

Welcome to Teach Yourself, a series read and trusted by millions for nearly a decade. Although you may have seen the Teach Yourself name on other books, ours is the original. In addition, no Teach Yourself series has ever delivered more on the promise of its name than this series. That's because IDG Books Worldwide recently transformed Teach Yourself into a new cutting-edge format that gives you all the information you need to learn quickly and easily.

Readers told us that they want to learn by doing and that they want to learn as much as they can in as short a time as possible. We listened to you and believe that our new task-by-task format and suite of learning tools deliver the book you need to successfully teach yourself any technology topic. Features such as our Personal Workbook, which lets you practice and reinforce the skills you've just learned, help ensure that you get full value out of the time you invest in your learning. Handy cross-references to related topics and online sites broaden your knowledge and give you control over the kind of information you want, when you want it.

More Answers . . .

In designing the latest incarnation of this series, we started with the premise that people like you, who are beginning to intermediate computer users, want to take control of their own learning. To do this, you need the proper tools to find answers to questions so you can solve problems now.

In designing a series of books that provide such tools, we created a unique and concise visual format. The added bonus: Teach Yourself books actually pack more information into their pages than other books written on the same subjects. Skill for skill, you typically get much more information in a Teach Yourself book. In fact, Teach Yourself books, on average, cover twice the skills covered by other computer books — as many as 125 skills per book — so they're more likely to address your specific needs.

WELCOME TO TEACH YOURSELF

...In Less Time

We know you don't want to spend twice the time to get all this great information, so we provide lots of timesaving features:

- ▶ A modular task-by-task organization of information: Any task you want to perform is easy to find and includes simple-to-follow steps.
- ▶ A larger size than standard makes the book easy to read and convenient to use at a computer workstation. The large format also enables us to include many more illustrations — 500 screen illustrations show you how to get everything done!
- ▶ A Personal Workbook at the end of each chapter reinforces learning with extra practice, real-world applications for your learning, and questions and answers to test your knowledge.
- ▶ Cross-references appearing at the bottom of each task page refer you to related information, providing a path through the book for learning particular aspects of the software thoroughly.
- ▶ A Find It Online feature offers valuable ideas on where to go on the Internet to get more information or to download useful files.

- ▶ Take Note sidebars provide added-value information from our expert authors for more in-depth learning.
- ▶ An attractive, consistent organization of information helps you quickly find and learn the skills you need.

These Teach Yourself features are designed to help you learn the essential skills about a technology in the least amount of time, with the most benefit. We've placed these features consistently throughout the book, so you quickly learn where to go to find just the information you need — whether you work through the book from cover to cover or use it later to solve a new problem.

You will find a Teach Yourself book on almost any technology subject — from the Internet to Windows to Microsoft Office. Take control of your learning today, with IDG Books Worldwide's Teach Yourself series.

Teach Yourself
More Answers in Less Time

Search through the task headings to find the topic you want right away. To learn a new skill, search the contents, chapter opener, or the extensive index to find what you need. Then find — at a glance — the clear task heading that matches it.

Go to this area if you want special tips, cautions, and notes that provide added insight into the current task.

Learn the concepts behind the task at hand and, more important, learn why the task is relevant in the real world. Timesaving suggestions and advice show you how to make the most of each skill.

After you learn the task at hand, you may have more questions, or you may want to read about other tasks related to that topic. Use the cross-references to find different tasks to make your learning more efficient.

Working with Records

As you enter and edit data, Access helps you along by displaying the following visual aids in the record selector box to the left of the fields (shown in the upper-left and upper-right figures):

▶ **Asterisk.** The asterisk marks the blank record Access automatically adds; it will not be saved when you close the table.
▶ **Arrowhead.** An arrowhead, displayed to the left of the record, indicates the current record (the one you have moved to).
▶ **Pencil.** A pencil replaces the arrowhead to indicate that changes have been made in the current record, but have not yet been saved. Moving to a new record automatically saves the changes made to the previous record.

Selecting a Record

You can select a record by clicking its record selector box. When you select a record, all its fields are highlighted, as shown in the lower-left figure.

You can select groups of records in the following ways:

▶ Click the record selector box of one field, hold down the mouse button, and drag up or down across the boxes of adjacent records to select all these records.
▶ Select a record, and hold down the Shift key while you click the record selector box of another record to select it and all the records between them.

You can also select records by choosing Edit ⇨ Select Record to select the current record.

Deleting a Record

To delete a record, first select it or move the cursor to it, and click the Delete Record button, or press the Delete key, as shown in the lower-right figure. If you have selected multiple records, you can delete them all in the same way.

Access displays a dialog box telling you the number of records deleted and lets you confirm or cancel your change.

TAKE NOTE

▶ **CANCELING AN ENTRY**
When you make a new entry or edit an existing record, the pencil displays to the left of the record. As long as the pencil is displayed, you can cancel all changes in the current field by pressing Esc. You can cancel all the changes you made in the record by pressing Esc again.

▶ **SAVING AN ENTRY**
Changes you make to a record are automatically saved when you move the highlight to another record, so there is usually no need to save your data. However, you may want to save a record while you are still working on it — for example, if you have to leave the computer to look something up before finishing the entry. To save the current record while you are still working on it, press Shift+Enter. After you do this, you cannot cancel the entry by pressing Esc.

44

CROSS-REFERENCE
For information on how to move to a record based on its contents, see the section "Finding Records" later in this chapter.

SHORTCUT
To select all the records in a table, choose Edit ⇨ Select All Records.

Use the Find It Online element to locate Internet resources that provide more background, take you on interesting side trips, and offer additional tools for mastering and using the skills you need. (Occasionally you'll find a handy shortcut here.)

The current chapter name and number always appear in the top right-hand corner of every task spread, so you always know exactly where you are in the book.

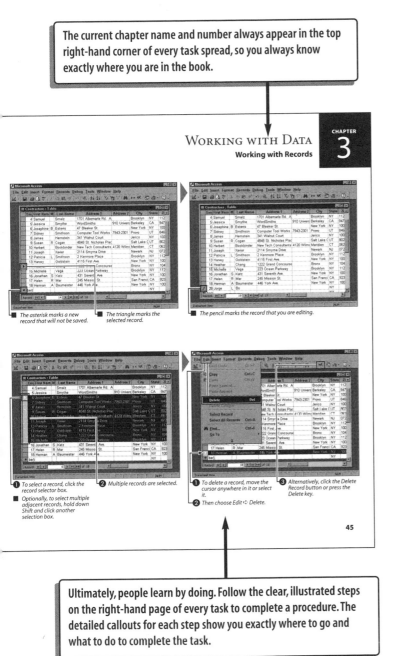

WORKING WITH DATA
Working with Records

CHAPTER
3

■ *The asterisk marks a new record that will not be saved.*　■ *The triangle marks the selected record.*

■ *The pencil marks the record that you are editing.*

❶ *To select a record, click the record selector box.*

■ *Optionally, to select multiple adjacent records, hold down Shift and click another selection box.*

❷ *Multiple records are selected.*

❶ *To delete a record, move the cursor anywhere in it or select it.*

❷ *Then choose Edit ➪ Delete.*

❸ *Alternatively, click the Delete Record button or press the Delete key.*

45

Who This Book Is For

This book is written for you, a beginning to intermediate PC user who isn't afraid to take charge of his or her own learning experience. You don't want a lot of technical jargon; you *do* want to learn as much about PC technology as you can in a limited amount of time. You need a book that is straightforward, easy to follow, and logically organized, so you can find answers to your questions easily. And, you appreciate simple-to-use tools such as handy cross-references and visual step-by-step procedures that help you make the most of your learning. We have created the unique Teach Yourself format specifically to meet your needs.

Ultimately, people learn by doing. Follow the clear, illustrated steps on the right-hand page of every task to complete a procedure. The detailed callouts for each step show you exactly where to go and what to do to complete the task.

Personal Workbook

It's a well-known fact that much of what we learn is lost soon after we learn it if we don't reinforce our newly acquired skills with practice and repetition. That's why each Teach Yourself chapter ends with your own Personal Workbook. Here's where you can get extra practice, test your knowledge, and discover ideas for using what you've learned in the real world. There's even a Visual Quiz to help you remember your way around the topic's software environment.

Feedback

Please let us know what you think about this book, and whether you have any suggestions for improvements. You can send questions and comments to the Teach Yourself editors on the IDG Books Worldwide Web site at **www.idgbooks.com**.

Personal Workbook

Q&A

❶ What are two ways to enter data in a Yes/No field?

_____

_____

_____

❷ What data can you enter in a Hyperlink field?

_____

_____

_____

❸ How do you edit a Hyperlink field?

_____

_____

_____

❹ How do you save your data entries? How often should you do this?

_____

_____

_____

❺ What is the fastest way to enter a record that is almost identical to an existing record?

_____

_____

_____

❻ How do you move a column to make it the first column displayed in the datasheet?

_____

_____

_____

❼ What is the fastest way to sort records alphabetically by Last Name?

_____

_____

_____

❽ What should you do if you want to print a table, but it is a bit too wide to fit on a standard page?

_____

_____

_____

ANSWERS: PAGE 344

64

After working through the tasks in each chapter, you can test your progress and reinforce your learning by answering the questions in the Q&A section. Then check your answers in the Personal Workbook Answers appendix at the back of the book.

Another practical way to reinforce your skills is to do additional exercises on the same skills you just learned without the benefit of the chapter's visual steps. If you struggle with any of these exercises, it's a good idea to refer to the chapter's tasks to be sure you've mastered them.

WORKING WITH DATA
Personal Workbook

CHAPTER **3**

Read the list of Real-World Applications to get ideas on how you can use the skills you've just learned in your everyday life. Understanding a process can be simple; knowing how to use that process to make you more productive is the key to successful learning.

EXTRA PRACTICE

❶ Enter sample data in the mailing list table you created in Chapter 2.

❷ Create a table to list your favorite Web sites, and add Hyperlink fields to link to these sites.

❸ Hide all the fields in the Mailing List table except First and Last Name, City, and State.

❹ Sort the Mailing List table by Last Name.

❺ Make the display font 12-point Times New Roman, and make the rows tall enough to hold the new font.

❻ Display the table in the Print Preview window and print it.

REAL-WORLD APPLICATIONS

✔ Before calling a client, you display your Client table and use a find to look up the client's name.

✔ Before telephoning a list of clients, you hide all the fields except the Name and Telephone Number fields, to make it easier to see the phone numbers without scrolling.

✔ One of the telephone area codes where you do business has been split into two area codes. You do a find and replace with the old area code as the Find value and the new one as the Replace value. Before replacing, you look at the city for each record to see if it is in a location with a new area code.

Visual Quiz

The figure shows a Mailing List table with the data display altered. What steps are necessary to display the data in this way?

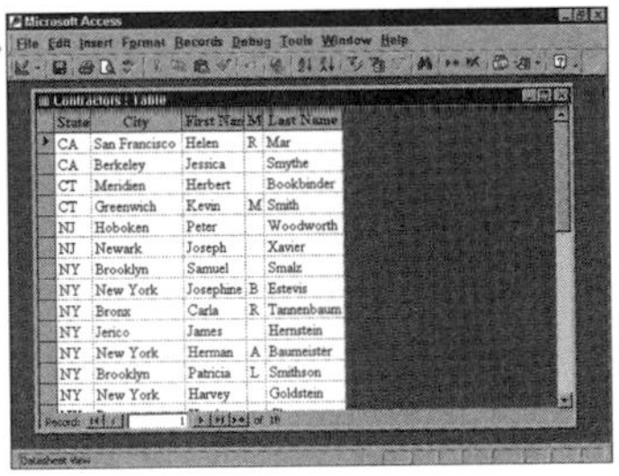

_____

_____

_____

_____

_____

65

Take the Visual Quiz to see how well you're learning your way around the technology. Learning about computers is often as much about how to find a button or menu as it is about memorizing definitions. Our Visual Quiz helps you find your way.

Acknowledgments

Thanks to all the people at IDG Books Worldwide who helped with this book, particularly to my editors, Debra Williams Cauley, Grace Wong, Chip Wescott, and Tim Borek, and the technical reviewer, Eileen Steele.

Contents

CONTENTS

CONTENTS

Teach Yourself®
Microsoft®
Access 2000

Contents of 'Desktop'

Name

My Computer

Network Neigh

Internet Explore

Microsoft Outloo

Recycle Bin

My Briefcase

3252-9

3259-6

3261-8

3262-6

3281-2

3286-3

DE Phone List

Device Manager

In

Iomega Tools

Access the Easy Way

Access is such a rich and powerful application that most people do not know where to begin when they start using it.

Access makes it easy for users — even beginners — to work with databases. You can create tables, edit data, and use queries to find the data you want with very little effort, and Access includes wizards that can do the work of designing data-entry forms, reports, and mailing labels for you.

Access also makes it easy for developers to create applications. It includes an entire programming language, Visual Basic for Applications, and its interface is so powerful that developers can create many custom applications without programming.

The book is unique because Part I, Access the Easy Way, introduces the features of Access that you need to work with your own data in the simplest way possible. It teaches how to create databases and tables, to add and edit data, to find the data you want, and to use wizards to produce your forms and reports. Most books on Access make you wade through long discussions of power features to learn about the simple features that you need to do your work. Part I of this book gives you just the basics. After you have finished it, you can go on to learn power features of Access from the rest of the book, or you can begin immediately to do practical work.

CHAPTER 1

Getting Started

A *database* is a system of organizing related pieces of information. Let's say that you want to keep records of all your customers' purchases. In Access, tables hold all the data, including customer name, address, phone number, and invoices. Each customer is a *record*, or separate row, in the table. The categories (Name, Address, Phone Number, and so on) are called *fields*, and they appear in separate columns. In Access, you can only have one entry in each field, so if your customer has two phone numbers, you need two fields (like Phone1 and Phone2). If you have a loyal customer who has made many purchases, instead of creating a dozen Invoice fields, you can simply create a separate invoice table and link it to the first table.

In a comparable paper-based filing system, you might have a separate file for each customer. If you want a list of all your customers' names and phone numbers, you would have to pull up each file and compile the information. If you need to see the March invoices of a group of customers, it might take several hours to piece those together. And if someone removes or misplaces one of the files, you are out of luck!

Access is a database tool that replaces the manual filing system. Although you still have to organize your information by creating tables, Access does the rest of the hard work, not you. If you only want to see some of the database information (just names and phone numbers), you can easily view just those fields. If you want to find the customers who have not placed an order in six months, Access can quickly sort the records according to your criteria. You can link separate tables and display data from them all; thus, keeping records up to date is only a matter of making the change in one table so it can be automatically applied to the other linked tables.

This chapter provides a quick overview of a database. Linked tables are used to create relational databases, and we will take a quick look at them in this chapter. Everything mentioned here is covered thoroughly in later chapters. For now, just look at the illustrations in this chapter to get a general idea of how Access databases work.

Using a Database

The primary function of Access is to store information in databases. However, Access makes it easy for you to manage or use the data by providing several types of *objects*, each of which let you work with your data in a different way.

You will use four main objects in Access. It is helpful to get an overview of each object's capabilities and limitations.

▶ *Tables* hold data. Each row of the table is a *record*. Each column is a *field*. In order to store data effectively, you may need to break it up into several tables (see Chapters 2 and 3).

▶ *Queries* create tables that are subsets of an underlying table and let you control what data is displayed. For example, you can create a query using only certain fields (such as names and phone numbers), only certain records (such as customers who have not ordered in the last six months), or a combination of fields and records (last names beginning with *D*). Queries can also be used to sort your data according to designated fields (see Chapters 4 and 11).

▶ *Forms* let you control how the data is displayed onscreen. You can have different form designs, but most people use forms to enter information vertically, rather than horizontally (as you do in a table) (see Chapters 6, 8, and 9).

▶ *Reports* let you control how the data is printed. Reports allow you to organize data according to groups and subgroups (for example, all customers grouped by region and then by state within each region). Reports can be any size or shape and include formats such as mailing labels, business cards, and Rolodex cards (see Chapters 6 and 10).

You are less likely to use three other objects when you are an intermediate or advanced user:

▶ *Data access pages* let you control how the data is displayed on the World Wide Web (see Chapter 15).
▶ *Macros* save you time by automating repetitive tasks (see Chapter 12).
▶ *Modules* hold programs, and they are not covered in this book.

Keeping track of tables, queries, reports, and forms may seem difficult, but fortunately, Access groups these objects by type in the Database window (see lower-left figure), which is displayed whenever you open a database (see upper figures). To work with an object, you must first select its type in the Database window's left panel.

TAKE NOTE

▶ MANAGING OBJECTS

To rename an object, select it and then choose File ⇨ Rename or click it a second time to turn the filename into editable text. Then simply type over the existing name to change it. To delete an object, select it and click the Delete button or press the Delete key

CROSS-REFERENCE

For information on using groups in the Database window, and on utilities that you use to manage objects in the Database, see Chapter 17.

SHORTCUT

You may find it easier to open a database and start Access by double-clicking the filename in Windows Explorer.

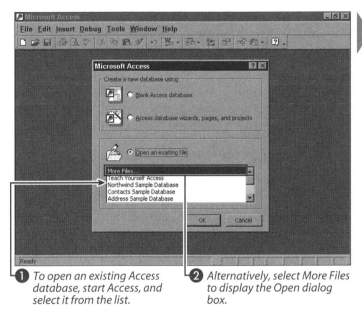

❶ To open an existing Access database, start Access, and select it from the list.

❷ Alternatively, select More Files to display the Open dialog box.

❸ If necessary, click the Up One Level tool to display the level above the current folder.

❹ Double-click the file you want to open, or select it and click Open.

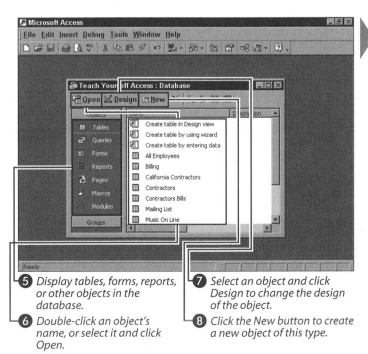

❺ Display tables, forms, reports, or other objects in the database.

❻ Double-click an object's name, or select it and click Open.

❼ Select an object and click Design to change the design of the object.

❽ Click the New button to create a new object of this type.

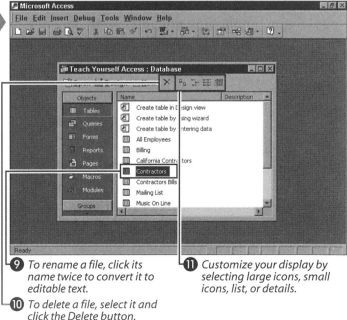

❾ To rename a file, click its name twice to convert it to editable text.

❿ To delete a file, select it and click the Delete button.

⓫ Customize your display by selecting large icons, small icons, list, or details.

Viewing Database Objects

Access provides a couple of different ways to display your records: Datasheet view and Form view. You can also use Design view to change the design of any object. Datasheet view lets you look at multiple records in a table layout. Form view lets you look at one record at a time in a rolodex-like layout. Design view lets you lay out the design of any object. To view the results, you must use either Datasheet view or Form view, where you can enter and edit data, but you cannot make any changes to the format or design. In contrast, Design view allows you to make changes to the format or design, but you cannot view the results. However, you can easily switch, or toggle, between the views by using the View button.

Tables

The upper-left figure shows a table in Datasheet view. You can see that an Access table holds a list of repetitive data, such as names and addresses.

The upper-right figure shows the same table in Design view. You can see that this view includes the name, data type, and definition of each field in the table. For example, the second field in the table is named First Name. Its Data Type is Text, and the panel below shows that the Field Size is 50, meaning that it can hold up to 50 characters of text.

Queries

The lower-left figure shows a query in Datasheet view. Though it looks similar to a table, a query includes only some of the table's data. You can see that that this query includes only names and addresses from New York state.

A query can specify which fields are displayed, which records are displayed, and the sort order of the records. It can be based on one table or on several.

The lower-right figure shows the same query in Design view. You can see that you specify which records are included by entering **NY** under the State field.

Continued

TAKE NOTE

▶ **UNDERSTANDING RECORDS AND FIELDS**

A *record* is all the data about one entity. A *field* is one piece of data that appears in each record. For example, if you have a list of names and addresses, the last name might be one field, and the street address might be another field. Because of how they are arranged in the table, records are also called *rows* and fields are also called *columns*.

▶ **USING OTHER TYPES OF QUERIES**

You have just looked at a *select query*, which lets you specify which data is displayed. Some queries, such as *action queries*, which let you change the data in a table, are more advanced. Advanced queries are covered in Chapter 11.

CROSS-REFERENCE

Tables are covered in Chapters 2 and 3. Queries are covered in Chapter 4.

SHORTCUT

For some purposes, rather than using queries, it is faster to use *filters*, which are covered in Chapter 5.

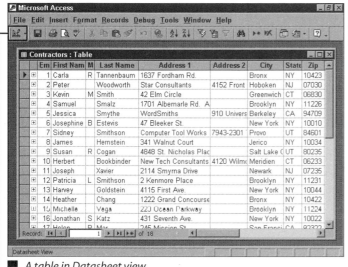

■ A table in Datasheet view.

■ Click the View button to switch to Design view.

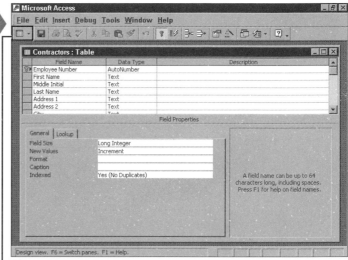

■ A table in Design view.

■ Click the View button to switch to Datasheet view.

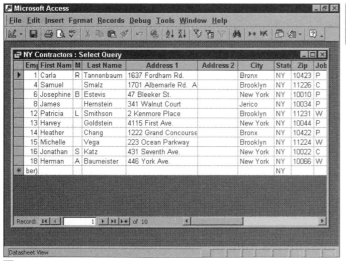

■ A query in Datasheet view.

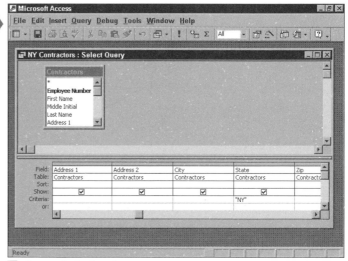

■ A query in Design view.

Viewing Database Objects
Continued

Forms

A table displays each record on a single line, which lets you look at a many records at the same time, but generally does not let you see all the information in each record.

A *form* usually displays one record at a time. You can select which fields to include in the form, and you can arrange the fields on the screen in a way that lets you see them all at once. You can also include graphics in a form.

The upper-left figure shows a form in Form view, which lets you control how data is displayed onscreen.

The upper-right figure shows the same form in Design view, which lets you lay out the form.

You can click the View button to display Forms in Datasheet view, with the records arranged in a table, as well as Form view or Design view.

Access includes easy-to-use Form Wizards that design forms for you. They are powerful enough that many users do not need to use Design view to create custom forms.

Reports

The objects you have looked at so far are usually used to display data from a table on the screen. *Reports* also let you control how the data is displayed, but they are meant specifically for printing data from a table, and they have a Preview button in the Database window instead of the Open button that other objects have.

You cannot edit data displayed in reports as you can in tables, queries, and forms. Instead, the Print Preview window displays them in a way that makes it easy for you to see how they will appear when they are printed. The lower-left figure shows a report in the Print Preview window.

The lower-right figure shows the Report window in Design view, which is similar to the Form window in Design view, but has more features. Access includes a Report Wizard that designs reports for you, and many users can get by without using Design view to create custom reports.

Mailing Labels are a type of report in Access, and there is a Mailing Label Wizard that makes it easy to create them.

TAKE NOTE

USING PAGES, MACROS, AND MODULES

You can display three other types of objects in the Database window. A *data access page* is like a form, but it can also be used on the World Wide Web. Pages are covered in Chapter 15. A *macro* is a list of actions. Access performs all the actions in the list when you run the macro. They let you automate and speed up your work, and they are also used when you develop applications. Macros are covered in Chapter 12. A *module* contains programs in Visual Basic. This book does not cover programming.

CROSS-REFERENCE

Chapter 6 covers using the wizards to create forms, reports, and mailing labels.

SHORTCUT

It is often easiest to create forms or reports using wizards and then to customize them in Design view.

■ *A form in Form view*

■ *A form in Design view*

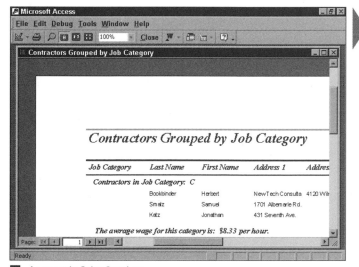

■ *A report in Print Preview*

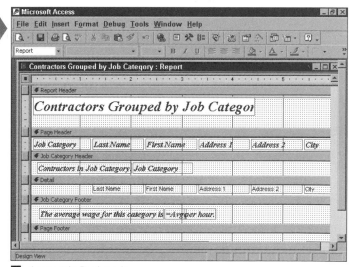

■ *A report in Design view*

Creating New Objects

After a new database, you will first create a table. After you create a table, you can then create forms, reports, and queries based on that table. Creating all of these objects involves common procedures, so learning how to create one helps you understand how to create others.

Let's use tables as an example. Clicking the Tables button in the Database window displays a list like the ones for Queries, Forms, and Reports. You can select from the list of existing tables (if there are any), or you can click the New button from the toolbar to create a new table.

If you click the New button, Access displays the New Object dialog box, which lets you choose how to create the table. You can create a table from scratch in Design view or use a wizard. It is a good idea to use the Wizard the first time, because it helps you learn all of the design features that might not yet be familiar to you. If you are creating a form or report, you can click AutoForm and AutoReport, which create standard layouts instantly. With the Auto features, there is very little flexibility: What you see is what you get. With wizards, you always have the option of choosing your own design modifications.

You can bypass this dialog box by double-clicking Create table in Design view or Create table by using wizard in the Database window—or the equivalent for other objects.

Using a Wizard

Wizards let you create new objects by going through a series of steps with instructions in plain English.

Each step lets you make choices to specify certain features of the object. Many include directions and pictures that illustrate your choices as you make them (as seen in the upper-right figure).

All steps have the same buttons at the bottom, which you use to move through the wizard. Generally, you will just provide information in each step and click Next.

A wizard's final step lets you name and create the object. This step also has radio buttons that let you specify how the object is displayed when it is created. Usually, you can display the object with data or display it in Design view to customize the wizard-generated design.

TAKE NOTE

USING THE NEW OBJECT TOOL

You can also create new objects clicking the New Object button, shown in the lower-right figure. For most of the options for this tool, Access displays the New dialog box for the selected object. However, the first three options of this tool, AutoForm, AutoReport, and AutoPage let you instantly create a form, report, or data-access page based on the table or query currently selected in the Database window.

CROSS-REFERENCE
All the steps of the Form Wizard are covered in Chapter 6.

SHORTCUT
You can also use the Insert menu to create new objects; it has the same options as the New Object button.

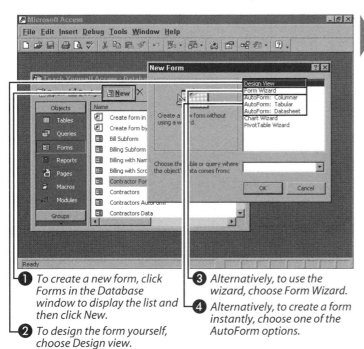

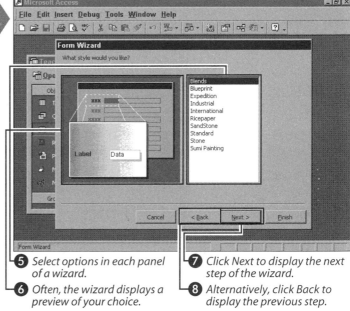

❶ To create a new form, click Forms in the Database window to display the list and then click New.

❷ To design the form yourself, choose Design view.

❸ Alternatively, to use the wizard, choose Form Wizard.

❹ Alternatively, to create a form instantly, choose one of the AutoForm options.

❺ Select options in each panel of a wizard.

❻ Often, the wizard displays a preview of your choice.

❼ Click Next to display the next step of the wizard.

❽ Alternatively, click Back to display the previous step.

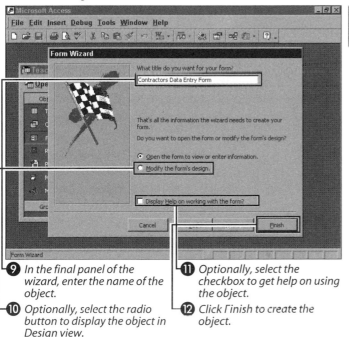

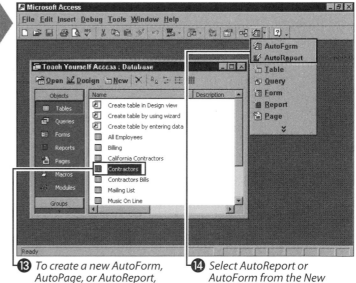

❾ In the final panel of the wizard, enter the name of the object.

❿ Optionally, select the radio button to display the object in Design view.

⓫ Optionally, select the checkbox to get help on using the object.

⓬ Click Finish to create the object.

⓭ To create a new AutoForm, AutoPage, or AutoReport, select a table or query in the Database window.

⓮ Select AutoReport or AutoForm from the New Object drop-down menu.

Using Multitable Databases

Many business applications require multitable databases because there are types of data that you cannot store effectively in a single table. A multitable database is often called a *relational database*, because you must relate the tables to each other.

Let's say that you are creating a database to record the number of hours that contractors work for you. You create a single table with fields for each contractor's name, address, date worked, and hours worked, as shown in the upper-left figure.

The first time a contractor works for you, you enter the date worked and hours worked. But what do you do the second time that same contractor works for you? There is no space for more dates and hours in the record, and you do not want to create a new record and re-enter the name and address each time a contractor works for you.

The way to deal with this is to create two tables, one for basic data, such as the name and address, and another for the dates and hours, and relate them. Relating two tables involves establishing the same *key field*, such as Employee Number, in each table which links tables. Any data changed in one table is changed on all other tables sharing that key field.

One of the best reasons for relating tables is to save time when editing specific fields. Let's say that your customer changes his or her address. You will only have to change the address in one table.

The key field should have a field name and data that will not be altered. If you do change the data in a key field, tables will no longer be related properly. Access lets you set up key field so data is not changed in ways that will break links between tables.

TAKE NOTE

LOOKING FOR ONE-TO-ONE RELATIONSHIPS

To put data in one table, there has to be a one-to-one relationship between that data and each record. For each record, there must be only one possible value for each field. For example, each contractor has just one name, one address, and one Social Security Number, so you can store all this data in one table. But the contractors do not just work once for you. Each client has many Dates Worked and Hours Worked, so you cannot store this in the same table with the name, address, and basic data; you must create another table. When creating a table, make sure that all its fields are in a one-to-one relationship with the record.

CROSS-REFERENCE
Chapter 7 covers relational databases in detail.

FIND IT ONLINE
To learn more about Access, you may want to join a users group. For a listing of users groups, see **http://www.yahoo.com/ Computers_and_Internet/Software/Databases/Access/ User_Groups/**.

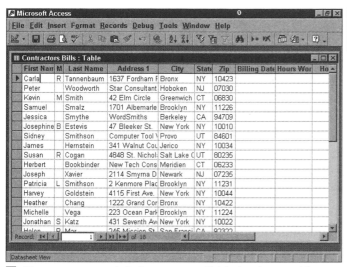

■ *The wrong way to do it: Do not enter all this data in one table.*

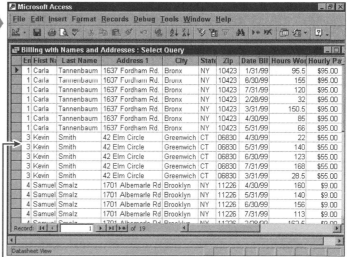

➊ *The right way to do it: Enter the basic data in one table, with a key field such as the Employee Number.*

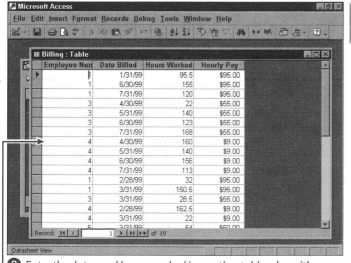

➋ *Enter the dates and hours worked in another table, also with an Employee Number field to link it to the first table.*

➌ *If you want to work with all the data, create a query to relate or link the tables.*

Personal Workbook

Q&A

1 What is the definition of a *database* in Access, and how is it different in other database applications?

_____

_____

_____

2 What are *records* and *fields*? What else are they called?

_____

_____

_____

3 What are the four most important objects in Access databases, and why are they used?

_____

_____

_____

4 What object would you use to let people work with data through the World Wide Web?

_____

_____

_____

5 What is the fastest way of creating a form, report, or data-access page?

_____

_____

6 If you are looking at the data in an object and you realize that you have to change its design, what should you do?

_____

_____

_____

7 What should you look for to decide whether to keep data in one table or to break it up into multiple tables?

_____

_____

8 If you break up data into multiple tables, what field must you include to relate them?

_____

_____

_____

ANSWERS: PAGE 342

EXTRA PRACTICE

① Open the Northwind sample database that is distributed with Access (Nwind.mdb). If it is not installed on your hard disk, you can find it on the distribution CD-ROM in the file \Pfiles\Msoffice\Office\Samples\.

② Display a table first in Datasheet view and then in Design view. Then close it.

③ Click the Query button and display a query first in Datasheet view and then in Design view. Then close it.

④ Click the Form button and display a form first in Datasheet view and then in Design view. Then close it.

⑤ Click Reports and display a report first in Datasheet view and then in Design view. Then close it.

REAL-WORLD APPLICATIONS

✔ You run a mail-order business, and you use Access to keep track of your inventory and of your customers' names, addresses, and orders.

✔ You are a realtor, and you use Access to keep track of the properties you are selling. You include a picture of each property in the table, so you can use Access to show clients the properties on your computer.

✔ You run a music store, and you use Access to maintain a list of the recordings you have in stock, with a sample from each that customers can play by double-clicking that field.

✔ You manage a library, and you use Access to create an online catalog to replace your card catalog.

Visual Quiz

How would you open the C:\Business\Personnel\Employees.mdb database using the Open dialog box displayed on the right?

_____

_____

_____

_____

_____

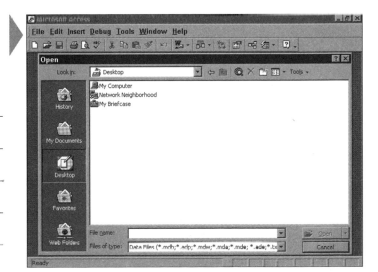

CHAPTER

2

Creating Databases and Tables

When you create a database, the first thing you should do is turn off the computer and take some time to think about what tables and fields it needs. If you take a bit of time to design it properly, you will save yourself many problems in the long run. For instance, your customer database may include Name, Address, and Phone Number fields. If you decide that you want to add data regarding customer orders, such as order dates, delivery dates, and amount of order, you should think about whether to put all these fields in one database to create a new table for the new data. Since each customer can have many orders, you should create two tables for this database.

It is also important to break the data properly into fields. In general, it is best to break up the data into more fields, rather than fewer. It is better to have fields for First Name and Last Name, than to have just one field for Name, and

it is better to have City, State, and Zip Code fields than to have just one field for City/State/Zip. If you are going to create a form letter and insert fields for salutations, you will want to create a field for titles such as Mr., Ms., Dr., and so on.

You must also put data in a separate field if it needs to be sorted. For example, if you plan to sort the table in alphabetical order according to last name, you will need a separate Last Name field. Likewise, if you plan to use a database to generate mailing labels, creating a single City/State/Zip field will prevent you from sorting by Zip Code or searching for all the records from a single state or city. It may be impossible to determine all of the fields you will need for future sorting, so the best advice is to break up the fields into the smallest possible segments.

In addition, be sure that all the fields in your table have a one-to-one relationship with each other, as explained in Chapter 1.

Creating a Database

Before you create a table, you must create a database to hold it. You can create a database in two ways:

▶ Create a blank database and then create the tables and other objects you need.
▶ Use the Database Wizard to create a database based on a template distributed with Access.

The Database Wizard can save you time, but you must have a good grasp of Access to know exactly which tables and other objects you need. It is best to work with a blank database when you are learning Access.

Creating a Blank Database

To create a blank database, choose File ➪ New to display the New dialog box, select the Blank Database icon, and click OK. If you select the Blank Database radio button of the dialog box displayed when you start Access, Access skips the New dialog box and immediately creates a blank database. (If you select the Database Wizard radio button of this dialog box, Access displays the New dialog box.)

Access displays the File New Database dialog box to let you name the new database. Enter a name in the File name box. Access suggests names such as DB1 or DB2, but you should use a meaningful name. Access automatically gives the file the extension .mdb, which stands for Microsoft Database, but this extension may not be displayed for everyone.

If necessary, open the folder in which you want to save the database. The current folder is listed in the Save in drop-down list at the top of this dialog box.

To open folders in the current folder, double-click them. To open the folder above the current folder, click the Up One Level button. The Save in drop-down list lets you move quickly among drives and folders.

Continued

Continued

TAKE NOTE

▶ VIEWING YOUR DATABASE FILES

In the File New Database dialog box, the buttons on the left let you display some key files and folders. History displays databases you have used recently. My Documents displays the folder named My Documents, where you probably keep your work. Desktop displays your desktop. Favorites displays Web pages and "bookmarked" files.

You can also use the drop-down list shown in the lower-right figure to control how your files and folders are displayed and how they are sorted:

▶ List displays only the names of folders and files.
▶ Details displays the name and type of folders and files and the size and last modification date for files.
▶ Properties displays a list of files and folders in the left half of the box, and the properties of the selected file to the right.
▶ Preview displays a list of files and folders in the left half of the box, and a preview of the selected file to the right.

CROSS-REFERENCE
For an overview of the Database window, see Chapter 1.

SHORTCUT
To create a new database, press Ctrl+N instead of choosing File ➪ New.

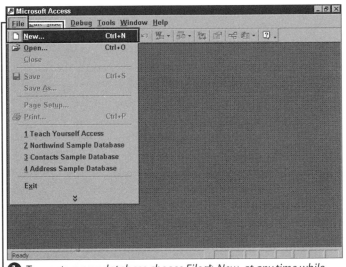

1 To create a new database choose File ⇨ New, at any time while you are using Access.

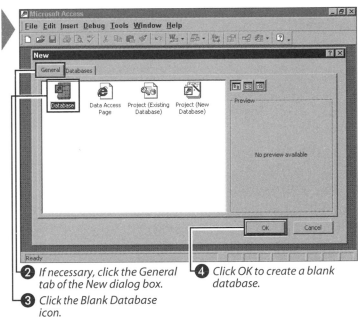

2 If necessary, click the General tab of the New dialog box.

3 Click the Blank Database icon.

4 Click OK to create a blank database.

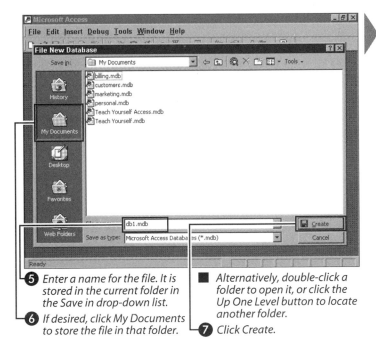

5 Enter a name for the file. It is stored in the current folder in the Save in drop-down list.

6 If desired, click My Documents to store the file in that folder.

■ Alternatively, double-click a folder to open it, or click the Up One Level button to locate another folder.

7 Click Create.

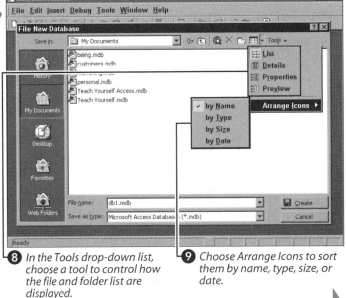

8 In the Tools drop-down list, choose a tool to control how the file and folder list are displayed.

9 Choose Arrange Icons to sort them by name, type, size, or date.

Creating a Database Using the Database Wizard

You can create each object of a database individually in Design view, but that requires some knowledge of Access. If you are not comfortable jumping into the deep end just yet, you should look at using the Database Wizard. The Wizard is a good choice, because the last step in the Wizard gives you the opportunity to open the database in Design view and customize your design. This way, you can let Wizard do most of the work, and you can do the final tweaking.

To create a database using the Wizard, return to the New dialog box, shown in the upper-left figure, and display its Databases tab. Select one of the database templates distributed with Access. The databases are designed for specific purposes and each contains the typical tables, queries, forms, and reports that you might need.

Access displays the File New Database dialog box, described on the previous pages. After you have named the database, Access displays the Database Wizard, which walks you through the steps to customize your chosen database template.

To determine if a particular template in the Wizard has enough of the fields you require to make this worth your while, you can open up each of the templates to see which fields are included, and what characteristics accompany these fields. If you do not like what you see in one, cancel the process and try another. If you like what you see, go ahead and use the Wizard; it will make creating the database much easier. Remember, you can always make changes in Design view before finalizing the table.

Though the Wizard seems simple, this appearance can be deceptive. Before you can use it effectively, you have to understand how the tables in the new databases that it creates are related to each other. It is best to first learn to create tables, queries, and other database objects, and to learn about relational databases so you understand how multiple tables relate to one another, before you use the Wizard to create databases.

TAKE NOTE

▶ ORGANIZING ACCESS FILES

In other Windows database applications, it is usually best to create a new folder for every database with which you work, to keep all of its files organized in one place. In Access, all the objects of the database are kept in a single file, so it is not necessary to create separate folders to keep them organized.

▶ OVERWRITING A FILE

You can create a new file with the same name as an existing file, but this will overwrite the existing file and destroy all the data in it. Access asks for confirmation before overwriting a file. If you want a name similar to the name of an existing file, you can click that file in the list to display its name in this box, and then edit its name.

CROSS-REFERENCE

See Chapter 1 for instructions on how to use a wizard.

FIND IT ONLINE

For information on creating a database using the Database Wizard, see **http://www2.winona. msus.edu/stc/Classes/Access_begin/part_b.htm**.

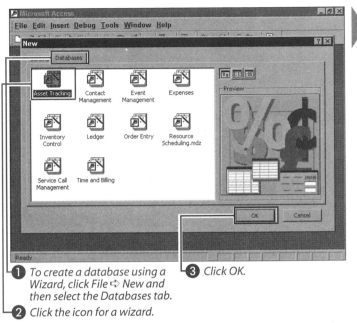

① To create a database using a Wizard, click File ⇨ New and then select the Databases tab.

② Click the icon for a wizard.

③ Click OK.

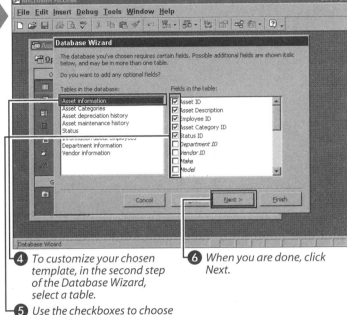

④ To customize your chosen template, in the second step of the Database Wizard, select a table.

⑤ Use the checkboxes to choose fields from that table.

⑥ When you are done, click Next.

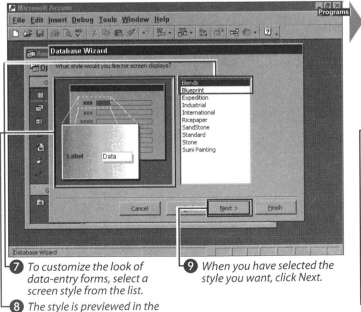

⑦ To customize the look of data-entry forms, select a screen style from the list.

⑧ The style is previewed in the box on the left.

⑨ When you have selected the style you want, click Next.

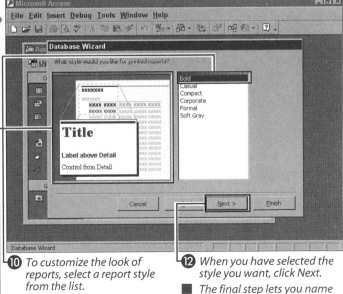

⑩ To customize the look of reports, select a report style from the list.

⑪ The style is previewed in the box on the left.

⑫ When you have selected the style you want, click Next.

■ The final step lets you name and save the database.

23

Creating a Table Using the Wizard

The Table Wizard includes a variety of standard tables, and lets you customize them to fit your needs exactly. You can use the Database window to select this option, as shown in the upper-left figure.

The first step of this wizard lets you choose a standard table and some or all of its fields, so you can create a table quickly without defining each field individually. To include these fields in the table, click the > button to move one field, or click the > button to move all fields. Click the buttons pointing in the other direction to remove the fields in the same way.

These table templates come with predetermined field names and specifications. For example, the Address template provides field names like Title, Last Name, First Name, Address, and includes fields for E-mail Address and Notes. The fields are also pre-configured. For example, in some tables, the Phone Number field does not allow you to separate out the area code or exchange. As you can see, the Wizard is efficient, but limited.

The second step of the Wizard lets you enter a name for the table and choose whether to have Access create a primary key field for the table or set one up yourself. *Primary keys*, which are identifying fields such as Employee Number or Customer Number, are covered later in this chapter; for now, it is easiest to let Access create one.

Access may display a step asking if the table is related to any other table in the database; this is useful in relational databases, which are discussed in Chapter 7, but you should just click Next to skip it for now.

The next step lets you create the table. You can display it in Design view so you can modify it or you can enter data immediately into the table or into a form that the wizard creates.

After you learn to create a table in Design view, you will find this Wizard a handy shortcut. You will be able to customize these tables in Design view, if necessary, to fit your own needs exactly.

TAKE NOTE

CREATING A TABLE BY ENTERING DATA

The Database window also lets you create a new table by entering data. This option creates a new table and displays it in Datasheet view, so you can immediately enter data. The new table has fields, with names like Field 1, which you can rename by double-clicking their column headings and editing their names. When you first save the table, Access determines the data type of each field based on the data you entered. It is occasionally convenient to create a table in Datasheet view if you want to quickly enter data, but it can lead to problems in the long run.

CROSS-REFERENCE
See Chapter 1 for instructions on how to use a Wizard.

FIND IT ONLINE
For information on creating a table using the Table Wizard, see http://www2.winona.msus.edu/stc/Classes/Access_begin/part_c.htm.

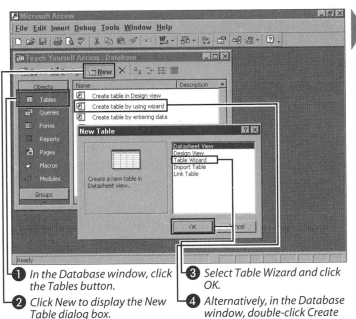

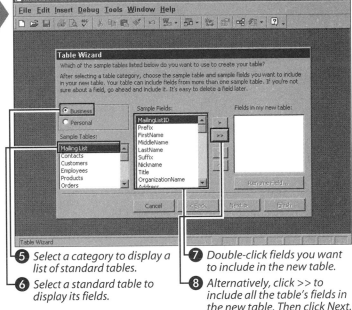

❶ In the Database window, click the Tables button.

❷ Click New to display the New Table dialog box.

❸ Select Table Wizard and click OK.

❹ Alternatively, in the Database window, double-click Create table by using wizard.

❺ Select a category to display a list of standard tables.

❻ Select a standard table to display its fields.

❼ Double-click fields you want to include in the new table.

❽ Alternatively, click >> to include all the table's fields in the new table. Then click Next.

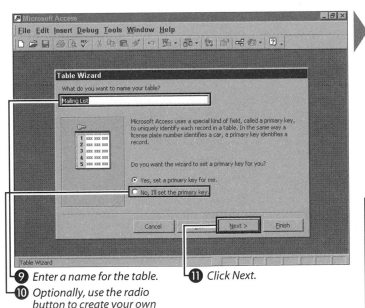

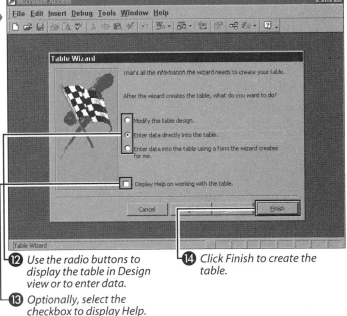

❾ Enter a name for the table.

❿ Optionally, use the radio button to create your own primary key field for the table.

⓫ Click Next.

⓬ Use the radio buttons to display the table in Design view or to enter data.

⓭ Optionally, select the checkbox to display Help.

⓮ Click Finish to create the table.

25

Creating a Table Using Design View

Design view gives you much more control over your table's design than the Table Wizard does. You may want to use it to create tables that are not available as standard tables in the Wizard or to customize tables that you created using the Wizard, so the fields have exactly the properties you want. Once you are accustomed to it, Design view is as easy to use as the Wizard. When you specify the fields of a table in this way, it is called *defining the structure of the table*, or simply, designing the table.

To use Design view, double-click Create table in Design view in the Database window, shown in the upper-left figure. For each field you can enter:

- ▶ **Field name.** The name of the field
- ▶ **Data type.** The characteristics of the field (that is, numbers only, text only, and so on)
- ▶ **Description.** A description displayed as a help line when the user enters data in this field

You do not need to memorize all the types of data, as Access provides a drop-down list of all available data types, as shown in the upper-right figure. Some data types give you additional options. For example, if your data is a date, Access asks you if you are particular about how the date is entered. You can be very specific and accept only one date format, such as mm/dd/yy, or you can tell Access to accept the full range of date formats, and always display them in text format. This means that dates entered as 11/03/91, Nov. 3, 1991, and 3 Nov 91 would all appear as November 3, 1991 in the result. The table on the following page lists data types and their uses.

You can also add field descriptions that would be helpful during data entry. This is a useful option if someone else will be entering data and they do not know or remember what data is valid for the fields. This is a good choice if your office employs temporary help on a regular basis. If you enter a description, it is displayed as a Help line in the status bar when that field is selected in the table or form, as shown in the lower-left figure. The Description column is optional.

You can use the panel in the bottom half of the window to specify different properties for different fields. Most of these properties are only needed by advanced users. The most important properties are described in the next task.

Continued

Continued

TAKE NOTE

▶ GETTING HELP

The Table window includes a Help panel on its lower right, with brief context-sensitive Help. Press F1 to display the Help system with more extensive context-sensitive Help.

CROSS-REFERENCE

See Chapter 13 for more advanced techniques for defining a table.

SHORTCUT

You can choose a data type by moving the highlight to the Data Type column and entering its first letter, rather than using the drop-down list.

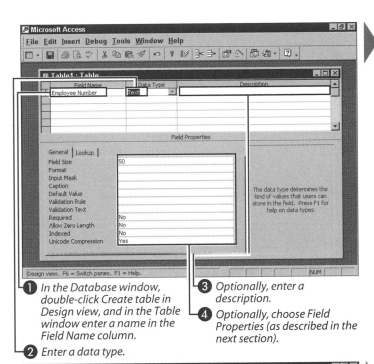

1 In the Database window, double-click Create table in Design view, and in the Table window enter a name in the Field Name column.

2 Enter a data type.

3 Optionally, enter a description.

4 Optionally, choose Field Properties (as described in the next section).

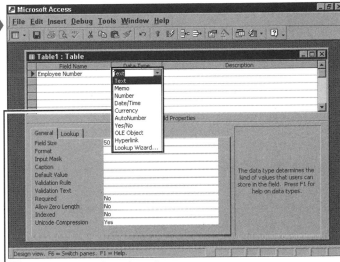

■ The Data Type drop-down list.

■ The Description is displayed as a Help line when you enter data in Datasheet view.

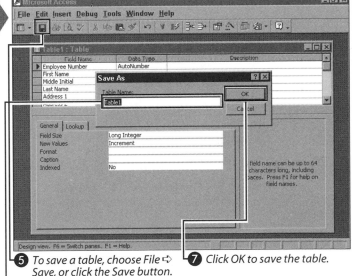

5 To save a table, choose File ⇨ Save, or click the Save button.

6 Enter the name of the table in the Save As dialog box.

7 Click OK to save the table.

Creating a Table Using Design View *Continued*

You must be careful to choose the right data type for each field. The most common data types used to hold the basic data that you will need to store are *Text*, *Number*, *Currency*, and *Date/Time*. *Memo* is also very useful for holding longer, unstructured forms of text data, such as a Note field with general remarks on each of your customers. *AutoNumber* is useful for creating key fields, such as Customer Number and Employee Number, discussed later in this chapter. *OLE objects* are sometimes needed to hold pictures, sounds, and similar data. *Hyperlinks* let you link to Web pages or other documents. The following table summarizes data types and their uses.

ACCESS DATA TYPES

Data Type	Description
Text	Holds up to 255 characters, including letters, numbers, and special characters.
Memo	Holds text of up to 65,000 characters. Unlike Text fields, Memo fields are variable length; you do not specify a maximum size for them.
Number	Holds numbers actually used in calculations. The type of number it can hold and accuracy of calculations depends on the size you give to the Number field. Some Number fields hold only integers and others can hold numbers with many decimal places.
Date/Time	Holds dates and times. Whether you can enter a date or a time depends on the format you give to the field.

Data Type	Description
Currency	Holds numbers used as amounts of money, or any numbers used in calculations with up to four decimal places of accuracy.
AutoNumber	Holds sequential numbers that Access automatically enters. Access places the number *1* in this field in the first record you add to the table, the number *2* in the second record, and so on. You cannot change the numbers that Access enters in this field.
Yes/No	Holds only two values, defined as Yes/No, True/False, or On/Off, depending on the format you give it in the Field Properties panel. By default, Yes/No fields appear in tables as checkboxes.
OLE Object	Holds data from other Window applications that support *Object Linking and Embedding* (OLE). This field can be used to attach pictures, sound files, or any other type of data available from other Windows applications that support OLE.
Hyperlink	Holds the address of an object, document or Web page, which you can display simply by clicking the field (see Chapter 15).
Lookup Wizard	Lets you create a field that lets the user choose values from a list (see Chapter 13).

CROSS-REFERENCE

See Chapter 3 for more information on the techniques you use to move among the cells of a table.

SHORTCUT

Instead of choosing Insert ⇨ Rows or Edit ⇨ Delete Row, just click the Insert Row or Delete Row toolbar button.

While you are defining the table, you move through the rows and columns of Design view in the same way that you move through the fields and records of a table when you are entering data. You can move among the Field Name, Data Type, and Description columns by clicking them with the mouse or by using the cursor keys. You can also press the Tab key to move one column to the right and Shift+Tab to move one column to the left. You can also edit the entries in the same way that you edit data.

To insert a new field between two fields that you have already defined, move the cursor into the row and choose Insert ⇨ Rows. To delete a field, move the cursor to the row and choose Edit ⇨ Delete Row.

In general, it is easiest to type in entries or make choices from drop-down lists, and then press Tab to go to the next column, or to the next row when you finish with a column.

Saving and Naming the Table

You can save changes at any time while you are defining the table by choosing File ⇨ Save, or clicking the Save button.

Alternatively, when you have finished defining the table, you can simply close the Table window, or you can click the View button to display the table in Datasheet view. If you have not saved it already, Access prompts you to save and name the table.

The first time you save the table, Access displays the Save As dialog box to let you name the table (shown in the lower-right figure of the previous spread). This dialog box is not like the Save As dialog box that you are familiar with from other Windows applications, because it does not let you select drive and folder where the table is located. This is because the table is part of the database file, whose drive and folder you specified when you first created it. Just enter a name for the table.

Using Access Naming Conventions

All Access objects, including tables and fields, must be given names that follow these naming conventions:

▶ Names can be up to 64 characters long.
▶ Names can include any characters except the square brackets ([and]), the period (.),and the the exclamation point (!).
▶ Names cannot include control characters (characters that cannot be entered by typing in the ordinary way).
▶ Names cannot begin with a space but they can include spaces.

These conventions let you give Access tables and other objects complete and meaningful names.

Using Essential Field Properties

You have seen that when you move the cursor to a field in Design view, a panel with all of that field's properties is displayed in the bottom half of the Table window.

You use this panel to specify properties such as the maximum size of the data that can be entered in the field, the format of the field, and validation rules that check the data. Properties vary for different data types.

Only advanced users need most of these properties, but the following may be essential:

▶ **Text fields.** You may want to use the Field Size property of Text fields, shown in the upper-left figure, to specify the maximum number of characters that the field can hold. In general, you can leave the default value of 50 here, but in some cases, you may want to allow more text in the field, or restrict the user to entering less text. For example, you would normally allow only two characters in a state field. The maximum size of a Text field is 255 characters, and you must use a memo field to hold longer amounts of text.

▶ **Number fields.** You must select the Field Size of a Number field, as shown in the upper-right figure. These sizes are a bit difficult to understand. In general, it is easiest to use a Number field and select Long Integer if the field will never hold fractions or decimals or to select Double if the field will hold fractions or decimals. It is easiest to select a Currency field to hold money amounts.

Access automatically validates data entry based on field type. For example, you can enter only numbers in Number fields, and you can enter only valid dates in Date fields. If a user tries to enter inappropriate data in the field, it will not be accepted, and the user will receive an error message.

TAKE NOTE

▶ **USING NUMBER AND CURRENCY FIELDS**

The real difference between Number and Currency fields is that internal calculations are done differently for them. The sizes of number fields determine their accuracy. Number fields with the Double size perform the most accurate calculations. Currency fields do calculations more quickly, but are only accurate to four decimal places. As you can see in the lower-left figure, Currency fields do not have a size because they always have the same degree of accuracy.

▶ **FORMATTING NUMBER AND CURRENCY FIELDS**

You can use the Format property of either a Number or Currency field to determine how data is displayed. Simply click the Format box for a Number or Currency field to add a drop-down arrow to the box, and then choose a format from the drop-down list, as shown in the lower-right figure.

CROSS-REFERENCE

For complete information on field properties, see Chapter 13.

SHORTCUT

Press F6 to move the cursor to the Properties Panel.

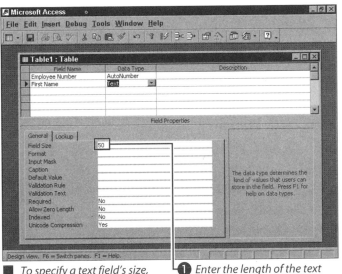

■ To specify a text field's size, display the table in Design view, and put the cursor anywhere in that field's line.

1 Enter the length of the text field.

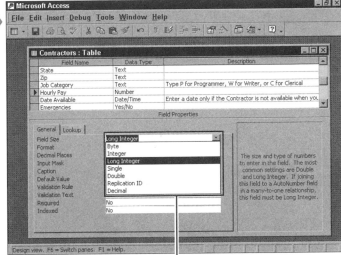

■ To specify a Number field's size, display the table in Design view, and put the cursor anywhere in that field's line.

2 Choose the field size of the Number field.

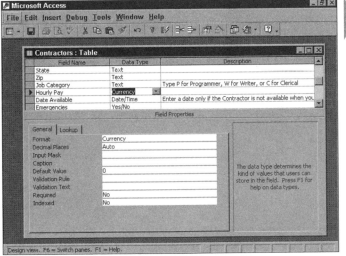

■ A Currency field does not have a field size.

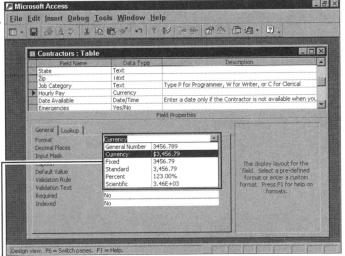

3 However, a Currency field can be formatted like other Number fields.

Creating the Primary Key Field

A *primary key* is a field orbasic description of combination of fields that identifies each record in a table. The most common primary key is a sequentially numbered field, such as Employee Number or Customer Number, which is given a unique value for each record in the table. This field is the key that identifies each record.

Access can retrieve data more quickly if you make sure that each table has a primary key. In other database programs, key fields are only needed when you work with relational databases. Access, on the other hand, uses the primary key to keep track of the records internally, so it always works more efficiently if a table has a primary key.

It is best to create primary keys by using the AutoNumber data type. For example, you could create an Employee Number field to use as a primary key, and make it the AutoNumber data type. By default, Increment is the New Values property of AutoNumber fields: this means that 1 is automatically entered in the first record, 2 in the second record, and so on.

You cannot edit AutoNumber fields. This prevents you from changing the value of the primary key by mistake, which would cause data loss if you were working with a relational database.

You can create your own primary key or let Access create one for you automatically. If you close the Table window without including a primary key when you define a table, Access displays the dialog box shown in the lower-right figure. Click Yes to create a primary key field. If one of the fields in the table is the AutoNumber data type, Access makes it the primary key. Otherwise, Access adds a new AutoNumber field to the table and gives it the name ID. Access displays a key graphic to the left of the primary key field.

You may choose No and work without a primary key field, but Access will perform more slowly.

TAKE NOTE

DO NOT USE MEANINGFUL FIELDS AS PRIMARY KEYS

Primary key fields must contain unique entries, and the field has to have an entry for each record. It is possible to use meaningful fields as primary keys, but I don't recommend it. For example, you might decide to use the last name as a primary key, because everyone in your table has a different name. But then you could not add a new person to the Table who has the same name as someone who has already been entered. If someone changes his or her name, you could also lose data in a relational database. A social security number is the only meaningful field that can sometimes be used as a primary key, because each U.S. citizen has a unique number that never changes. You could use it, if you are sure that everyone who you will enter in your table will have one.

CROSS-REFERENCE
See Chapter 13 for more information on the properties of AutoNumber fields.

SHORTCUT
Click the Primary Key button instead of choosing Edit ⇨ Primary Key.

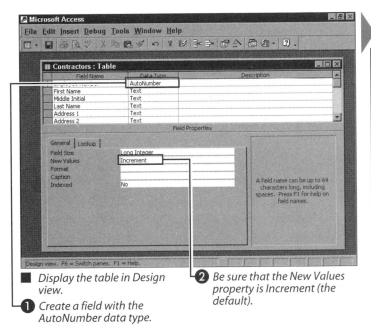

■ *Display the table in Design view.*

① *Create a field with the AutoNumber data type.*

② *Be sure that the New Values property is Increment (the default).*

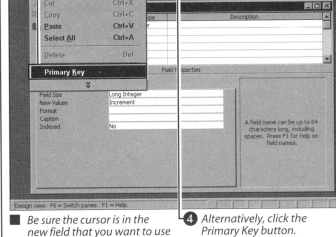

■ *Be sure the cursor is in the new field that you want to use as key field.*

③ *Choose Edit ➪ Primary Key.*

④ *Alternatively, click the Primary Key button.*

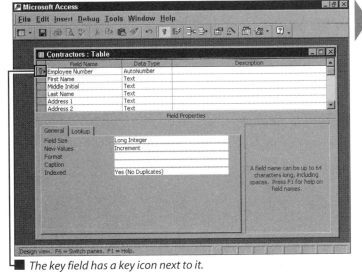

■ *The key field has a key icon next to it.*

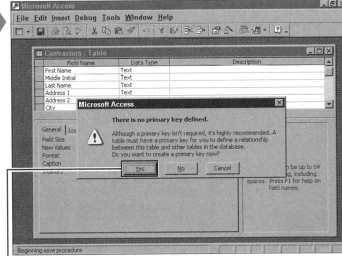

■ *If you do not create a primary key, Access asks if you want one when you leave Design view. Click Yes to have Access create a primary key field for you.*

Modifying the Design of a Table

If you are working on a table and suddenly realize that you need to make a change in it, such as adding another field, you can switch to Design view and modify the design of the table at any time. Use the same methods you use to create the table to change its field names, data types, descriptions, and properties.

Watch Out for Data Loss

However, when you modify the design of a table that already has data, there is a danger of data loss. If you have changed the design in a way that might destroy data, Access warns you when you try to save the change.

If you delete a field, you will lose all data you entered into that field.

If you make a field size smaller, you lose data that cannot fit into the new size of the field. For example, if you reduce the size of a Text field from 50 to 20 characters, fields with data longer than 20 characters keep only the first 20 characters.

If you change the size of a Number field, data is rounded to fit into the new size. For example, if you change the size of a Number field from Double to Long Integer, all values are rounded to the nearest integer and decimal places are lost.

If you change a field's data type, all data that cannot be held in the new field type is lost. For example, if you change a Text field to a Number field, any character that is not a number is lost.

If you make a field a primary key, any records with duplicate data in that field are discarded, because a primary key must have a unique value in each field.

TAKE NOTE

MODIFYING TABLE DESIGN IN DATASHEET VIEW

You can add, delete, or rename the fields of a table in Datasheet view. Simply right-click a column's heading to display its pop-up menu, shown in the lower-right figure, and choose one of the following options to change its definition:

▶ Choose Rename Column to edit the column's heading and change the field's name.

▶ Choose Insert Column to add a new column to the left of the column whose menu you used. It will have a name such as Field1 and will be a Text field with the size 255. You can rename it using the method that was just described, and change its properties using Design view.

▶ Choose Delete Column to remove the selected column from the table.

▶ Choose Lookup Column to display the Lookup Wizard and change this field into a Lookup Field, which has a value you select from a list.

Other options on the shortcut menu do not affect the table's design.

CROSS-REFERENCE

Chapter 13 covers lookup fields and the Lookup Wizard.

SHORTCUT

To create a new table similar to an existing one, select the existing table in the Database window, copy and paste it, and modify its structure as necessary.

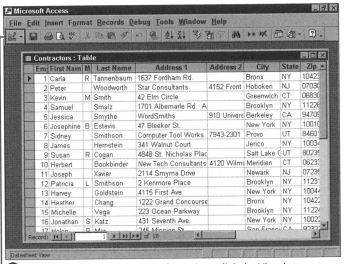

1 *While using the table in Datasheet view, click the View button to switch to Design view.*

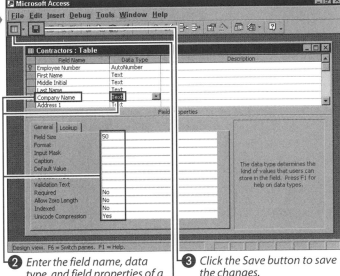

2 *Enter the field name, data type, and field properties of a new field.*

■ *If necessary, change the properties of existing fields.*

3 *Click the Save button to save the changes.*

4 *Click the View button to switch back to Datasheet view.*

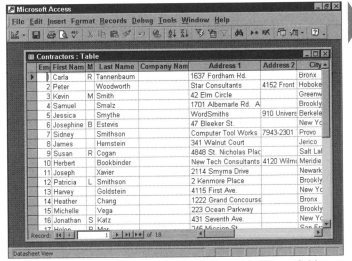

■ *Access displays the table in Datasheet view with the new field.*

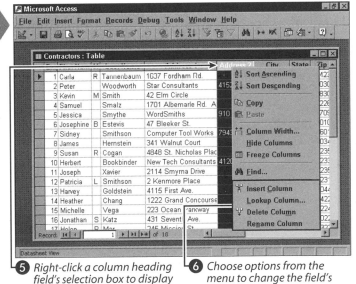

5 *Right-click a column heading field's selection box to display its pop-up menu.*

6 *Choose options from the menu to change the field's definition.*

Personal Workbook

Q&A

1 Which data type should you use for an Employee Number field, and why?

_____

_____

2 Which data type should you use for a field that holds general notes on each record?

_____

_____

_____

3 Which data type should you use for a field that holds zip codes?

_____

_____

_____

4 What are two reasons why you would want to change the field size of a Text field?

_____

_____

_____

5 What field size should you use for a Number field where you must perform calculations that are accurate to many decimal places?

_____

_____

_____

6 Should you ever use the Currency data type for fields that do not hold amounts of money?

_____

_____

_____

7 Can you lose data if you add a new field to an existing table?

_____

_____

_____

8 What sort of data loss is possible if you change the size of a field in an existing table?

_____

_____

ANSWERS: PAGE 343

EXTRA PRACTICE

1 Create a database using the Database Wizard, based on the standard Time and Billing database.

2 Open the database you created and look at its tables to make sure they have the fields you specified.

3 Create a blank database.

4 Use the Wizard to create a Mailing List table in this database.

5 Open this table in Design view and modify its design so you can enter longer last names.

6 Use Design view to create a second Mailing List table. Include fields that you think you actually would need in an address book.

REAL-WORLD APPLICATIONS

✔ You convert your Rolodex into a database with tables to hold the names, addresses, and phone numbers of your friends and business contacts, so you can look up addresses more quickly and create mailing labels.

✔ You are setting up a page of links to related sites for your company's Web site. You create a table with names and descriptions of sites and a hyperlink to each, which your co-workers can review to decide which links to include.

✔ You are starting a mail-order business, and you create a database to hold information about the products you sell and your customers.

Visual Quiz

Why is Long Integer the wrong size for the Hourly Pay field?

_____

_____

_____

_____

_____

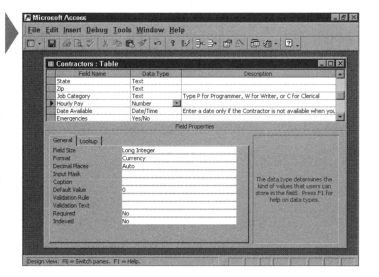

CHAPTER **3**

MASTER
THESE
SKILLS

▶ **Navigating in Datasheet View**

▶ **Entering and Editing Data**

▶ **Working with Records**

▶ **Working with Special Data Types**

▶ **Using Data-Entry Shortcuts**

▶ **Finding Records**

▶ **Working with Columns**

▶ **Changing the Data Display**

▶ **Printing and Previewing the Datasheet**

Working with Data

A database without data is like a piano without keys. The piano may look great, but it will not make any music, which is what it was designed to do. All the hard work you have done in creating the database — determining the fields and their specifications — is about to pay off as you learn how to add data to your database and use the database as it was designed to work.

First, you must add data to your database before you can work with it. The fact is that much of your time using Access will be spent doing the most fundamental tasks: entering and viewing data in a table. As your data needs grow and change, you will add, delete, and edit data, and fortunately, doing all of this is easy to learn.

You probably will work with data most often in Datasheet view. You can enter and edit data in Datasheet view, which as you learned previously, is just a grid with fields in the columns and records in the rows. In Datasheet view, you enter data horizontally one record at a time, vertically one field at a time, or both. Datasheet view is especially useful if you need to jump around a lot among records or if you have just added a field to the database and need to make entries for all of your records. Because of this flexibility, using Datasheet view is considered the easiest approach.

Some people prefer designing their own forms for data entry. Forms are great for when you wish to enter and edit data one record at a time (Forms are covered in Chapter 6). Although Access automatically generates a Datasheet for your table, you need to create a form before you can use it.

The basic methods of entering, viewing, and editing data are so simple that you should be able to do much of your work intuitively. This chapter introduces you to other techniques that will make your work faster and easier.

Navigating in Datasheet View

While editing data, you will often want to move among the records of a table or to select records so you can delete or copy them. With a large table, you can quickly move among records by using the Record buttons at the bottom of the Table window, shown in the upper-left figure.

At other times, you may find it easier to move among a Datasheet's rows and columns by tabbing, clicking, or using the cursor movement keys. As in a spreadsheet, you can press Tab to move one field to the right and press Shift+Tab to move back one field to your left. If the data in a field is selected (highlighted), you can use any of the arrow keys to move one field in the direction of the arrow (as opposed to moving one character in other Windows applications), which then selects all the data in that field. If you need to jump around a lot, you can always click your cursor in the field you want.

While these are the popular navigation methods, Access provides a host more. Try the methods in the table below to see which you find most comfortable. Sometimes finding just the right method makes a world of difference.

CURSOR MOVEMENT KEYS IN DATASHEET VIEW

Key	Selected Data	Insertion Point
Left or right arrow	Moves one field left or right	Moves one character left or right
Up or down arrow	Moves one record up or down	Moves one record up or down
Ctrl+left arrow or Ctrl+right arrow	Moves one field left or right	Moves one word left or right
Ctrl+up arrow or Ctrl+down arrow	Moves to top or bottom of column	Moves to top or bottom of column
PgUp or PgDn	Scrolls up or down one window	Scrolls up or down one window
Ctrl+PgUp or Ctrl+PgDn	Scrolls left or right one window	Scrolls left or right one window
Home or End	Moves to first or last field of record	Moves to beginning or end of field
Ctrl+Home or Ctrl+End	Moves to first or last field of table	Moves to beginning or end of field
Tab	Moves to next field	Moves to next field
Shift+Tab	Moves to previous field	Moves to previous field
Enter	Moves to next field	Moves to next field

CROSS-REFERENCE

For information on finding the data you want, see the section "Finding Records" later in this chapter.

SHORTCUT

The simplest method of viewing data is to use the mouse to scroll through the Table window, just as you scroll through any window.

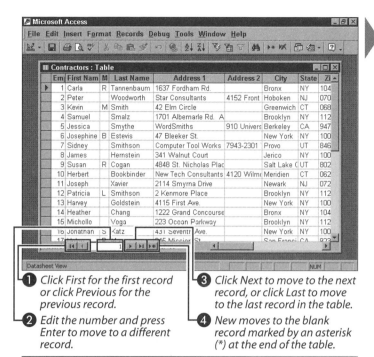

① Click First for the first record or click Previous for the previous record.

② Edit the number and press Enter to move to a different record.

③ Click Next to move to the next record, or click Last to move to the last record in the table.

④ New moves to the blank record marked by an asterisk (*) at the end of the table.

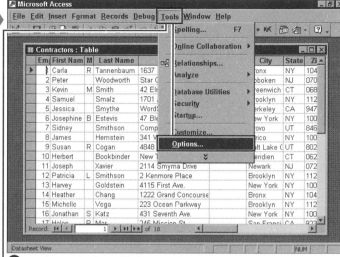

⑤ To change keyboard behavior, choose Tools ➪ Options.

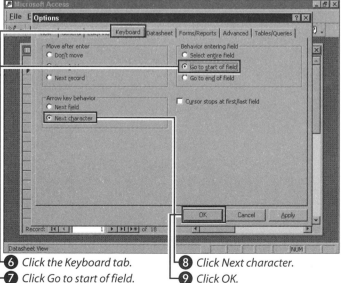

⑥ Click the Keyboard tab.

⑦ Click Go to start of field.

⑧ Click Next character.

⑨ Click OK.

TAKE NOTE

CHANGING KEYBOARD BEHAVIOR

If you are not comfortable using the cursor movement keys in this way, you can easily change it by choosing Tools ➪ Option and using the Options dialog box, as shown in the upper-right and lower-left figures.

SCROLLING WITHOUT MOVING THE CURSOR

If you are entering data in a field and need to see the contents of another field beyond the screen display, but you want keep your cursor in the current field, use the horizontal and vertical scroll bars. You may also want to use the page up and page down keys, to move more quickly.

Entering and Editing Data

Once you place your cursor in the right field, it is time to get down to business and actually enter and edit some data. Entering data is as simple as placing your cursor in the right field and typing in the entry. Moving to another record saves your previous entry. To add a new record to the table, just move the cursor to the blank record that Access automatically adds to the end of the table, which is marked with an asterisk, and type the data. If you are adding one record after another, you can just press Tab when you finish each record to move to the first field of the next record.

At other times, moving to a new record in one of these ways is easiest:

► Click the New Record button of the toolbar. Click the New button at right of the Record buttons located at the bottom of the Table window.

► Press Ctrl++ (hold down the Ctrl key and press the + key).

Sometimes, adding new records without displaying the records already in the table is more convenient. To do this, choose Records ⇨ Data Entry, as shown in the upper-right figure. Access hides all the existing records in the table and displays a blank record. You make entries in the usual way, but the table displays only the new data you enter.

Once fields contain data, editing data in Access is similar to editing text in other Windows applications.

If you need to completely replace the data, you can use the cursor movement keys to move to the field. Navigating using the keyboard highlights the entire contents of each field as your cursor lands on it. Once the field is selected, you do not need to press Delete or Backspace — just type and your data is automatically replaced.

Sometimes, you need to only make a few changes to the data, such as changing the name McGregor to MacGregor. To do this, press F2 or click the field in the space that needs the *a*. Once you have an insertion point in a field, you are in edit mode, and you can use the backspace and delete keys as you would in with any other text. You can also use the cursor movement keys to move the insertion point within the field. The F2 key is a toggle. If you are working with an insertion point, you can press it again to select all the data in the field. After you are done, you can press Tab to move to the next field or Shift+Tab to move to the previous field.

TAKE NOTE

USING INSERT AND OVERSTRIKE MODE

If you press the Insert key while working with an insertion point, you toggle from *insert mode* to *overwrite mode,* and each character you type replaces a character of the existing text. Press Insert again to toggle back to insert mode.

CROSS-REFERENCE

Certain data types require special techniques for data entry, which are covered later in this chapter.

SHORTCUT

The fastest way to add new records is to keep pressing the Tab key to move the next field and next record.

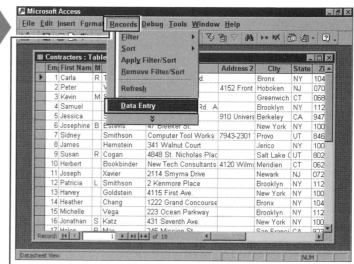

① *To go to a new record, click the New Record button.*

② *Alternatively, click the New button at right of the Record buttons.*

■ *Alternatively, press Ctrl++ (hold down the Ctrl key and press the + key).*

③ *To display only the new record, use data-entry mode by choosing Records ⇨ Data Entry.*

Working with Records

As you enter and edit data, Access helps you along by displaying the following visual aids in the record selector box to the left of the fields (shown in the upper-left and upper-right figures):

- ▶ **Asterisk.** The asterisk marks the blank record Access automatically adds; it will not be saved when you close the table.
- ▶ **Arrowhead.** An arrowhead, displayed to the left of the record, indicates the current record (the one you have moved to).
- ▶ **Pencil.** A pencil replaces the arrowhead to indicate that changes have been made in the current record, but have not yet been saved. Moving to a new record automatically saves the changes made to the previous record.

Selecting a Record

You can select a record by clicking its record selector box. When you select a record, all its fields are highlighted, as shown in the lower-left figure.

You can select groups of records in the following ways:

- ▶ Click the record selector box of one field, hold down the mouse button, and drag up or down across the boxes of adjacent records to select all these records.
- ▶ Select a record, and hold down the Shift key while you click the record selector box of another record to select it and all the records between them.

You can also select records by choosing Edit ➪ Select Record to select the current record.

Deleting a Record

To delete a record, first select it or move the cursor to it, and click the Delete Record button, or press the Delete key, as shown in the lower-right figure. If you have selected multiple records, you can delete them all in the same way.

Access displays a dialog box telling you the number of records deleted and lets you confirm or cancel your change.

TAKE NOTE

▶ **CANCELING AN ENTRY**

When you make a new entry or edit an existing record, the pencil displays to the left of the record. As long as the pencil is displayed, you can cancel all changes in the current field by pressing Esc. You can cancel all the changes you made in the record by pressing Esc again.

▶ **SAVING AN ENTRY**

Changes you make to a record are automatically saved when you move the highlight to another record, so there is usually no need to save your data. However, you may want to save a record while you are still working on it — for example, if you have to leave the computer to look something up before finishing the entry. To save the current record while you are still working on it, press Shift+Enter. After you do this, you cannot cancel the entry by pressing Esc.

CROSS-REFERENCE

For information on how to move to a record based on its contents, see the section "Finding Records" later in this chapter.

SHORTCUT

To select all the records in a table, choose Edit ➪ Select All Records.

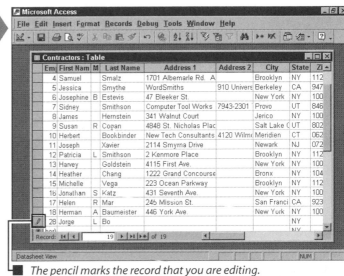

The asterisk marks a new record that will not be saved.

The triangle marks the selected record.

The pencil marks the record that you are editing.

1 To select a record, click the record selector box.

■ Optionally, to select multiple adjacent records, hold down Shift and click another selection box.

2 Multiple records are selected.

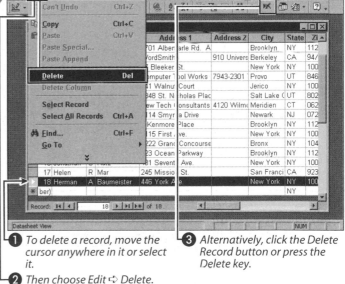

1 To delete a record, move the cursor anywhere in it or select it.

2 Then choose Edit ⇨ Delete.

3 Alternatively, click the Delete Record button or press the Delete key.

Working with Special Data Types

You have seen how to type values (text and numbers) into fields, but a few data types are entered differently. If you have specified a field as Yes/No, it is displayed as a checkbox, as shown in the upper-left figure. Check and uncheck it either by clicking it or by pressing the spacebar.

Hyperlink fields let you store addresses of documents and Web pages, and can be entered as data. To enter them, type the address in the field, as shown in the upper-right figure. Because you have defined the field as a hyperlink, Access automatically displays the entry underlined and in blue (the standard appearance of hyperlinks). When the pointer is placed on one, it displays as a hand with the index finger extended. The person viewing this entry only needs to click it to go directly to the linked document.

You cannot click a Hyperlink field to edit it because Access will jump to its address. Instead, tab to the field and press F2 to place an insertion point. A # sign is added at either side of the address, to indicate that it can be edited, as shown in the lower-left figure. When you move the cursor to another field, the # sign is automatically removed.

If you have created a lookup field, a drop-down arrow is displayed when you place the cursor in it. Select an entry from the drop-down list, as shown in the lower-right figure.

Entering and editing data in Memo fields is similar to entering and editing in ordinary Text fields, with some minor differences. If you want to enter more than one paragraph in a Memo field, you must press Ctrl+Enter to add a line break, because pressing Enter moves you to the next field rather than beginning a new paragraph. After you have added multiple paragraphs, you can use the up- and down-arrow keys to move the insertion point among them, unless you are in the first or last paragraph. It is difficult to work with multiparagraph Memo fields in Datasheet view and easier to create a form to work with them.

OLE fields let you use Object Linking and Embedding to store objects from other Windows applications, such as pictures, sounds, spreadsheets, or videos, in Access databases.

TAKE NOTE

▶ HYPERLINK FIELD CONTENTS

Data you enter in a Hyperlink field must be one of the following:

▶ **Internet addresses.** Enter the *Uniform Resource Locator* (URL) of the Web page you want displayed. For example, **http://www.microsoft.com/ pagename.html**.

▶ **Local Area Network addresses.** Enter the *Universal Naming Convention* (UNC) path name for the object, which includes the server name. For example, enter **//servername/pathname/filename.doc**.

▶ **Files on your own computers.** Enter the full path name of the file. For example, enter **C:\My Documents\filename.doc**.

CROSS-REFERENCE

See Chapter 16 for information on working with OLE objects.

SHORTCUT

Copy an address from your Web browser and paste it into a Hyperlink field.

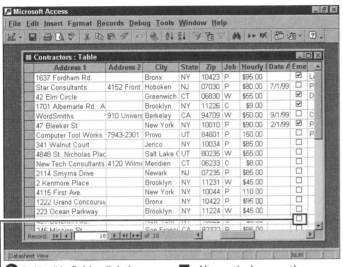

❶ In Yes/No fields, click the checkbox to add or remove the check mark.

■ Alternatively, press the spacebar to add or remove the check mark.

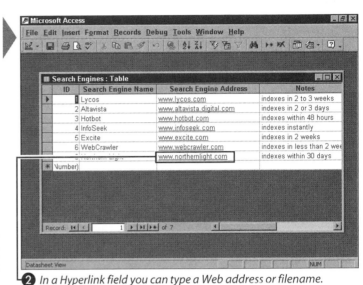

❷ In a Hyperlink field you can type a Web address or filename.

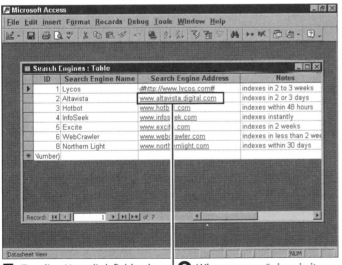

■ To edit a Hyperlink field, tab to it rather than clicking it.

■ Press F2 to put an insertion bar in it.

❸ When you see # signs in it, you can edit it in the usual ways.

■ Move to another field to stop editing and to remove the # signs.

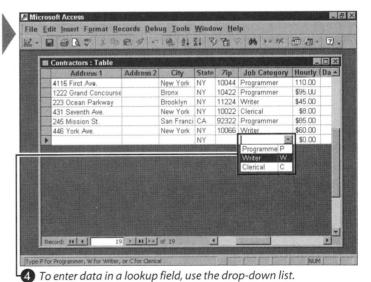

❹ To enter data in a lookup field, use the drop-down list.

Using Data-Entry Shortcuts

lthough most people find the basic methods of entering, viewing, and editing data fairly easy and more than adequate, additional methods can make your work faster and easier. These are fondly referred to as shortcuts. (Something we all need from time to time!)

If you need to enter the same data over and over again, such as a company name, you can enter it once, copy it, and then move to each field where this value should be entered and paste it instead of manually entering data.

If you want to create multiple records containing similar information, such as a company address, use the Paste Append command. While Paste just lets you place the copied text where the cursor is, Paste Append lets you copy an entire record and append it to the table. As you learned earlier, you can also select multiple records in a table by clicking and dragging the mouse through their selection boxes. You can copy and Paste Append them all to a table.

You can copy data from the same field of the previous record by pressing Ctrl+' or Ctrl+". (Hold down the Ctrl key and type either an apostrophe or quotation mark.)

To insert the current date, press Ctrl+;. To insert the current time, press Ctrl+:. (Hold down the Ctrl key and type a semicolon or colon.)

If you have defined a default value for a field (the Default Value property is described in Chapter 13), you can enter it in the field by pressing Ctrl+Alt+ spacebar. (Hold down both the Ctrl and Alt keys and then press the spacebar.) The default value is entered in the field automatically when the record is created, but you may want to use this key combination to re-enter the default value in a field that you edited earlier.

CROSS-REFERENCE

See Chapter 13 for information on how to create default values for fields, which enter data automatically.

SHORTCUT

Press Ctrl+X to cut, press Crtl+C to copy, and press Ctrl+V to paste.

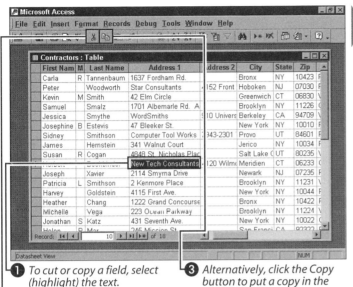

1 To cut or copy a field, select (highlight) the text.

2 Click the Cut button to remove it and put it in the Clipboard.

3 Alternatively, click the Copy button to put a copy in the Clipboard.

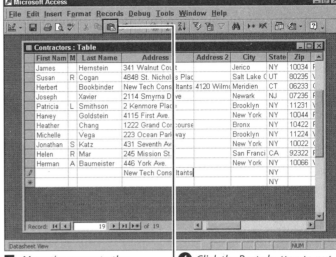

■ Move the cursor to the location where you want to place the text.

4 Click the Paste button to put the text in the new location.

5 To copy an entire record, click the record selection box to select it.

6 Click the Copy button to copy the record.

7 Choose Edit ⇨ Paste Append to add a copy of the record to the table.

■ You may have to display the full Edit menu.

49

Finding Records

Working with a database involves more than just entering and editing data. From the mountains of data, you may need to find a lone field or record. For example, you might need to look up someone by name to find their phone number. *Finds* (also called *searches*) let you look for information in fields that hold text or numbers.

The simplest way to find a single record is to place the cursor in a field that contains the data you want to search for, and choose Edit ➪ Find, or click the Find button. In the Find and Replace dialog box, enter the text or numbers that you are searching for in the Find What text box and click Find Next until you locate the record.

For example, if you are searching for the record of someone whose last name is Smith, and you think the record is near the beginning of the table, place the cursor in the Last Name field of the first record in the table, enter **Smith** in the Find What text box, and click the Find Next button to go to the first Smith in the table. If that is not the right person, click the Find Next button repeatedly until you get to the right Smith. When you find the right person, click the Cancel button to close the Find and Replace dialog box and return to the table to work with that record.

If the Find and Replace dialog box covers up your database, simply click and drag it to move it to a more convenient location.

If Access cannot find the record, it displays a message saying it has finished searching the records and the search item was not found, as shown in the lower-left figure. (If you have the Assistant turned on, you will get a different message from the one shown.)

You can use Finds to find more than one entry — for example, all the fields containing the entry N/A — but it will stop at each one until you tell it to find the next. If you want to display all the found records, you should create a filter or a query.

Continued

TAKE NOTE

▶ USING INDEXED FINDS

Finds are faster with indexed fields. For example, if you often search for a last name, you should create an index on the Last Name field. It is particularly important to use an index if you are working with table that has a very large number of records. Indexes are covered in Chapter 17.

▶ FINDS VERSUS QUERIES

Queries let you use much more sophisticated criteria to isolate one or more matching records; for example, you can use queries to search for values in several fields. Finds are the easiest way to search for a record with a single value in one of its fields.

CROSS-REFERENCE

For more information on queries, see Chapter 4.

SHORTCUT

You can press Ctrl+F instead of choosing Edit Find.

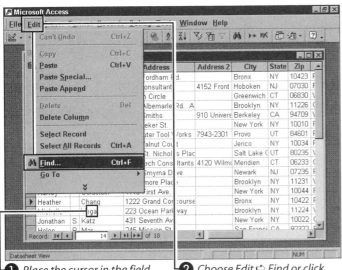

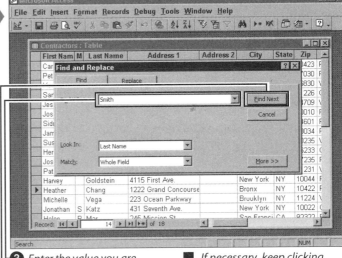

① *Place the cursor in the field with the data you are searching for.*

② *Choose Edit ➪ Find or click the Find button to display the Find and Replace dialog box.*

③ *Enter the value you are searching for in the Find What text box.*

④ *Click the Find Next button to find the next record with that value.*

■ *If necessary, keep clicking Find Next until you find the record you want.*

■ *Click Cancel to work with that record.*

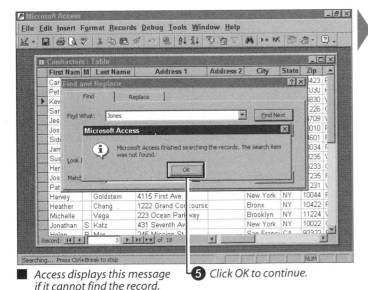

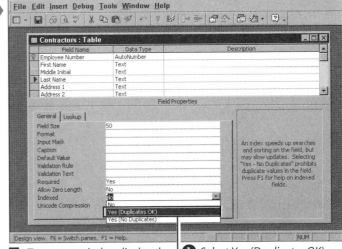

■ *Access displays this message if it cannot find the record.*

⑤ *Click OK to continue.*

■ *To create an index, display the table in Design view.*

■ *Place the cursor in the field you want to Index.*

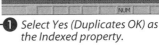

① *Select Yes (Duplicates OK) as the Indexed property.*

Finding Records
Continued

The Find and Replace dialog box offers a few other options. By default, the value you enter in the Find What text box must be the same as the entire entry in the field. You can use the Match drop-down list, shown in the upper-left figure, to search for partial matches. Start of Field finds all records that begin with the value you entered. Any Part of Field finds records that have the value anywhere in the field.

By default, the Find option searches for the value only in the field where the cursor was when you began the search. If you choose the name of the table in the Look In drop-down list, it searches for the value in all the fields of the table.

The Search drop-down list lets you search All of the table, search Up until you reach the beginning, or search Down until the end.

By default, finds do not distinguish between upper- and lowercase letters. Select the Match Case checkbox if you want to find records with the text capitalized exactly as you have entered it.

Select the Search Fields as Formatted checkbox if you want to search for the values displayed according to the display format you specified for the field. For example, if you search for a date by entering **11/15/99** in the Find What text box, the search ordinarily finds matching records whether they are formatted as 11/15/99, 15-Nov-99, November 15, 1999, and so on. If you select the Search Fields as Formatted option, Access only finds records that were input as 11/15/99.

Rather than entering an exact value in the Find What text box, you can use the wildcard characters shown in the following table as part or all of the value for which you are searching.

Find and Replace

You might want to use Find and Replace if data changes in the same way in many records. For example, if a company changes its name, you can use the feature to change the company name of everyone in your mailing list who works for this company.

WILDCARD CHARACTERS FOR FINDS

Character	Meaning	Example
?	Matches any single character.	Sm?th matches Smith, Smyth, Smeth, and so on.
*	Matches any number of characters.	Sm* matches Smith, Smyth, Smithson, Smythers, and so on.
[ ]	Matches all options enclosed in brackets.	Sm[iy]th matches Smith or Smyth but not Smeth.
[!]	Matches all options not enclosed in brackets.	Sm[!i]th matches Smyth or Smeth but not Smith.
[–]	Matches a range of characters.	[a-d]* matches any value beginning with a, b, c, or d.

CROSS-REFERENCE

For a more complete discussion of wildcards, see Chapter 4.

SHORTCUT

Press Ctrl+H to display the Find and Replace dialog box.

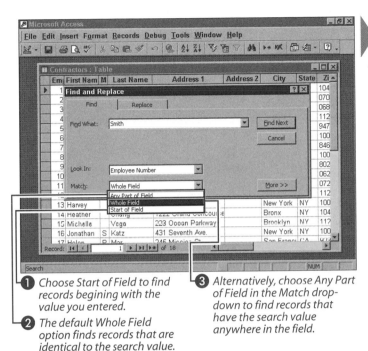

① *Choose Start of Field to find records begining with the value you entered.*

② *The default Whole Field option finds records that are identical to the search value.*

③ *Alternatively, choose Any Part of Field in the Match drop-down to find records that have the search value anywhere in the field.*

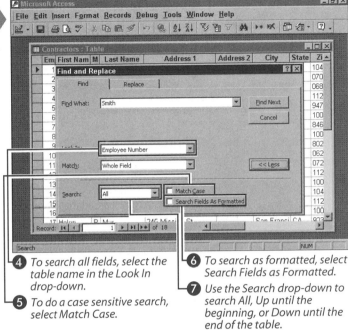

④ *To search all fields, select the table name in the Look In drop-down.*

⑤ *To do a case sensitive search, select Match Case.*

⑥ *To search as formatted, select Search Fields as Formatted.*

⑦ *Use the Search drop-down to search All, Up until the beginning, or Down until the end of the table.*

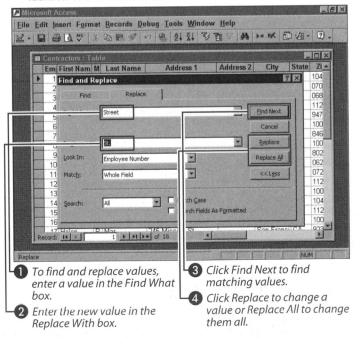

① *To find and replace values, enter a value in the Find What box.*

② *Enter the new value in the Replace With box.*

③ *Click Find Next to find matching values.*

④ *Click Replace to change a value or Replace All to change them all.*

TAKE NOTE

SPEEDING UP SEARCHES

Searching all fields is much slower than searching only the current field, so you should use this option only if you have some special reason. A formatted search also slows down the find, and you should use it only with good reason.

Working with Columns

The main limitation of Datasheet view is that you usually cannot see all the fields of a record. For example, if you want to look at a list of names and phone numbers, the name fields may disappear beyond the left edge of the screen when you scroll right to see telephone number. Also, in Datasheet view, some columns are unnecessarily wide while others are too narrow to display all the data in them. You can solve these problems by resizing or moving the columns.

Resizing Columns

There are several ways to resize columns. You can click and drag the right edge of a column to the desired width, or you can use the Column Width dialog box (under the Format menu) to enter the character width you want to display.

You can also right-click a column heading and select Column Width to specify its width. If you select multiple columns and then select Column Width, they are all resized to the new width.

You can make columns as wide or as narrow as you need them, when you need them. For example, if you just need to see the Name and Phone Number fields, you can make the columns in between narrow, so you can see the two fields without scrolling. The data in the middle columns will not be readable, but it does not need to be. You can widen the columns when you need to read the data.

Moving Columns

You may also choose to move a field closer to another one. To do this, simply click its column heading and drag it to where you want to place it; all of its entries follow. To select multiple adjacent columns, select a single column, hold down the Shift key, then select another column; click and drag to move them all.

If the new location is between two columns, the columns to the right move over one column (but no data is replaced or overwritten). You cannot cut a column and then paste it in the position you want. If you try to do this, nothing happens.

Continued

TAKE NOTE

GETTING THE BEST FIT

If you click the Best Fit button of the Column Width dialog box, the columns will automatically be sized to fit the longest entry in the column, including the data and the title of the column. This option is useful sometimes, but other times it is not really the best fit. For example, if your table has a Middle Initial field, it only needs to hold one letter. Selecting Best Fit would make the column wide enough to display the column heading Middle Initial — much wider than you actually need it in order to see the data.

CROSS-REFERENCE
For information on resizing rows, see the next section.

SHORTCUT
You can also select a range of columns by clicking the first column heading and dragging through all the other headings.

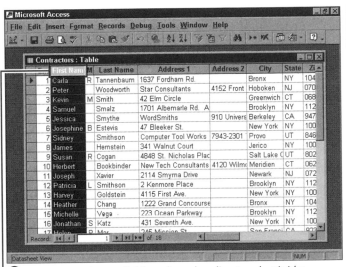

1 To move a column, click its column heading to select it (the selected column is highlighted). Then click and drag the column heading to its new location and release the mouse.

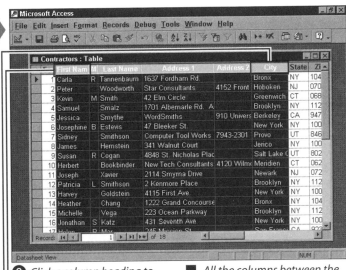

2 Click a column heading to select the first column you want.

3 Hold down the Shift key and click the column heading of the last column you want.

■ All the columns between the two are selected.

■ Click and drag a column heading to move them all.

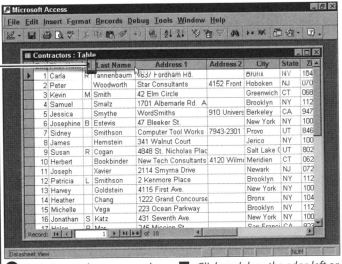

4 To resize a column, move the pointer to the right edge of a column heading. It is displayed as a vertical bar with arrows pointing left and right.

■ Click and drag the edge left or right to narrow or widen the column.

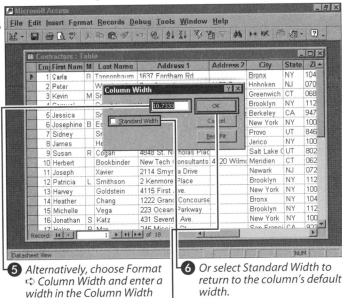

5 Alternatively, choose Format ⇨ Column Width and enter a width in the Column Width dialog box.

6 Or select Standard Width to return to the column's default width.

7 Click OK.

Resizing and moving columns will usually be enough to make it easy to work with your Datasheet, but there are a couple of other options that should be considered: hiding and freezing columns.

Hiding Columns

Hiding columns removes columns from view. You can hide columns when you do not need to work with them, so you can move through the Datasheet with greater ease. For example, if there are three columns between the Name and Phone Number fields of your database, you could hide them so the two fields appear side by side. The data in the hidden columns is pulled out of the table and held by Access so it will not be displayed. When you use Tab or the Arrow key with columns hidden, the cursor moves to the next visible column. The upper-left figure shows how to hide columns and the upper-right figure shows how to make hidden columns reappear.

Freezing Columns

Sometimes it is convenient to freeze columns so that they are always displayed, even as you scroll right to see additional fields. For example, you might want to display the First Name and Last Name fields permanently at the left edge of the table as you scroll right to see all the other data for these people.

Freezing columns involves "drawing a line" down the right side of a field and telling Access to freeze all of the columns to the left. When you scroll to the right, the frozen columns do not scroll, but all columns to the right of the freeze line scroll by and seem to disappear under the frozen columns. The lower-left figure shows how to freeze columns and the lower-right figure shows how to unfreeze them.

Both hiding and freezing are options on the extended menu, so you may have to click the arrow at the bottom of the Format menu to use them.

Notice that deleting a column is not an option in Datasheet view. If you select a column, you do not have a menu choice to delete it, which would be tantamount to deleting the field. You have to delete fields in Design view.

TAKE NOTE

▶ **HIDING COLUMNS SELECTIVELY**

You can also use the Unhide Columns dialog box to hide columns selectively. In the dialog box, click the checkboxes to remove check marks for the columns you want hidden and to add check marks to the ones you want displayed. Then click Close.

▶ **USING QUERIES**

You can also hide columns by running a query that only includes specific fields. To do so, select the fields that you want to show in your query, but run it with no criteria, so you get every record. Queries are covered in detail in Chapters 4 and 9.

CROSS-REFERENCE
To control the display more completely, see Chapters 8 and 9 for information on creating a custom form.

SHORTCUT
If you only have to edit data in certain fields, hiding columns can save time.

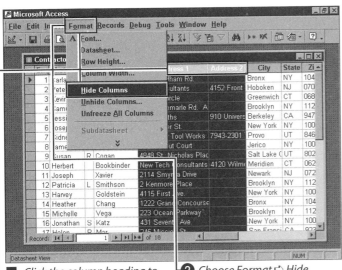

■ Click the column heading to select the column you want to hide.

❶ Hold down the Shift key during column selection to select more than one.

❷ Choose Format ➪ Hide Column.

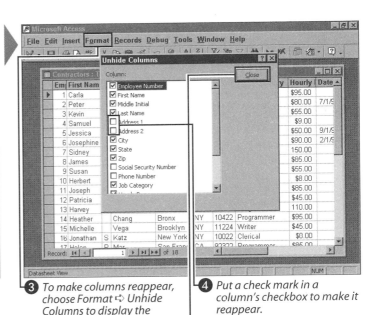

❸ To make columns reappear, choose Format ➪ Unhide Columns to display the Unhide Columns dialog box.

❹ Put a check mark in a column's checkbox to make it reappear.

❺ Select Close.

❻ To freeze columns, click the column heading to select a column. Hold down the Shift key during column selection to select more than one.

❼ Choose Format ➪ Freeze Columns.

❽ The frozen columns are automatically moved to the left. Chose Format ➪ Unfreeze All Columns when you want to unfreeze them.

■ You may need to move the columns back to their original location using the techniques described in Moving Columns.

Changing the Data Display

Usually, you will want to create forms or reports to control how your data is displayed, but there are times when it is easier to use the following quick methods to change the way your data is displayed in the Datasheet.

Use a quick sort if you want to arrange your records alphabetically or by date. An Ascending sort is alphabetical for Text fields, from lowest to highest value for Number fields, and from earliest to latest date for Date fields. Descending sorts are particularly useful in Date fields, to put the most recent dates at the top of its list. To sort, put the cursor in any record in the field on which you want the sort to be based, then click the Sort Ascending or Sort Descending button depending on what you want.

You can also make changes to the appearance of the data by changing fonts, alignment, and row and column sizes.

The first thing you should look at is formatting the text and the font. Serif fonts (like Arial) are ideal for numeric data; text data reads better in a nonscript serif font, such as Times New Roman. You can also apply color to the text. However, any changes you make apply to the heading and all the records and fields in the datasheet, so you must choose the one that is best for displaying all your data. Choose

Format ➪ Font to display the Font dialog box, shown in the upper-right figure, and use it to select a typeface, type size, and other effects.

After making your changes, it is time to see how everything looks on screen. You may need to make the rows shorter and the columns narrower in order to make everything fit. On the other hand, if you think more space will make your table easier to read, you might want to do the opposite. The quick way to resize rows is to move the pointer to the line between any two record selector buttons (for rows) and then click and drag. The height of all rows is changed.

You can use these changes to enhance screen viewing or a quick printout of data (more about this in the next task).

TAKE NOTE

SAVING DATASHEET SETTINGS

You can choose File ➪ Save at any time to save changes to the table layout, including the changes in columns described in the previous section and the changes in format described here. If you close the Table window without saving changes, Access displays a dialog box that asks you if you want to Save layout changes.

CROSS-REFERENCE

To better control how your data is printed, see Chapter 10 for information on designing custom reports.

SHORTCUT

Press Ctrl+S instead of choosing File ➪ Save.

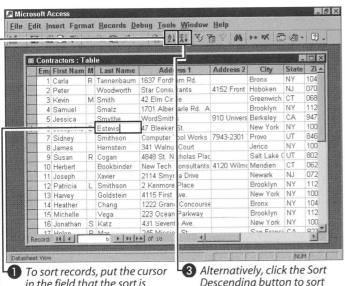

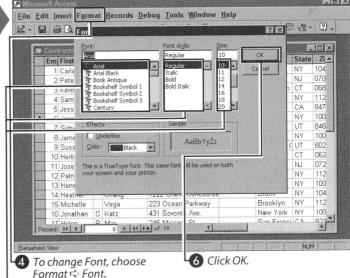

① To sort records, put the cursor in the field that the sort is based on.

② Click the Sort Ascending button to sort from A to Z, or lowest to highest value.

③ Alternatively, click the Sort Descending button to sort from Z to A, or highest to lowest value.

④ To change Font, choose Format ➪ Font.

⑤ Choose font, font style, size, and other effects.

⑥ Click OK.

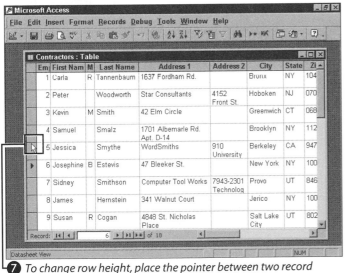

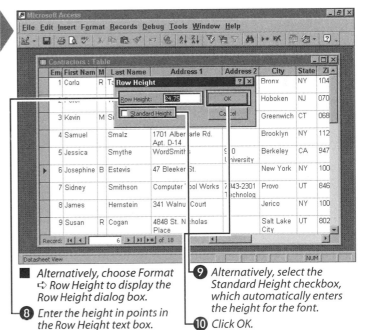

⑦ To change row height, place the pointer between two record selection boxes and click and drag. All row heights are changed.

■ Alternatively, choose Format ➪ Row Height to display the Row Height dialog box.

⑧ Enter the height in points in the Row Height text box.

⑨ Alternatively, select the Standard Height checkbox, which automatically enters the height for the font.

⑩ Click OK.

Printing and Previewing the Datasheet

It is sometimes easier to print the Datasheet than to create a report. For example, if you want to print out names and telephone numbers to call people on your address list, you can simply hide the unnecessary columns and print a list of names and phone numbers. You can also change the font and make other formatting changes in the Datasheet, as described previously.

When selecting data to print, you are not limited to selecting columns or pages, you can also select just a few rows (records). The Print dialog box's Print Range area lets you select how much of the table you want to print. You can print it all, print the selected rows, or print only certain pages. If you have a large table, you may want to print only one page as a sample, to make sure it is right, before printing the entire table. Access includes the column headings by default.

The Print dialog box's Number of Copies spinner allows you to indicate how many copies you want to print. The Collate Copies checkbox is selected by default, so that if you print more than one multipage Datasheet, each copy of the Datasheet is printed from beginning to end before the next one is printed.

Most people print directly from the Datasheet for quick glances at information. When you print a table, Access automatically includes the table name and the date as the header, which can be useful if you have to search through several printouts to find the latest version your boss needs to approve.

You may want to modify the margins, especially if a table is a bit too wide to fit on the page. This can be done in the Margins Tab of Page Setup. If your data is too wide to fit in the ordinary page width, you should use Landscape rather than Portrait orientation. The Page Tab in Page Setup enables you to select the orientation of your printed data. This tab also lets you specify the size and source of the paper and choose a printer other than the default printer. For datasheets too wide for even Landscape orientation, you might want to consider using legal size paper in Landscape orientation. If you are not sure which look will be best for your data, you can preview your results with Print Preview.

Continued

TAKE NOTE

PRINTING TO DISK

The Print to File checkbox lets you store the contents of the table and all the printer codes needed to print it on disk. After you select OK, Access displays a dialog box that lets you name the file. Anyone who has the printer named on the top of this dialog box can print this file, even if they do not have Access. For example, you can use this feature if you want the file printed by an assistant, who does not have Access.

CROSS-REFERENCE

See the next section for information on how to Preview the Datasheet before printing it.

SHORTCUT

Press Ctrl+P instead of choosing File ⇨ Print.

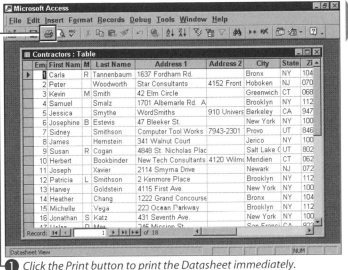

1 Click the Print button to print the Datasheet immediately.

2 Alternatively, choose File ⇨ Print to display the Print dialog box.

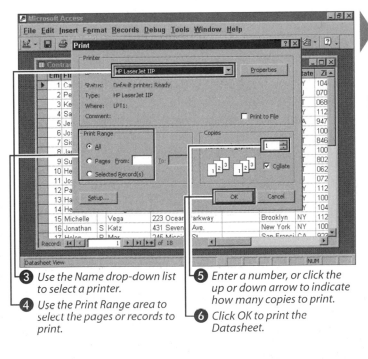

3 Use the Name drop-down list to select a printer.

4 Use the Print Range area to select the pages or records to print.

5 Enter a number, or click the up or down arrow to indicate how many copies to print.

6 Click OK to print the Datasheet.

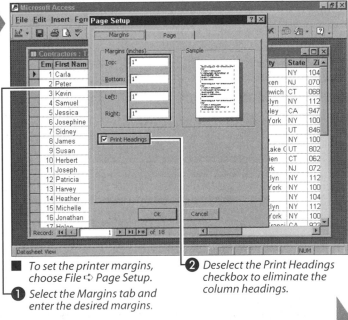

■ To set the printer margins, choose File ⇨ Page Setup.

1 Select the Margins tab and enter the desired margins.

2 Deselect the Print Headings checkbox to eliminate the column headings.

Printing and Previewing the Datasheet *Continued*

Before you print, it is often best to display the Datasheet in the Print Preview window. When you first open Print Preview, it provides you with an exact, scaled down version of the Datasheet that allows you to see how each page of the Datasheet will look when it is printed.

In Print Preview, you can get a good look at margins, page breaks, and overall number of pages. You might use this view to look for places where you might adjust data for more logical breaks from one page to the next. To do this, you may need to take a closer look at the data. Simply use the magnifying glass pointer or the Zoom tool to click the preview and display it in actual size or make it to small enough to see a full page. You can also use the Zoom drop-down list to choose among a wider range of sizes, ranging from 200 percent to 10 percent of actual size. Choose Fit to make the page small enough to fit in the window.

To display the table one or two pages at a time, you can click the One Page or Two Page button. Or you can view several pages at once by clicking the Multiple Page button and selecting the number of pages to display on screen. This feature can be useful if you want to look quickly through a long document and get an idea of its overall layout.

If you find that you need a little more space, you can click the edge of the page to bring up margin handles. Click and drag these handles to resize the margins until the layout meets your needs. Be careful about leaving too little margin, however. You may be able to see all of the data in Print Preview, but your printer may not be able to handle it, and you may still cut off some of the data. While you can make changes to the margins in Print Preview, you cannot change data or field names. To do this, you have to return to Datasheet view.

You can go directly from Print Preview to Page Setup by right-clicking the Print Preview page and selecting Page Setup.

If you decide the preview is satisfactory, you can print directly from the Print Preview screen by clicking the Print button, but you will not be able to make adjustments such as choosing a different printer or number of copies. To do so, you need to go back to Datasheet view and select Print from the File menu.

TAKE NOTE

MOVING AMONG PAGES IN PRINT PREVIEW

You can use the page controls at the bottom of the Print Preview window to specify which pages are displayed. These work just like the record controls and record indicator at the bottom of the Datasheet, discussed earlier in this chapter, in the section "Working with Records."

CROSS-REFERENCE

See Chapter 10 for more information on the Page Setup dialog box.

SHORTCUT

Press PgDn and PgUp to move quickly among pages in Print Preview.

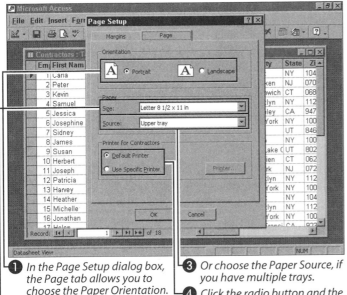

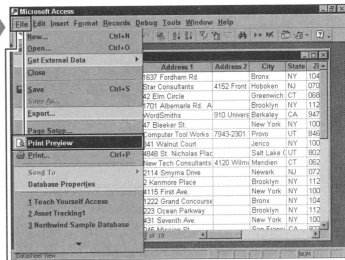

1 In the Page Setup dialog box, the Page tab allows you to choose the Paper Orientation.

2 Choose the paper size.

3 Or choose the Paper Source, if you have multiple trays.

4 Click the radio button and the Printer to choose a different printer.

5 To see what your document will look like printed, choose File ➪ Print Preview or click the Print Preview button.

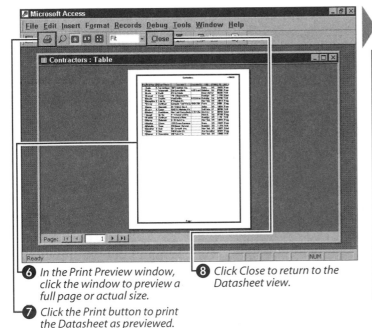

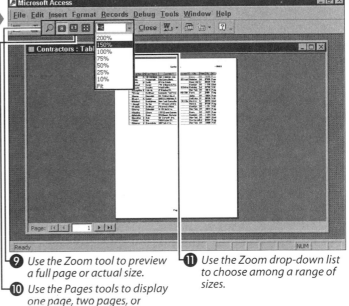

6 In the Print Preview window, click the window to preview a full page or actual size.

7 Click the Print button to print the Datasheet as previewed.

8 Click Close to return to the Datasheet view.

9 Use the Zoom tool to preview a full page or actual size.

10 Use the Pages tools to display one page, two pages, or multiple pages.

11 Use the Zoom drop-down list to choose among a range of sizes.

Personal Workbook

Q&A

1 What are two ways to enter data in a Yes/No field?

_____

_____

_____

2 What data can you enter in a Hyperlink field?

_____

_____

_____

3 How do you edit a Hyperlink field?

_____

_____

_____

4 How do you save your data entries? How often should you do this?

_____

_____

_____

5 What is the fastest way to enter a record that is almost identical to an existing record?

_____

_____

6 How do you move a column to make it the first column displayed in the datasheet?

_____

_____

_____

7 What is the fastest way to sort records alphabetically by Last Name?

_____

_____

_____

8 What should you do if you want to print a table, but it is a bit too wide to fit on a standard page?

_____

_____

_____

ANSWERS: PAGE 344

EXTRA PRACTICE

1 Enter sample data in the mailing list table you created in Chapter 2.

2 Create a table to list your favorite Web sites, and add Hyperlink fields to link to these sites.

3 Hide all the fields in the Mailing List table except First and Last Name, City, and State.

4 Sort the Mailing List table by Last Name.

5 Make the display font 12-point Times New Roman, and make the rows tall enough to hold the new font.

6 Display the table in the Print Preview window and print it.

REAL-WORLD APPLICATIONS

✔ Before calling a client, you display your Client table and use a find to look up the client's name.

✔ Before telephoning a list of clients, you hide all the fields except the Name and Telephone Number fields, to make it easier to see the phone numbers without scrolling.

✔ One of the telephone area codes where you do business has been split into two area codes. You do a find and replace with the old area code as the Find value and the new one as the Replace value. Before replacing, you look at the city for each record to see if it is in a location with a new area code.

Visual Quiz

The figure shows a Mailing List table with the data display altered. What steps are necessary to display the data in this way?

_____

_____

_____

_____

_____

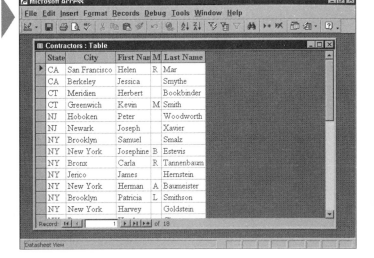

CHAPTER 4

MASTER THESE SKILLS

▶ **Creating a Query Using the Wizard**

▶ **Creating a Query in Design View**

▶ **Including Fields in the Result**

▶ **Controlling Sort Order and Field Display**

▶ **Entering Criteria**

▶ **Using the Query**

Using Queries

Tables are wonderful tools for managing large numbers of records. However, some tables can become bulky, and you may want to create subtables that show only a few fields or a few records. To bring an overgrown table down to size, you can create a *query*. Queries can be used to create an independent object containing all the records with only a few fields, some of the records with only a few fields, or some of the records with all of the fields.

Queries aren't always needed to bring a bulky table under control. If there are a few unwanted fields, you might simply hide them. Most people create a query when they need to see subsets of an existing table as a separate table.

Queries can be used like tables as the basis of a form, report, or data-access page. Tables and queries both contain sets of fields and records; so either can provide the raw information for a form, report, or page. However, when you create a query, you can specify which fields and records of a table are displayed and the order in which they are displayed. For example, if you

have a table that holds your customers' contact information, you can create a query that displays only the name and telephone number fields of people from New York state, listed alphabetically by name.

There are two basic types of queries: *select* queries and *action* queries. Select queries include simple select, summary, and parameter queries. This chapter only covers *simple select queries*, which let you specify which fields and records of a table are displayed. Advanced queries, such as action queries that let you modify the data in tables, are discussed in Chapter 11.

An alternative to a query is a *filter*. Filters work like select queries, except that they are not independent tables. Chapter 5 covers filters.

Because the query and parent table are related (the term is a *dynaset*), any changes you make to the data in the query are reflected in the parent table and vice versa. Be especially wary about making deletions in a query because they cannot be undone (Access warns you of this before you complete the deletion).

Creating a Query Using the Wizard

The easiest way to create a query is by using the Simple Query Wizard. Although not as powerful as creating a query in Design view, it is often a fast, efficient tool that takes much of the hassle out of manually creating a table. Where it really stands out is in its ability to make combining multiple tables of relational databases a fairly painless process. You learn about queries with relational databases in Chapter 7.

Using the Simple Query Wizard may not always be the best choice. It is easy to hide a table's fields in the Table window or to create a query in Design view that specifies which fields are included, so you rarely have occasion to use this Wizard when working with a simple, single-table database. However, the last choice in the Wizard enables you to switch to Design view so you can modify the query and take advantage of the Design view features. The Wizard also enables you to create the query without any further modifications.

The Simple Query Wizard presents clear, step-by-step instructions to help you create your query. After you select the table you want to query, the Wizard provides the listing of available fields. Use the field picker to move the fields you want to include from the Available Fields list to the Selected Fields list. If you want to change the order of the fields after they've been selected, click the field and then click the arrow pointing back to the original list. Then select it again and reinsert it by clicking the field positioned above where you want it. Be sure you like the order of the fields before you click Finish, because it's difficult to go back and make modifications unless you switch to Design view.

The Wizard also asks you whether you're creating a *detail query,* which shows all the fields you selected in all the records of the table, or a *summary query,* which displays a Sum, Average, Minimum, or Maximum value in numeric fields (see Chapter 11).

The last step lets you open or modify the table, or you may modify the query design.

TAKE NOTE

▶ QUERYING A QUERY

You can actually create a query from an existing query. Queries create independent tables, which appear in the Tables/Queries listing. Simply identify the query to use as the basis for the query.

▶ OPENING EXISTING QUERIES

To open an existing query in Datasheet view, click the Queries button in the Database window, select the query name in the list box, and then click Open. To open an existing query in Design view, click Queries in the Database window, select the query name from the list, and then click Design.

CROSS-REFERENCE
If you do not know how to use a wizard, see the section "Creating New Objects" in Chapter 1.

SHORTCUT
In the field picker, you can also move fields from one list to the other by double-clicking them.

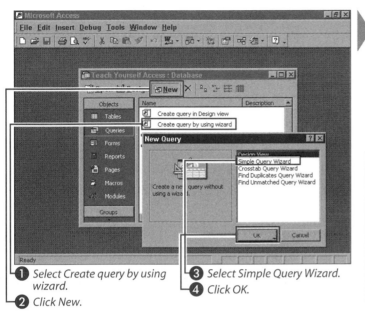

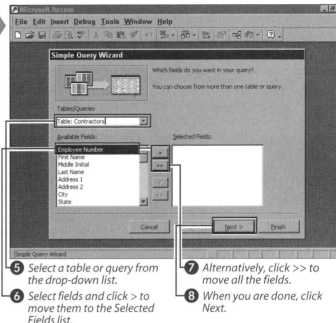

① *Select Create query by using wizard.*

③ *Select Simple Query Wizard.*

④ *Click OK.*

② *Click New.*

⑤ *Select a table or query from the drop-down list.*

⑥ *Select fields and click > to move them to the Selected Fields list.*

⑦ *Alternatively, click >> to move all the fields.*

⑧ *When you are done, click Next.*

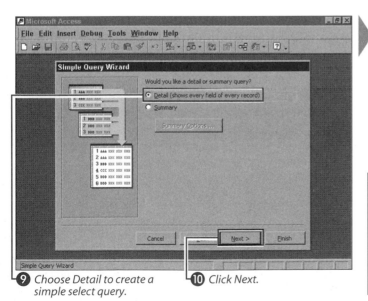

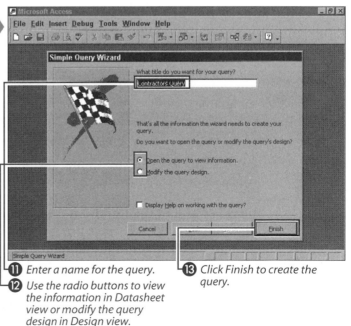

⑨ *Choose Detail to create a simple select query.*

⑩ *Click Next.*

⑪ *Enter a name for the query.*

⑫ *Use the radio buttons to view the information in Datasheet view or modify the query design in Design view.*

⑬ *Click Finish to create the query.*

Creating a Query in Design View

Design view allows your creativity to shine. You control where the fields appear in the query and how they will appear. While the Simple Query Wizard can be helpful, once you work with Design view a few times and see how easy it is to be on your own, you will probably bypass the Wizard.

The modification possibilities in Design view are seemingly endless. Design view lets you control which records are displayed and their sort order, as well as which fields are displayed. You can specify a criterion, such as all the customers from New York, and create a query containing only your New York customers. Or you can create a query with several criteria, like all the customers from New York whose last name begins with S and who owe you more than $10,000. You can hide any fields, which means you don't need to see the state of residence or the customer number if you don't want to. You can also pull fields from several different tables and sort them many different ways, which I cover in Chapter 7.

The lower-right figure shows a query design. You can see some similarities in table design, but the query design allows you to designate a sort order and criteria after you select the fields. To run the query, you must click the Run button (the red exclamation

point on the toolbar). Once a query has been created, you can further refine it if you like. You can modify or build a query as many times as you need or create as many queries as you want, which is great if you have a huge database and only need to see several specific records.

TAKE NOTE

WORKING WITH COLUMNS

You can select, move, and resize columns in the design grid just as you do in a table. Click the selector box above a column to select it, and then click or drag it to move it. Move the pointer to the right edge of the selector box, where it's displayed as a vertical line with arrows pointing in both directions, and click and drag to resize the column. You can also add a column (Insert ⇨ Column) and delete a selected column by right-clicking and selecting Cut.

QUERY BY EXAMPLE

In the Criteria line of the Select Query window's design grid, you identify the criterion by simply typing an example of how a typical record entry will appear. So to select only records from New York, you need to type **NY**.

CROSS-REFERENCE

See the section "Working with Columns" in Chapter 3 for more information on moving and resizing columns.

SHORTCUT

Double-click Create query in Design view to bypass the New Query dialog box and immediately display the Show Table dialog box.

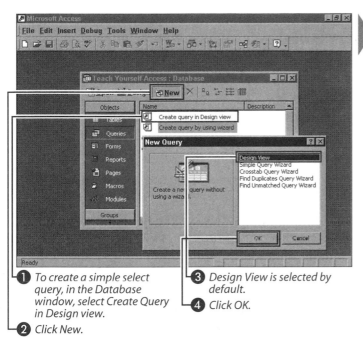

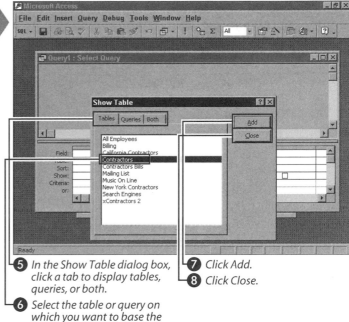

❶ To create a simple select query, in the Database window, select Create Query in Design view.

❷ Click New.

❸ Design View is selected by default.

❹ Click OK.

❺ In the Show Table dialog box, click a tab to display tables, queries, or both.

❻ Select the table or query on which you want to base the query.

❼ Click Add.

❽ Click Close.

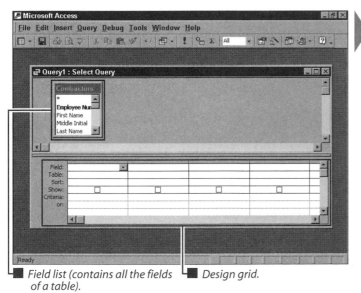

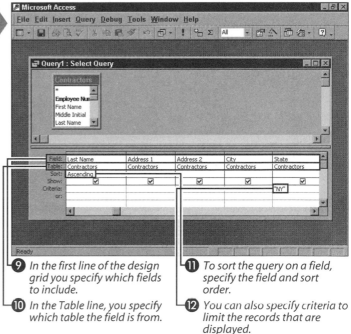

■ Field list (contains all the fields of a table).

■ Design grid.

❾ In the first line of the design grid you specify which fields to include.

❿ In the Table line, you specify which table the field is from.

⓫ To sort the query on a field, specify the field and sort order.

⓬ You can also specify criteria to limit the records that are displayed.

Including Fields in the Result

One purpose in creating a query is to view a select group of fields from some or all of your records. In Design view, there are several easy ways to specify query fields.

Perhaps the easiest method is to click in the Field cell of the design grid and use the field name drop-down list. Another option is to click and drag the field name from the Field List to a Field cell. Or you can simply double-click the selected field in the Field List to place the field in the next available column. If you type the name in the Field cell, the names of fields beginning with the letters that you type are displayed in the cell. For example, when you type **S**, the field name "State" might be displayed, and when you type **So**, the name "Social Security Number" might be displayed. This is an easy way of entering field names.

If you want future changes in the parent table to automatically appear in the query, select and place the asterisk from the field list. The asterisk represents all the fields in a table. If you select and place each field individually, any later additions to the parent table will not be shown in your query. You will have to manually update it.

While using the asterisk method is an easy way to copy a table, it doesn't allow you to enter criteria or sort. To do this, you must individually select the fields you want to manipulate and add them to the Design Grid alongside the asterisk entry. Of course, these fields will show up twice in the results unless you uncheck the Show box for the field column. This may seem like a lot of work, but it is the only way to link the parent table and the query, which keeps the query current and manipulate the query's data.

TAKE NOTE

ADDING MULTIPLE FIELDS

If you select multiple fields in the field list, you can click and drag them to a Field cell, and they will all be placed in separate Field cells. To select multiple fields, hold down the Ctrl key when you click them. To select a group of fields, click the first field, hold down the Shift key, and then click the last field; all the fields between these two are selected.

WHEN TO USE THE ASTERISK

While using the asterisk makes your work easier, it can make it a bit more difficult to sort or enter criteria for the fields. Generally when working with a single table, adding all the individual field names is easiest. The asterisk is most useful when you are including all fields from additional tables in a relational database.

CROSS-REFERENCE

See Chapter 7 for information on adding fields from multiple tables.

SHORTCUT

To select all fields, double-click the field list's title bar.

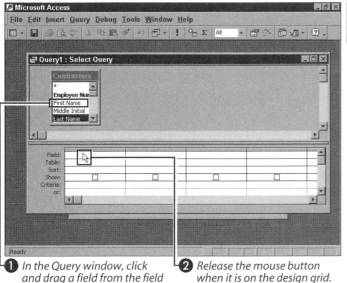

1 In the Query window, click and drag a field from the field list.

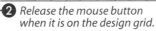

2 Release the mouse button when it is on the design grid.

■ Alternatively, double-click the field in the field list to place it in the next available column.

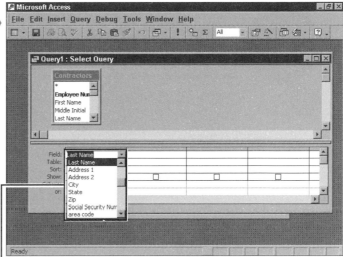

3 Alternatively, use the Field drop-down list to add the field to the design grid.

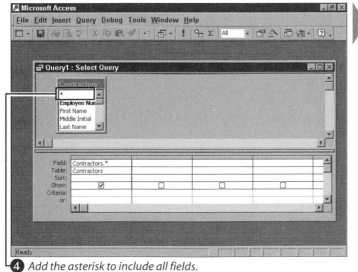

4 Add the asterisk to include all fields.

5 If you want to sort or specify criteria for a field, click and drag it from the field list to the design grid.

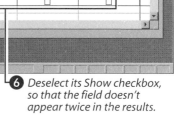

6 Deselect its Show checkbox, so that the field doesn't appear twice in the results.

Controlling Sort Order and Field Display

One of the most popular uses of a query is to sort records according to a specific field. The query's result records can be sorted according to one field or multiple fields. As in most tables, fields can be sorted in ascending or descending order, and you can turn off the sort option at any time.

As you learned earlier, a simple sort on one field can be done without a query. But when you need to sort on multiple fields, you need to use a query, and if you have many records in your table, you often need to sort the table on more than one field. For example, to alphabetize records by name, you need to sort on both the Last Name and the First Name fields to make sure that Aaron Jones comes before Zazu Jones. To do this, select Ascending in the Sort cell of both the Last Name and the First Name fields.

When you sort on multiple fields, Access bases the sort on the leftmost field and uses fields to its right as tie-breakers when values in the leftmost field are the same. To sort by name, you must place the Last Name field to the left of the First Name field, as shown in the upper-right figure.

You can also combine ascending and descending sorts. For example, you might sort your customers by name in alphabetical order, and also sort their orders with the most recent first. If you no longer want to sort on a field that you sorted on previously, select (**not sorted**) in the Sort cell.

You may need to change the order of fields in the design grid if you are sorting on multiple fields. You move a field in the design grid in the same way that you move a column in a table: Click its title to select it, and then click and drag its title to move it. This can be handy when the most important field to see in the query isn't the first field in the design grid.

You can also insert or delete columns to change field order or to add or remove fields. Place the cursor in a field, choose Insert ⇨ Columns to insert a blank column to its left, and use the drop-down list to select a field. To delete a field, place the cursor in the column and choose Edit ⇨ Delete Column.

TAKE NOTE

UNDERSTANDING SORT ORDER

In an ascending sort, text fields are sorted in alphabetical order, and the sort does not take account of capitalization. Number, Currency, and AutoNumber are sorted from the smallest to the largest number. Date fields are sorted from the earliest to the latest date. You cannot sort on other data types. Descending sorts are useful for Date fields, to get the most recent records at the top of the list.

CROSS-REFERENCE

For more information on moving fields, see "Working with Columns" in Chapter 3.

SHORTCUT

To insert a column, click and drag a field to the location you want, and the other fields will move to the right.

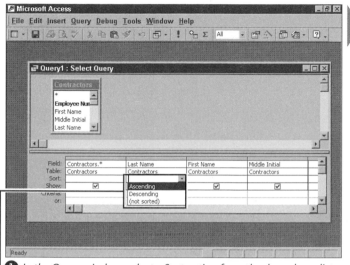

❶ In the Query window, select a Sort option from the drop-down list of the design grid.

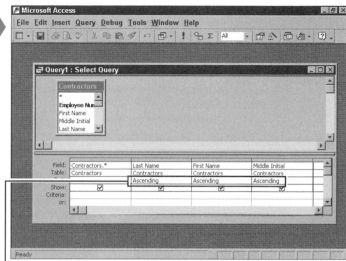

❷ To sort by name, place the last name to the left of the first name and select Ascending sort for both.

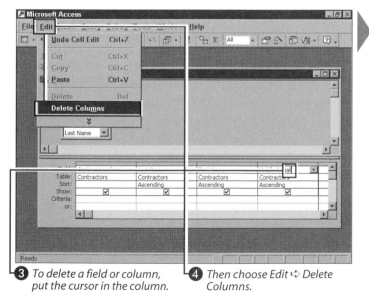

❸ To delete a field or column, put the cursor in the column.

❹ Then choose Edit ➪ Delete Columns.

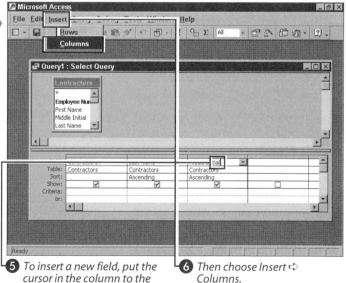

❺ To insert a new field, put the cursor in the column to the right of where you want it to appear.

❻ Then choose Insert ➪ Columns.

Entering Criteria

Sorting records simply rearranges all the records in the table in a particular order. To look at specific records in the table, you must enter a criterion in the Criteria line of the design grid under the desired field. When you enter criteria in a query, only records that match the criteria will be displayed in the result.

For text fields, values are marked by quotation marks ("NY"). Numeric fields are marked by pound symbols (#3000#). You can type in these *delimiters*, as they are called, as you enter the value, or simply type in the value, and Access automatically puts the delimiters around it. You can also type **ny**, and Access will still find and display all records from New York, because text field queries are not case sensitive.

Most people use criteria to search for specific text or numeric values (State, or Postal Code, for example). But criteria can take on a much broader scope. Access can also search for yes/no criteria. Entering Yes, True, On, or 1 tells Access to search for all Yes records. Entering No, False, Off, or 0 tells Access to search for all No records. If you create a field in your client directory for all clients who have renewed their membership for the year, you can easily identify those who need a follow-up call by entering No as the criterion for that field.

When searching for values, you may need to look for all clients from New York, New Jersey, or Connecticut. The Or line enables you to enter additional criteria, and Access searches for all records that have any one of the criteria. This is called a *logical OR*. You may also need to search for records that have specific values in more than one field (clients in New York who are also named Smith). Entering each criterion in the appropriate field tells Access to search for records that satisfy both criteria. This is called a *logical AND*. If you need to find all the people who are named Smith and also live in NY, NJ, or CT, you can combine logical AND with logical OR by entering several lines of criteria, each with values under several fields. If you do this, you must enter **Smith** on each line, so it applies to each state.

Continued

TAKE NOTE

▶ ENTERING NUMERIC CRITERIA

When entering numeric criteria, do not use currency signs or number separators. For example, enter 3000 rather than $3,000.

▶ ENTERING DATE CRITERIA

For Date fields, values are marked with pound symbols (#1/1/99#). With dates, you can enter dates in number or text format. In the United States, for example, you can enter 1/1/99, Jan 1 99, 1-Jan-99, or any other valid U.S. date order. Access displays any of these as #1/1/99#.

CROSS-REFERENCE
See Chapter 11 for more advanced information on entering criteria.

FIND IT ONLINE
For a discussion of logical AND and OR, see http://soda.gsw.peachnet.edu/DM/chapters/review1.1.html#CS.

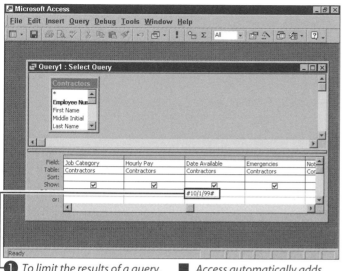

① *To limit the results of a query, enter a criterion.*

■ *Access automatically adds delimiters such as # or ".*

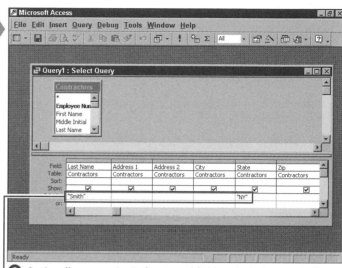

② *Optionally, enter criteria for several fields to include records that match them all.*

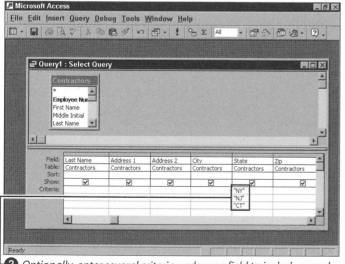

③ *Optionally, enter several criteria under one field to include records that match any of them.*

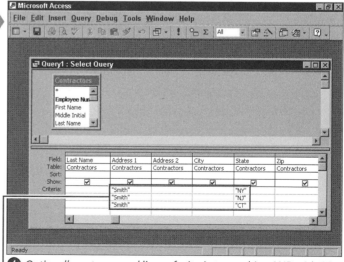

④ *Optionally, enter several lines of criteria to combine AND with OR.*

Entering Criteria

Continued

Most people think of using criteria to search for exact matches. This doesn't help if you want to find all of your clients who do not live in New York. Rather than enter criteria matching the other 49 states, Access provides the <>, or the "is not equal to" symbol. If you type <>NY in the State/Province field, Access will search for all clients who do not live in New York.

Finding a range of values

With numeric values, you may need to find a range of values rather than an exact match by using the comparison operators shown in the table to the right. You are probably familiar with these operators from mathematics. For example, to find all your employees who earn more than $50 per hour, you can use the query shown in the upper-right figure. Bear in mind that in Access, they can be used with text and dates as well as with numbers, so you can use this feature to find all customers who have been with you prior to January 1984 (if, of course, you have a field dating customer inception).

If you need to broaden your search to include all Postal Codes beginning with 462—, you can use the wildcard characters. These are the same characters used with Searches (Finds) in the Access database.

** represents any group of characters.

*? represents any single character.

When you enter a value that includes a wildcard in a criterion cell, Access automatically adds the Like operator. Thus, if you want to find all last names beginning with *A*, you can enter the criterion **A*** in the Last Name field. Access automatically displays this as Like "A*" when you leave the cell.

You can also use the * wildcard to search for part of a field's value. For example, to find everyone in a table who lives on Main St., you can enter the criterion ***Main*** in the Address field. (Note that this method would also include someone who lived on Main Ave. or North Main St.)

COMPARISON OPERATORS

Operator	Meaning
=	Is equal to
>	Is greater than
>=	Is greater than or equal to
<	Is less than
<=	Is less than or equal to
<>	Is not equal to

TAKE NOTE

QUERYING MEMO FIELDS

You almost always use the * operator in order to query memo fields. For example, to find all your employees who program the user interface, use a query with the criterion *interface* in its memo field to isolate all records that have that word anywhere in the memo field.

CROSS-REFERENCE

See Chapter 3 for the use of Wildcard characters in Finds.

SHORTCUT

You can omit the = operator. The criterion "Ny" is exactly equivalent to the criterion = "NY".

Finding Empty Fields

You may need to find all records in which you have not yet entered a customer ID. In this case, you can use the criterion *Is Null* (or just *Null*, as Access will add the word *Is* for you) to find these empty fields. Is Null can also be used to find data-entry errors. For example, the query in the lower-right figure finds employees whose last name has not been entered.

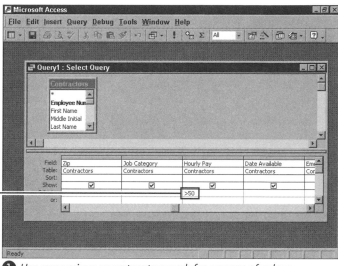

① *Use comparison operators to search for a range of values.*

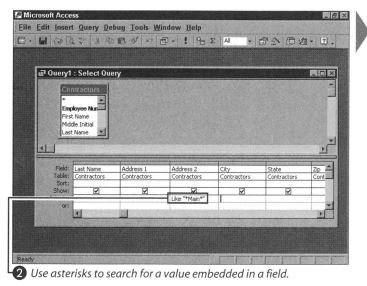

② *Use asterisks to search for a value embedded in a field.*

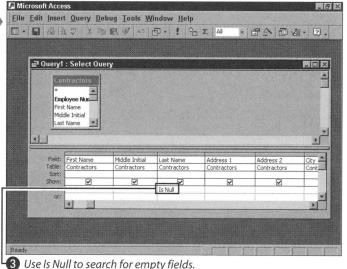

③ *Use Is Null to search for empty fields.*

Using the Query

Once you've created your query, you are ready to run it. This is where the query accesses the table, searches for all the selected fields, selects the records that meet the criteria, sorts the records, and finally displays them in Datasheet view — all in the blink of an eye.

When you run the query, the results are displayed in Datasheet view. You can look at your results, analyze them, and act on them. For example, if you searched for all the records of people who owe you money, you could now start calling or writing to those people.

Many times, after looking over the records in your query, you will want to adjust the query. Maybe you want to sort it by a different field, or you want to add another field to the query. Luckily, you can immediately switch back and forth between Datasheet view and Design view any time in the design process to see how the design's changes are implemented.

Switching views is especially helpful when you are working with a complex query with multiple criteria. You can toggle between views to refine the query. As you make each modification to the design, you can switch to Datasheet view to make sure it's doing what you expected before making further modifications. You don't want to build a complex query with multiple criteria and find out when you run it that you don't get the correct results.

Like your tables, you want your queries to be as readable as possible. You can make it so by applying the standard formatting features found in Datasheet view. You can use the Format menu to change font, row height, column width, and to hide, show, freeze, and unfreeze columns. In fact, with the proper formatting, the query can be transformed into a concise report that you can print out and present.

TAKE NOTE

▶ LOOKING AT ADVANCED FEATURES

Though advanced query features are not covered in this chapter, you should know about a few of them. *Delete queries* are used to delete a group of records that meet some criterion. Likewise, *update queries* are used to change the data in a group of records that meet some criterion. Queries with totals and groups are useful for summarizing your data. For example, you can use them to find each customer's average purchase. *Crosstab queries* are useful for cross-tabulating data. For example, you can use them to find the average salary for each Job Category in each State. These advanced features of queries, and many others, are covered in Chapter 11.

CROSS-REFERENCE
See Chapter 3 for methods of formatting and printing tables, which can also be used for queries' datasheets.

FIND IT ONLINE
For a general discussion of Access queries with more examples, see http://technology.niagarac.on.ca/courses/comp464/lecture_4.htm.

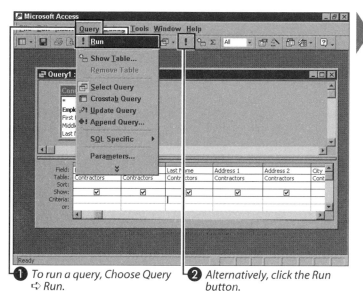

❶ To run a query, Choose Query ⇨ Run.

❷ Alternatively, click the Run button.

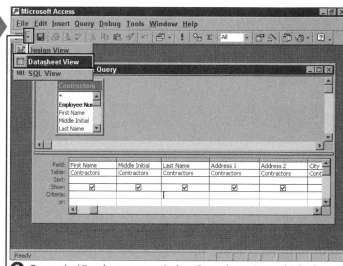

❸ Or use the View button to switch to Datasheet view, which also runs the query.

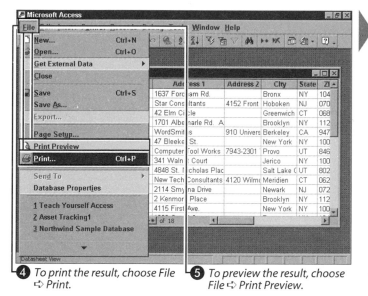

❹ To print the result, choose File ⇨ Print.

❺ To preview the result, choose File ⇨ Print Preview.

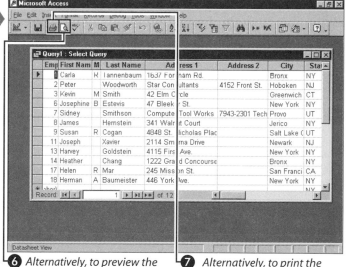

❻ Alternatively, to preview the result, click the Print Preview button.

❼ Alternatively, to print the result, click the Print button.

Personal Workbook

Q&A

1 What are four ways to add a field to the query's design grid?

_____

_____

_____

2 What is the easiest way to select all fields in the field list?

_____

_____

_____

3 What are two ways to include all fields in the result of the query, and how do they differ?

_____

_____

_____

4 Why would you want to hide a field?

_____

_____

_____

5 What does it mean if there are several criteria on one line?

_____

_____

_____

_____

6 What does it mean if there are several criteria, one above another, on different lines?

_____

_____

_____

_____

_____

7 What are three ways to run a query?

_____

_____

_____

_____

ANSWERS: PAGE 345

EXTRA PRACTICE

① Use the Query Wizard to create a query that displays just the name fields of a table.

② Use Design view to modify the query created in question 1, so it sorts these records in alphabetical order.

③ Create a query that uses the asterisk to include all fields and also sorts records alphabetically by name, without including the name fields twice in the results.

④ Modify the query in question 3 so it also sorts in descending order by date.

⑤ Create a query to display records from Kansas City, Missouri.

⑥ Create a query to display the records from three different states.

REAL-WORLD APPLICATIONS

✔ To do targeted bulk mailings, you create a query that includes the names and addresses of customers from selected zip codes, sorted by zip code. Then you create form letters and mailing labels based on this query.

✔ To do telemarketing to customers who ordered most recently, you create a query that includes names and telephone numbers and is sorted in descending order by date of order.

✔ A customer wants to compare four different products that you sell. You create a query based on your Products table to display only the records for these four products.

✔ You are a realtor, and clients often ask you what houses are available in different cities. You have queries ready that display listings for each city.

Visual Quiz

What do you think the user is trying to do with this query? Is there anything wrong with the query's design?

_____

_____

_____

_____

_____

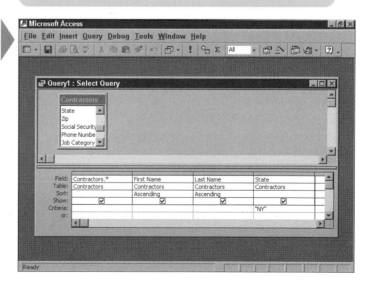

CHAPTER **5**

MASTER
THESE
SKILLS

▶ **Using Simple Filters**

▶ **Using Advanced Filters**

▶ **Working with Filters**

Using Filters

Filters are similar to queries in that they extract specific records. Queries are used when you must extract specific records or specific fields to an independent object or when you must combine records from relational databases. When you are working with a single table, and do not need the results in a separate object, you can apply a *filter* rather than use a query. A filter is easy to apply, and can be turned on and off with a simple click of a button. There are, though, two differences in using a filter: Filters must show all fields (fields cannot be selected, as in a query), and you can only create one filter at a time, because creating a new filter automatically replaces the previous one.

Filters produce results that are a subset of the table or form — in fact, filters are a part of the table or form, not a separate object. A filter simply hides the records that don't meet its criteria in the table or form. When you remove the filter, all the records again appear in the table. When you apply a filter, the other Access tools work only on the displayed records. For example, if you apply a filter before doing a Find, Access will only search through the displayed records.

Filters are best used when you need two distinct views for a single table, and you must switch between views. For example, you may want to create a filter that identifies clients who have not called you in the past two days, so you can follow up with them. When you're done calling them, you can easily switch back to the main table or form.

If you need to see multiple filters' results at the same time, or you need to save the filter for future use, you need to convert the filter to a query. Access enables you to create queries from existing filters. Likewise, you can create filters from existing queries (more about these later in the chapter). While this may sound like splitting hairs, occasionally a query is too much, and other times a filter is not enough. These subtle refinements make Access the best tool, whatever your data-viewing needs.

Using Simple Filters

The two simplest ways of creating filters are *Filter By Selection* and *Filter For*. You can use these to create filters that use a single criterion. For example, if you have a mailing list, you can create a filter to display just the records from California.

To create a Filter By Selection, display the table or form it will be based on, and highlight the value you want to find in any of the records where it appears. Then choose Records ⇨ Filter ⇨ Filter by Selection, or click the Filter By Selection button, as shown in the upper-left figure.

The value you highlight can also be part of a field. For example, to find every record with a company name that includes the word *Computer,* highlight just that word in a record's Company Name and click the Filter By Selection button. If you highlight only part of the word or the wrong part of the word, you won't get correct results.

You can also display all records except those that include a certain value. Select the value you want to exclude and then choose Records ⇨ Filter ⇨ Filter Excluding Selection, or right-click the value to display the shortcut menu and select Filter Excluding Selection, as shown in the upper-right figure.

To search for an exact match, you can use Filter For. To use Filter For, simply right-click any field in the column and then enter a criterion in its shortcut menu. For example, in the lower-left figure, the user has right-clicked the State field column and is creating a filter to display all the records from New York.

Using the computer store example, if you entered the word *computer,* a Filter For would only find entries that read exactly "Computer" and not find every company with that word in its name, as a Filter By Selection would.

A Filter For can also be used to find ranges of numeric values, expressions, and other more complex criteria. For example, to display records of employees earning more than $50 per hour, you can right-click the Hourly Pay field and enter >**50** in the Filter For box; or to display the employees who earn between $50 and $75, you can enter >=**50 And** <=**75** in the Filter For box.

TAKE NOTE

▶ USING FILTERS WITH MULTIPLE CRITERIA

After using Filter by Selection or Filter Excluding Selection, you can further narrow down which records are displayed by using these same methods again. For example, after displaying only records from New York, you can highlight "Bronx" in the City field and choose Records ⇨ Filter ⇨ Filter Excluding Selection, as shown on the lower right, to display all records of people from New York except those from the Bronx. The criteria have a logical AND relationship. All the criteria you specify must be satisfied for the record to be displayed.

CROSS-REFERENCE

Instead of using a filter for simple queries, you can use a Find, covered in Chapter 3.

SHORTCUT

You can right-click a field to select its entire contents and display its shortcut menu. Then select Filter By Selection from the shortcut menu.

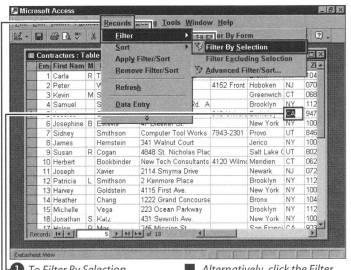

1 To Filter By Selection, highlight the value you want to find in any record.

2 Choose Records ➪ Filter ➪ Filter By Selection.

■ Alternatively, click the Filter By Selection button.

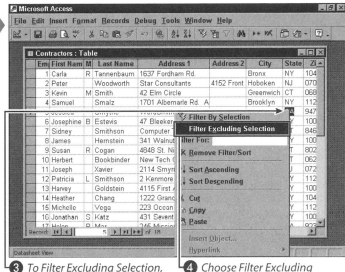

3 To Filter Excluding Selection, select the value you want to exclude.

■ Right-click the table to display its shortcut menu.

4 Choose Filter Excluding Selection.

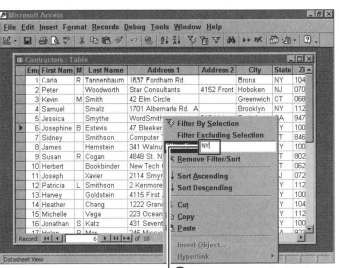

■ To use Filter For, right-click the desired field column to display its shortcut menu.

5 Enter a criterion in the Filter For box.

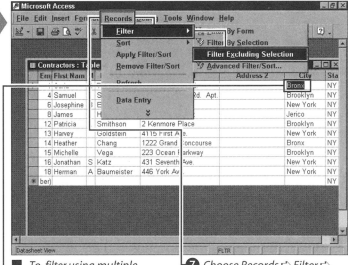

■ To filter using multiple criteria, use Filter By Selection or Filter For to enter one criterion.

6 Highlight the value you want to select or exclude in a field.

7 Choose Records ➪ Filter ➪ Filter By Selection or Filter Excluding Selection to filter by a second criterion.

Using Advanced Filters

I
f you need to create a filter using multiple
criteria, you can use either *Filter By Form* or
Advanced Filter/Sort. Filter By Form is the
easier of the two to use, and it is efficient for
quickly entering criteria in many fields.

Filter By Form displays one record of the table,
laid out exactly as it is in Datasheet view, with no
entries in any of the fields. (This view is called a
form, because it is not the actual table, just a form
based on your selected table.) You can type in the criteria for each field, or select from current entries
from the drop-down list (Access automatically adds
delimiters to the value you enter). Apply the filter by
choosing Records ⇨ Apply Filter/Sort, or click the
Apply Filter button, or right-click the filter and
choose Apply Filter/Sort from its shortcut menu.
Only the records that meet the criteria you specified
will be displayed.

If you need to specify a sort order in addition to
using multiple criteria, you must use Advanced
Filter/Sorts. You can also create a filter by displaying
a table or form and choosing Records ⇨ Filter ⇨
Advanced Filter/Sort (shown in the lower-left figure)
to display the Filter window shown in the lower-right
figure.

The Filter window is almost identical to the Select
Query window. You need to specify which fields to
sort on, and enter criteria to determine which records

are displayed. Unlike a query, a filter displays all the
fields of the table or form, so it does not have a Show
line in its design grid. You can drag fields from the
field list to the design grid to enter criteria under
them, but this does not affect which fields are
displayed. You apply this filter in the same way as
Filter By Form.

TAKE NOTE

▶ USING FILTER BY FORM WITH LOGICAL AND AND LOGICAL OR

If you enter multiple criteria on the same row, they
will be in a logical AND relationship, as in queries.
To enter criteria in an OR relationship, click the Or
tab at the bottom of the Filter by Form window to
display a new sample record on a new row, and fill
out criteria in it. Using multiple Or tabs is like entering criteria on multiple lines of a query form.

▶ MODIFYING FILTERS

Once you create a filter, you can go back and make
modifications. Regardless of how you first created
the filter, you must display it as either a Filter By
Form or an Advanced Filter/Sort to
modify it.

CROSS-REFERENCE
See Chapter 4 for complete information on using the
Select Query window.

SHORTCUT
Click the Apply Filter button to apply a query. The
button looks depressed when the query is applied.

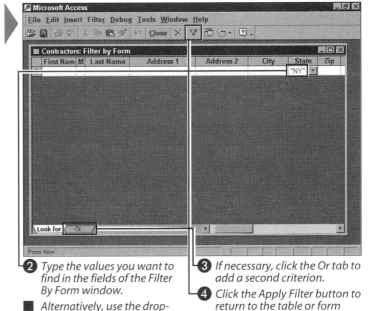

■ To create a Filter By Form, display a table or form.

1 Choose Records ➪ Filter ➪ Filter By Form, or click the Filter By Form button.

2 Type the values you want to find in the fields of the Filter By Form window.

■ Alternatively, use the drop-down list in each field to select a value.

3 If necessary, click the Or tab to add a second criterion.

4 Click the Apply Filter button to return to the table or form with the filter applied.

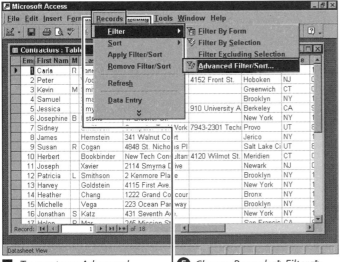

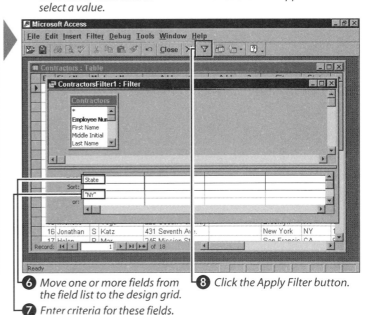

■ To create an Advanced Filter/Sort, display a table or form.

5 Choose Records ➪ Filter ➪ Advanced Filter/Sort.

6 Move one or more fields from the field list to the design grid.

7 Enter criteria for these fields.

8 Click the Apply Filter button.

Working with Filters

To view the table in its original form with all its records, you have to turn off the filter. The filter is saved whenever you save changes in the design of the table or form and available for future use. This is one of the primary benefits of a filter: It can be turned on and off with the simple click of a button. If you close a table with the filter on, it will be on when you next open the table. If you close a table with the filter off, the next time you open it, the same filter is still available.

Whenever you use Filter By Form or the Advanced Filter window, Access displays the current filter, if there is one, no matter how the current filter was created. You can use the Filter By Form or Advanced Filter window to modify its design.

Because a table can have only one filter, the current filter is lost when you create a new one. If you think the current filter may be useful later, you should save the filter permanently as a query, as shown in the upper-right figure. Once you do this, you lose the ability to turn the filter on and off because it is now a query and not a filter. However, you can always load the query as a filter if you need the on/off feature again. If you have already saved the filter as a query, you don't need to worry about losing it when you need to replace it with a new filter.

You may want to turn a query on and off as easily as a filter. To do this, you can load a filter from an existing query. You can only do this if it is a select query based solely on the table you want to filter; queries based on multiple tables cannot be used. (Access only lists queries that can be applied as filters to this object in the Applicable Filter dialog box, shown in the lower-right figure.) When you create a filter from a query, the original query remains unchanged. This feature is used primarily when you use several different views frequently within a single query. You can make copies of these queries and apply different filters to each one.

TAKE NOTE

▶ USING A FILTER ON A QUERY

Filters can be applied to any queries as well as tables. Simply use the same procedures. You can even create a filter, save the filter as a query, and then apply a filter on this query (which used to be a filter).

▶ USING A FILTER ON QUERIES WITH SELECT FIELDS

Filters loaded from queries still display all the parent table's fields, even if the query selected only some of the fields.

CROSS-REFERENCE
See Chapter 2 for information on using the Save As box to name an object.

SHORTCUT
The Apply Filter button looks depressed when the filter is applied. You can click it to remove the query.

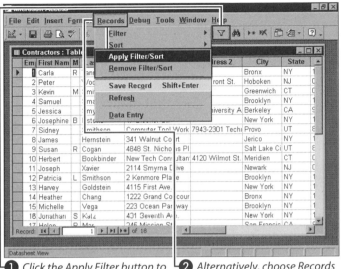

❶ Click the Apply Filter button to apply or remove the filter.

❷ Alternatively, choose Records ⇨ Apply Filter/Sort or Records ⇨ Remove Filter/Sort.

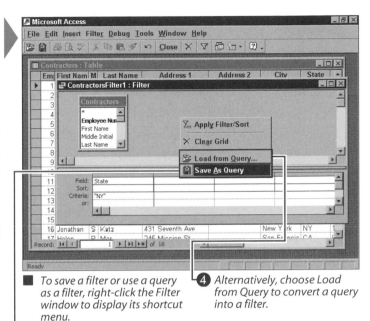

■ To save a filter or use a query as a filter, right-click the Filter window to display its shortcut menu.

❹ Alternatively, choose Load from Query to convert a query into a filter.

❸ Choose Save As Query to save the filter as a query.

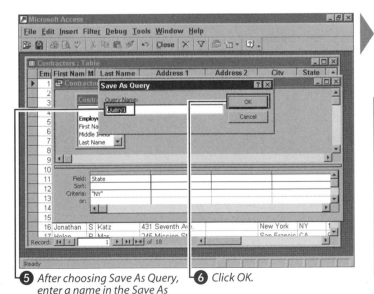

❺ After choosing Save As Query, enter a name in the Save As Query dialog box.

❻ Click OK.

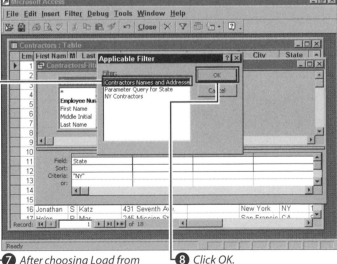

❼ After choosing Load from Query, select the query in the Applicable Filter dialog box.

❽ Click OK.

Personal Workbook

Q&A

1 What are the four ways of creating a filter?

_____

_____

_____

2 How do you create a Filter By Selection?

_____

_____

_____

3 How do you create a Filter By Selection or Filter Excluding Selection with multiple criteria?

_____

_____

_____

4 How do you create a Filter For?

_____

_____

_____

5 How do you create a Filter By Form?

_____

_____

_____

6 How do you create an Advanced Filter/Sort?

_____

_____

_____

7 What are three ways to display all records except those from California?

_____

_____

_____

8 How do you modify a filter?

_____

_____

_____

ANSWERS: PAGE 345

EXTRA PRACTICE

1 Create a Filter By Selection to display only records from one state.

2 Create a Filter Excluding Selection to display all records except those from one state.

3 Create a Filter For to display the records from one state.

4 Use Filter By Form to modify the filter in Extra Practice #3,, so it includes records from three different states.

5 Use Advanced Filter/Sort to modify the filter in Extra Practice #4, so the records are sorted by state.

6 Save the filter from Extra Practice #5 as a query.

REAL-WORLD APPLICATIONS

✔ You work in the Human Resources department, and sometimes you need a list of all employees, while other times you need a list of employees who have taken training courses. You create a filter that displays only the employees who have taken courses, and apply it or remove it off as needed.

✔ Your telemarketers either call all customers or customers who have not made purchases recently. You create a filter that displays customers who have not recently made purchases, so they can apply it as needed.

✔ You are working on a research project. You create a table to hold references, with a field that identifies which section each reference is for. When you are writing the report, you create a Filter By Selection to display only the references for your current working chapter.

Visual Quiz

Here is a filter used with a table that lists employees, with a one-letter code for their job category. What does this filter do?

_____

_____

_____

_____

_____

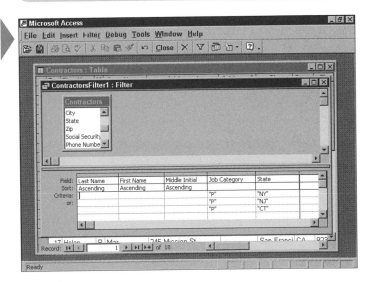

CHAPTER 6

MASTER
THESE
SKILLS

▶ **Creating Forms**

▶ **Using the Form Wizard**

▶ **Working with Forms**

▶ **Creating Reports**

▶ **Using the Report Wizard**

▶ **Creating Mailing Labels**

Fast Forms, Reports, and Labels

So far, we have been working in Access 2000 using *Datasheet view*. Datasheet view displays your data in a table layout with columns and rows. This table is a logical matrix of all the fields and records in your database, but it is not optimal for entering records or creating printed reports. Because it always displays every record, it can be hard on your eyes when you are entering new records. And since the data is always presented as a matrix, Datasheet view is not a good design for reports either.

The good news is that Access allows you to enter records using *Form view*. Form view allows you to change the screen layout so that you can enter one record at a time. The main function of a form is to facilitate entry and editing of data, so forms usually display fields so you can see them on the screen all at once.

Usually when you want to print data, you want to be able to choose which fields are printed, and how they are laid out on the printed page. Though you can print a form, you can get better results by designing a report.

Report view allows you to change the layout so that your printed results are easy to read and understand. You can print traditional reports that organize individual records or mailing labels (another type of report).

Like other database management programs, Access lets you design custom forms and reports by working in Design view. But Access also gives you easier ways of creating forms and reports. The simplest way is to use *AutoForms* and *AutoReports* that automatically arrange all the fields of a table or query in a standard layout—all you have to do is click a toolbar button. Access also includes wizards that do most of the work of designing forms, reports, and mailing labels for you. These wizards are sophisticated enough that many users can get by without designing custom forms or reports.

Using the standard forms and reports of Access wizards is often all you need to accomplish most of your home and office tasks. For the truly inspired, customizing forms is covered in Chapters 8 and 9, and customizing reports is covered in Chapter 10.

Creating Forms

Many people find it inconvenient to view and enter data directly in Access tables (Datasheet view). The format is dense, and you usually cannot see all the fields of a record. Most people find it easier to enter data one record at a time, and to work down a screen, rather than across. To do this, you need to create a form.

The easiest way to create a form is to use AutoForm. By default, the AutoForm displays the fields of each record one above another, rather than side by side. The fields are nicely spaced, which makes data entry infinitely easier.

Access also lets you create a tabular AutoForm, in which the data is displayed similar to the datasheet view. The records are still presented horizontally, but rather than the dense configuration of the Datasheet view, the grey records are broken apart and separated by a distinct, colorful background. AutoForm also provides a Datasheet view, which is exactly like the table you started with.

Using AutoForm helps the beginner make sure they have not forgotten anything. A common error beginners make is to click the AutoForm button without identifying a table or query to base it on. When you do this, Access presents a dialog box informing you of your error. AutoForm also takes all of the detail work out of creating a form, such as lining up the fields exactly right, and providing just the right amount of space consistently between fields.

You cannot float the phone number in the upper right-hand corner, but that is a small price to pay for the neatness some might otherwise never achieve in a form.

Apart from AutoForms, you create, open, and design forms in the same way you do other objects by first clicking the Forms button in the Database window. Then, to use an existing form, select it, and click the Open button. To change the design of a form, select it and click the Design button. To create a new form, click the New button to display the New Form dialog box, which gives you a host of other choices, including Design view, in which you create a form from scratch. Design view takes a bit more effort, and the how-to's are covered in Chapters 9 and 10. You can also select from among three wizards to use, and you look at them in detail later.

TAKE NOTE

▶ USING FORMS BASED ON QUERIES

Queries are particularly useful for adding versatility to AutoForms, because tables often have too many fields to fit on a screen. You can get a useful, compact form if you create a query to control which fields are displayed, as well as the records and their order, and then base an AutoForm on that query. You can also use a filter, but they do not control which fields are displayed (see Chapter 5).

CROSS-REFERENCE

See Chapters 8 and 9 for a complete discussion of the Form window in Design view.

SHORTCUT

To bypass the New Form dialog box and display the wizard immediately, double-click Create form by using wizard.

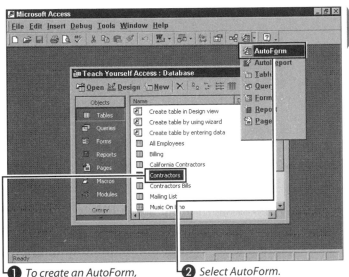

1 To create an AutoForm, display the Database window and select a table or query.

2 Select AutoForm.

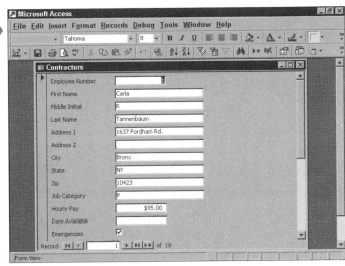

■ A sample AutoForm.

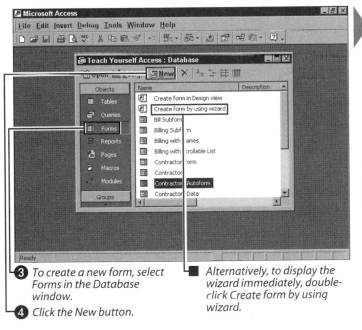

3 To create a new form, select Forms in the Database window.

4 Click the New button.

■ Alternatively, to display the wizard immediately, double-click Create form by using wizard.

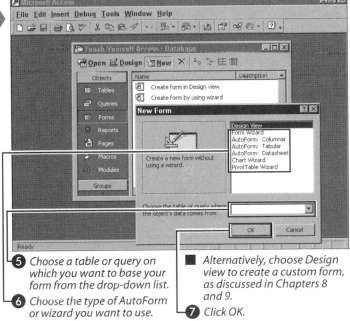

5 Choose a table or query on which you want to base your form from the drop-down list.

6 Choose the type of AutoForm or wizard you want to use.

■ Alternatively, choose Design view to create a custom form, as discussed in Chapters 8 and 9.

7 Click OK.

Using the Form Wizard

AutoForm is a nice feature, but it does have its limits, the most noticeable being that it still displays all of the fields from the table, whether you need them or not. To control the layout of the form, the fields that it contains, and its style and title, you can use the Form Wizard. Like other wizards, the Form Wizard guides you through a series of steps that let you enter information that is used to generate your form.

In the first step of the Form Wizard, you must choose which fields of the underlying table or query will be displayed in the form. The field picker is used like the ones described in Chapter 2. If you are working with a relational database, you can use the drop-down list to include multiple tables and queries in the form (as covered in detail in Chapter 7).

In the second step of the Form Wizard, you choose how the fields are laid out. As you can see in the upper-right figure, you can lay them out in a columnar, tabular, Datasheet, or justified arrangement. The first three choices are the same ones available when you create AutoForms; the fourth, Justified, adjusts the sizes of the field so each line of the form is the same width. The layout that you select is illustrated in the box to the left.

The third step of the Form Wizard is where you get to break out of the traditional mold. You can choose from a wide variety of styles, which control the appearance of labels and data in the form. As you scroll through the options in the list, the one that is selected is illustrated to the left.

Before you click Finish in the final step, be sure to specify a title for the form. It is easy to overlook this in the excitement of wanting to see how your form will actually look.

By default, the form is displayed with data after it is created. If you still want to tweak the design a bit (maybe you really want the phone number in the upper right-hand corner), select the Modify the form's design radio button, and the form will be displayed in Design view when you click the Finish button to create it. It is common to begin creating custom forms and reports by using a wizard, and then make further changes to them in Design view.

TAKE NOTE

LEAVING OUT THE KEY FIELD

Notice in the first figure that all the fields are included except the Employee Number, the primary key field of the table. Since this field is an AutoNumber, its value is entered automatically when you add new records. This form prevents the user from accidentally editing the key field, which can cause data loss if you are using a relational database.

CROSS-REFERENCE

If you do not know the basic techniques of using wizards, such as how to move from one dialog box to the next, see the section on wizards in Chapter 1.

FIND IT ONLINE

For information on using the Form Wizard, see http://www2.winona.msus.edu/stc/Classes/Access_begin/part_d.htm.

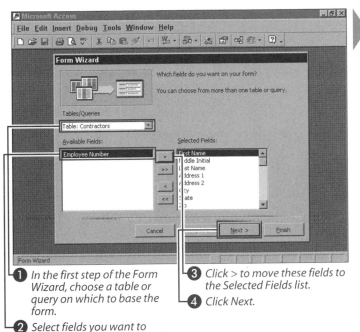

1 In the first step of the Form Wizard, choose a table or query on which to base the form.

2 Select fields you want to include in the form.

3 Click > to move these fields to the Selected Fields list.

4 Click Next.

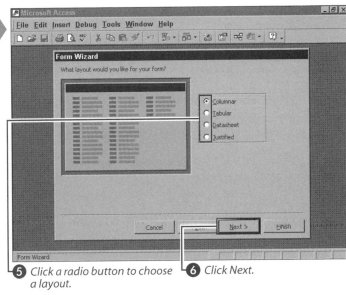

5 Click a radio button to choose a layout.

6 Click Next.

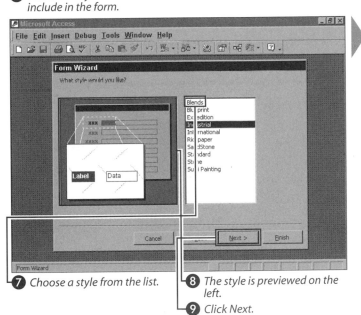

7 Choose a style from the list.

8 The style is previewed on the left.

9 Click Next.

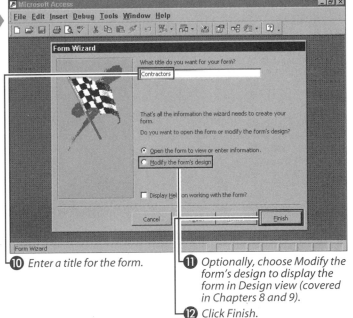

10 Enter a title for the form.

11 Optionally, choose Modify the form's design to display the form in Design view (covered in Chapters 8 and 9).

12 Click Finish.

Working with Forms

Once you have created a form, you are ready to begin entering and editing data, one record at a time. Remember that the form is tied to a table, so as soon as you enter a new record it is immediately put in a table. The form is simply an easy-to-use data entry point to the table.

You can add and delete records at any time by clicking the New Record or Delete Record buttons. If you are using AutoNumber as your key field, the new record will receive the next number available and it will be the last record in the table.

If you are not sure which record contains the data you are looking for, use the Find button (or choose Edit ⇨ Find) to bring up the standard Find dialog box and search for the record.

Navigation within an individual record is most easily handled with the Tab key; to move among records, use record indicator and arrow buttons at the bottom of the Form window. The record indicator does not reflect the AutoNumber, but the actual order of the records according to the latest sort. If your key field is Employee Number, but you have just sorted according to Last Name, then the order of the records as reflected by record indicator is based on Last Name.

The View button drop-down list, shown in the upper-right figure, includes three tools. The Form View button lets you view the data in the Form, and the Design View button lets you change the design of the Form, as with other objects. Click the Datasheet View button (or choose View ⇨ Datasheet) to display the form as a datasheet, as shown in the lower-left figure. Notice that this Form looks just like the Datasheet view of your table, except that it has a small Form icon at the left edge of the title bar and it only displays the fields that are included in the form.

As you enter and edit data, you can view the results in the table by toggling between the Form and Datasheet views clicking the View button. To do this, you can create an AutoForm to use as the main object. In this way, you can work with one record in Form view or a list of records as a datasheet, just by clicking one button.

TAKE NOTE

▶ USING FILTERS WITH FORMS

You can apply filters to forms just as you do with tables (see Chapter 5). As with tables, filters are attached to the form, and you can only use one filter at a time.

CROSS-REFERENCE

For more detail on how to work with data in forms and tables, see Chapter 3.

SHORTCUT

To move among records, press PgUp and PgDn or Ctrl+Home (to go to the first record) and Ctrl+End (to go to the last record).

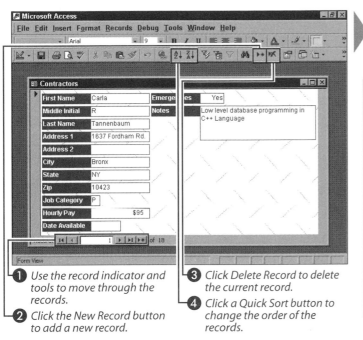

1 Use the record indicator and tools to move through the records.

2 Click the New Record button to add a new record.

3 Click Delete Record to delete the current record.

4 Click a Quick Sort button to change the order of the records.

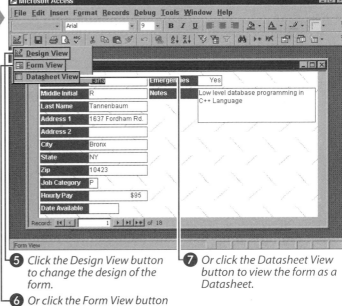

5 Click the Design View button to change the design of a form.

6 Or click the Form View button to view the data in the form.

7 Or click the Datasheet View button to view the form as a Datasheet.

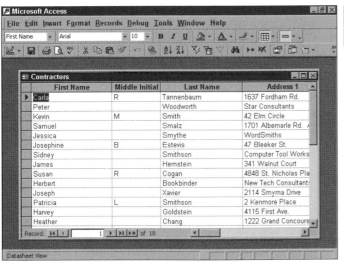

■ Work with a form in Datasheet view as you would work with a table.

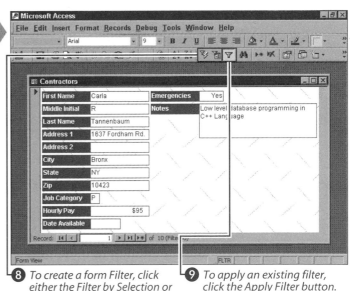

8 To create a form Filter, click either the Filter by Selection or the Filter by Form button.

9 To apply an existing filter, click the Apply Filter button.

■ To remove the filter, click the Apply Filter button again.

Creating Reports

You can print forms or tables, but a much better way to show off your results is to create a report. By selecting the Reports button in the Database window, you can create many types of printed reports including mailing labels.

An Access *report* is any output designed to be printed and is based on a table or query. You cannot create a report directly from an open table or query. Instead, you should click the Report button of the Database window, then New, and use the drop-down list in the New Report dialog box to select the table or query that the report is based on. You can then select one of the following options:

- ▶ Design View to create a custom report from scratch (using methods described in Chapter 10).
- ▶ AutoReport: Columnar (default).
- ▶ AutoReport: Tabular (useful for queries with a few fields).
- ▶ A Wizard: Report, Chart (for graphs), or Label. The Report and Label Wizards are discussed later in the chapter.

As with forms, you can also create a report by selecting a table or query in the Database window and selecting the New Report button (or choosing File ➪ New ➪ Report) to display the New Report dialog box with that table or query already entered in its drop-down list.

Although AutoReport is sometimes the easiest way to dump the data on paper, like the AutoForm, it displays all of the fields in your table in a record-by-record vertical listing. This may not be any easier to read than printing the form or table itself.

One way to make an AutoReport more useful is to first create a query that includes only the few fields you want to display and use it as the basis of the AutoReport. Of course, you can also use the query to specify which records to include in the report and their sort order. So if you want to create a report containing Last Name, First Name, and Extension Number, create a query specifying this order and select AutoReport.

Because a report is meant to be printed, Access displays it in the Print Preview window when you view it. You cannot edit data displayed in reports. To do so, you must view the report as a table, query, or form. If the report is not the way you want, or does not contain the information you want, switch to Design view and make the necessary adjustments.

TAKE NOTE

▶ USING QUERIES WITH REPORTS

You cannot add filters to reports, as you can to tables and forms. If you want to control which records are included in a report, create a query to isolate these records first, as described in Chapter 4, and use the query as the basis of the report rather than a table.

CROSS-REFERENCE
For more information on Print Preview, see Chapter 3.

FIND IT ONLINE
For information on creating a Report using the Report Wizard, see **http://www2.winona.msus.edu/stc/ Classes/Access_begin/part_e.htm.**

1 To create an AutoReport, select the table or query on which you want to base it.

2 Click AutoReport.

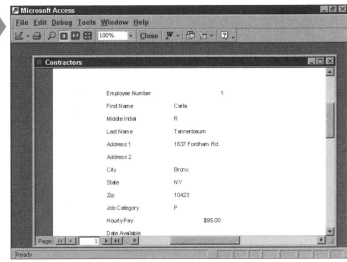

■ The AutoReport has the fields arranged one above another.

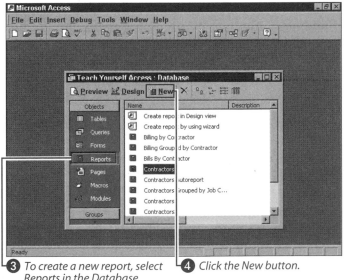

3 To create a new report, select Reports in the Database window.

4 Click the New button.

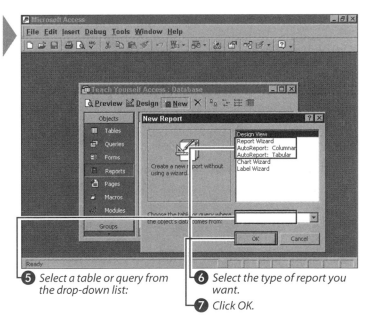

5 Select a table or query from the drop-down list:

6 Select the type of report you want.

7 Click OK.

Using the Report Wizard

Most of the time, people create reports for someone like their boss or a client, so it is important to make a good impression. While AutoReport is the easiest way to create a report, it can leave much to be desired in terms of presentation. Design view has many more options, but the Report Wizard is much easier to use and is adequate for most purposes. A word of caution: Report Wizard has many more options than Form Wizard, so create a few dummy reports to familiarize yourself with the process and presentation possibilities.

When you use the Report Wizard, you must first select the table or query on which to base the report. Then, choose which fields to display in the report. You can select all the fields or just some of the fields.

When you are selecting fields, think about what type of layout you are planning to create. If you want to use a tabular layout, be sure the fields you select will fit in the width of a page. Select fields from a single table or query, unless you are working with a relational database, described in Chapter 7.

One of the best features of Report Wizard is that it helps you create grouped reports. For example, you could create a report that groups records by State. If the table you are working with contains numeric values and you select a single field to group on, the report can provide subtotals for each group and a grand total for the table. If you do not select fields to group by, the report can provide grand totals of its numeric fields.

You can also group on multiple fields. For example, you can produce a report on a customer table that groups them by state, so all the records from each state are together. Within each state, you can group by city. The report can include a grand total, subtotals for each state, and sub-subtotals for each city You can use up to four levels of grouping. Click the up and down arrows to change the order of the grouping.

Reports are automatically sorted by group. For example, if you group by state, the states will be listed alphabetically. If you group by city within each state, the cities of each state will be listed alphabetically.

Continued

TAKE NOTE

SELECTING GROUPING OPTIONS

The Grouping Options button, which is enabled if you create groups, lets you group by a range of values. You can group your Date/Time fields by time intervals ranging from Minutes to Years by using the dropdown list shown in the lower-left figure. You can group text fields by one or more characters (select Normal to group records only if they contain the same values). Numeric data can also be grouped by a range of values (see lower-right figure).

CROSS-REFERENCE

For information on how to use the field picker, see Chapter 2.

SHORTCUT

It is often fastest to click > to add all fields, and then double-click the fields you want to remove.

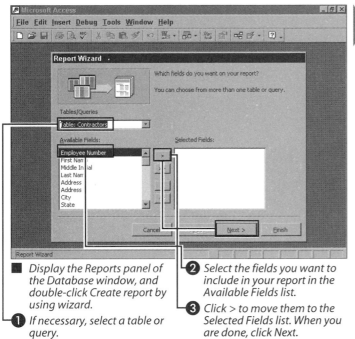

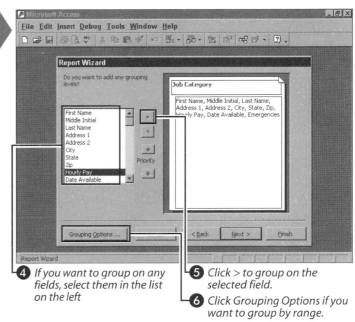

■ *Display the Reports panel of the Database window, and double-click Create report by using wizard.*

1 *If necessary, select a table or query.*

2 *Select the fields you want to include in your report in the Available Fields list.*

3 *Click > to move them to the Selected Fields list. When you are done, click Next.*

4 *If you want to group on any fields, select them in the list on the left*

5 *Click > to group on the selected field.*

6 *Click Grouping Options if you want to group by range.*

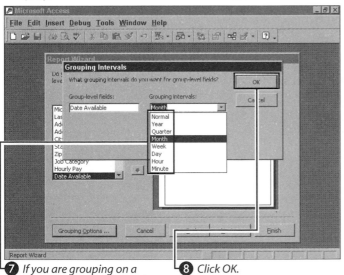

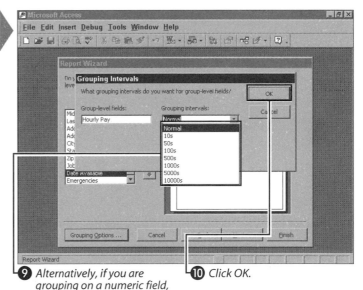

7 *If you are grouping on a Date/Time field, select a time range in the drop-down list.*

8 *Click OK.*

9 *Alternatively, if you are grouping on a numeric field, select a number range in the drop-down list.*

10 *Click OK.*

Using the Report Wizard

Continued

The next step of the Report Wizard, shown in the upper-left figure, lets you choose the sort order of the records in each group. You can sort according to any of the available fields in the dropdown list, and toggle the Sort button to change between ascending and descending order. For example, if you want to sort by name, choose Last Name in the top dropdown, First Name in the next dropdown, and Middle Initial in the third dropdown. This only determines the sort order of the records within each group, not the sort order of the groups themselves (which will be alphabetical). And this sort is only pertinent to the report: the table is not sorted.

From here, it can get a little complicated. If you have not grouped any fields, Report Wizard gives you the standard options of Columnar (fields one above another), Tabular, or Justified (width of fields are adjusted so the lines are the same length) layout. If you have grouped fields, fields are displayed in Tabular layout (one next to another), and you can specify how the group and subgroup headings are laid out. Click the radio buttons to display samples of available layouts to the left.

It is a good idea to create sample reports in each layout to really see how they present the data. You can keep these samples on hand for future reports, so you can choose the best layout ahead of time, without going through the trial-and-error process again.

You can adjust the page orientation or adjust the width of the fields to try and make everything fit onto a page. It is often better to use Landscape Orientation for a Tabular report, to fit more fields across the page. If field widths are much too wide for the page, some data will not be printed.

Once you have the format of the layout you like, you can choose the report style. Report Wizard provides you with a variety of styles, from conservative to snazzy (illustrated on the left as you scroll through), and it can be fun to liven things up a bit!

In the final step of the Report Wizard you get to enter a title, which is displayed at the top of the report as a header. Like other Wizards, this last window also lets you select Modify this design before choosing Finish, so you can tinker even further with the layout design. Report Design view has all the same options as Form Design view.

TAKE NOTE

USING SUMMARY OPTIONS

If numeric fields are included in the report, the Sort Order step will also have a Summary Options button, which displays a dialog box that lets you choose which fields to total on, and whether to include their Sum, Average, Minimum value, or Maximum value.

CROSS-REFERENCE

For information on creating summary reports, see Chapter 14.

SHORTCUT

Rather than using the drop-down list to select the field you sort on, you can enter the field's first letter in the drop-down list's text box.

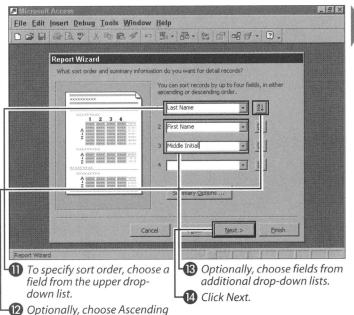

11 To specify sort order, choose a field from the upper drop-down list.

12 Optionally, choose Ascending or Descending sort.

13 Optionally, choose fields from additional drop-down lists.

14 Click Next.

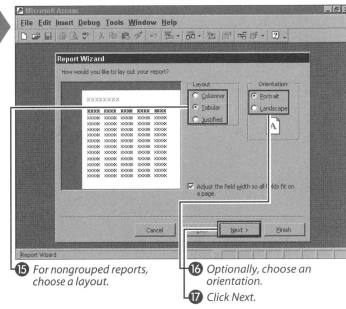

15 For nongrouped reports, choose a layout.

16 Optionally, choose an orientation.

17 Click Next.

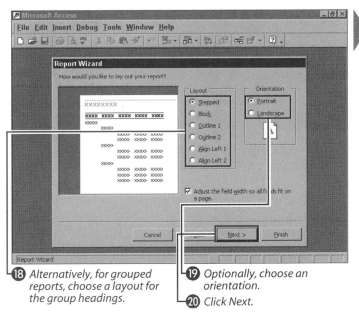

18 Alternatively, for grouped reports, choose a layout for the group headings.

19 Optionally, choose an orientation.

20 Click Next.

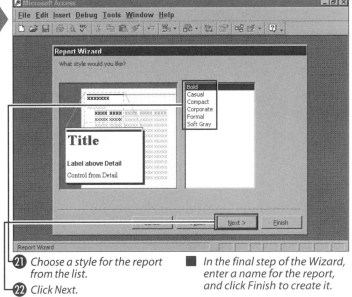

21 Choose a style for the report from the list.

22 Click Next.

■ In the final step of the Wizard, enter a name for the report, and click Finish to create it.

Creating Mailing Labels

One of the most popular uses of reports is to create mailing labels. With Access-generated labels, bulk mailings are a breeze. You can send all your customers notices about an upcoming sale in no time at all! To make things even easier, Access provides a Label Wizard that takes all the guesswork out of this task.

Creating labels can be broken down into two parts: identifying the dimensions of the labels, and then determining how the selected fields will be displayed. Before you begin to create a label, you must know exactly which labels you will be using, because the dimensions will determine the layout. So make sure you have the actual blank labels first.

The easiest way to create labels is to use the Label Wizard. Create a new report and click Label in the New Report dialog box to display the Label Wizard, which lets you specify the size of the label, lay out the fields on it, and specify the typeface and sort order of the labels. Label Wizard saves you the trouble of measuring the labels and figuring out exactly how to space them, by providing a dropdown to let you choose from standard label sizes according to major label manufacturers, like Avery. (Actually, Avery number is often the product number on the package of labels, regardless of manufacturer.)

If the labels you are using do not appear in the list, you need to create a custom label. To add custom label sizes to the list of standard labels, click the Customize button to display the New Label Size dialog box, shown in the lower-left figure. This dialog box includes any custom labels you have created in the past.

To create a new label, click New, and input the unit of measure, label type, and orientation, and name the label. Use the Number across text box to specify how many labels fit across a page. Edit the dimensions in the text boxes on the illustration of the sample labels to indicate the height and width of each label, the right and left margins, the top and bottom margins, the vertical and horizontal space between labels, and the distance of the text on the label from the label's top and left edge. This takes a bit of work, and once you have it right, you will definitely want to save it for future use. To edit a custom label size, select it and click the Edit button instead of New.

Continued

TAKE NOTE

CHOOSING WHICH LABEL FORMS ARE LISTED

If you create custom label sizes, in the first step of the Wizard, select the Show custom label sizes checkbox to display only these custom sizes in its list, or deselect this checkbox to display only the standard label sizes. The radio buttons below the list box let you specify which labels are displayed in the list.

CROSS-REFERENCE

For information on how Page Setup is used to control the layout of mailing labels, see Chapter 10.

SHORTCUT

Use a standard label like the one you want to create a custom size, and change its dimensions as needed.

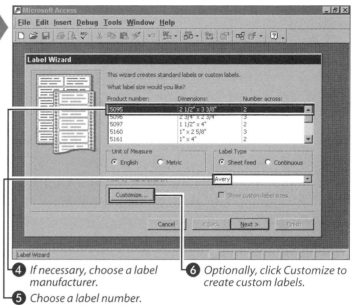

■ *Display the Report panel of the Database window and click the New button.*

1. *Choose Label Wizard in the New Report dialog box.*

2. *Choose the table or query the labels are based on.*

3. *Click OK.*

4. *If necessary, choose a label manufacturer.*

5. *Choose a label number.*

6. *Optionally, click Customize to create custom labels.*

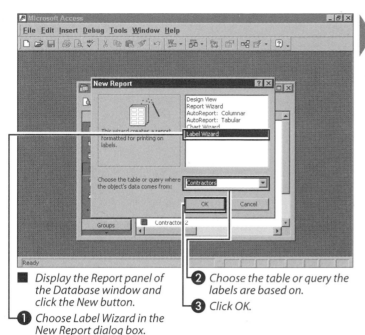

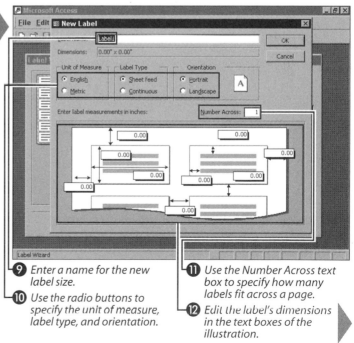

7. *Select a custom label size and click Edit button.*

8. *Alternatively, click the New button.*

9. *Enter a name for the new label size.*

10. *Use the radio buttons to specify the unit of measure, label type, and orientation.*

11. *Use the Number Across text box to specify how many labels fit across a page.*

12. *Edit the label's dimensions in the text boxes of the illustration.*

Creating Mailing Labels

Continued

Once you have determined the label size, you are ready to select a typeface for the label. Access asks you to specify the font, font weight, font size, and other formatting, such as bold, italics, underlined, and colors. These formats will be applied to all fields; you cannot mix and match formats among the fields. Obviously, don't bother with color unless you have a color printer!

After this, you are ready to lay out the label. Labels are significantly smaller than a standard size report. The number of lines depends on your label size and font size. You select fields as you do in other Wizards, with one important difference: each field you select will automatically be deposited in the next available space to the right (fields will not wrap at the edge of the label). Label Wizard provides you with a prototype label with your selected fields and dimensions, so you can see exactly how your label will look.

In addition to adding fields, you can also type text directly into the Prototype label. For example, you must add a space after the First Name before adding the Middle Initial field. And then, type a period and space after the Middle Initial field before adding the Last Name field. Field names are enclosed in curly brackets to distinguish them from other text.

To add new lines to the label, simply press the down arrow or Enter key or click a location on the Prototype label. For example, after adding the name, you press the down arrow or Enter key and add the address field on the next line. You must actually place fields as you want them to appear on the label.

You can click to place the cursor anywhere on the prototype label, and press the backspace or Del keys to delete text or fields.

You can then sort the labels just as you do any other report, which is helpful if you must organize bulk mailings by zip code or you need to organize letters by name so you can add a personalized form letter.

The final step lets you name the labels and display them in the Print Preview window or in Design view, as in other Wizards.

TAKE NOTE

CHOOSING FONTS

The options that will be displayed to let you choose font name and size depend on the fonts that you have installed in Windows. You should be careful to choose a font that is small enough to let names and addresses fit on the labels. The default is 8 points, and though this size is too small for most text, it is ideal for labels.

PREVIEWING YOUR REPORT

Labels are expensive, so it is a good idea to print a dry run on plain paper, so you do not waste labels on addresses where the postal code runs off the edge.

CROSS-REFERENCE

For information on customizing mailing labels, see Chapter 10.

SHORTCUT

Rather than clicking Next, you can press Enter to move to the next step of a wizard.

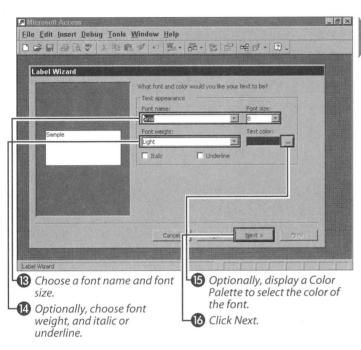

13 Choose a font name and font size.

14 Optionally, choose font weight, and italic or underline.

15 Optionally, display a Color Palette to select the color of the font.

16 Click Next.

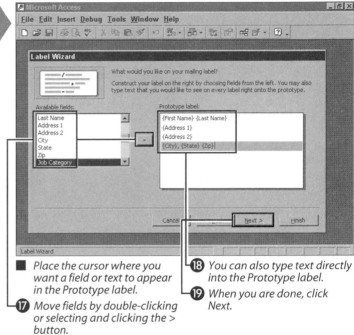

■ Place the cursor where you want a field or text to appear in the Prototype label.

17 Move fields by double-clicking or selecting and clicking the > button.

18 You can also type text directly into the Prototype label.

19 When you are done, click Next.

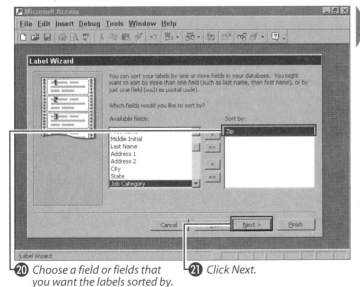

20 Choose a field or fields that you want the labels sorted by.

21 Click Next.

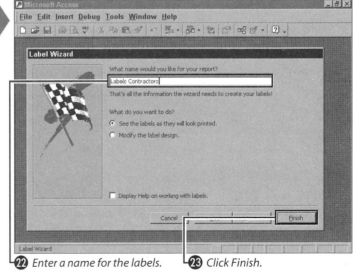

22 Enter a name for the labels.

23 Click Finish.

Personal Workbook

Q&A

1 What is the fastest way to create a form and a report?

_____

_____

_____

2 What is the one field that should usually be left out of data-entry forms? Why should it be left out?

_____

_____

_____

3 Describe the three views in which you can display a form.

_____

_____

_____

4 How do you add a filter to a form or a report?

_____

_____

_____

5 Describe the two views in which you can display a report.

_____

_____

_____

6 Describe the three basic report layouts for nongrouped reports.

_____

_____

_____

7 On which ranges of values can you group reports?

_____

_____

_____

8 What are the summary options for grouped reports?

_____

_____

_____

ANSWERS: PAGE 346

EXTRA PRACTICE

1. Create an AutoForm for your sample table.

2. Create an AutoReport for your sample table.

3. Use the Form Wizard to create a form for your sample table, and leave out the primary key field.

4. Use the Report Wizard to create an ungrouped report for your sample table, and be sure that all the fields fit in the width of the page.

5. Use the Report Wizard to create a grouped report with a summary line for your sample table. Include a numeric field to total on.

6. Use the Label Wizard to create mailing labels for your sample table, sorted by zip code.

REAL-WORLD APPLICATIONS

✔ You have hired a temporary worker to do data entry. You create a form that leaves out the Client Number field, so it is not changed by mistake, and that leaves out the Notes field, where you sometimes enter confidential information, to protect your clients' privacy.

✔ You work for a nonprofit organization that publishes salary surveys for a number of industries. You want to determine if there is any difference in the salaries between male and female employees of the same rank. You create a report on employees grouped by job category and subgrouped by gender, which includes summary lines with the average wage for each job category for each gender.

Visual Quiz

What is wrong with the prototype label shown on the right, and how can you correct it?

_____

_____

_____

_____

_____

_____

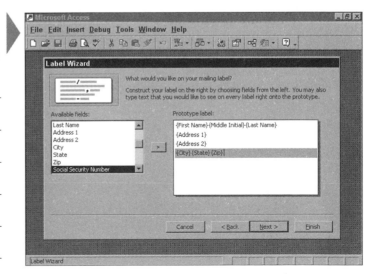

PART

II

Contents of 'Desktop'

Name

My Computer

Network Neigh

Internet Explore

Microsoft Outloo

Recycle Bin

My Briefcase

3252-9

3259-6

3261-8

3262-6

3281-2

3286-3

DE Phone List

Device Manager

In

Iomega Tools

Adding Power

In Part I, you learn the basic techniques that let you begin working with Access as quickly as possible. Part II lets you expand these skills by learning power techniques that let you use Access more effectively.

Most important, you learn how to work with *relational databases*, which enable you to use data from multiple tables. Even though Access can be simple to use, the data you work with is often complex. You must use relational databases to work effectively with complex data.

You also learn in Part II to create custom forms, reports, and advanced queries. Finally, you learn to automate your work by creating *macros*, or scripts, to perform repetitive tasks. You can easily create macros that perform a series of actions for you, and run them by clicking a button or pressing a key.

By the end of this part, you will be at the edge of developing applications for users. If you create all the tables, queries, forms and reports needed in an application, and you create macros that let the user click buttons to work with these objects, you can then create custom applications that make it easy for people to use Access, without doing any programming.

CHAPTER 7

MASTER THESE SKILLS

▶ Working with Many-to-One Relationships

▶ Working with Many-to-Many Relationships

▶ Working with More Complex Relationships

▶ Creating a Default Relationship in Access

▶ Using Queries with Relational Databases

▶ Using Reports with Relational Databases

▶ Using Forms with Relational Databases

Using Relational Databases

In Part I of this book, you learned the basic techniques that you need to work with a single-table database. This chapter teaches you to use these basic techniques to deal with more complex data stored in multiple tables.

You must know how to use relational databases in order to work with data more complex than a simple mailing list of names and addresses. By using Access's basic features and the introduction to relational databases in this chapter, you can use Access for almost any job, however complex the data.

When you use relational databases, you break up data into multiple tables that are related to each other using common *key fields*. For example, you might have a table that lists your employees, with an Employee Number in each record, and a second table listing the hours each employee worked each week, also with an Employee Number in each record. The Employee Number is the key field that enables you to relate the two tables.

Access makes it easy to relate tables, but before you can do any hands-on work with a relational database, you must have a basic understanding of database theory. You need to know enough theory to know how to break up the data into different tables, which you then relate to each other using common key fields.

In database terminology, this is called *normalizing* data. This book does not cover the technical rules of normalization, which are discussed in textbooks on database theory. Instead, it gives you some simple common-sense guidelines, which are easy to apply when you understand why multitable databases are sometimes necessary and when you understand the two basic types of relationships that require multitable databases — the many-to-one and the many-to-many relationship.

After you understand the basics of database design, you learn the techniques used in Access to work with relational databases, to relate the tables, and to create the queries, forms, and reports you need to work with them.

Working with Many-to-One Relationships

When you first learned to design a table, you saw that there must be a one-to-one relationship between each field and the entire record. For example, if you have a table with a list of contractors who work for you, each record would contain one first name field, one last name field, one address field, one job category field, and so on.

However, there will probably be information on contractors that you cannot store in a single table, such as the invoices that contractors send to bill you. Since each contractor sends an invoice periodically — say, at the end of each month — you will get many invoices for each contractor, and you will have to enter many invoice records for each contractor record. This billing data is in a *many-to-one* relationship with the contractor records.

Many problems arise if you enter this data in the same table as the contractors' names and addresses. To record this data, you should create a separate table for it, called, for example, Billing, which has fields for the employee number, the billing date, the hours worked, and so on. Each record in the original Contractors table must also have an Employee Number key field. So both the Billing table and the Contractors table have an Employee Number field. You can see in the upper-right figure how these key fields are used to relate the two tables in a many-to-one relationship.

The figure shows some of the data that would appear in the Billing table, the bills for Employee 1 to Employee 4 for the first three months of 1999. The arrows make it easy for you to see how Access can use the key field to look up the record in the Contractors table that goes with each record in the Billing table. By finding the Contractor record with the same Employee Number as each Billing record, you know the name and address of the person who worked those hours.

The figure in the lower left shows how these records can be joined, with data from a Contractor record added to the data from each Billing record.

Continued

TAKE NOTE

▶ DOING IT THE WRONG WAY

Imagine that an inexperienced user designed a table that included fields for billing date and hours worked in the same record as the contractor's name and address. It would be easy to enter the date and hours of the first bill, but how would you enter the data on the second bill you got? You might try adding a new contractor record to hold this data, but then you would have to re-enter all the basic name and address data for a contractor each time you got a bill. You might try adding new fields to the table called Billing Date 2, Hours Worked 2, Billing Date 3, Hours Worked 3, and so on, but then you would have an unwieldy table with many empty fields for contractors who work on fewer jobs. You would also have trouble producing reports that summarize billing data kept in fields with different names. This is why you must use relational databases.

CROSS-REFERENCE
For the basics of designing a table, see Chapter 2.

FIND IT ONLINE
For more on data normalization and Access, see http://www.fmsinc.com/tpapers/datanorm/index.html.

One-to-One Relationships

If data is in a one-to-one relationship, you can break it into several tables, and then you can relate the tables. However, it is usually best to keep all the data in a single table, even if you only have to use some of the fields at any time. Rather than breaking it into multiple tables, store all data with a one-to-one relationship in one table, and create queries to display only the fields you want to work with at any time.

Access makes it possible to join tables in a one-to-one relationship, but this is useful only in special cases. For example, you might join two tables used in two different applications that you later have some special reason for combining. The tables would have to have some field, such as the social security number, which you could use as the common key field.

EmpNo	Bill Date	Hours	Name	Etc.
1	1/31/99	95.5	Carla Tannenbaum	...
1	2/28/99	32.0	Carla Tannenbaum	...
1	3/31/99	150.5	Carla Tannenbaum	...
3	3/31/99	28.5	Kevin Smith	...
4	2/28/99	162.5	Samuel Smalz	...
4	3/31/99	22.0	Samuel Smalz	...

Joining tables in a many-to-one relationship adds data from the "one" (Contractors) table to each record from the "many" (Billing) table.

BILLING TABLE			CONTRACTORS TABLE		
EmpNo	Bill Date	Hours	EmpNo	Name	Etc.
1	1/31/99	95.5	1	Carla Tannenbaum	...
1	2/28/99	32.0			
1	3/31/99	150.5			
3	3/31/99	28.5	3	Kevin Smith	...
4	2/28/99	162.5	4	Samuel Smalz	...
4	3/31/99	22.0			

Working with Many-to-One Relationships *Continued*

In the example shown in the figures on the previous page, the key field is used differently in the Contractors and the Billing Table. By thinking carefully about how a many-to-one relationship works, you can understand the difference between these two types of key fields.

The Primary Key

The Employee Number is the primary key of the Contractors table, which identifies each record.

You can see why a primary key must be unique to each record. If the Billing table has a record for a bill from Employee Number 1, there must be only one record in the Contractor table with that Employee Number. You have to be able to identify just one contractor who sent that bill.

The Foreign Key

On the other hand, the Employee Number field in the Billing table is not that table's primary key. It is called a *foreign key,* because it refers to a primary key in another table.

The key field in the "many" table of a many-to-one relationship is not unique for each record. By definition, a many-to-one relationship can always have more than one record in the "many" table with the same key as each record in the "one" table to which it is related. In our example, there can be many bills from each contractor.

The Billing table should have its own primary key, called Bill Number (or some other similar name), but it cannot use the Employee Number field as its primary key.

CROSS-REFERENCE

For information on how to Access checks for referential integrity, see "Creating a Default Relationship" later in this chapter.

FIND IT ONLINE

For more on key fields, see **http://www-c. developer.com/reference/library/0672308320/ ch02.htm#E69E20.**

One-to-Many Relationships

It is sometimes more convenient to look at this relationship from the opposite direction, as a *one-to-many* relationship rather than as a many-to-one relationship. For example, you may want to look up all the bills for a contractor.

If you compare the figure on this page and the one on the previous page, you will see that you can use exactly the same tables in both a many-to-one and a one-to-many relationship. However, if you use a one-to-many relationship, you cannot find a single record in the table on the "many" side that matches each record in the table on the "one" side. The Billing table contains several records for each Name and Address field in the Contractors table. You must display one record from the Contractors table (or other table on the "one" side) with several records from the Billing table (or other table on the "many" side) below it.

If you are looking for one invoice, it is useful to use a many-to-one relationship, with the contractor's name and address added to the billing data. If you are looking for all invoices from a contractor, it is useful to use a one-to-many relationship, with all billing records listed under the contractor record.

Displaying Data

To display a one-to-many relationship, you can to create a form with a subform. The main form holds data from the Contractors table (or other "one" table), and the subform has multiple lines to hold the corresponding records of the Billing table (or other "many" table).

CONTRACTORS TABLE			BILLING TABLE		
EmpNo	Name	Etc.	EmpNo	Bill Date	Hours
1	Carla Tannenbaum	…	1	1/31/99	95.5
			1	2/28/99	32.0
			1	3/31/99	150.5
3	Kevin Smith	…	3	3/31/99	28.5
4	Samuel Smalz	…	4	2/28/99	162.5
			4	3/31/99	22.0

Working with Many-to-Many Relationships

Not all relational databases are based on many-to-one relationships. Some data is more complex. For example, you have seen that there is a many-to-one relationship if you hire contractors, because each contractor bills you many times. But what if you run a referral agency for contractors? The contractors bill you and you bill the employers for their work.

You need tables with data on each contractor and on each employer, but you cannot relate these to each other using a many-to-one relationship. Because each contractor can work for many different employers, and each employer can hire many different contractors over the course of the year, this is a many-to-many relationship.

You work with a many-to-many relationship by breaking it up into two separate one-to-many relationships. You do this by creating a third table that is in a one-to-many relationship with each of the two original tables.

In the case of the contractor-referral business, you would create a Billing table, like the one shown in the upper-left figure, which has two foreign keys. One foreign key is the Employee Number field, and is the primary key of the Contractors table, just as it was in the previous example. The other foreign key is the Employer Number field, which is the primary key of a table that holds data about employers.

You can relate this Billing table to the Contractors table by using a many-to-one relationship, just as you did in the previous example, as shown in the upper-right figure.

You could also use the same methods to join this Billing table with an Employer table, as shown in the lower-left figure. The Employer table would hold all the data on each employer, including the employer number and name, address, and contact person. It can be joined in a many-to-one relationship with the Billing table, just as the Employee table is.

You can always break down a many-to-many relationship between two tables into two many-to-one relationships. You just need to create a third table that has records that include the primary key fields from the two other tables, plus any other data that is in a many-to-one relationship with those tables.

TAKE NOTE

INCLUDING EXTRA FIELDS

When you join the Employee table with the Billing table, you could also add a bit of information on the employers each one worked for, because each record in the Billing table has a foreign key that refers to only one record in the Employer table. You could print a report to send out with employees' paychecks that not only lists the hours they worked each month, but also includes the name of the their employers. Likewise, when you join the Employer table with the Billing table, you could pull in some fields from the Employee table. For example, you could send a bill with the employee's name next to his hours worked.

CROSS-REFERENCE

Before reading this section, see the previous section, "Working with Many-to-One Relationships."

FIND IT ONLINE

For a discussion of using joined tables in queries, see http://www.cse.bris.ac.uk/~ccmjs/accsql.html#join.

BILLING TABLE

Employee No	Employer No	Bill Date	Hours
1	14	3/31/99	150.5
3	25	3/31/99	28.5
4	25	2/28/99	162.5
4	14	3/31/99	22.0

Students and Classes

Another common example of a many-to-many relationships is students and classes in a school. Each student can take many different classes, and each class can enroll many different students.

You need a table of Enrollments that has the student number and the class number in each record, to link the Student table and the Classes table. The Enrollments table lets you look up all the students in a given class, or all the classes that a given student is taking.

To link two tables that are in a many-to-many relationship, create a third table that includes the primary keys of both as its foreign keys. You can relate this third table to either of the original two tables.

BILLING TABLE			CONTRACTORS TABLE		
EmpNo	Bill Date	Hours	EmpNo	Name	Etc.
1	3/31/99	150.5			
3	3/31/99	28.5	3	Kevin Smith	...
4	2/28/99	162.5	4	Samuel Smalz	...
4	3/31/99	22.0			

BILLING TABLE				EMPLOYER TABLE		
Employee No	Employer No	Bill Date	Hours	Employer No	Name	Etc.
1	14	3/31/99	150.5			
3	25	3/31/99	28.5	25	XYZ Co.	...
4	25	2/28/99	162.5			
4	14	3/31/99	22.0			

Working with More Complex Relationships

Databases that are more complex must be broken down into more than three tables. An example is a database that records sales. Each salesperson deals with many customers, and each customer deals with many salespeople. This many-to-many relationship can be broken down into two one-to-many relationships, like the one discussed previously. As shown in the upper-left figure, you need an Employee table with Employee Number as its key field, a Customer table with Customer Number as its key field, and an Invoice table with fields for the Employee Number, Customer Number, other information about each sale, and with Invoice Number as its own primary key. With these three tables, you could easily print a list of when each customer made purchases and when each salesperson made sales.

However, you also need to record all the products sold in each sale. Since any number of products could be sold in a sale, products are in a many-to-one relationship with invoices. To handle this relationship, create a separate Invoice Line table, which includes fields for the invoice number, the price of each product, the quantity sold of the products, and other data. Use the Invoice Number field to join the Invoice Line table with the Invoice table.

The invoice heading includes

▶ The date from the Invoice table
▶ The customer's name, found in the Customer table for the record whose primary key matches the Invoice table's customer number

▶ The salesperson's name, which you find by looking in the Employee table for the record whose primary key is the same as the employee number in the Invoice table

Under this heading, you print all the lines of the invoice, which you find by looking in the Invoice Line table for records that have this invoice number as their foreign key.

You would also want to include the product's name in each line of the invoice. You probably already would have a Product table, with product number and other data on each product, as shown in the upper-right figure. Include the product number as a foreign key in each invoice line to use the product name from the Product table.

TAKE NOTE

▶ BREAK IT INTO MANY-TO-ONE RELATIONSHIPS

This example includes different types of data stored in many tables, but it is finally broken down into a number of one-to-many relationships. The Invoice table is in a many-to-one relationship with the Customer table. The Invoice table is in a many-to-one relationship with the Employee table. The Invoice table is in a one-to-many relationship with the Invoice line table. No matter how complex the data, it can be broken down into many-to-one relationships. Thus, you can work with even complex data using the techniques that are shown next.

CROSS-REFERENCE

Before reading this section, see the previous two sections on many-to-one and many-to-many relationships.

FIND IT ONLINE

For more on managing complex databases, see http://www.hawkesbury.uws.edu.au/faculties/management/IS/MCom/CP805A/M3t5.htm.

Normalization Made Easy

The technical rules of *data normalization*, covered in advanced textbooks on database theory, are useful in complex cases. In most cases, you can do just as well by using these common-sense rules:

▶ Be sure a one-to-one relationship exists between each field and the record in your tables. In other words, the field should have only one value for each record. For example, an employee has only one address and one zip code, so these fields can go in the Employee table, but if the employee generates many invoices, these should not go into the Employee table.

▶ If there is a one-to-many relationship between the table and some data, put this data into a second table that includes the primary key of the first table as its foreign key.

For example, to record the employee's invoices, create a Billing table that includes the Employee Number field as a foreign key.

▶ Break up a many-to-many relationship between two tables into two many-to-one relationships by creating a third table that includes the original tables' primary keys as its foreign keys. For example, if each employee sends invoices to many customers and each customer receives invoices from many employees, then the Employee table and the Customer table are in a many-to-many relationship, and you need a Billing table with both the Employee Number and Customer Number fields as foreign keys.

If you keep looking for one-to-many and many-to-many relationships and breaking them down into separate tables, you can generally normalize even complex data.

CUSTOMER TABLE			INVOICE TABLE				EMPLOYEE TABLE		
CustNo	Customer Name	Etc.	InvNo	CustNo	EmpNo	Date	EmpNo	EmpName	Etc.
111	John Smith	...	222	111	23	3/3/99	23	Jane Jones	...

INVOICE LINE TABLE			PRODUCT TABLE		
InvNo	ProdNo.	Quantity	ProNo.	Product Name	Price
222	23	1	23	MS Office Upgrade	$199.00
222	25	1	25	MS Windows Upgrade	$99.00

Creating a Default Relationship in Access

In general, you should begin creating relationships in Access by using the Relationships window to define the default relationships among tables. The default relationship will be used whenever you work with the tables, unless you specify some other relationship.

You save time if you begin by defining the relationship you need most often as the default relationship. Then you will only need to define the relationship for individual queries, forms, or reports where there is some special reason for not using the default relationship.

To create a default relationship, open the database and select Tools ⇨ Relationships from the Tools menu. The first time you do this, Access displays the Show Table dialog box, shown in the upper-right figure, which lets you choose the tables or queries you want to include in the Relationships window.

The Relationships window includes field lists for the tables you added, as shown in the lower left figure. Notice that name the primary key field for each table is the top-most field and is displayed in darker type.

To create the relationship, click and drag from a field in one table to a field with matching values in another table. For example, you could click and drag the Contractors table's Employee Number field to the Billing table's Employee Number field.

When tables are joined in this way, Access displays a line connecting the fields on which that the join is based. Notice the number 1 near the Contractors table, and the infinity symbol near the Billing table,

indicating that this is a one-to-many relationship. There can be an infinite number of billing records associated with each contractor's record.

Modifying the Relationship

To modify a Default Relationship, choose Tools ⇨ Relationships to display the Relationships window. To delete a relationship, click the line that represents it and press Delete. To remove a table from the Relationships window, select it by clicking anywhere on the field list, and press Delete.

To add new tables to the Relationships window, choose Relationships ⇨ Show Table, or click the Show Table button to use the Show Table dialog box again. To move a table, click and drag its title bar. It is sometimes convenient to move tables in complex databases to make it easier to see their connections.

Continued

> ### TAKE NOTE
>
> #### USING THE PRIMARY TABLE
> Dragging from the "one" table's key field side of the relationship is best. For example, you should drag the Employee Number field from the Contractors table to the Billing table. The table you begin dragging from is that relationship's *primary table*. As you will see, you must use the "one" table as the primary table to enforce referential integrity. If you use the "many" table, you will be unable to enforce referential integrity.

CROSS-REFERENCE
For more information on the Show Table dialog box, see Chapter 4.

SHORTCUT
You can also add a table to the Relationship window by double-clicking it in the Show Table window.

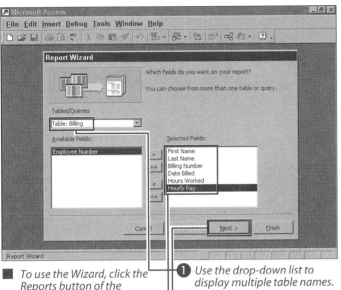

■ To use the Wizard, click the Reports button of the Database window and double-click Create Report by using wizard.

❶ Use the drop-down list to display multiple table names.

❷ Add the fields to the Selected Fields list by clicking >.

❸ Click Next.

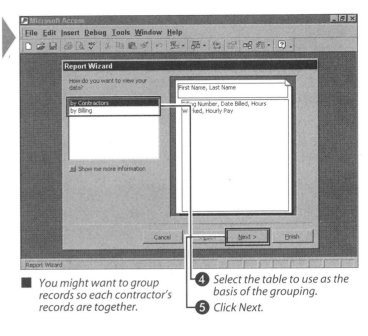

■ You might want to group records so each contractor's records are together.

❹ Select the table to use as the basis of the grouping.

❺ Click Next.

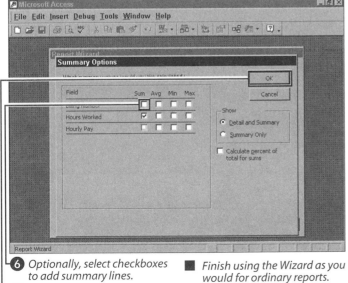

❻ Optionally, select checkboxes to add summary lines.

❼ Click OK.

■ Finish using the Wizard as you would for ordinary reports.

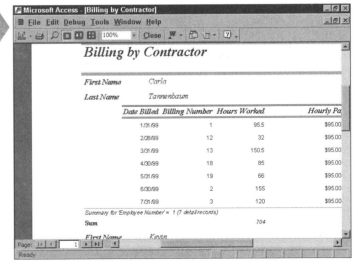

■ An example of a grouped report for a relational database.

Defining the Relationship

When you click and drag to create a relationship, before displaying the line that represents the relationship, Access displays the Edit Relationships dialog box shown here in the upper-left figure. The primary table or query is listed on the left, and the related table or query is listed on the right.

A record in the "many" table whose foreign key does not refer to any record in the "one" table is sometimes called an *orphan record*. For example, if you had a Billing record with a Contractor Number not found in the Contractor table, it would be an orphan record. If you select the Enforce Referential Integrity checkbox, Access will not let you add or edit records in the "many" table or delete records from the "one" table, if it creates an orphan record. Unless you have some special reason not to, you should always select the Enforce Referential Integrity checkbox.

You can use the two checkboxes below Enforce Referential Integrity to override the usual protections in the following ways:

▶ If you select Cascade Update Related Fields, you can edit the primary key field in the "one" table, and Access automatically makes the same change to the foreign key in the "many" table, so the records are still related.

▶ If you select Cascade Deleted Related Records, you can delete records in the "one" table even if there are related records in the "many" table.

Access automatically deletes the related records in the "many" table, so it does not have orphan records.

After a cascading update or delete, the database still has relational integrity, but records in the "many" table may have been changed without the user knowing. Nonprogrammers should avoid cascade updates and deletes, since they override many of the protections built into Access. They are useful to programmers, who can build similar protections into their programs.

If you want to change the definition of a relationship, you can display the Edit Relationships dialog box at any time by clicking the line that represents the relationship choosing Relationships ⇨ Edit Relationship.

TAKE NOTE

▶ SELECTING THE DATA TYPE OF THE FOREIGN KEY

As you know, using AutoNumber as a primary key's data type is usually best. If you want to enforce referential integrity and relate a foreign key to an AutoNumber primary, you should make the foreign key the Number data type with the Long Integer field size. If you use any other data type, Access displays an error message saying that the relationship must be based on fields with the same data types. Access considers a Number with the size Long Integer to be the same data type as the AutoNumber field, which also has the size Long Integer.

CROSS-REFERENCE

For an explanation of why you need to protect referential integrity, see "Working with Many-to-One Relationships" earlier in this chapter.

SHORTCUT

You can display the dialog box to change the definition of a relationship by double-clicking the line that represents the relationship.

Selecting Join Types

The Join Properties dialog box lets you control which records are included when you use the default relationship. Click the Join Type button of the Relationships dialog box to display this dialog box, shown here. If you are working with a one-to-many relationship, the options are as follows:

1. Include only records that are in both tables. In the example, a record must have the same Employee Number in both the Contractor table and the Billing table for it to be included in queries, forms, reports, or data access pages that use this default relationship.

2. Include all records from the "one" table and only the records from the "many" table related to these records.

3. Include all records from the "many" table and only their related "one" table records.

When working with a one-to-many relationship, Options 1 and 3 should be equivalent. In the sample application, both would display only contractors who sent bills. But Option 1 would hide orphan records in the Billing table; Option 3 would not. It is always better to use Option 3, so that your errors are detected. Whether you should use Option 2 or 3 depends on your reason for joining the tables. Choose whichever is most convenient as the default, and change it for individual queries or reports as needed. If you do not use this dialog box, Access uses Option 1.

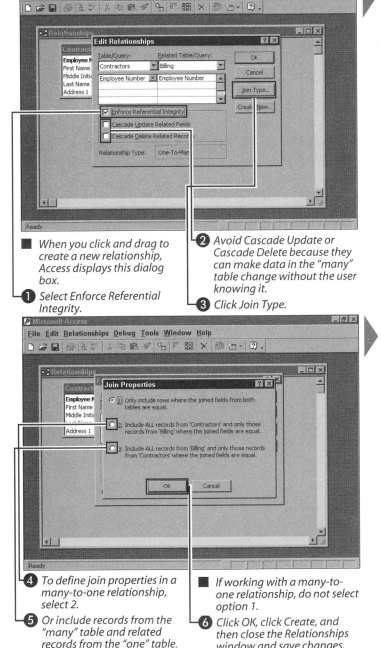

■ *When you click and drag to create a new relationship, Access displays this dialog box.*

1 *Select Enforce Referential Integrity.*

2 *Avoid Cascade Update or Cascade Delete because they can make data in the "many" table change without the user knowing it.*

3 *Click Join Type.*

4 *To define join properties in a many-to-one relationship, select 2.*

5 *Or include records from the "many" table and related records from the "one" table.*

■ *If working with a many-to-one relationship, do not select option 1.*

6 *Click OK, click Create, and then close the Relationships window and save changes.*

Using Queries with Relational Databases

I t would be hard to use the "many" table of a many-to-one relationship by itself. For example, a Billing table that has contractors' employee numbers but not their names is not that useful. You do not want to look at the employee number and try to remember who it is; you want to see the contractor's name.

You can easily display fields from both tables by using a query. After including related tables, you use the Query window as you do when you are creating a query based on a single table.

For example, you could create a query that is an extended version of the record in the Billing table, with the Name field as a bit of extra information.

Use the Show Table dialog box to include both Contractor and Billing tables in the Query window, and Access automatically includes the default relationship, as you can see in the upper-left figure. Then add the fields you want to the design grid, as shown in the upper-right figure. Optionally, use the other features of the Query window, as you do with single-table queries. (In the illustration, records are sorted by last name.)

Save the query and run it as usual. The result includes the name of each contractor as well as the billing data.

It is much easier to use the query than to use the Billing table. If you enter an employee number, the employee's name is automatically displayed in the name column, as you can see in the lower-left figure.

Continued

TAKE NOTE

▶ EDITING DATA IN THE QUERY

You can add records, edit records, and work with the result of this query in other ways, just as you work with any table or query in Datasheet view. But there are a few traps into which you can fall. If you change the Employee Number field from the Contractor table, all the relations to it from records in the Billing table will be lost. (This is not a problem if you used an AutoNumber as the primary key, because you cannot edit an AutoNumber.) If you change the Employee Number field, and it was taken from the Billing table, the values in the Last Name and First Name fields also change, as Access looks them up in the Contractor table on the basis of the Employee Number field. If you edit any field from the Contractors table, the value changes in that table, so it changes in all the fields where it appears in the query, as you see in the lower-right figure.

CROSS-REFERENCE
For basic information on creating queries, see Chapter 4.

SHORTCUT
The fastest way to create a query is to double-click Create query in Design view in the Database window.

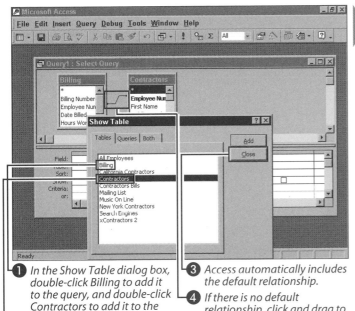

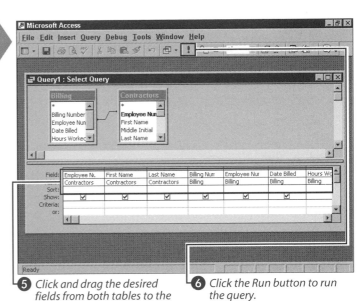

1 In the Show Table dialog box, double-click Billing to add it to the query, and double-click Contractors to add it to the query.

2 Click Close.

3 Access automatically includes the default relationship.

4 If there is no default relationship, click and drag to create one, as you do in the Relationships window.

5 Click and drag the desired fields from both tables to the design grid.

6 Click the Run button to run the query.

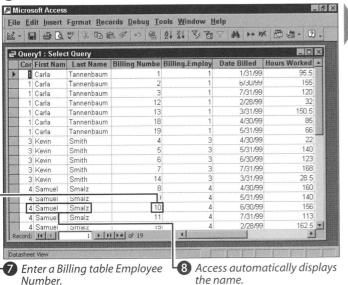

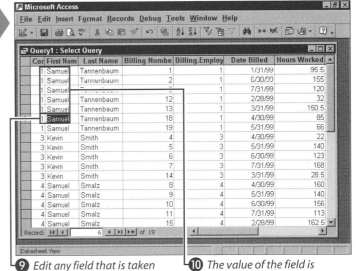

7 Enter a Billing table Employee Number.

8 Access automatically displays the name.

9 Edit any field that is taken from the Contractor table.

10 The value of the field is changed in all records.

Using Queries with Relational Databases *Continued*

Remember that the records displayed in the result of the query depend on the Join Properties of the relationship. You learned that, when you create a default relationship, you can choose to display all records in the "one" table or to display a record in the "one" table only if there is a matching record in the "many" table.

In the example, you would probably want records in the Contractors table to be displayed only if there were an equivalent record in the Billing table, as shown in the upper-left figure. You would not want to clutter the table with records of contractors who have not billed you recently, as shown in the upper-right figure.

However, there may well be times when you want to use this sort of query and display all the records in the "one" table. For example, this would be useful if you wanted to see which contractors have not worked for you. To handle the exceptions, you can create a query and change its join properties, rather than using the default.

To change join properties of the relationship, right click the line representing the Join and choose Join Properties from its pop-up menu to display the Join Properties dialog box. Use this dialog box to specify the Join Properties for this query, as you did when you created the default relationship.

You can see from the illustrations that it is usually best to display only records from the "one" table that have related records in the "many" table. Unless you have some special reason not to, you should choose this as the default relationship, and alter it in the exceptional queries and reports where it is not used.

TAKE NOTE

▶ MODIFYING A QUERY WITH RELATED TABLES

There are a few special changes you might want to make in queries based on relational databases. To add new tables or queries, select Query ⇨ Show Table and use the Show Table dialog box to add them, as usual; then, relate them to other tables by clicking and dragging a key field from one table to another as you do when you create a default relationship. To delete a join, click the line representing the join to select it and then press Delete, or right-click the line and select Delete from its pop-up menu.

▶ DISPLAYING RELATED RECORDS IN A TABLE

For some purposes, it is sufficient to display related records in the table rather than creating a query. After you relate tables, Access adds a + next to each record in the "one" table, and you can click it to display all related records in the "many" table, as shown in the lower-right figure.

CROSS-REFERENCE
It is also useful to use lookup fields, covered in Chapter 13, to add the foreign key to the "many" table.

SHORTCUT
You can double-click the line representing the join to display the Join Properties dialog box.

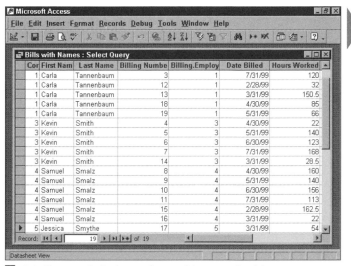

Join Property 3 displays only matching records of the Contractors table.

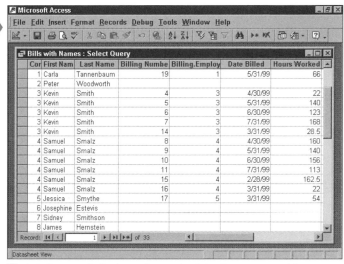

Join Property 2 displays all records of the Contractors table.

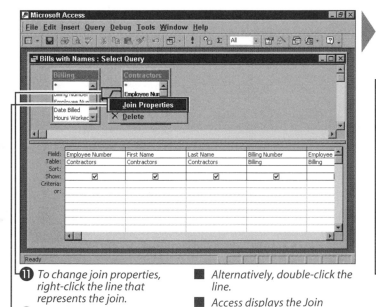

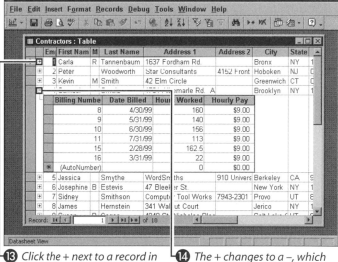

⑪ To change join properties, right-click the line that represents the join.

⑫ Choose Join Properties from the shortcut menu.

■ Alternatively, double-click the line.

■ Access displays the Join Properties dialog box, described above.

⑬ Click the + next to a record in the table to display related records.

⑭ The + changes to a –, which you click to hide the related records.

Using Reports with Relational Databases

In general, you can use the Report Wizard with multiple tables just as you would do with a single table. You can create a query that joins tables and use it as the basis of the report. Or you can use the Wizard's Tables/Queries drop-down list to select multiple tables and add fields from them, just as you would add fields from a single table. The tables will be joined using the default relationship.

Grouped reports are particularly useful when you are working with a many-to-one relationship, because there is repetitive data that you often want to group. In the sample query you have been looking at, there are many billing records for each contractor. It would be useful to create a report that groups these records by contractor name and provides a summary line with the total number of hours worked by each contractor.

A few extra features of the Wizard that are especially relevant to relational databases are covered here.

In the first step of the Report Wizard, add fields from two or more tables to the report, as shown in the upper-left figure, or add fields from a query that joins the tables.

The next step, shown in the upper-right figure, is added when you create a report on a multitable database. Be sure that the "one" table is selected as the basis of the grouping: In the example, you want to group on the Contractors table, as shown in the upper-right figure, so that the billing records for each contractor are grouped together.

Use the other steps to add groups based on fields, select the sort order, select the style, and then name and create the report just as you do with ordinary reports.

An example of the grouped report is shown in the lower-right figure. The billing records for a contractor are displayed under that contractor's name, with a summary line for each contractor.

You can see that this report would be improved if the contractors' names were placed on a single line in the group header, rather than on two lines, and if there were a better description on the summary line. In Chapter 10, you learn to design custom reports, which let you make this change.

TAKE NOTE

ADDING SUMMARY LINES

It is often useful to add summary of numeric fields to grouped reports on relational databases. To do this, click the Summary Options button on the step that lets you sort detail fields to display the Summary Options dialog box, shown in the lower-left figure. For example, you might want a summary line with the total hours each contractor has worked, as shown in the illustration.

CROSS-REFERENCE

See Chapter 6 for more information about using the Report Wizard.

SHORTCUT

The fastest way to create a report is to double-click Create Report by using wizard in the Database window.

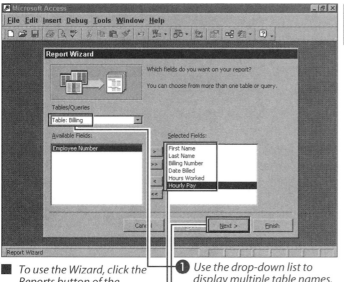

■ To use the Wizard, click the Reports button of the Database window and double-click Create Report by using wizard.

❶ Use the drop-down list to display multiple table names.

❷ Add the fields to the Selected Fields list by clicking >.

❸ Click Next.

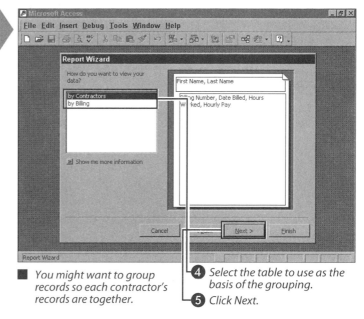

■ You might want to group records so each contractor's records are together.

❹ Select the table to use as the basis of the grouping.

❺ Click Next.

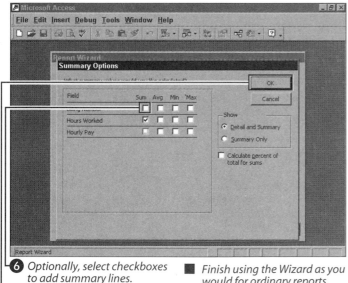

❻ Optionally, select checkboxes to add summary lines.

❼ Click OK.

■ Finish using the Wizard as you would for ordinary reports.

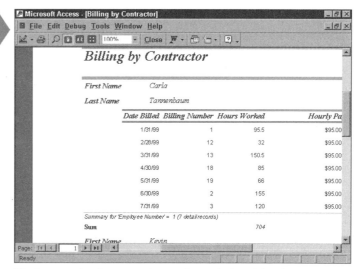

■ An example of a grouped report for a relational database.

Using Forms with Relational Databases

You can create simple forms for relational databases very easily by basing the form on a query that joins two tables and using the Form wizard to create the report in the usual way.

Forms with subforms are particularly useful when working with relational databases. When you display a record from the "one" table in the main form, all the related records from the "many" table are displayed in the subform under it. Forms with subforms are best if you want to take a one-to-many approach and display all the records from the "one" table and related records from the "many" table.

In the first step of the Form Wizard, you must include fields from both tables in the form, as you can see in the upper-left figure.

In the second step, which lets you choose the grouping of the form, you must group by the "one" table.

If you select Form with subform(s) in this step, the Form Wizard will create a single form with fields from the "one" table in its upper half and corresponding fields from the "many" table listed under it. For example, you could create a form with the name of the contractor in the upper half and all the records from the Billing table for that contractor in a panel in the bottom half. If there are too many Billing table records to display at once, a scroll bar will be added to the panel to let you view them all.

If you select Linked forms, the Form Wizard will create a form with fields from the "one" table that has a button you can click to display a second form with the corresponding fields from the "many" table. This is useful if you want to display so many fields that they can't all fit in a single form.

Other steps let you choose a layout (Tabular or Datasheet) for your subform and a style. The final step lets you enter two titles, one for the main form and one for the subform or linked form, as you can see in the lower-left figure.

Click Finish to create the form with subform, as shown in the lower-right figure. Notice that there is a scroll bar and a separate set of record controls for the subform to let you move through its records.

TAKE NOTE

CREATING THE RELATIONSHIP FIRST

Before you use the Report Wizard or the Form Wizard, make sure you have created the default relationship you need. The Report and Form Wizards relate the tables using the default relationship. If you are working with more complex data, the Form Wizard also lets you create forms with multiple subforms or with multiple linked forms, and you must set up the default relationships among all the tables before you use it.

CROSS-REFERENCE

See Chapter 6 for complete information on using the Form Wizard.

SHORTCUT

The fastest way to create a form is to double-click Create Form by using wizard in the Database window.

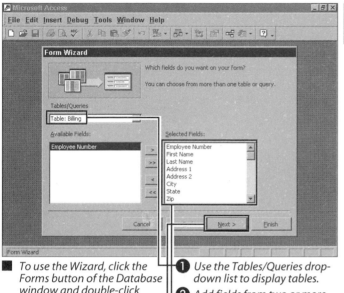

■ To use the Wizard, click the Forms button of the Database window and double-click Create Form by using wizard.

❶ Use the Tables/Queries drop-down list to display tables.

❷ Add fields from two or more tables to the Selected Fields list by clicking >.

❸ Click Next.

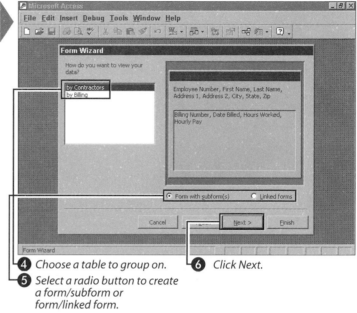

❹ Choose a table to group on.

❺ Select a radio button to create a form/subform or form/linked form.

❻ Click Next.

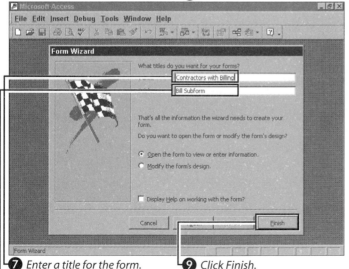

❼ Enter a title for the form.

❽ Enter a title for the subform.

❾ Click Finish.

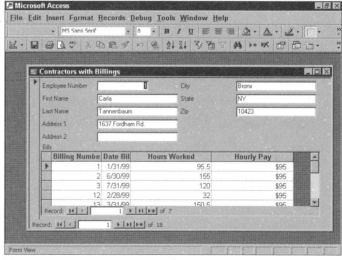

■ A sample form and subform.

Personal Workbook

Q&A

1 What relationship should each field have to the record it is in?

_____

_____

_____

2 Give an example of a one-to-many relationship.

_____

_____

_____

3 Give an example of a many-to-many relationship.

_____

_____

_____

4 How do you normalize a one-to-many relationship?

_____

_____

_____

5 How do you normalize a many-to-many relationship?

_____

_____

_____

6 When is a primary key valid, and how can you be sure that only valid values are entered?

_____

_____

_____

7 When is a foreign key valid, and how can you be sure only valid values are entered?

_____

_____

_____

8 What data type should you use for a foreign key?

_____

_____

_____

ANSWERS: PAGE 347

EXTRA PRACTICE

1. Define a second table that is in a one-to-many relationship to the sample table you have been using so far. Be sure to include a numeric field.

2. Create the default relationship between the two tables.

3. Create a query joining the two tables.

4. Display the query in Datasheet view and use it to enter sample data in the second table.

5. Create a grouped report that includes the two tables, with a group summary that uses the numeric field.

6. Create a form with subform that displays data from the two tables.

REAL-WORLD APPLICATIONS

✔ You run a mail-order business. Your database includes one table with your customers' names and addresses and a second related table with their orders. You cannot keep this data in a single table, because each customer can have multiple orders.

✔ You are creating a list of reports arranged by authors. You keep information about the authors in one table, and information about all the reports in a second related table, and you create a form with subform to let the user display any author's name with all the reports by that author underneath it. The Reports table also has a hyperlink field that the user can click to display the report online.

Visual Quiz

The picture here shows a data-entry form for two tables in a many-to-one relationship, which does not use a subform. How was this form created?

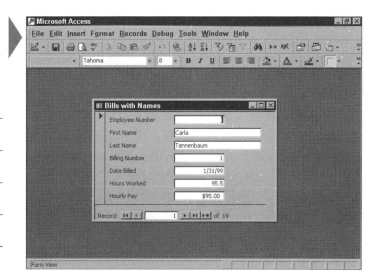

CHAPTER 8

MASTER THESE SKILLS

▶ **Getting Oriented with Form Design**

▶ **Working with the Form**

▶ **Working with Bands**

▶ **Working with Controls**

▶ **Using the Layout Tools**

▶ **Working with Text**

▶ **Adding Colors and Effects**

Designing Custom Forms

In Chapter 6, you learned to create AutoForms and forms using the Form Wizard. Although these forms are adequate for many purposes, customizing them is often useful.

For one thing, if you include many fields in the forms you create using the Wizard, you may not be able to fit them all into a single screen. To create a form that is easier to work with, you will want to customize the form by resizing and moving the fields so you can see them all at once. This is easy to do: You just switch to Design view and then click and drag the fields. Another reason for customizing forms is to add instructions that tell users how to use the form.

When you create a new form, the New Form dialog box gives you the option of creating a new form in Design view. If you do this, Access displays a blank form, and you can add fields to the form design yourself. However, most people find it easier to use a wizard to select fields, so you have all the fields you need placed in the Form window when you begin. In general, even when you are creating a custom form, it is best to begin by using the Form Wizard or creating an AutoForm. The last dialog box of every Form Wizard has a button that lets you display the form in Design view so you can customize it.

As you learn to design custom forms, you will see that the Access Form window in Design view lets you easily make some changes, such as moving and resizing fields, yet it also gives you tremendous power. For example, it enables you to create drop-down lists or radio buttons used to enter data. This chapter covers basic techniques for working with forms in Design view. It focuses on teaching you how to change objects that the Wizard places on the form. The next chapter covers advanced ways in which you can use Design view to add new objects to the form.

Getting Oriented with Form Design

All the items included in a form, such as fields, labels (text objects) and checkboxes, are called controls. Access features three fundamentally different types of controls:

▶ *Bound controls* are associated with data in the table. All the fields in a form are bound controls. The information displayed in them is connected (or bound) to the data in the table.

▶ *Unbound controls* are independent of the data in the table. If you add a title at the top of a form, it would be an unbound control. It always remains the same, regardless of the data in the table.

▶ *Calculated controls* are created using expressions. In the upper-left figure, the field that displays Total Pay multiplies Hours Worked by Hourly Pay. These calculated controls require expressions, which are described in Chapter 14.

The upper-right figure shows three important Form window features that you can display or hide by clicking toolbar buttons.

▶ Click the Field List button to display or hide the field list (used to add fields to the form).

▶ Click the Toolbox button to display or hide the toolbox (used to add new controls).

▶ Click the Properties button to display a property sheet for the selected object. This sheet contains properties for the entire form, a band, or a control, depending on which is selected.

▶ Click the Code button to display the Visual Basic code for the form.

If a feature is displayed, its tool button will be depressed, and you can click the button again to hide the object (except for code, which is displayed in its own window). Access remembers which features are being used when you close the form, and it displays them the next time you open the Form window in Design view.

Because people often change the fonts, colors, or "look" of forms, Access makes this easy by automatically displaying a special toolbar, called the Formatting toolbar, below the standard toolbar when you are working with a form.

The lower-left figure identifies the buttons used for formatting text ; they are accessible only when an object that includes text is selected. The other formatting buttons are identified in the lower-right figure. When you select an object, these buttons display its current font, size, and colors.

TAKE NOTE

▶ **CHOOSING FEATURES TO DISPLAY**

It is usually most convenient to display the toolbox and property sheet only when you need them, so they do not get in your way. Beginners should not display the code, which is only meant for programmers. If you click the Code button by mistake, close this window in one of the usual ways (for example, by clicking its Close button) to return to the Form window.

CROSS-REFERENCE

For information on creating forms using the Form Wizard, see Chapter 6.

SHORTCUT

You can also right-click the form and use its pop-up menu to display and hide the toolbox and property sheet.

- ■ Bound Controls.
- ■ Unbound Control.
- ■ Calculated Control.

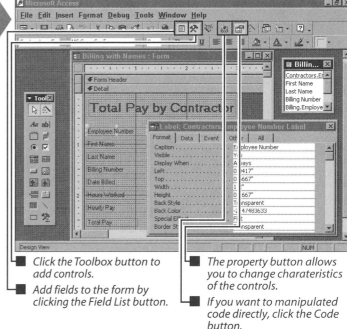

- ■ Click the Toolbox button to add controls.
- ■ Add fields to the form by clicking the Field List button.
- ■ The property button allows you to change charateristics of the controls.
- ■ If you want to manipulated code directly, click the Code button.

- ■ Select Object to be changed.
- ■ Fonts can be changed with the Font Name drop-down list.
- ■ Font Sizes are changed with Font Size drop-down list.
- ■ Left Align, Center, and Right Align are helpful when placing labels close to objects.

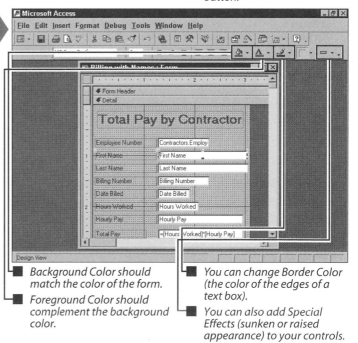

- ■ Background Color should match the color of the form.
- ■ Foreground Color should complement the background color.
- ■ You can change Border Color (the color of the edges of a text box).
- ■ You can also add Special Effects (sunken or raised appearance) to your controls.

143

Working with the Form

You might want to customize a form in several ways. For example, you may want to change the size of the entire form so it has room for more objects; change the header band of the form so you can fit your company logo in it; or change the size of an individual text box so it is big enough to display long names that you entered in the field. In the next few sections, you learn how to select and work with the form as a whole, with bands of the form, and with individual controls on the form.

You can tell which of these objects is selected because its name is displayed in the Select Object drop-down list of the Formatting toolbar. You can also select objects by choosing them from this drop-down list.

Selecting the Form

Once you have displayed a form in Design view, you can select the whole form in any of these ways:

- ▶ Choose Edit ➪ Select Form. (This option is on the extended menu, so you may have to click the arrows at the bottom of the Edit menu to display it.)
- ▶ Choose Form in the Select Object drop-down list.
- ▶ Click the Form Selector box in the upper-left corner of the form.

The Form Selector box has a black square displayed in it whenever the form is selected, as shown in the lower-left figure.

As you learn near the end of this chapter, you can display a property sheet for the whole form as you can for other objects you select, but this is useful primarily for programmers. After selecting the form, you cannot manipulate it in many of the simple ways that you can with bands and controls.

Resizing the Form

The only feature of the entire form that nonprogrammers commonly work with is its size. To resize the form, simply place the pointer on the form's right edge, as shown in the lower-right figure, so that it is displayed as a vertical line with arrows pointing in both directions. Then drag left or right to make the form narrower or wider. If you have maximized the form, you must click the Restore button first in order to resize it.

TAKE NOTE

▶ DISPLAYING FORMS

Once you have created a form, you can use the toolbar to display it in Design view, Form view, or Datasheet view using the View menu or the View tool drop-down list. You learned in Chapter 6 how to use Form view and Datasheet view. In this chapter, you learn to work in Design view.

CROSS-REFERENCE

In Design view, you work with reports and forms in the same way. See the beginning of Chapter 10 for a quick summary of the basics.

FIND·IT ONLINE

For information on creating Forms, see http://www.istis.unomaha.edu/isqa/wolcott/ isqa3310/accform.htm.

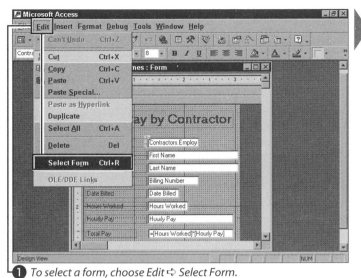

❶ To select a form, choose Edit ➪ Select Form.

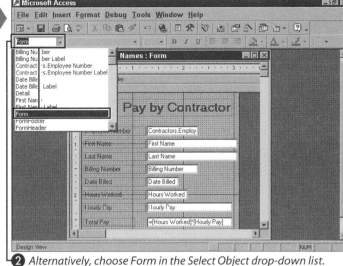

❷ Alternatively, choose Form in the Select Object drop-down list.

❸ Alternatively, click the Form Selector Box.

❹ To resize a form, place the pointer on its right edge.

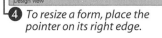 ■ Click and drag to change the form's width.

Working with Bands

The Form design window is divided into bands or sections, as shown in the upper-left figure. The band where you place a control determines how that control is used when you print the form or display it on the screen.

Forms can have the following bands:

- ▶ Detail section of the form scrolls on the screen, and it is repeated for each record when you print the form. It includes the fields of the table.
- ▶ Form Header and Form Footer are displayed at the top and bottom of the screen when you view the form on the screen. When you print the form, they are printed once at the beginning and end of the printout.
- ▶ Page Header and Page Footer are not displayed on the screen. They are printed at the top and bottom of each page when you print the form.

The upper-left figure shows a form in Design view with a header and a footer, and the upper-right figure shows the form: The scroll bar only moves the data, not the header and footer.

To select a band in Design view, click it or choose it in the Select Object drop-down list of the Formatting toolbar. You can also press Tab or Shift+Tab to select the bands in turn. The bar with the band's name on it is shaded when it is selected. After you have selected it, you can change the color or other properties of the band using methods described later in this chapter.

To resize a band, place the pointer on it and click and drag its lower border downward to make the band larger or upward to make it smaller.

A form must have a Detail band, but you can choose whether to have Form Header, Form Footer, Page Header, and Page Footer bands. To add or remove bands, right-click any band to display its pop-up menu, and choose Page Header/Footer and Form Header/Footer, which are toggles that add or remove these headers and footers, as shown in the lower-right figure.

Selecting either of these options adds both a Header and Footer. If you want just a Header or just a Footer, you must add both, and then resize the one you do not want to zero.

The figure in the lower right shows a form with a Page Footer added.

TAKE NOTE

▶ AVOIDING DATA LOSS

If you remove form or page headers and footers, Access also removes all the controls in them, so that you lose all the previous work you did in designing them. Access displays a warning telling you this before removing headers and footers. Because Access cannot undo this change, it is best to save your work before removing a header and footer. Then you can undo the change after seeing its effect, if necessary, by closing the Form window without saving changes.

CROSS-REFERENCE

Reports also allow Group Headers and Footers, covered in Chapter 10.

SHORTCUT

You can right-click the Form and use its pop-up menu to display or hide Page Header/Footer and Form Header/Footer.

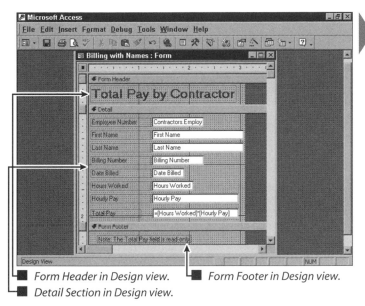

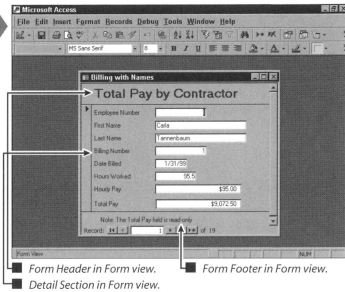

■ *Form Header in Design view.* ■ *Form Footer in Design view.*
■ *Detail Section in Design view.*

■ *Form Header in Form view.* ■ *Form Footer in Form view.*
■ *Detail Section in Form view.*

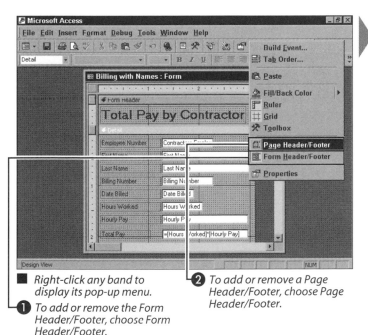

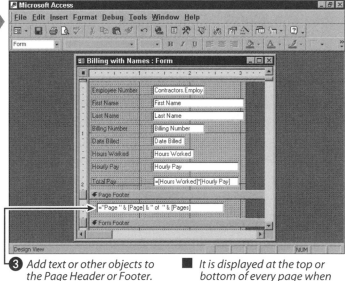

■ *Right-click any band to display its pop-up menu.*

❶ *To add or remove the Form Header/Footer, choose Form Header/Footer.*

❷ *To add or remove a Page Header/Footer, choose Page Header/Footer.*

❸ *Add text or other objects to the Page Header or Footer.*

■ *It is displayed at the top or bottom of every page when you print the form.*

Working with Controls

One of the most common and easiest ways to modify a form generated by the Wizard is to resize and move its controls to make the form easier to view. You can group like controls together, such as all the phone numbers (Home, Office, Cell, and Fax) on one side of the form.

To do this, first select a control by clicking it or choosing it from the Select Object drop-down list of the Formatting toolbar. To deselect a control, click anywhere in the Form window outside of the control.

When a control is selected, it has two types of handles, the Resize handle and the Move handle (the larger one). To move a control, simply click and drag its Move Handle in any direction. When it is on the Move Handle, the pointer is displayed as a hand with its index finger extended. To resize a control, click and drag one of its Resize handles. When it is on a Resize handle, the pointer is displayed as a two-headed arrow, indicating the directions you can drag that handle (shown in the lower-left figure).

To delete a control, select it and press Del. Access does not display a warning before deleting it, but you can click the Undo tool (or select Edit ⇨ Undo) if you delete a control by mistake.

Working with Fields and Labels

If you are rearranging controls, you may want to move both a field and its label to a new location, or you may want to move just one. For example, you may want to put the label above the field instead of to its left.

In the lower-right figure, the Hourly Pay field frame is selected and has both the Resize and Move handles. The box that holds the field's name, called the field's *label*, has only the Move handle. Whenever you select a field or its label, the other has just a Move handle. If you drag the Move handle to move the control, only it moves. If you drag the control's edge to move it, the label and field move together. To do this, you must click and drag the control that has both Move and Resize handles, and the one with just a Move handle will move along with it. Be careful where you move controls, however, because Access will overlap controls if that is where you put them.

If you delete a field, its label is automatically deleted, but if you delete a label, the field remains.

Continued

TAKE NOTE

MOVING CONTROLS IN ONE DIRECTION

To make it easier for you to keep controls in proper alignment, Access lets you move a control (or all selected controls) in only a horizontal or vertical direction. Hold down the Shift key and then click and drag the control using its Move handle, and it will only move horizontally or vertically.

CROSS-REFERENCE

For information on how to add new controls to a form, see Chapter 9.

SHORTCUT

After you move or resize or delete a control, you can click the Undo button to get rid of the change.

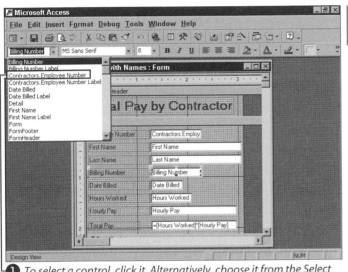

1 To select a control, click it. Alternatively, choose it from the Select Object drop-down list.

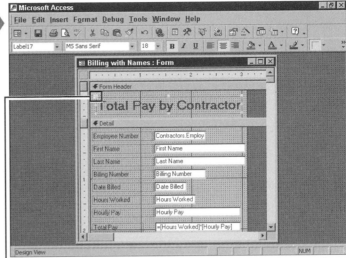

2 To move a control, click and drag its Move handle. Alternatively, click and drag any edge.

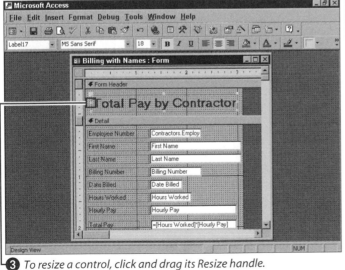

3 To resize a control, click and drag its Resize handle.

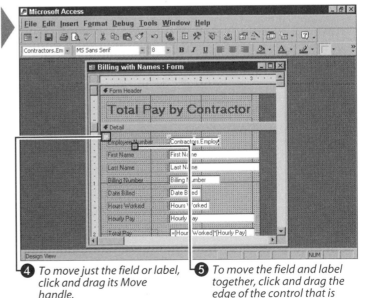

4 To move just the field or label, click and drag its Move handle.

5 To move the field and label together, click and drag the edge of the control that is selected.

Working with Controls

Continued

Selecting Multiple Controls

You can often save time by selecting multiple controls, and then moving and resizing them all. This is a good idea when you have created the basic form in the Wizard. All of the field labels and field boxes will be uniform in size. If you resize them all at the same time, you can be sure that the result will also be uniform.

You can also perform other operations, such as changing the background and text color of the controls. You might group certain types of field by color for easy identification. Or you could distinguish required fields (fields that must have an entry) by giving them a different color than fields that do not require an entry.

You can select multiple controls using the Shift+Click method. If the controls are in the same general vicinity, you can select them all by clicking and dragging through the controls. Access displays a rectangle when you release the mouse button, as shown in the upper-left figure. To select all the controls in the form, choose Edit ⇨ Select All.

When multiple controls are selected, if you resize one of them, all the others are resized in the same way. If you move one control by clicking and dragging its edge, all the selected controls move in the same way. Moving and resizing using click and drag requires a keen eye, a steady hand, and a smooth mouse, so if you make a mistake, remember the Undo button. Pressing Delete deletes all the selected controls.

Changing Stacking Order and Tab Order

At times, you might want to place two objects on the form so that they overlap; for example, you might want to place a colored rectangle behind a text box to emphasize it. When you do this, the object that you place second appears to sit on top of the one that you placed earlier. You can rearrange this layering by using the Format ⇨ Bring to Front or Send to Back options.

You can also specify the tab order of controls on the form, that is, the order in which the user accesses them when they press Tab and Shift+Tab. If you have moved controls or added new controls, pressing Tab no longer moves through the controls from top to bottom and left to right, so you should reset the Tab order.

TAKE NOTE

WORKING WITH CONTROLS THAT USE SPECIAL EFFECTS

If you use the Wizards to create controls with a Chiseled, Shadowed, or Boxed style, Access creates these effects by using two controls, one behind another, to give the impression of depth or shadow. If you simply click and drag one of these controls, the other is left in place. To move or resize this sort of control, you must first click and drag around it to select both controls.

CROSS-REFERENCE

After you select controls, you can control their properties using the methods described in the rest of this chapter.

SHORTCUT

You can choose tab order from the pop-up menu of either a control or the form.

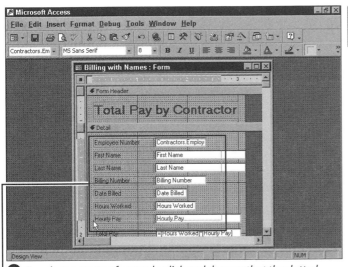

❶ To select a group of controls, click and drag so that the dotted rectangle encloses them all.

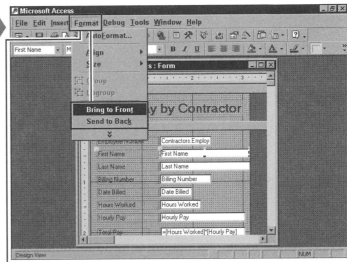

❷ Choose Format ➪ Bring to Front to place a control above others. Or choose Format ➪ Send to Back to place a control behind others.

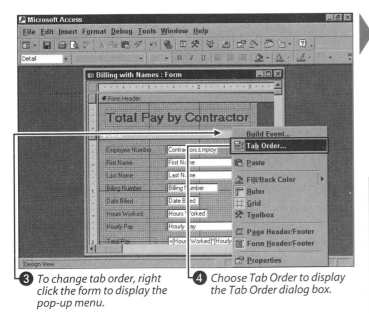

❸ To change tab order, right click the form to display the pop-up menu.

❹ Choose Tab Order to display the Tab Order dialog box.

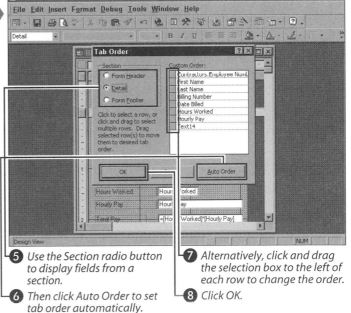

❺ Use the Section radio button to display fields from a section.

❻ Then click Auto Order to set tab order automatically.

❼ Alternatively, click and drag the selection box to the left of each row to change the order.

❽ Click OK.

Using the Layout Tools

Clicking and dragging is usually the fastest method for rearranging the layout of the form, but the results can sometimes be messy: Labels do not line up nicely and field sizes vary. Fortunately, Access provides rulers and grids to make it easier for you to work these controls on the Form.

The rulers above and to the left of the grid are highlighted when you move an object to help you align it, as shown in the upper-left figure.

A grid of dots is also displayed in Design view by default, and controls are automatically aligned with this grid when you move them. If you try to place an object so its edge is not on the grid, it will move, or snap, to the grid. You can turn off this feature off if you want one or more controls to stand out by not being aligned with the others.

You can also select a number of controls and align them with each other. Choose Format ⇨ Align and choose Left, Right, Top, or Bottom from the submenu to align all the controls to the edge you select. Choose To Grid from the submenu to align upper-left corners of the selected controls to the nearest grid points. This is useful if you have turned off Snap to Grid.

You can select one or more controls and have Access size them by choosing Format ⇨ Size and one of these options from its submenu, shown in the lower left figure:

▶ Choose To Fit to adjust the size of the control to fit the font of the text it contains.

▶ Choose To Grid to adjust the size of the control so all of its edges fit the grid. This is useful if you have changed the spacing of the gridlines, so that controls that you placed earlier do not fit exactly into the new grid.

You can also use this command to make a number of controls the same width or height. Select several controls and choose To Tallest, To Shortest, To Widest, or To Narrowest, in order to make them all as high as the tallest or shortest or to make them all as wide as the widest or narrowest.

You can adjust the spacing of controls by choosing Format ⇨ Horizontal Spacing or Vertical Spacing. Both of these have a submenu with the options Make Equal, Increase, and Decrease, as shown on the lower right, which you can use to space all the selected controls evenly or to increase or decrease the spacing between them uniformly.

TAKE NOTE

▶ **HIDING THE RULER AND GRID**

You can hide and display the ruler and the grid by right-clicking the form and choosing Ruler or Grid from its pop-up menu. Though you will rarely want to hide the ruler, it is often useful to hide the grid to see how certain design effects look without the grid in the way.

CROSS REFERENCE

You can change the spacing of the gridlines by using the Form's property sheet, covered in the next chapter.

SHORTCUT

To move controls one gridline in any direction, select them and press Ctrl+arrow key.

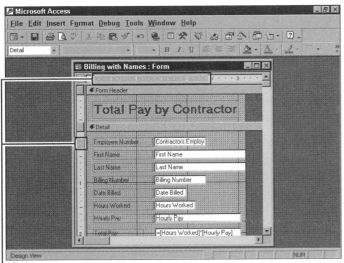

1 *The ruler is highlighted when you select and move an object to help you align it.*

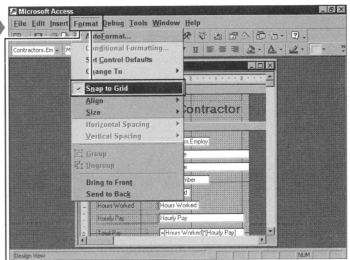

2 *Choose Format ➪ Snap to Grid to enable or disable automatic alignment of the controls with the grid.*

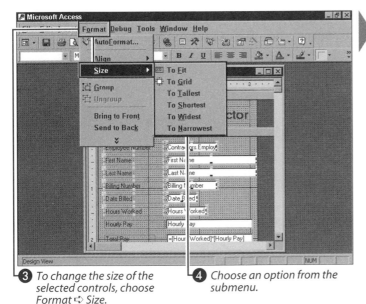

3 *To change the size of the selected controls, choose Format ➪ Size.*

4 *Choose an option from the submenu.*

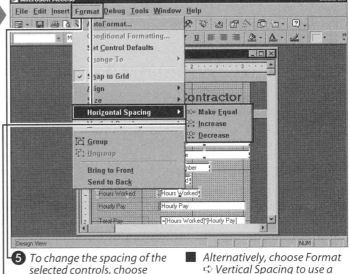

5 *To change the spacing of the selected controls, choose Format ➪ Horizontal Spacing.*

6 *Choose an option from the submenu.*

■ *Alternatively, choose Format ➪ Vertical Spacing to use a similar submenu.*

Working with Text

Occasionally, you may want to edit the text in a label and in some other types of controls, and you can do this directly in Design view. You can change the text, font, font size, font style, and the color, among other things. These modifications can enhance labels and call attention to their fields, but don't go overboard — if every single label and field has a unique appearance, the main benefit is lost.

Changing text is similar to editing in other applications: Place an insertion point or highlight text and then type. When you edit text, you can only select one control at a time.

In contrast, you can apply other modifications, such as typeface, style, and alignment, to more than one label, as well as to any other control containing text (like fields). When you select one or more controls containing text, the buttons on the Formatting toolbar used for working with text are enabled. You may then select Font Name, Font Size, Font Bold, Font Italic, Left Alignment, Center Alignment, or Right Alignment (to determine how the text is aligned within its control).

Formatting changes can be a lot of fun, because the possible combinations are virtually endless. The important thing to remember is that forms are supposed to make entering and editing text easier, so making everything italic may not fly. If you make changes that affect size and spacing (for example, font size), the text may no longer fit in the text box or field, so it is best to save your resizing for after you have changed the text. If you have to resize a control to hold a larger font size, the easiest way to do this is to choose Format ⇨ Size ⇨ To Fit.

TAKE NOTE

APPLYING FORMATTING

Formatting features must be applied to an entire control. You cannot, for example, use a different typeface for some of the letters in a label. They can be applied to many controls at once simply by selecting all of the controls before applying them.

EDITING TEXT ON OTHER CONTROLS

The label of a field is a text object, and you can edit it, though the text in the field itself cannot be edited in Form view, because it depends on the data in the table. You can also edit the text on some other controls, such as command buttons that you add to the form. To change the text in most other controls, however, you must work with the dialog boxes that you use to define them, described in the next chapter.

CROSS-REFERENCE
For information on adding new text to the form, see Chapter 9.

SHORTCUT
To view text and other controls as they will be printed, choose File ⇨ Print Preview.

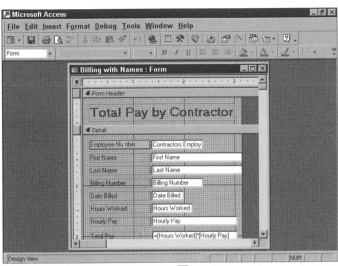

- To edit a field label, click it to select it.
- Click again to place an insertion point in it, and type to insert new text.

- Or click and drag to select text and type to replace the selected text.

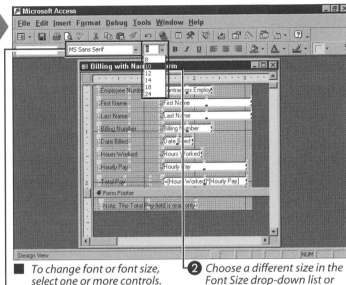

- To change font or font size, select one or more controls.
- ❶ Choose a different font in the Font drop-down list.

- ❷ Choose a different size in the Font Size drop-down list or type in the desired size.

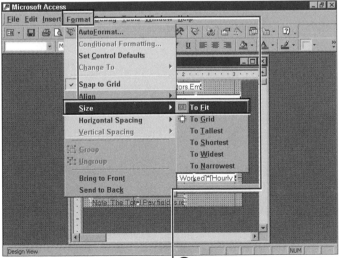

- If the new type no longer fits in the text boxes, resize the controls so it fits.

- ❸ Choose Format ➪ Size ➪ To Fit.

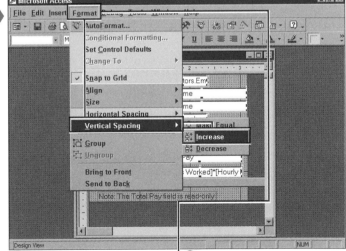

- If the controls are too cramped or too far apart, adjust the spacing around the controls.

- ❹ Choose Format ➪ Vertical Spacing ➪ Increase.

Adding Colors and Effects

You can also use the Formatting toolbar to specify the colors of objects and the type of border they have, and to create special effects, such as a raised or lowered look. This is especially helpful if you want to clearly distinguish between the labels and the fields. Typically, forms have raised labels and the fields look flat, but you can change this if you want.

First, you must select a band of the form or one or more controls (not all options on the toolbar are available if you select a band).

Most controls have three elements whose colors you can specify, as shown in the upper-left figure: the font or other foreground element, the fill or background color, and the line or border element.

To specify colors for these, use the Font/Foreground, Fill/Background, or Line/Border color tool. Simply select the controls that you want to change, click the tool's drop-down arrow to display a color palette, as shown in the upper-right figure, and select a color to apply it to the selected objects.

The Line/Border Width button, shown in the lower-left figure, lets you change the thickness of the border around a field. A thicker border around summary fields can call attention to results.

The Special Effect button, shown in the lower-right figure, creates a border that gives a lowered, raised, or shadow effect.

Back Color and Border Color tools both have a Transparent option: If you select this, the background

or border will be invisible. That is, you will be able to see other objects through the background of the control or the control will appear not to have any border. The color that is selected is shown in a small rectangle below each of the color buttons' icons. If Transparent is selected, the line around the rectangle is white; otherwise, it is black.

TAKE NOTE

▶ DEFINING A DEFAULT FORMAT

If you are adding many new controls, you can save time by defining the default properties. Simply select any control that already has those properties, and choose Format ⇨ Set Control Defaults. Then all new controls that you add will have these properties.

▶ USING THE FORMAT PAINTER TOOL

You can also save time by applying the properties of an existing control to other controls using the Format Painter tool. Select the control whose properties you want to use, and click the Format Painter button. The pointer is displayed with a paintbrush next to it. Then click any other control to apply these properties to it.

▶ USING AUTOFORMATS

You can apply a predefined format to a form by choosing Format ⇨ AutoFormat to display the AutoFormat dialog box and selecting a format. This feature is similar to the one in the Form Wizard.

CROSS-REFERENCE
For information on selecting a band or controls, see "Working with Bands" and "Working with Controls" earlier in this chapter.

SHORTCUT
You can also right-click an object and use its pop-up menu to specify its colors and special effects.

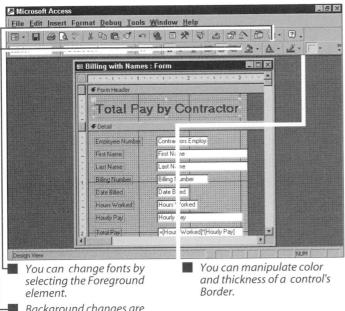

■ You can change fonts by selecting the Foreground element.

■ Background changes are made with the Fill/Background element.

■ You can manipulate color and thickness of a control's Border.

① To change a control's line or border color, click the drop-down arrow of the Line/Border button.

② Choose a color from the color palette.

■ Click the Font/Foreground or Fill/Background button to change these properties using a similar palette.

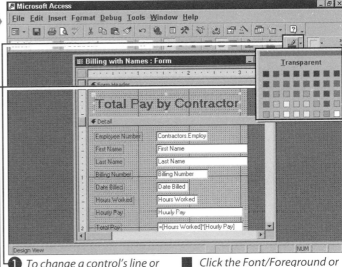

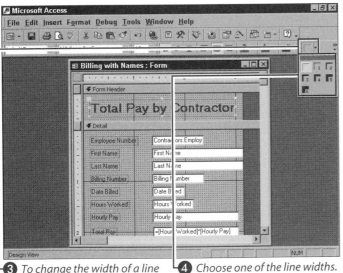

③ To change the width of a line or border, click the drop-down arrow of the Line/Border Width button.

④ Choose one of the line widths.

⑤ To give a control a raised, sunken, etched, shadowed, chiseled, or flat look, click the drop-down arrow of the Special Effect button.

⑥ Choose one of the special effects.

157

Personal Workbook

Q&A

1 What are the three types of controls in Access forms?

_____

_____

_____

2 What are three features of the Form window that you display or hide by clicking buttons on the toolbar? What is their purpose?

_____

_____

_____

3 What are three ways of selecting an entire form?

_____

_____

_____

4 What are three ways of selecting multiple controls in a form?

_____

_____

_____

5 How can you move a field and move its label at the same time?

_____

_____

_____

6 How can you move a field without moving its label?

_____

_____

_____

7 What is *tab order* and how do you change it?

_____

_____

_____

8 What are the three elements of an object whose color you can change?

_____

_____

_____

ANSWERS: PAGE 348

EXTRA PRACTICE

Change the sample form that you created in Chapter 6 in the following ways:

1 Change the fonts in the fields and their labels to 12-point Times New Roman.

2 Resize the fields and their labels so the larger font fits into them. You can do this in one step.

3 Resize the form and move the fields to make them easier to read.

4 Try several different combinations of colors and effects for the fields.

5 Try different combinations of colors and effects for the fields' labels, such as giving them a sunken special effect and changing their text color.

REAL-WORLD APPLICATIONS

✔ You create an AutoForm to use for data entry of your mailing list, but you have to scroll to view all the fields. You could move the fields so they can all be displayed on the screen at once.

✔ You have trouble reading your address book table on your laptop computer. You could create a special data entry form to use on this computer and give it larger size fonts.

Visual Quiz

This form was created by modifying an AutoForm, using techniques covered in this chapter. How do you change an AutoForm to produce this Form?

_____

_____

_____

_____

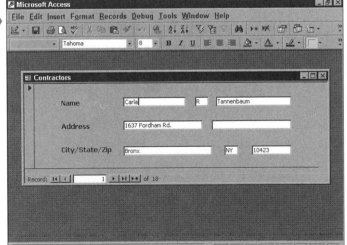

CHAPTER **9**

MASTER
THESE
SKILLS

▶ **Using the Field List and Toolbox**

▶ **Adding Labels and Text Boxes**

▶ **Adding an Option Group**

▶ **Adding Toggle Buttons, Option Buttons, and Checkboxes**

▶ **Adding List Boxes and Combo Boxes**

▶ **Adding Command Buttons**

▶ **Adding Other Controls**

▶ **Adding Page Breaks and Tabs**

▶ **Adding Hyperlinks**

▶ **Looking at Property Sheets**

Designing Custom Forms — Advanced Techniques

In the previous chapter, you looked at basic techniques for customizing forms, which let you make simple changes, such as moving controls that the Form Wizard placed on a form. In this chapter, you will look at more advanced techniques, focusing on how to add new controls to a form.

You will often want to add extra controls to a form, even if you use the Wizard to add all the fields you want. For example, you may want to add simple graphic enhancements (such as lines and boxes), add text that gives extra information to the reader, or include a company logo or other picture.

You may also want to add more advanced controls that make the user's work easier and more accurate. You can replace fields with radio buttons and drop-down lists so the user can enter data simply by choosing an option. For example, it's easier for a user to select the correct state from a drop-down list than to remember if Massachusetts is abbreviated MA, MS, or MT. If a user is making a selection from several radio buttons, it reduces the possibility of typing errors and incorrect answers. And if you add Command Buttons, the user can click to execute commands, rather than choosing commands from the menu system. When you do this, you are moving to the edge of programming — anticipating the user's needs and setting up the application so they can work with it even if they know little about Access.

This chapter briefly discusses property sheets. You can display a property sheet for the form, each of its bands, and each of its controls, and use it to set properties that control its appearance and behavior. Property sheets are an advanced feature of Access, used largely by programmers, but this chapter introduces you to them and the properties that are most valuable for ordinary users.

Using the Field List and Toolbox

In the last chapter, you learned how to work with controls that are already in the form design. You can add new controls to a form by using the *field list* and *toolbox* in Design view, shown in the upper-left figure. While not as easy a moving and resizing controls, adding controls is far less complicated than actually programming a design. You can display and hide the field list and toolbox by clicking the Field List and Toolbox buttons.

The field list includes all the fields in the table or query on which the form is based. To add a field to a form, simply click and drag the field's name from the field list to the form. You can also add several fields at once by clicking and dragging a group selected using the Shift+Click or the Ctrl+Click method. To select all the fields, double-click the title bar.

If you add a field from the field list, the form will include both a label with the field's name and a text box to enter data in the field, as shown in the upper-right figure.

Adding a different type of control, such as a drop-down list or radio button, is as easy as adding a field. The toolbox holds a number of icons, each representing a different type of control (see lower-left figure). If you're not sure what an icon does, hover your pointer over it to bring up the tool tip. Click the toolbox on the type of control you want to add. Your pointer changes to indicate that you can now place that control on the form by clicking (and dragging, if

you need to indicate size, as shown in the lower-right figure). Until you click another icon in the toolbox or in the Select Objects icon, your pointer is still operating under that control type.

When you release the mouse button, Access may display a wizard to help you define the control. Wizards guide you through the available options for that control. For example, if you are using the Combo Box button to add a drop-down box, Access displays a wizard to guide you through its creation. Access does not display the wizard when you add a simple control such as a rectangle, because no information beyond its size and location is needed to define it.

TAKE NOTE

USING THE SELECT OBJECTS AND CONTROL WIZARDS TOOLS

The toolbox has two buttons that don't add controls. The Select Objects button turns the pointer back into an arrow. If you select a tool, but decide not to add it, use this button to cancel the operation of adding a new control. The Control Wizards button enables or disables the wizards used to define new controls that you add to the form. Most users should always work with the wizards; click this button to restore wizards if they are disabled.

CROSS-REFERENCE

See Chapter 8 for information on altering these controls after you place them on the form.

SHORTCUT

You can also right-click the form and use its pop-up menu to display the toolbox.

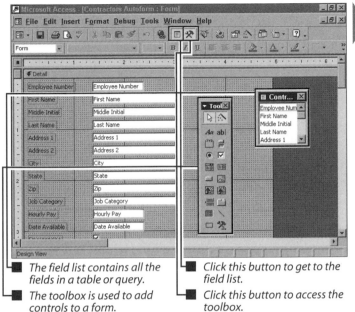

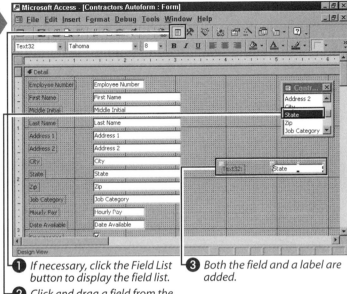

■ *The field list contains all the fields in a table or query.*

■ *The toolbox is used to add controls to a form.*

■ *Click this button to get to the field list.*

■ *Click this button to access the toolbox.*

➊ *If necessary, click the Field List button to display the field list.*

➋ *Click and drag a field from the field list to add it to the location where you want it on the form.*

➌ *Both the field and a label are added.*

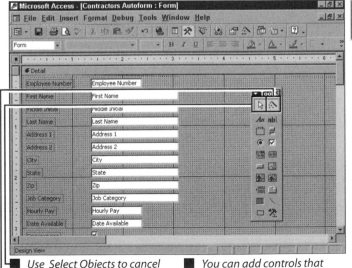

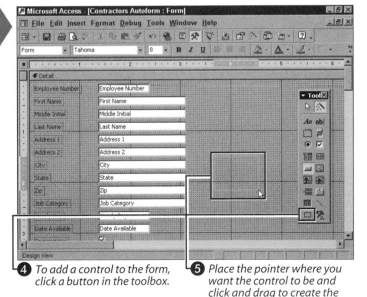

■ *Use Select Objects to cancel the addition of a control or to modify a control.*

■ *The Control Wizard guides you through any options you might want to change.*

■ *You can add controls that aren't predefined with Custom Controls.*

➍ *To add a control to the form, click a button in the toolbox.*

➎ *Place the pointer where you want the control to be and click and drag to create the size of the control you want.*

Adding Labels and Text Boxes

We've been talking about labels as they refer to fields. When you add a field, a label with its name automatically appears next to the field. However, you can add labels that are not tied to any field. You may want to add labels to hold form headings, explanatory text, or some other text.

To add new text to the form, click the Label button, and click and drag to create a label box, or simply start typing anywhere on the form. If you click and drag, after you the release the mouse button, the box displays the text you type. When you are done, press Enter or click anywhere outside the label box to leave the label box.

Labels can be any size you want, and Access tries to be as accommodating as possible. If the box is large enough for several lines of text, the text automatically wraps to the next line when you fill a line in the label box. If you type too much text, the box automatically expands vertically to accommodate your entry. If you want to create a new paragraph, press Ctrl+Enter, because pressing Enter takes the cursor out of the label box. If you change the label box size later, the text automatically adjusts to fit the new size.

You can still edit the text later as you do any text, by selecting the label and then clicking it to plan an insertion bar in it, as shown in the lower-left figure.

In contrast, text boxes display a field or expression's value and can be independent or attached to a field label. you can use a text box to display a calculated value by typing an expression in it, in place of the word "Unbound." See Chapter 14 for a complete explanation of Access expressions and how to use them to create calculated fields.

TAKE NOTE

ATTACHING A LABEL TO A CONTROL

If you deleted the label for a field, you can use the Text button to create another one and attach it to the control. Create the label as usual. When you are done, select and cut it, and then select the control you want to attach it to and paste.

CROSS-REFERENCE
You can change the font, color, border, and other label or text box features any time using the methods described in Chapter 8.

FIND IT ONLINE
For an advanced discussion of using forms, see http://www.unibo.it/stse/serinf/bldapps/chapters/ba03_1.htm.

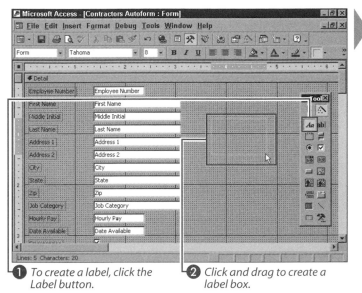

1 To create a label, click the Label button.

2 Click and drag to create a label box.

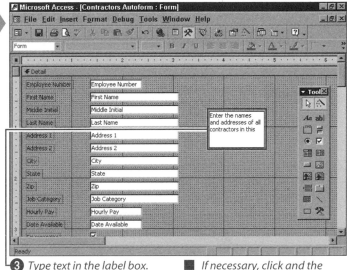

3 Type text in the label box. Then press Enter or click outside of the label box.

■ If necessary, click and the drag the label box to change its location.

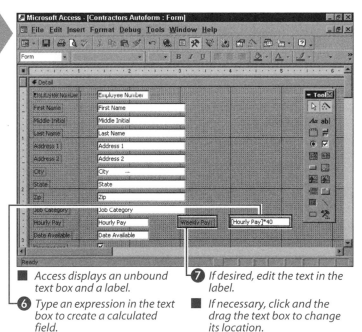

4 To create a text box, click the Text Box button.

5 Click and drag to create a text box.

■ Access displays an unbound text box and a label.

6 Type an expression in the text box to create a calculated field.

7 If desired, edit the text in the label.

■ If necessary, click and the drag the text box to change its location.

Adding an Option Group

An *option group* is a group of controls that work together to let the user enter data in a field that has only a few possible entries. Option groups can save time and simplify data entry. For example, you may want a user to choose Large, Medium, or Small on an order form by clicking a button instead of typing in a size. The only problem is the programming code in Access doesn't recognize text; it only recognizes numbers (integers), like 1, 2, and 3. To create an option group, you need to type each result (Large) and attach it to a value (3). In the form, when the Large button is selected, Access enters the value 3 in the field.

While creating option groups sounds relatively simple, it employs programming techniques that may be confusing for beginners. You can achieve a similar, but more limited, result by using the Combo Box button from the toolbar. If you want to limit the input choices to specific options, try adding an option group.

An option group is usually made up of option buttons, but it can be checkboxes or toggle buttons. In any case, if the user selects one of the options, the others are automatically deselected.

To add an option group, click the Option Group button, and then click and drag to place the group on the form. When you release the mouse button, Access displays the Option Group Wizard. The Wizard lets you choose a name and a number value for each option, select the field where the selected value will be entered, and control the appearance of the option group, as shown on the opposite page

You can use the Option Group Wizard to specify a default option that is selected when the form is displayed, to decide whether to bind the option group to a field (nonprogrammers should select this), and to choose whether the buttons will be option buttons, checkboxes, or toggle buttons. You can also use the Wizard when deciding whether the group will have a normal, boxed appearance or a raised or sunken look.

In the final step, the Option Group Wizard lets you enter a name to label the entire option group and to create the option group.

If the option group replaces one of the form fields, you should delete that field from the design if it was initially included in it.

TAKE NOTE

PICKING WHICH CONTROL TO USE

In general, it is best to use radio buttons in option groups, because users are accustomed to selecting options in this way. Groups of toggle buttons can be used to create special effects. Groups of checkboxes may confuse users, since a checkbox is conventionally used to enter data in a field that can have only two values, most often a Yes/No field.

CROSS-REFERENCE

See "Adding List Boxes and Combo Boxes" in this chapter for a better method of letting the user choose among entries.

SHORTCUT

You can usually save time by creating a default choice, even if it is not used more frequently than other options.

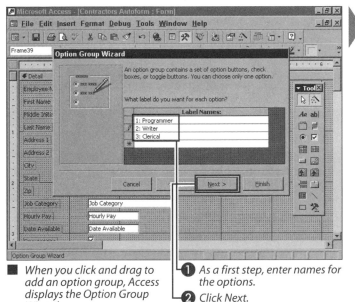

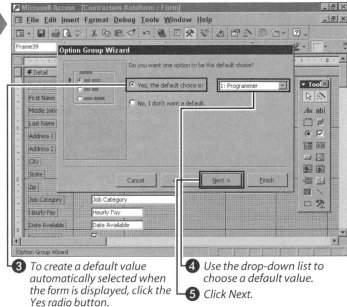

■ When you click and drag to add an option group, Access displays the Option Group Wizard.

❶ As a first step, enter names for the options.

❷ Click Next.

❸ To create a default value automatically selected when the form is displayed, click the Yes radio button.

❹ Use the drop-down list to choose a default value.

❺ Click Next.

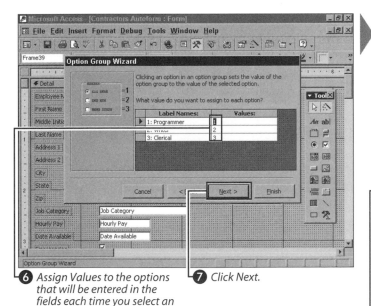

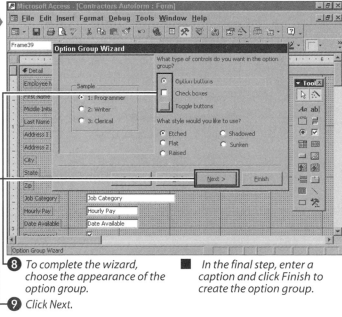

❻ Assign Values to the options that will be entered in the fields each time you select an option.

❼ Click Next.

❽ To complete the wizard, choose the appearance of the option group.

❾ Click Next.

■ In the final step, enter a caption and click Finish to create the option group.

Adding Toggle Buttons, Option Buttons, and Checkboxes

Option groups are best used when you have several choices from which to select. Another common scenario requires a simple Yes or No entry. For example, you might have a field that asks whether an applicant is a resident of the United States. They either are or they are not, so a Yes or No control is perfect for this situation.

If you have Yes/No fields in your Form, you can add a single toggle button, option button, or checkbox to represent that field. If any of these controls is selected, Yes is entered in the field; if it is not, No is entered in the field. This is the way a checkbox is commonly used in Windows applications.

The easy way to create one of these controls is to display both the field list and the toolbox. Click the Toggle Button, the Option Button, or the Checkbox button in the toolbox. Then use this pointer to click and drag a Yes/No field from the field list to the form. Access creates a toggle button, option button, or checkbox that is bound to that field.

You can also add one of these controls by clicking the Toggle Button, the Option Button, or the Checkbox button and then clicking and dragging on the form to create an unbound toggle button, radio button, or checkbox, as shown in the lower-left figure. Then you can display the property sheet of the unbound control and use its Field property to bind it to a field, as shown in the lower-right figure.

This method is obviously harder than just clicking and dragging a Yes/No field. It is useful for developers who want to control some later action of an application on the basis of the option selected in one of these controls, rather than using it to enter data in a field. It is not advisable for nonprogrammers.

TAKE NOTE

▶ THE RIGHT CONTROL FOR A YES/NO FIELD

Checkboxes are best for entering values in a Yes/No field, because this is the conventional method of selecting Yes or No in Windows applications, and users are accustomed to it. You may sometimes want to use a toggle button for special effects, but you should be sure to make it clear what the button is for, so as not to confuse users who are used to clicking buttons to take an action. You can confuse users by using an option button to enter data in a Yes/No field, because option buttons are conventionally used in groups to let users select one of several options. Be particularly careful not to use several option buttons that are near each other to enter values in several Yes/No fields. When users see a group of option buttons like this, they expect to be able to select only one of them.

CROSS-REFERENCE

See the final section of this chapter for information on using property sheets.

SHORTCUT

You can right-click these controls and use their pop-up menus to display their property sheets, as described later in this chapter.

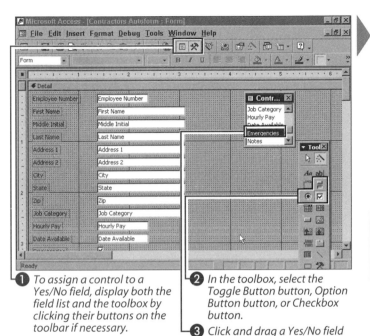

① To assign a control to a Yes/No field, display both the field list and the toolbox by clicking their buttons on the toolbar if necessary.

② In the toolbox, select the Toggle Button button, Option Button button, or Checkbox button.

③ Click and drag a Yes/No field from the field list.

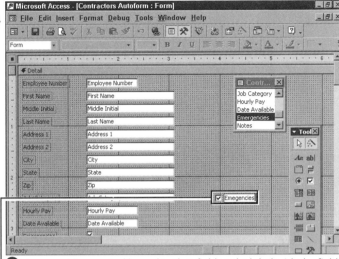

④ Access adds a control bound to that field and a label with the field name to the form.

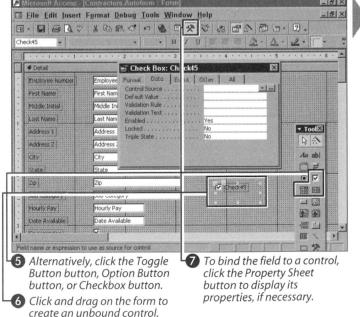

⑤ Alternatively, click the Toggle Button button, Option Button button, or Checkbox button.

⑥ Click and drag on the form to create an unbound control.

⑦ To bind the field to a control, click the Property Sheet button to display its properties, if necessary.

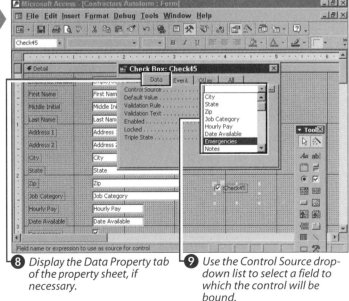

⑧ Display the Data Property tab of the property sheet, if necessary.

⑨ Use the Control Source drop-down list to select a field to which the control will be bound.

Adding List Boxes and Combo Boxes

List boxes and combo boxes let users choose a field's entries from a list. These controls can streamline data entry and help reduce the number of typing errors.

A list box's choices appear in a scrolling list that is always displayed. The entries in a list box are limited to just the choices on the list — you cannot manually type in an entry. List boxes are useful when the entries in the list are not likely to change; for example, a list of U.S. states. List boxes work with either a short or a long list of options.

A combo box gives the user the flexibility of choosing from a list or typing the entry. A combo box is best used when there are frequently selected entries, but the list is not exclusive. For example, if you have a survey that asks people which color they prefer in a car, an individual could either select from the list or type their favorite color if it doesn't appear in the list. Combo boxes, which drop down and are not scrolled, generally work best with a fairly short list of options to choose from, and they are used to save space on crowded forms.

Whether you choose to use a list box or combo box, the wizards used to define them are identical. The first step of these wizards lets you choose from three fundamentally different ways of defining the values in the list. Two of the ways make data entry easier by letting you enter new data in a field using the combo box or list box: You can type values in the wizard, or you can use values from a table or query. The third saves time in lookups by letting the user move to a record in the form by selecting a value.

Typing the Values

It is useful to type the values you want if there are a fairly small number of options. If you select this in the first step, the Combo Box Wizard displays the steps shown on the facing page. The example shows how to create a combo box for a Job Category field that only has one letter entered: The job category is written out in the first column, which is displayed on screen, and the letter that is entered is in the second column.

Continued

TAKE NOTE

LIMITING CHOICES IN A COMBO BOX

By default, if you create a combo box, the user can either choose an option from the drop-down list or make an entry in the text box. You may want to change this to let the user only make choices from the drop-down list. To do this, display the combo box's property sheet and choose Yes as the Limit to List property in the Data tab.

CROSS-REFERENCE

Chapter 13 illustrates how you can create a drop-down list to choose the value in a field by using a lookup field.

SHORTCUT

You can display a combo box's property sheet by right-clicking it and using its pop-up menu.

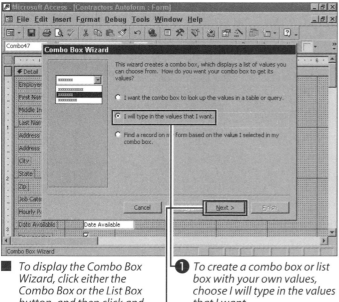

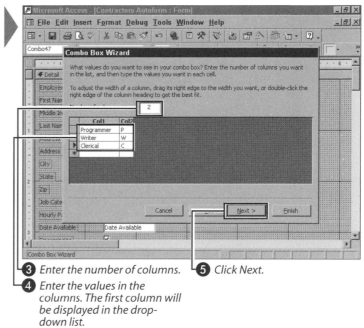

■ To display the Combo Box Wizard, click either the Combo Box or the List Box button, and then click and drag on the form.

❶ To create a combo box or list box with your own values, choose I will type in the values that I want.

❷ Click Next.

❸ Enter the number of columns.

❹ Enter the values in the columns. The first column will be displayed in the drop-down list.

❺ Click Next.

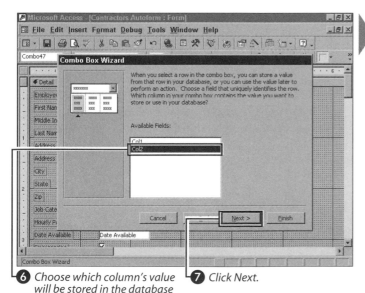

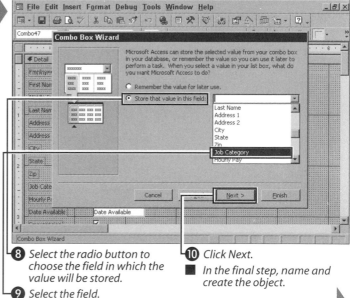

❻ Choose which column's value will be stored in the database table.

❼ Click Next.

❽ Select the radio button to choose the field in which the value will be stored.

❾ Select the field.

❿ Click Next.

■ In the final step, name and create the object.

Adding List Boxes and Combo Boxes *Continued*

Using Values from a Table or Query

When you work on a relational database, it is useful to enter the value in the foreign key field in the "many" table by using a list box that enters values from the "one" table. For example, a user could enter the employee number in a Billing table by choosing from a list of employee numbers and names in the Contractor table. This is the easiest way to enter this value, and if any new records are added to the Contractor table, they are automatically added to the list. You also may want to create tables used only to look up values, such as a table with the names and abbreviations of all the states.

Access provides a wizard for this process, because it can get complicated working from table to table. In the first step of the Combo Box Wizard, choose to look up values from a table or query.

The second step of the Wizard displays a list that lets you choose the table or query: Choose the "one" table of the database — for example, the Contractors table in Chapter 7.

In the third step, shown in the upper-left figure, choose the fields you want to display in the drop-down list. Choose the key field plus fields that identify it, such as name.

The next step, shown in the upper-right figure, lets you decide how these values are displayed. Click and drag to size the columns. You must select the checkbox to display the key field to have the option of storing its value.

The next step, shown on the lower left, lets you choose the field whose value will be stored. Choose the key field of the one table.

The next step, shown on the lower right, lets you choose the field in which to store the value. Choose the foreign key of the many table.

The final step lets you name and create the form.

Moving to a Record

You can use the combo box or list box to move to a record. For example, you might create a drop-down list of all your contractors' names, so you can select a name to display that record immediately, rather than searching for it. If you select this option in the first step, the Wizard provides you with a different series of steps that do not require the identification of values and key fields.

TAKE NOTE

▶ DECIDING HOW TO DEFINE VALUES

In general, it is best to type in the values if there are only a few of them that will not change. It is best to use the values in a table or query when there are many values. This is useful in a relational database, as you have seen, and you also can create special tables to be used as the basis of combo boxes or list boxes.

CROSS-REFERENCE
For information on relational databases, see Chapter 7.

SHORTCUT
If you need to enter the same values in more than one table, you can save time by creating a look-up table to use as the basis of controls in all the tables.

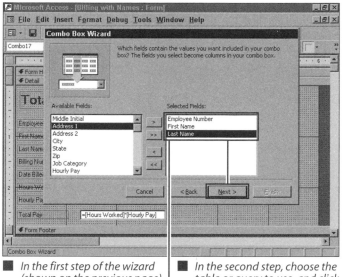

■ In the first step of the wizard (shown on the previous page), choose "I want the combo box (or list box) to look up the values in a table or query" and click Next.

■ In the second step, choose the table or query to use, and click Next.

❶ Choose the fields you want to display in the list, and then click Next.

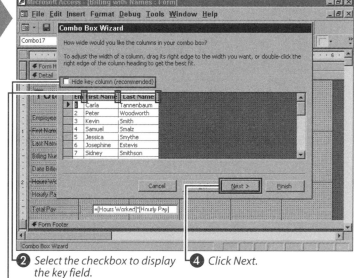

❷ Select the checkbox to display the key field.

❸ Click and drag to change the width of the fields.

❹ Click Next.

❺ Choose the Key field as the field to store.

❻ Click Next.

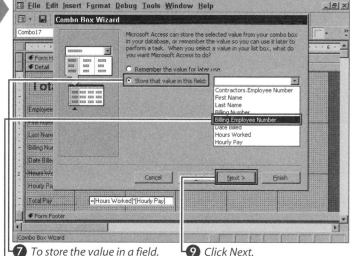

❼ To store the value in a field, select the radio button.

❽ Use the drop-down list to choose the field in which to store the value.

❾ Click Next.

■ In the final step, enter a label for the control and click Finish.

Adding Command Buttons

The Command Button Wizard makes it easy to create buttons that perform many standard actions. For example, you can easily add to the form buttons that let you move to the first, previous, next, and last records, and that let you search for a record. Many of these are useful primarily for developers creating applications that do not have the usual Access toolbars or menus, but you can also use command buttons as a quick way to perform tasks you do frequently.

To add a command button to a form, click the Command Button button and then click and drag to define the location and size of the Command button, as shown in the upper-left figure. When you release the mouse button, Access displays the Command Button Wizard.

The Wizard first lets you select categories to display lists of standard actions. Most of the listed actions are similar to actions that you can perform from the Access interface, for example, Find Record or Go to Last Record.

When you select an action, you see a representation of the command button with an icon in the left window. If you don't like the icon, the next step of the Wizard lets you select a new icon for that command from among all of the standard icons (by selecting the Picture radio button and the Show All Pictures checkbox), or from just the suggested icons for that particular command (by deselecting the Show All Pictures checkbox). You can also use bitmap files by clicking the Browse Command button. If you

use an icon, select one that relates to the command, such as a magnifying glass icon for Find. If you don't want an icon, you can always create a text command button by selecting the Text radio button and typing in your own text.

It is a good idea to group all your command buttons in one place on the form. That way you will always know where to look for them. Because you can have several command buttons on a form, you must name each one. Try to be as clear as possible, because when you go to make modifications, Access will provide a listing of all buttons by name, and Button1 won't be of much help.

In the Wizard's final step you name and create the command button.

TAKE NOTE

DEFINING CUSTOM ACTIONS

You can also use command buttons to perform custom actions that you cannot perform by using the Access interface. Programmers can write programs and attach them to a command button. It is easy for nonprogrammers to use a button to run a macro, which automatically performs a series of steps, such as making menu choices or typing text. If a user often does repetitive work with many steps, you can save them time by creating macros and attaching them to command buttons.

CROSS-REFERENCE

See Chapter 12 for information on creating macros and attaching them to command buttons.

SHORTCUT

After placing a command button with text on it, you can edit the text simply by clicking it to put an insertion bar in it.

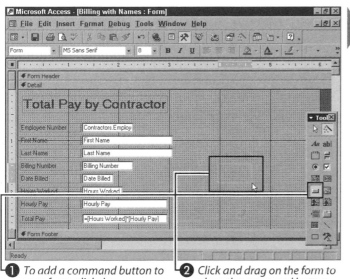

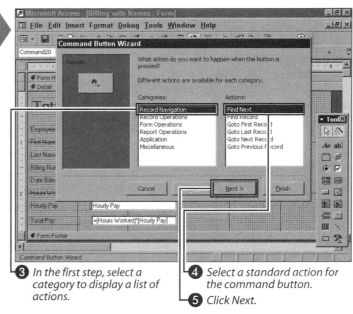

1 To add a command button to your form, click the Command Button button.

2 Click and drag on the form to place the command button. When you release the mouse button, the Command Button Wizard is displayed.

3 In the first step, select a category to display a list of actions.

4 Select a standard action for the command button.

5 Click Next.

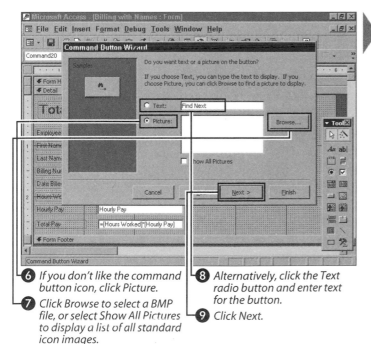

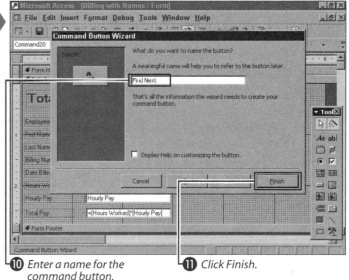

6 If you don't like the command button icon, click Picture.

7 Click Browse to select a BMP file, or select Show All Pictures to display a list of all standard icon images.

8 Alternatively, click the Text radio button and enter text for the button.

9 Click Next.

10 Enter a name for the command button.

11 Click Finish.

Adding Other Controls

Image frames, unbound OLE objects, bound OLE objects, lines, rectangles, and subforms are added using the buttons labeled in the upper-left figure.

You might want to use a Picture control to include your company logo in a form. To add this, click the Image Frame button and click and drag to define the frame for the picture. Access displays the Insert Picture dialog box, shown in the upper-right figure, which you use to select the file containing this picture.

OLE objects let you include objects from other applications in Forms. To add an OLE object to the form, click the Unbound Object Frame or Bound Object Frame button and then click and drag to create the frame that holds the OLE object. A bound OLE object frame displays the contents of an OLE object field, while an unbound OLE object frame displays an OLE object that remains the same as you move through the records. For example, if you insert an Excel graph as a bound object, it will be updated in the Form whenever it is updated in Excel. If you insert it as an unbound object, it will remain unchanged, even if it has been updated in Excel.

Lines can be added to underline or emphasize parts of the form or to divide the form visually into several parts. To add a line to the form, click the Line button and then click and drag on the form.

Rectangles are commonly used to place a box around an area of the form, as shown in the lower-left figure. To add a rectangle to the form, click the Rectangle button and then click and drag on the form. Access adds a rectangle with opposite corners in the locations where you begin and end dragging.

You can use the Color, Line, and Special Effect tools to change the appearance of a line or rectangle. For example, for rectangles you might want a transparent back color; a boxed look, rather than a sunken look; and a thicker line as its border. To do this, give the rectangle some back color and choose Format ⇨ Send to Back.

Adding Subforms

You learned about subforms in Chapter 6. To add a subform in Design view, you must use the LinkChildFields and LinkMasterFields properties to link the form and subform. It is best for beginners to use the Form Wizard to create it and then to customize the form if necessary.

TAKE NOTE

▶ CHANGING CONTROL TYPE

You can change the type of an existing control by selecting it and then choosing Format ⇨ Change To from the menu to display the submenu shown in the lower-right figure. Only the types that the currently selected tool can be converted to are accessible on the submenu. In the figure, for example, a checkbox is selected, and you can change it to a toggle button or an option button.

CROSS-REFERENCE

OLE objects are covered in Chapter 16.

SHORTCUT

After inserting pictures or OLE objects, click and drag to resize the frame to an exact fit.

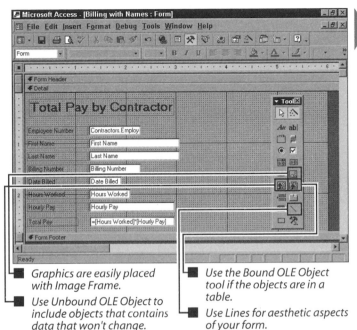

■ *Graphics are easily placed with Image Frame.*

■ *Use Unbound OLE Object to include objects that contains data that won't change.*

■ *Use the Bound OLE Object tool if the objects are in a table.*

■ *Use Lines for aesthetic aspects of your form.*

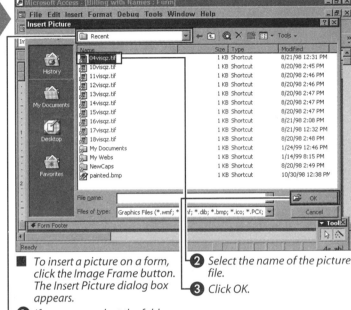

■ *To insert a picture on a form, click the Image Frame button. The Insert Picture dialog box appears.*

① *If necessary, select the folder that holds the picture file.*

② *Select the name of the picture file.*

③ *Click OK.*

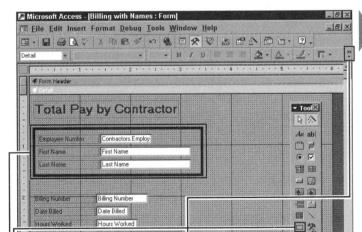

④ *To add a rectangle to highlight an area of the form, click the Rectangle button.*

⑤ *Then click and drag to create a rectangle that encloses the chosen fields.*

⑥ *Optionally, use the Formatting toolbar to change the appearance of the rectangle.*

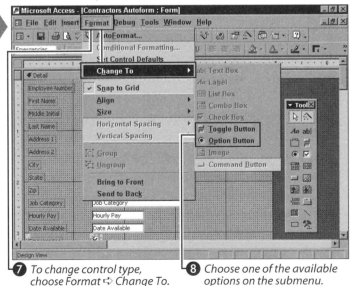

⑦ *To change control type, choose Format ➪ Change To.*

⑧ *Choose one of the available options on the submenu.*

Adding Page Breaks and Tabs

The Page Break and Tab Control tools enable you to break forms into multiple pages. Both are useful if a form is too large to fit on a single page.

Adding Page Breaks

If you use the Page Break tool to break the form into pages, the user moves among these pages with the PgDn and PgUp keys. You can control with page breaks exactly which parts of the form the user sees at one time. Page breaks also control how the form is printed. Forms longer than a page automatically break at the bottom of each page; if this makes the printout hard to read, you should add a page break elsewhere.

The page break is displayed as a dotted, horizontal line at the left margin (see the upper-left figure). You select and move it by clicking and dragging. Selecting it and pressing Delete removes the page break.

You can break the form into multiple pages for data entry, and control how they are displayed, by using the following steps:

1. Click the Page Break button and then click the form where you want to place the Page Breaks.
2. Display the form's Property sheet and select Current Page as the Cycle property in the Other tab. Then users cannot use the Tab key to move among pages. Select Horizontal only or Neither as the ScrollBars property .
3. Display the form in Form view and size the window so that only one page is visible. Now,

the only way to move among pages is by pressing PgDn and PgUp.

Adding Tabs

The tab control is a more sophisticated method of creating multipage forms, which you can use instead of page breaks. Each page displays as a tab of the form. Instead of scrolling, the user clicks a tab to display the page.

To create a tab control, click the Tab Control button and click and drag anywhere in the form: Access places a tab control with two pages. To change the number of pages, right-click the control's border, and select Insert Page or Delete Page from its pop-up menu. To change the tab order, select Page Order from the pop-up menu. Remove tab controls as you do other controls, by selecting them and then pressing Delete.

Clicking a tab displays its page. You can then place fields or other controls on it using the field list and the toolbox just as you place controls on a form.

TAKE NOTE

PRINTING SEPARATE RECORDS

One of simplest uses of the page break is to print the form with each record on a separate page. Just add a page break at the bottom of the form. When Access prints the form, it begins a new page whenever it reaches the page break.

CROSS-REFERENCE

For more information on printing, see Chapter 3.

SHORTCUT

You can add fields to tabs quickly by clicking one and then Shift-clicking another in the field list; then click and drag the entire group of fields to the tab.

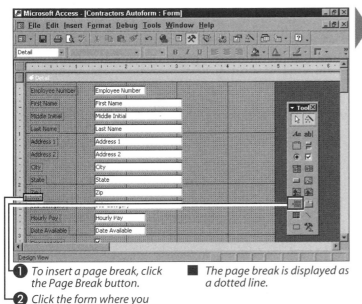

1 To insert a page break, click the Page Break button.

2 Click the form where you want to add the page break.

■ The page break is displayed as a dotted line.

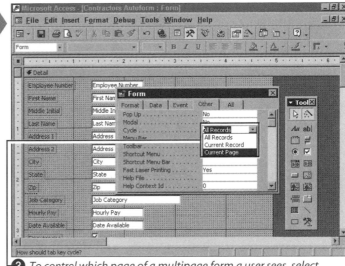

3 To control which page of a multipage form a user sees, select Current Page as the Cycle property.

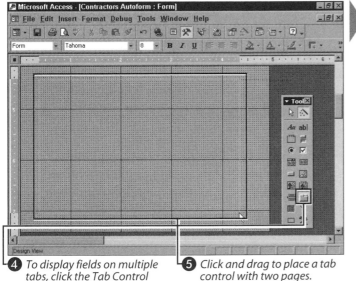

4 To display fields on multiple tabs, click the Tab Control button.

5 Click and drag to place a tab control with two pages.

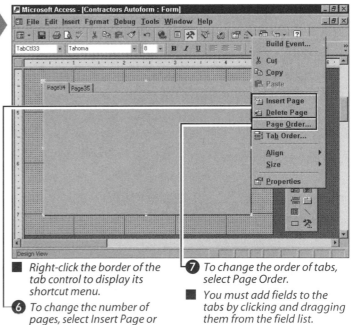

■ Right-click the border of the tab control to display its shortcut menu.

6 To change the number of pages, select Insert Page or Delete Page.

7 To change the order of tabs, select Page Order.

■ You must add fields to the tabs by clicking and dragging them from the field list.

Adding Hyperlinks

Forms can take on an even higher level of sophistication if you include a hyperlink. You can link to a Web page, to documents on your own computer, or to a local area network.

You may want to add two types of hyperlinks to a form:

▶ *Bound hyperlinks* are bound to a field and change when the record changes. For example, you may want a form with data on your suppliers to include each supplier's home page.

▶ *Unbound hyperlinks* are not bound to a field; they remain the same as records change. Unbound hyperlinks are useful when you need to link to a site that is not dependent on a field entry. For example, you might want your job application form to include a hyperlink to your company's home page.

To add a bound hyperlink to a form, simply include it as a hyperlink field when you define the table the form is based on. When you use AutoForm or the Form Wizard to create the form, Access adds the field as a hyperlink, which the user can click to jump to the linked document.

To add an unbound hyperlink to a form, choose Insert ➪ Hyperlink or click the toolbar's Insert Hyperlink button, shown in the upper-left figure. (Notice that this button is part of the toolbar, not of the toolbox.) In the Insert Hyperlink dialog box,

enter the Web page address or file path name manually, or use the buttons to select it from the list of recently opened files, recently browsed Web pages, or recently inserted links. Doing the latter reduces the chance of error in address entry.

You can also add a hyperlink to an object in the database or to a new document, as shown on the lower-left and -right figures. If you want to add a hyperlink to an e-mail address, in the Insert Hyperlink dialog box, click the E-mail Address button, and Access will ask you to enter the e-mail address and the text to display as its label.

You can also add a hyperlink to a command button or picture. To do this, you must use the object's property sheet, a technique covered in the next section.

TAKE NOTE

▶ ADDING HYPERLINKS TO OFFICE DOCUMENTS

You can also insert a hyperlink to other Microsoft Office documents using copy and paste or drag and drop. Copy the text in a document that you want to link to. Then return to the Access form and choose Edit ➪ Paste as Hyperlink. Alternatively, resize and move the application and document windows so you can view both the Access form and the document to which you are linking. Highlight the text in the other document that you want to link to. Then click the highlighted text with the right mouse button and drag it to the Access form. Access displays a pop-up menu. Choose Paste Hyperlink.

CROSS-REFERENCE

See Chapter 15 for more information on adding hyperlinks to forms.

SHORTCUT

Instead of choosing Insert ➪ Hyperlink, press Ctrl+K.

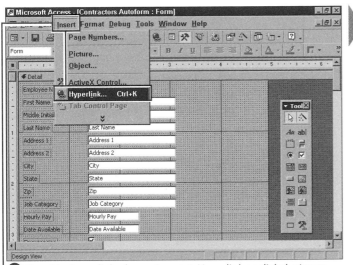

① To add a hyperlink, choose Insert ➪ Hyperlink or click the Insert Hyperlink button

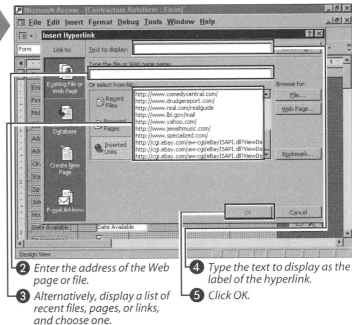

② Enter the address of the Web page or file.

③ Alternatively, display a list of recent files, pages, or links, and choose one.

④ Type the text to display as the label of the hyperlink.

⑤ Click OK.

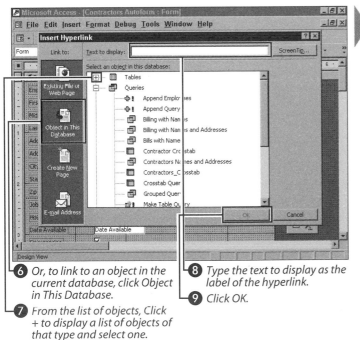

⑥ Or, to link to an object in the current database, click Object in This Database.

⑦ From the list of objects, Click + to display a list of objects of that type and select one.

⑧ Type the text to display as the label of the hyperlink.

⑨ Click OK.

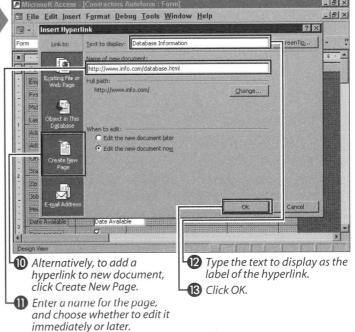

⑩ Alternatively, to add a hyperlink to new document, click Create New Page.

⑪ Enter a name for the page, and choose whether to edit it immediately or later.

⑫ Type the text to display as the label of the hyperlink.

⑬ Click OK.

Looking at Property Sheets

A *property sheet* is a list of an object's many features. For example, a property sheet for a field includes its size, its background, foreground and border colors, the source of its data, validation rules, and many other properties you have learned to control when you use tables and forms in Design view. You can change these properties in the property sheet to change the appearance of the object, but it is easier to make these changes in Design view. Nevertheless, it is important to look at property sheets, because objects also have properties that you can only change by using the property sheet.

You can display a property sheet for the entire form, for a band of the form, or for a control by right-clicking it and choosing Properties from its pop-up menu, or by selecting it and clicking the toolbar's Properties button, as shown in the upper-left figure

Once you display the property sheet, Access keeps it open and displays the properties of any object you select. To hide the property sheet, choose View ⇨ Properties, click the Properties button, or click the property sheet's Close Window button (*X*).

Since objects often have many properties, you can use the tabs at the top of the property sheet to limit the type of properties displayed. You can select Format, Data, Event, or Other Properties, or select All to display the Properties in a single list.

Some property sheets are useful primarily for programmers. Others are useful for everyone. Some will be covered here and others will be covered in later chapters. First, you should glance at a property sheet to get an idea of what sorts of properties objects have.

The figures show the property sheet for a field. The Format properties, shown in the upper right, control its appearance. The Data properties, shown on the lower left, control which field it is bound to and what data can be entered. The Event properties, shown in the lower right, let you attach macros or programs to the field, which will be executed before or after the control is updated, when it is clicked or double-clicked, and so on; in general, only developers use these event properties. The Other tab of the property sheet includes the objects name and many miscellaneous features.

Continued

TAKE NOTE

▶ GETTING HELP ON PROPERTIES

Property sheets have many features that may be useful on occasion, but are not generally needed by most people. The best way to learn about them is to look through some property sheets to get a general idea of what they contain, and to display Help on properties that you think you might want to use. You can display help for an individual property by moving the cursor to it and pressing F1.

CROSS-REFERENCE

Chapter 13 covers Data properties defined in the Table window. Chapters 8 and 9 cover Format properties defined with the Form window.

SHORTCUT

It is easiest to design a form or report if you hide the property sheet, except when you need to use it.

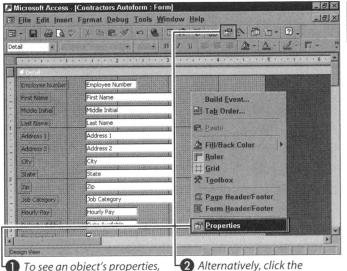

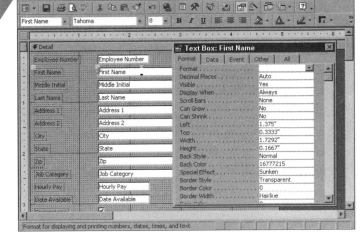

1 To see an object's properties, right-click the object and choose Properties from its pop-up menu.

2 Alternatively, click the Properties button.

■ Format properties for a field's text box control the text box's appearance.

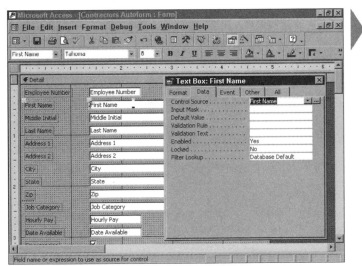

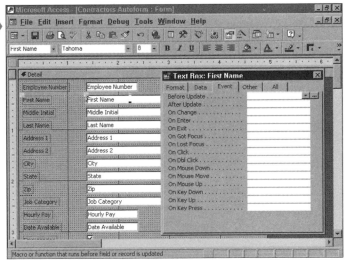

■ Data properties for a field's text box control the value in the text box.

■ Event properties for a field's text box let you attach macros or programs to the text box.

Changing Grid Fineness

You know that the Form window in Design view includes a grid of dots, which objects are automatically aligned to when you add or move them. You can change the *fineness*, or number of gridlines per inch, as shown in the upper-left figure. You can enter 4, for example, to place them just ¼ inch apart. Enter any integer from 1 to 64.

Preventing Users from Entering Data in a Combo Box

You learned earlier to add a combo box, which lets users enter data by choosing it from a drop-down list or by typing it into a text box. To limit the choices in the list and prevent users from entering other values, click the Format tab of the combo box's property sheet, and choose Yes in the Limit To List property (see the upper-right figure).

Choosing the Field Control Source

The Control Source property in the Data tab lets you bind a text box or other control to a field or an expression. You must use this property to create a calculated field, by binding the control to an expression.

As the lower-left figure shows, you can display a drop-down list for this property and then select any of the fields in the table or query that the form is

based on. Or you can delete the value in the field and leave it blank to create an unbound field.

You can also use this property to bind a text box to an expression. Enter the expression, or click the Build button to the right of this property to display the Expression Builder and use it to create the Expression.

Adding Hyperlinks to Command Buttons and Pictures

You can use the property sheet to add a hyperlink to a command button or picture. Add the command button or picture as described earlier in this chapter. Then display its property sheet, and in the Format tab, enter the address to link to as the Hyperlink Address property, as shown in the lower-right figure. Or you can click the Build button to its right to display the Insert Hyperlink dialog box and use it to add the address, as described in the previous section.

TAKE NOTE

USING THE BUILD BUTTON

Many properties display a Build button with three dots on it. Click this button to display a dialog box that lets you choose the property. Depending on what the property is, it might display the Expression Builder, the Insert Hyperlink dialog box, or some other dialog box that lets you choose the property, rather than typing it in.

CROSS-REFERENCE

Expressions are covered in Chapter 14, which has complete information on how to use them as the Control Source property.

SHORTCUT

If any property has a drop-down list, you can type the first letter of an option to choose it.

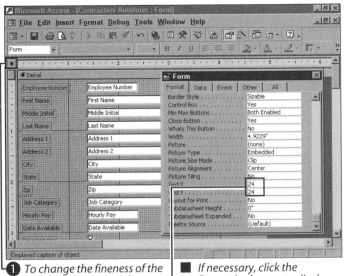

1 To change the fineness of the grid, click the Form Selector to select the entire form.

■ If necessary, click the Properties button to display the property sheet, and then click its Format tab.

2 Enter new values for Grid X and Grid Y.

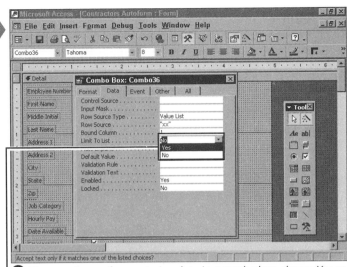

3 To prevent users from entering data in a combo box, choose Yes as the Limit to List Property.

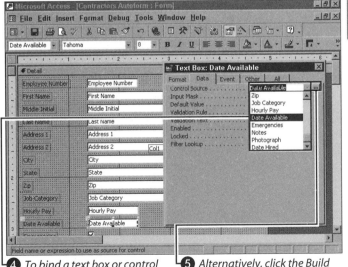

4 To bind a text box or control to a field or an expression, choose a field from the Control Source drop-down list.

5 Alternatively, click the Build button to display the Expression Builder, and use it to generate an expression.

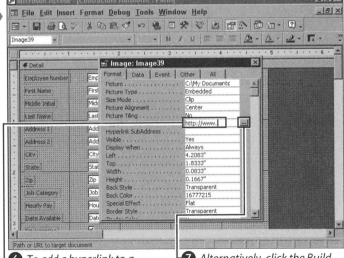

6 To add a hyperlink to a command button or picture, type in a Web address in the Hyperlink Address field.

7 Alternatively, click the Build button to display the Insert Hyperlink dialog box, and use it to select the address.

185

Personal Workbook

Q&A

1 How do you add a field to a form?

_____

_____

_____

2 What are two ways to add text to a form?

_____

_____

3 You want to add an option group enabling the user to choose from three values for a field. You also want to add a control enabling the user to choose a value for a Yes/No field. What is the best control to use for each?

_____

_____

_____

4 How do you add a drop-down list to a form to let the user choose from three possible entries for a field?

_____

_____

_____

5 How do you add a colored rectangle behind a group of four fields on your form, to highlight those fields?

_____

_____

_____

6 How do you make a form print out with basic information (such as name and address) on one page, and the other information for the record on a second page?

_____

_____

_____

7 You want your fields to be grouped on two tabs, so users can click a tab to display only the fields they need to see. How do you do this?

_____

_____

8 How do you control the fineness of the grid that is used to align controls on the form?

_____

_____

ANSWERS: PAGE 349

EXTRA PRACTICE

1. Add a title and help text to the form. The title should be in large letters, in a color that stands out. The help text should tell the user what data is entered in the form.

2. Add a heavy line under the basic data, such as name and address, to separate it from the other data on the form.

3. Add a World Wide Web hyperlink to the form.

4. Add a combo box to the form, and limit the user to the options available in the drop-down list.

5. Add a page break to the form to control how it is printed.

6. Change the fineness of the grid and move some controls so that you can see how this feature affects layout.

REAL-WORLD APPLICATIONS

✔ You add option buttons, drop-down lists, and scrolling lists to the data-entry form that your employees use, so they can enter new records more quickly and accurately.

✔ Your table has much more data than fits on the screen. You create a form with tabs, and you organize all the fields in logical groups on these tabs, which lets people find data more quickly than they could if they had to scroll through the form.

✔ You add your company's logo and a link to your company's Web site to all of its data-entry forms.

Visual Quiz

The figure shows a form that lets you enter the employee number in the Billing table by choosing from a scrolling list that includes the employee number and name from the Contractor table. How do you create this form?

_____

_____

_____

_____

_____

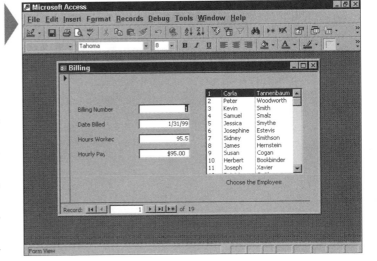

CHAPTER **10**

MASTER
THESE
SKILLS

▶ **Understanding the Basics of Report Design**

▶ **Sorting and Grouping**

▶ **Grouping By Range**

▶ **Creating Complex Sorts and Subgroups**

▶ **Using Page Setup**

Designing Custom Reports

Report design is similar in many ways to form design. When you design reports, you select, move, and resize objects, and you use the field list, toolbox, and property sheets just as you do when you design forms. However, reports differ from forms in a few important ways because they are meant to be printed rather than viewed on the screen.

This chapter summarizes the features that report design has in common with form design, but it concentrates on special features of reports.

One basic difference is that reports are displayed differently than forms. Because reports are meant to be printed rather than edited, Access does not provide an Open button in the Database window to let you view and edit data. Instead, it provides a Preview button to display the report in the Print Preview window, so you can see how your report will look if it is printed.

Reports usually display lists of records, and you may find it useful to create reports that group records and include summaries for each group. For example, you might want a report that groups your customers by state, with a summary line that tells you the number of customers in each state. This chapter includes a detailed discussion of the different types of grouping used in reports.

By definition, reports include all printed output in Access, including mailing labels. To produce mailing labels, Access reports have a special Page Layout feature that lets them display repeated items: To produce mailing labels, you just have to lay out the name and address once, and use this feature to indicate how it is repeated on the page. You will learn page layout and the special feature that creates repeating items.

Finally, you will learn how to print reports, including setting the margins, setting up the printer, and printing only data without graphics. These features also apply to forms, but they are covered here because although forms can be printed, they are primarily viewed on the screen.

Understanding the Basics of Report Design

The upper-left and upper-right figures show a simple report in Design view and in the Print Preview window. Look at them to see how similar report design is to form design. The most important differences in reports include the following:

▶ **Grouping.** Reports let you group records and add headers and footers with summary data on the groups.

▶ **Page setup.** Reports are meant to be printed. You must know how to set margins and how to set up the page in other ways to take full advantage of them.

Working with Bands

Recall from Chapter 8 that the band where you place a control determines how that control is used when displayed or printed.

The Page Header and Footer bands contain controls displayed at the top and bottom of each printed page. Page headers and footers must be added in pairs. To display just a header or just a footer, first add both, and then resize the one you do not want to 0.

The Report Header and Footer bands display controls at the beginning and end of the report. This is the place to insert more official information, such as the report's formal title, or in the footer, the company address and phone/fax numbers, as many letterheads employ.

Controls in the Detail band are displayed repeatedly on each page, once for each record in the table.

If you group records, reports also have Group Header and Footer bands, whose controls are displayed at the beginning and end of each group. Here you could insert a brief summary of the group's distinctive characteristics or some important data in each group. To resize a band, simply click and drag its lower border up or down.

Changing Views

When you first design the report, you will likely need to switch from Design view to Layout Preview so that you can make sure it's what you want. When you are satisfied with the design, you can change to Print Preview to see exactly how the report will print. These views are available from the View menu and the View button drop-down list in reports. Reports offer no Datasheet view.

Continued

TAKE NOTE

ADDING PAGE NUMBERS

To add page numbers to the page header or footer, choose Insert ➪ Page Number. Access displays a dialog box that lets you choose the location of the numbers.

CROSS-REFERENCE

For information on using the Page property to add a page number, see Chapter 14.

SHORTCUT

The fastest way to create a report is to double-click Create report by using wizard in the Database window.

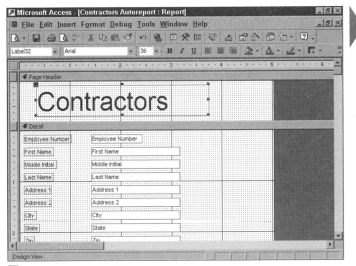

■ *A report in Design view.*

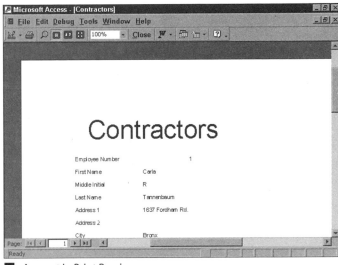

■ *A report in Print Preview.*

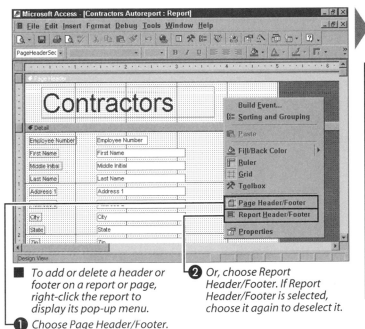

■ To add or delete a header or footer on a report or page, right-click the report to display its pop-up menu.

① *Choose Page Header/Footer.*

② *Or, choose Report Header/Footer. If Report Header/Footer is selected, choose it again to deselect it.*

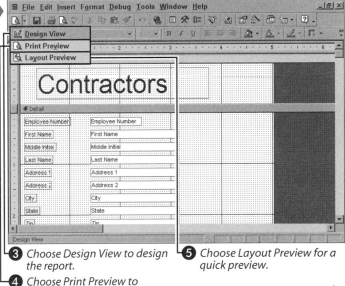

③ *Choose Design View to design the report.*

④ *Choose Print Preview to preview the entire report.*

⑤ *Choose Layout Preview for a quick preview.*

Understanding the Basics of Report Design *Continued*

Working with Controls

Every object you add to a report, whether it is text, fields, or graphics, is called a *control*. Knowing how to work with each control will help you improve the layout of your reports.

First, click a control to select it. Then, work with controls in reports as you do in forms:

- ▶ To resize a control, click and drag one of the Resize handles.
- ▶ To move a control, click and drag on the Move handle or anywhere on the control where the pointer is displayed as a hand.
- ▶ To delete a control, press the Delete key.
- ▶ To edit text, select a label, and then click again to place an insertion point in it.

Working with Other Features

Many of the features used in designing forms can be used in designing reports in the same way (shown in the lower-right figure):

- ▶ Click the field list button to display or hide a field list, which you can use to add fields to the report.
- ▶ Choose Toolbox or click the Toolbox button to display or hide the toolbox used to add new controls.
- ▶ Click the Properties button to display a property sheet with properties for selected objects, the entire form, a band, or a control.

- ▶ Use the pop-up menu to hide or display the rulers above and to the left of the window.
- ▶ Use the pop-up menu to hide or display the grid to which the controls are automatically aligned. Choose Format ⇨ Snap to Grid to turn on and off this automatic alignment. Use the property sheet of the entire report to change the fineness of the grid.

The toolbox, shown on the lower left, is also the same in reports as it is in forms, though you will never need to use some of its tools in reports. There is no reason to use the Combo Box tool to create a drop-down list control in a report. These features are the same to make it easier for you to learn to use the Form and Report windows.

The Formatting toolbar, shown on the lower right, is also the same in reports as in forms, and can be used in the same ways to specify the colors, fonts, and other properties that affect the appearance of report controls.

> **TAKE NOTE**
>
> ▶ **WHY LABELS ARE NOT ATTACHED TO FIELDS**
>
> When the Report Wizard helps create reports, labels and fields usually are not attached. Instead, the label with the field's name is in the Page Header band, with the field itself in the Detail band. The resulting report displays field names once at the top of each page and the data for all the records in columns under the field names.

CROSS-REFERENCE

For complete information on using all these features of the Form and Report windows, see Chapters 8 and 9.

SHORTCUT

To move a field label to the Page Header band, select and cut it; then click the header and paste it.

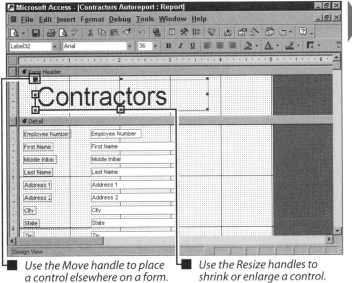

■ Use the Move handle to place a control elsewhere on a form.

■ Use the Resize handles to shrink or enlarge a control.

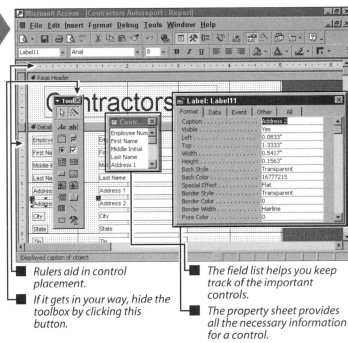

■ Rulers aid in control placement.

■ If it gets in your way, hide the toolbox by clicking this button.

■ The field list helps you keep track of the important controls.

■ The property sheet provides all the necessary information for a control.

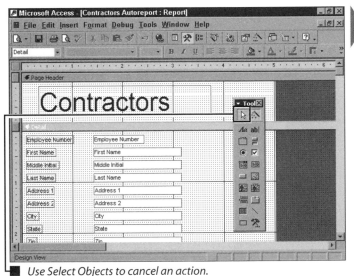

■ Use Select Objects to cancel an action.

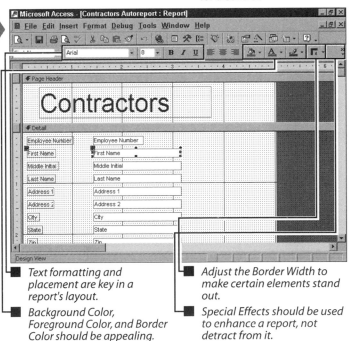

■ Text formatting and placement are key in a report's layout.

■ Background Color, Foreground Color, and Border Color should be appealing.

■ Adjust the Border Width to make certain elements stand out.

■ Special Effects should be used to enhance a report, not detract from it.

Sorting and Grouping

Now that you have reviewed the features of reports that are similar to forms, you should look at the most important feature of reports that does not apply to forms — sorting and grouping.

When you are designing printed reports, you often want to group records and include a header and a footer describing each group. For example, you may want to create a report on your employees that is grouped by job category, so programmers, writers, and clerical help are listed separately. You could include a header for each group that says something like "Contractors in Job Category (P)." You might also want a footer for each group that says something like "The average wage for this Category is . . . per hour." This report's design is shown in the upper-left figure, and sample output is shown in the upper-right figure.

You can include summary data for the group, such as the average wage, by creating a calculated field.

The Sorting and Grouping Dialog Box

To sort or group a report, click the Sorting or Grouping button or choose Sorting and Grouping from the pop-up menu to display the Sorting and Grouping dialog box, shown in the lower-right figure.

Use the drop-down lists to select the fields, or enter an expression that the report will be sorted on, and then specify whether they are sorted in ascending or descending order.

You must sort on the fields specified here to group on them. Any fields that you sorted using other methods are also included in this list.

Whether the data also is actually grouped on the fields or expressions that you sort them on depends on the Group Header and Group Footer properties that you specify in the lower half of this dialog box. By default, the Group Header and Group Footer properties are set to No when you add a new field or expression. The report is sorted on the field or expression but not grouped on it. To create groups, select Yes for one or both of these properties to add a header or footer that separates the group from other groups.

If you have defined a header or footer for the group, Access adds the Grouping symbol to its left in the Sorting and Grouping dialog box.

TAKE NOTE

WHY YOU MUST SORT TO GROUP

Understanding the connection between sorting and grouping is easiest by looking at an example. If you have a list of employees with the job categories Clerical Help, Programmers, and Writers, and you sorted by job category in ascending order, the clerical help would be listed first, then the programmers, and then the writers. However, the records would just follow one after another without being separated. If you also created a group header and footer for Job Category, then they would separate the records in one category from the others.

CROSS-REFERENCE

For information on using calculated fields in group summaries, see the "Using Expressions in Forms and Reports" section in Chapter 14.

SHORTCUT

Another way to choose a field name is to type the first letters of the name in the Field/Expression cell.

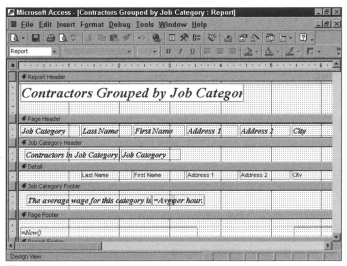

■ The design of a grouped report.

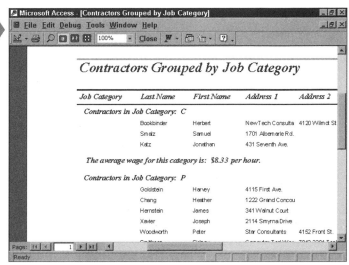

■ The output of a grouped report.

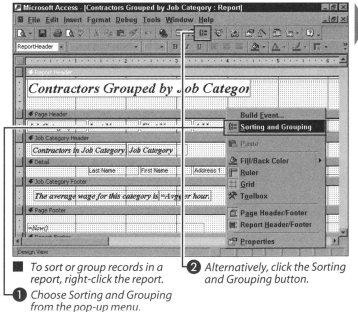

■ To sort or group records in a report, right-click the report.

① Choose Sorting and Grouping from the pop-up menu.

② Alternatively, click the Sorting and Grouping button.

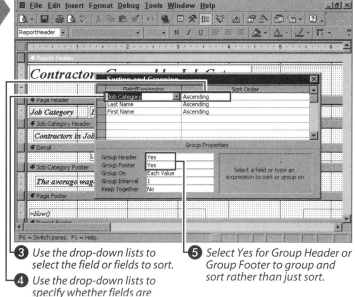

③ Use the drop-down lists to select the field or fields to sort.

④ Use the drop-down lists to specify whether fields are sorted in ascending or descending order.

⑤ Select Yes for Group Header or Group Footer to group and sort rather than just sort.

Grouping by Range

If you are working in Design view, you can use the Group On property of the Sorting and Grouping dialog box to group on a range of values. Your grouping options depend on the type of data entered in that particular field and the choices you have made. Normally, the Group On property is set to Each Value, so Access creates a new group whenever the value in the field or expression changes. For example, if you are grouping on the State field, there will be a new group for each state. However, if you are grouping and sorting a text field, you may choose Group On Prefix Characters instead.

To group a date/time field by range, just choose an interval such as Month or Year from the Group On drop-down list, as shown in the upper-left figure.

To group a text field by range, choose Prefix Characters as the Group On property and use the Group Interval property to specify how many characters the group is based on. For example, if you want to group records by the first letter of the last name, choose 1 as the Group Interval.

To group numeric data (including Number, Currency, or Counter fields) by a range of values, select Interval as the Group On property and select the number that represents the range as the Group Interval property. For example, you could group employees by their hourly pay, so employees who earn less than $10 per hour are included in one group, employees who earn more than $10 but less than $20 per hour are included in a second group, and so on. To do this, you would select Hourly Pay as the field to group on and 10 as the Group Interval property.

You can specify how groups are organized on the printed report by using the Keep Together property, shown in the lower-right figure. For presentation-quality reports, it is always better to select With First Detail rather than No. The header of a group should not be printed at the bottom of a page with no records following it.

TAKE NOTE

SORTING WHEN YOU GROUP BY RANGE

When you group by range, the sort also is based on the range. For example, Access might sort records by year but not by the date within the year. To sort properly, use the same field or expression twice, once as the basis of the grouping by range, and a second time as the basis of a sort grouped on each value. For example, use date as the basis of a sort (leave Group Header and Footer properties at No), with Each Value as the Group On property, so Access sorts all the records by date. In the second sort, set the Group Header and/or Footer property to Yes, and select a range such as Month as the Group On property, so Access groups by month.

CROSS-REFERENCE

See Chapter 6 for information on using the Report Wizard to group on a range of values.

SHORTCUT

An easy way of keeping groups together is to use the toolbox to add a page break at the bottom of the group footer.

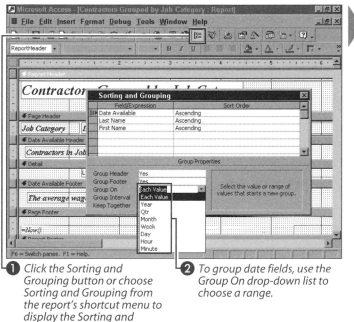

1 Click the Sorting and Grouping button or choose Sorting and Grouping from the report's shortcut menu to display the Sorting and Grouping dialog box.

2 To group date fields, use the Group On drop-down list to choose a range.

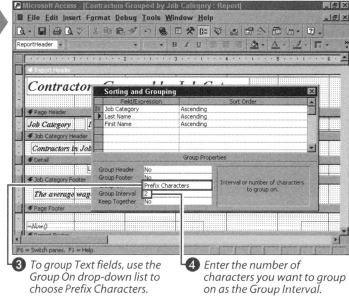

3 To group Text fields, use the Group On drop-down list to choose Prefix Characters.

4 Enter the number of characters you want to group on as the Group Interval.

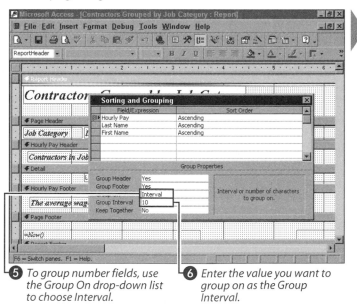

5 To group number fields, use the Group On drop-down list to choose Interval.

6 Enter the value you want to group on as the Group Interval.

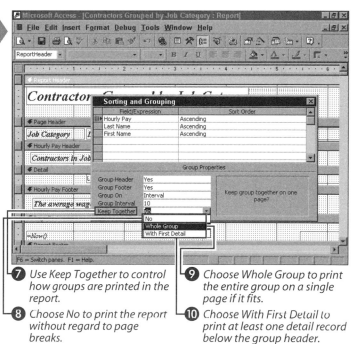

7 Use Keep Together to control how groups are printed in the report.

8 Choose No to print the report without regard to page breaks.

9 Choose Whole Group to print the entire group on a single page if it fits.

10 Choose With First Detail to print at least one detail record below the group header.

Creating Complex Sorts and Subgroups

So far, you have looked at how to sort and group on a single value, but you will sometimes want to sort and group on multiple values.

As you know, you cannot always sort on a single field. To sort alphabetically by name, for example, you have to use the first name and middle initial as tie-breakers, so that Aaron A. Smith comes before Zazu Z. Smith.

Or you might need your report sorted by department, then by managers, then by supervisors, and then by employees. So all the employees who work for Paul Hutko (supervisor), who works for Sally Smith (manager) in the Sales department, are grouped together.

To create complex sorts like this, simply select all the fields in the Field/Expression column, from the most important to the least important. For example, to sort alphabetically by name, select Last Name, First Name, and Middle Initial. The first field is the primary sort order, and the ones below are only used as tie-breakers.

You create groups with subgroups in the same way. Simply create a complex sort and select Yes as the Group Header and/or Group Footer property for all the groups.

For example, you might want to group by state, have all the records within each state grouped by city, and then have all the records within each city grouped by zip code. You can do this by sorting first on State, then on City, and finally on Zip, as shown on the upper right.

You can include a Header and Footer band for each of the groups. After you create this grouping in the Sorting and Grouping window, and specify that a footer should be included in each, Access displays the Report like the one shown in the lower-left figure. You can add text and expressions to each of the footers, as shown in the lower-right figure.

CROSS-REFERENCE

For more information on modifying the design of a table, see Chapter 2.

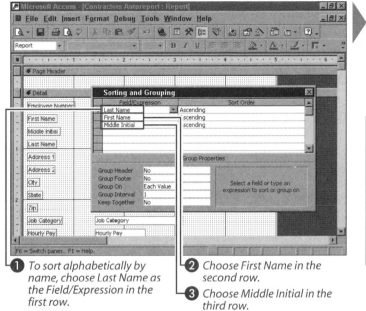

1 To sort alphabetically by name, choose Last Name as the Field/Expression in the first row.

2 Choose First Name in the second row.

3 Choose Middle Initial in the third row.

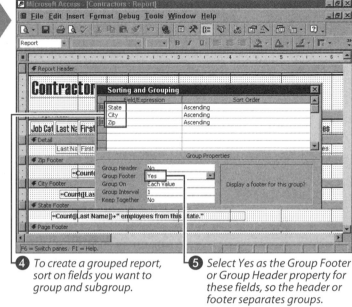

4 To create a grouped report, sort on fields you want to group and subgroup.

5 Select Yes as the Group Footer or Group Header property for these fields, so the header or footer separates groups.

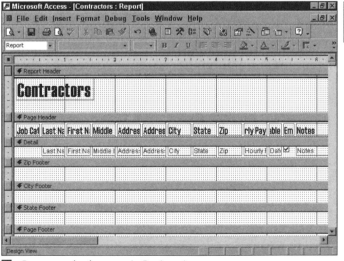

■ Groups and subgroups in Design view.

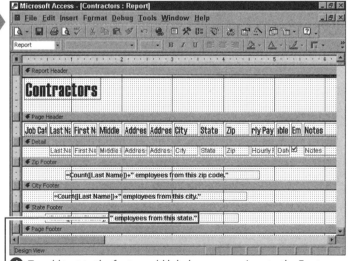

6 To add text to the footer, add labels or expressions to the Footer band.

Using Page Setup

The whole purpose of creating a report is to make the data easy to read. The Page Setup dialog box allows you to change many settings that affect how the report prints. For example, you may want to change the size of the margins or the orientation of the paper to fit the report into the width of the printed page. To display this dialog box, choose File ⇨ Page Setup.

You can specify margin size using the four Margin text boxes on the Margins tab, shown in the upper-left figure. If you just want to print a draft report or to print the data on a preprinted form, select the Print Data Only checkbox to leave out graphics and borders.

You can change the orientation of the items on the page (the default is usually Portrait) on the Page tab (see the upper-right figure). It is often useful to switch to Landscape to make room for more fields across the width of a page.

You can use the two Paper drop-down lists of the Page tab to specify the size and source of the paper on which you are printing.

Finally, if you select Use Specific Printer and click the Printer button, Access displays a dialog box with a drop-down list that lets you choose among available printers.

Reports with Repeating Items

The Columns tab is useful for creating reports with repeating items, such as mailing labels, name tags, business cards, and Rolodex cards. When you look at mailing labels in Design view, their design only takes up a small portion of the page. The Columns tab indicates how they are repeated on the page.

The lower-left figure shows an ordinary reports Columns tab, which does not contain repeating items. By contrast, the lower-right figure shows the Columns tab for mailing labels created using the Label Wizard. The single label that you see in Design view is laid out in multiple rows and columns on the page. If you are using Design view and not the Wizard, you may want to print the report on plain paper to make sure it lines up correctly with the dimensions of the labels or cards with which you are working.

When you are creating multicolumn reports, you must determine the number of columns, the spacing between columns and rows, the width and height of the item that is repeated on the page, and how the data is laid out, as shown in the lower-right figure.

TAKE NOTE

WATCH THE MARGINS

If a wizard creates unusual settings for the left and right margins, they are probably necessary to fit the data on the label forms and in the width of the page. If you change these margins, make sure that there is still room to display all the data on the line.

CROSS-REFERENCE

For information on printing a report or other object, see Chapter 3.

SHORTCUT

You do not have to display a report in the Report window to use Page Setup. You can just click it in the Database Window and choose File ⇨ Page Setup.

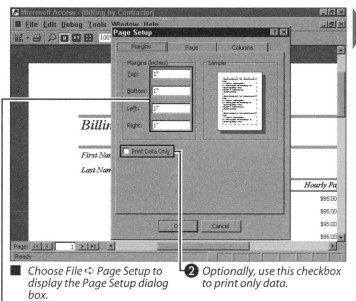

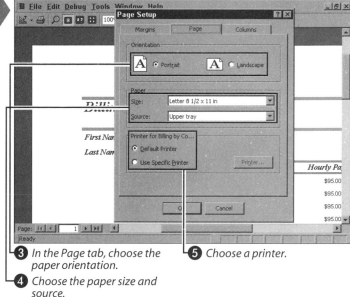

■ Choose File ➪ Page Setup to display the Page Setup dialog box.

❶ In the Margins tab, enter the width of the margins.

❷ Optionally, use this checkbox to print only data.

❸ In the Page tab, choose the paper orientation.

❹ Choose the paper size and source.

❺ Choose a printer.

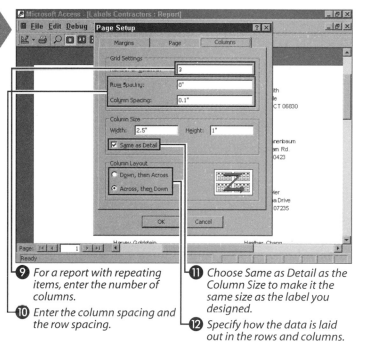

❻ In the Columns tab, you can enter the desired number of columns for your report.

❼ For a report without repeating items, enter 1 as the number of columns.

❽ For the Column Size, choose Same as Detail.

❾ For a report with repeating items, enter the number of columns.

❿ Enter the column spacing and the row spacing.

⓫ Choose Same as Detail as the Column Size to make it the same size as the label you designed.

⓬ Specify how the data is laid out in the rows and columns.

Personal Workbook

Q&A

1 What is the difference between *sorting* and *grouping?*

_____

_____

_____

2 How do you create a complex sort?

_____

_____

_____

3 How do you create groups with subgroups?

_____

_____

_____

4 How do you group records by month and sort them by date within each month?

_____

_____

_____

5 What should you do to make sure that a group's header is not printed at the bottom of a page, with the first record in that group printed on the top of the next page?

_____

_____

6 What are two ways that you can use Page Setup to fit more fields on each line of a report?

_____

_____

7 You use the Label Wizard to create labels sorted alphabetically by name, and you find that the names are listed across each row. How can you change the labels so the names are listed down each column instead?

_____

_____

8 How do you add a calculated field to a report?

_____

_____

ANSWERS: PAGE 350

EXTRA PRACTICE

1 Use the Report Wizard to create a report grouped on Last Name and First Name and that has a summary line with a count of the number of records in each group.

2 Customize this report so both first and last name are displayed on one line in the group header.

3 Customize this report so there is descriptive text in the summary line, in addition to the summary expression that the Report Wizard inserts.

4 Change the summary line fonts to make it stand out, and underline it with a heavy gray line.

5 Add a report title in the report header.

6 Add a summary line in the report footer, similar to the summary in the group footers.

REAL-WORLD APPLICATIONS

✔ You used the Report Wizard to create reports to include in your company's brochure, but the data does not all fit each row. You modify the report by resizing the fields, by changing their headings so the data fits, by adding graphics, and by changing colors to make it more attractive.

✔ You ran out of your usual three-column labels, so you have to do a mailing on some old two-column labels. Rather than using the Label Wizard to create new labels, you just use the Page Setup dialog box to modify your usual labels so they print on two columns.

Visual Quiz

You let someone else work on your computer, and when you came back, you found that your mailing labels looked like the figure. What can you do to correct them?

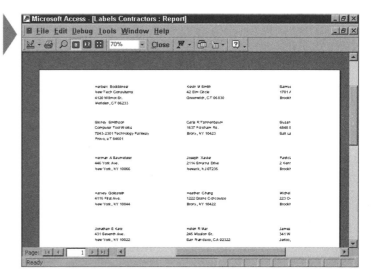

CHAPTER **11**

MASTER
THESE
SKILLS

▶ **Working with Parameter Queries**

▶ **Using Make-Table Queries**

▶ **Using Update Queries**

▶ **Using Append Queries**

▶ **Using Delete Queries and Correcting Errors**

▶ **Creating Queries with Totals and Groups**

▶ **Creating Crosstab Queries**

▶ **Using Properties in Queries**

Using Advanced Queries

In Chapter 4, you learned how to use simple select queries. You learned to add fields to the design grid to specify which fields of the underlying table the query displays. You also learned how to enter criteria specifying which records of the underlying table the query displays. Finally, you learned how to use the Sort checkboxes to specify the sort order of records in the query. This allowed you to extract all your New York customers from a table to a query and alphabetically sort them by last name. In this chapter, you learn more sophisticated forms of queries, such as parameter queries and action queries.

Parameter queries are a type of select query that lets you enter the criteria each time you run the query. For example, you can create a query to isolate records from a specific state, and enter the name of a different state each time you run the query.

In contrast, *action queries* let you change the data in the table. There are a number of different action queries:

▶ *Make-table queries* create a new table based on the underlying table or query.

▶ *Update queries* change the values in specified fields in some or all the records of the underlying table or query.

▶ *Append queries* add data from the underlying table or query to another existing table.

▶ *Delete queries* delete groups of records in the underlying table or query.

Queries also let you create sophisticated summaries of your data. You can include totals and groups in queries. For example, you can create a query that groups your employees by job category and displays the average wage for each job category. You can also create crosstab queries that display this sort of summary data in cross-tabulated form.

The Query menu and the Query Type drop-down list on the toolbar let you choose among different types of queries. After creating a new query in the usual way, select the tool or menu option for the type of query you want. The title of the Query window changes to reflect the type of query it is.

Working with Parameter Queries

In Chapter 4, you learned to enter criteria in the query form itself, but you might sometimes want to use a query with criteria that vary. For example, you know how to create a query that would isolate the names and addresses of records from New York State by entering "**NY**" in the Criteria cell for the State field. But if you regularly have to isolate records for individual states, you would not want to overcrowd your Database window by creating 50 different queries, one for each state.

A Parameter query lets you create a single query and enter a criterion in a dialog box that Access displays each time you run it. For example, you could use one query to find contractors from any of the states by entering the state in the dialog box when you run the query.

To create a parameter query, you design the query as usual, but you must enter a parameter, rather than an actual value, in one of the design grid's Criteria cells. The parameter should be a useful prompt, but must not be the name of a field. It must be enclosed in square brackets, as shown in the upper-left figure.

When you run the query, Access displays a small dialog box where the user enters the value for the criterion, with the parameter as its prompt.

In addition to entering the parameter in the design grid, you must define a data type for the parameter. To do this, choose Query ⇨ Parameters to display the Query Parameters dialog box, enter the parameter that you typed in the design grid in the left column,

and select its data type in the right column. The data type defines what data is acceptable. For example, if you select Date/Time for the data type, then only entries that are a date or a time will be accepted.

You can use criteria entered as parameters in the same ways that you use values in the design grid. For example, you can use a parameter in a logical AND or a logical OR relationship with some other value in the design grid, as you learned in Chapter 4.

You can also create a query with several parameters in a logical AND or a logical OR relationship. When you run the query, Access displays a dialog box for each parameter, with the prompt you specified.

TAKE NOTE

▶ COPYING AND PASTING THE PARAMETER

The easiest way to enter the parameter in the Query Parameters dialog box is by copying and pasting. This not only saves you time but also makes sure you will make the parameter exactly the same as in the design grid. After entering it in the design grid, select and copy it. Then display the dialog box and paste it.

CROSS-REFERENCE

See Chapter 4 for general information on creating select queries.

SHORTCUT

You may omit the square brackets around a parameter in the Query Parameters dialog box, but you must include them in the Query window.

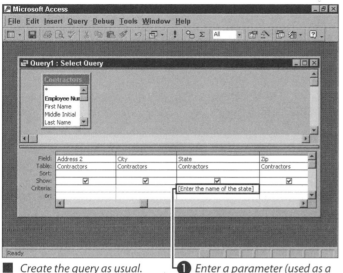

■ *Create the query as usual.*

① *Enter a parameter (used as a prompt) rather than a criterion in the Criteria line under the field to which it applies.*

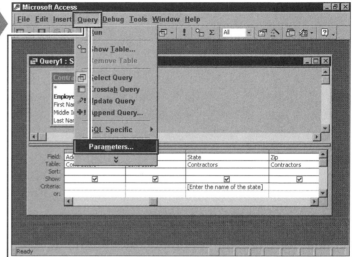

② *To define the parameter's data type, choose Query ➪ Parameters.*

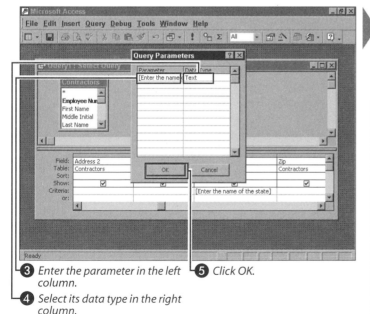

③ *Enter the parameter in the left column.*

④ *Select its data type in the right column.*

⑤ *Click OK.*

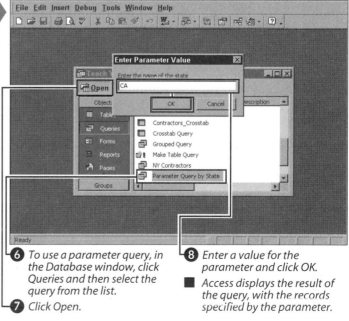

⑥ *To use a parameter query, in the Database window, click Queries and then select the query from the list.*

⑦ *Click Open.*

⑧ *Enter a value for the parameter and click OK.*

■ *Access displays the result of the query, with the records specified by the parameter.*

Using Make-Table Queries

Select queries just give you a different view of the data, but you can use a make-table query to create a new table with separate data based on the result of the query, or to replace all the data in an existing table with the result of the query. For example, if sales representatives want copies of your customer table, you could send tables with just the customers in the states where they work, not the entire table that lists all customers nationwide. You would use a make-table query to create these tables.

To do so, after displaying the Query window in Design view, choose Query ⇨ Make Table. The title bar of the Query window changes, to indicate that it is now a make-table query. Access displays the Make Table dialog box, which you use to specify the table in which the data will be stored.

If you want to store the data in a table in the current database, simply enter its name in the Table Name text box. If you enter the name of a new table, Access creates that table and stores the result of the query in it. If you enter the name of an existing table, Access replaces the data in that table with the result of the query. If you want to store the data in a table in another database, select the Another Database button, and enter the full path name of the MDB file in the File Name dialog box. Then enter the table name.

Use the Query window exactly as you do for a select query, to enter criteria to specify records and fields and to assign a sort order.

When you run the query, Access displays a dialog box warning you that the change is irreversible. The warning is appropriate if you are replacing data in an existing table, but there is nothing to worry about if you are creating a new table.

TAKE NOTE

▶ AVOIDING DATA LOSS

Make-table queries and other action queries all work quickly, and their results are irreversible. To avoid losing data, it is best to first run an action query as a select query. After you are sure that it isolates the records you want, convert it to an action query and run it.

▶ BACKING UP A TABLE

To avoid errors, you should also back up a table before performing an Action query on it. The easiest way to back up a table is to click the table to select it (highlight it) in Database window. Then choose Edit ⇨ Copy and then Edit ⇨ Paste. Access displays the Paste As dialog box, which lets you enter a new name for the copy of the table. The new, renamed table is accessible in the Database window, along with the original table.

CROSS-REFERENCE

For more information on copying and pasting a table, see Chapter 17, which covers Access utilities.

SHORTCUT

Run an action query as a select query by switching to Datasheet view. This displays the result, but does not perform the action.

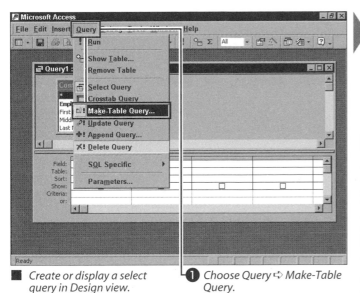

■ Create or display a select query in Design view.

❶ Choose Query ➪ Make-Table Query.

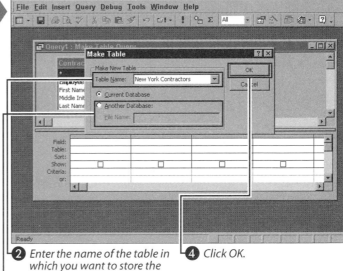

❷ Enter the name of the table in which you want to store the query's result.

❸ Optionally, select Another Database and enter a file name.

❹ Click OK.

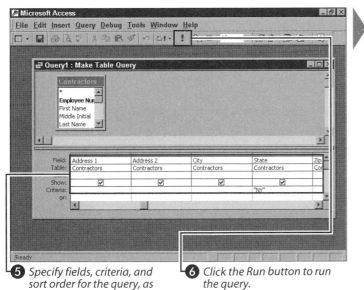

❺ Specify fields, criteria, and sort order for the query, as usual.

❻ Click the Run button to run the query.

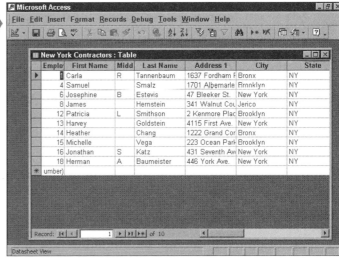

■ Access creates a new table with the query's result.

Using Update Queries

Update queries let you change the values in some or all of the records of a table by entering a new value for the field. For example, if some cities have a new telephone area code, you can enter it in all of them by using the query shown in the lower-left figure.

Usually, though, you use an expression in the Update To row that is based on an existing value in the field. For example, to give all your programmers a raise of $5 per hour, you could use the Update query shown in the lower-right figure.

After displaying the Query window in Design view, choose Query ⇨ Update, or choose Update Query from the Query Type drop-down list. The title bar of the Query window changes to show that you are working on an update query.

Access displays the Query window in the form shown in the lower-left figure. Notice that the Show and Sort rows of the design grid have been removed because they do not apply when you are changing the data in a table. Instead, an Update To row is added, in which you enter an expression that represents the new value for the field.

If you want only some of the records updated, enter criteria in the rows to specify the records you want changed, just as you do in a select query.

TAKE NOTE

▶ USING VALUES FROM OTHER FIELDS AND TABLES

You can update the table by using a value in another field in the same table, or an expression based on this value. You can also base the update on an expression that uses a value in a field in another table that is joined to the table, as long as the expression evaluates as a unique value.

▶ USING UPDATE QUERIES WITH RELATIONAL DATABASES

In a relational database, you can use a field from a table that the current table is in a many-to-one relationship with, because the expression would have only one value. For example, if you have an Employee table that includes the current hourly wage of each employee, and you have a Wages Paid table that has the hours worked and hourly wage of each employee for each month, you can update the Hourly Wage field of the Wages Paid table from the Hourly Wage field of the Employee table — because each employee in that table has only one hourly wage. You cannot, however, update the Hourly Wage field of the Employee table from the Hourly Wage field of the Wages Paid table — because there can be many hourly wages for each employee in that table (because their wages might have changed over time), and Access would not know which to use.

CROSS-REFERENCE

For more information on using expressions in update queries, see Chapter 14.

SHORTCUT

If you are using criteria, run a select query to make sure that they isolate the right records. Then choose Query ⇨ Update Query.

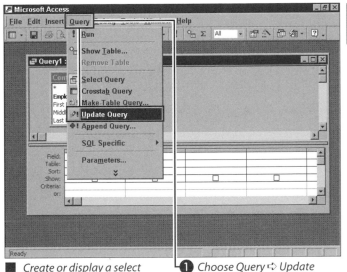

■ *Create or display a select query.*

❶ *Choose Query ➪ Update Query.*

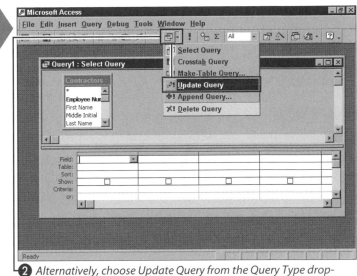

❷ *Alternatively, choose Update Query from the Query Type drop-down list.*

❸ *Enter a new value for the field you want to update.*

❹ *Optionally, enter criteria to update specific records.*

❺ *Click the Run button to run the query.*

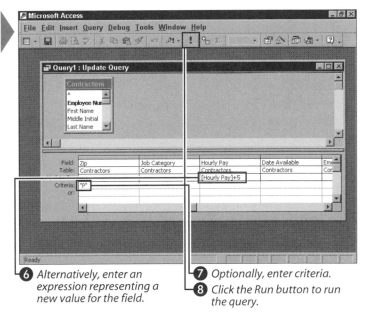

❻ *Alternatively, enter an expression representing a new value for the field.*

❼ *Optionally, enter criteria.*

❽ *Click the Run button to run the query.*

Using Append Queries

Append queries are similar to make-table queries except that the data is appended to an existing table without affecting the data already in that table. You can use an append query to specify which records from one table should be appended to another table.

For example, if you are using several national mailing lists to create a mailing list of people from Arkansas, you can use append queries to pull out the Arkansas records from each of the lists, and add them to an Arkansas list. Combining data from several tables using Append enables you to consolidate specific data in one table that you can then use for reports or queries. Of course, the table you take data from must have information that fits in the table you add the data to.

The Append To row of the Design Grid allows you to select specific fields in the table you are appending the data to. Click an Append To cell to display a drop-down list that lets you choose among the fields in the table to which you are appending. If you leave this cell blank, the field is not included in the appended data. If there are fields in the two tables with the same name, they are displayed in these cells by default. You must specify fields in the Append To row that are the proper data type to hold the data from the source field. Use the Sort and Criteria cells to specify which records are appended to the table and the order in which they are added to the end of the table.

TAKE NOTE

APPENDING AUTONUMBER FIELDS

An append query can append the values in the AutoNumber fields in two ways. If you do not include the AutoNumber field in the list of fields to be appended, it will be filled in automatically in sequence for all the records that are appended, just as if you appended these new records by hand. The value in the AutoNumber field in the table to which you have appended will have nothing to do with its value in the original table. Instead, it will just continue the sequence of entries already in that field. On the other hand, if you include the AutoNumber field in the design grid as one of the fields to be appended, the values that it has in the original table will be kept in this field in the appended records. This can create errors if the same value already exists in that field in the table to which you are appending records, because a AutoNumber field cannot have the same value in two records. In general, it is best not to include the AutoNumber field in the design grid as one of the fields to be appended, unless you have some special reason to.

CROSS-REFERENCE

For more information on AutoNumber fields, see Chapter 13.

SHORTCUT

Instead of choosing Query ➪ Append, you can choose the Append Query tool from the Query Type drop-down list.

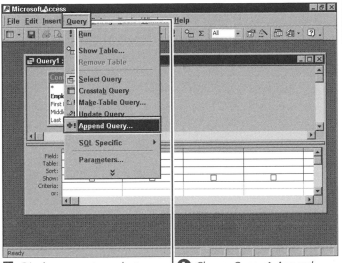

■ Display or create a select query.

❶ Choose Query ➪ Append Query, or choose Append Query from the Query Type drop-down list.

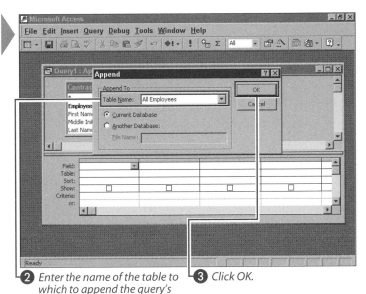

❷ Enter the name of the table to which to append the query's result.

❸ Click OK.

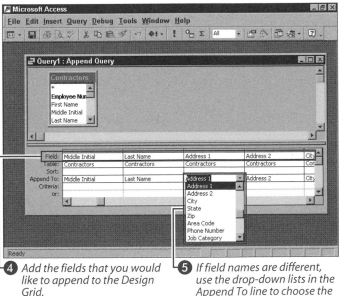

❹ Add the fields that you would like to append to the Design Grid.

■ If the two tables have fields with the same name, they are included in the Append To line by default.

❺ If field names are different, use the drop-down lists in the Append To line to choose the fields to which data will be added.

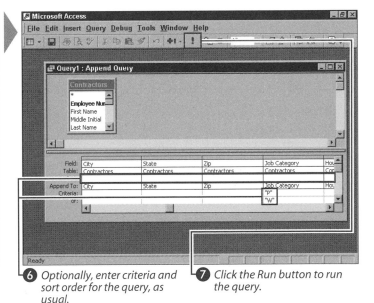

❻ Optionally, enter criteria and sort order for the query, as usual.

❼ Click the Run button to run the query.

Using Delete Queries and Correcting Errors

Delete queries are used to delete records that meet some criterion. For example, you may want to delete the records of inactive customers who have not ordered since a certain date.

To delete records, drag the asterisk from the field list to the design grid: The asterisk represents all of the fields in the table, and you must delete all the fields to delete the record. In addition, drag the individual fields that you will use to enter criteria. When you do this, the Delete line includes the word "From" below the asterisk name and "Where" below names of the individual fields, as shown in the upper-right figure. You can enter criteria only under fields.

Enter the criteria to specify which records are to be deleted. For example, the query in the illustration would delete everyone in Job Category C from the Contractors table.

Errors in Action Queries

When you enter data using an action query, Access displays a dialog box summarizing all the errors the query would create, as shown in the lower left and right figures. The possible errors are

▶ **Type conversion failure.** Data is not valid because of a field's data type; for example, you tried to add text to a Number field. To correct the error, change the data type of the field you are adding data to, or edit the data in the field the data comes from.

▶ **Key violations.** There is a duplicate value or no value in the primary key field. If you are using an append query and the primary key is an AutoNumber field, you can correct this error by not including this field in the fields to be appended, so its value is filled out automatically with numbers that continue the sequence that is already in the field.

▶ **Lock violations.** Someone else on the network is using records that you tried to change. To correct this error, simply try again when no one else is working on the table.

▶ **Validation rule violations.** The data you tried to enter violated a validation rule. To correct this error, check the table's validation rules by displaying it in Design view; then change the action query so it does not violate any validation rules, or eliminate the validation rule if it is not really necessary.

TAKE NOTE

▶ **CANCELING THE ERROR**

If you get error messages that say that Access "set fields to Null" or "didn't add records", you should remember that the table has not yet been changed. If an error message is displayed, it is best to select No in order to avoid performing the action query that creates the error. Then go back and redesign the query to avoid the error, and run it again.

CROSS-REFERENCE

For more information on Validation Rules, see Chapter 13.

SHORTCUT

Instead of choosing Query ⇨ Delete, you can choose the Delete Query tool from the Query Type drop-down list.

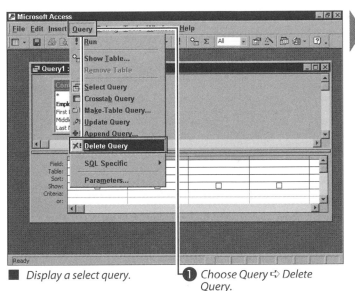

■ *Display a select query.*

① *Choose Query ⇨ Delete Query.*

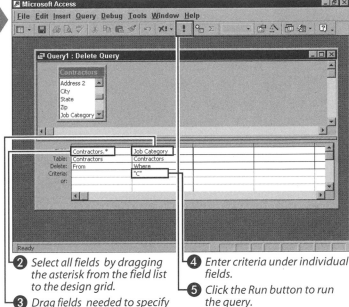

② *Select all fields by dragging the asterisk from the field list to the design grid.*

③ *Drag fields needed to specify which records to delete to the design grid.*

④ *Enter criteria under individual fields.*

⑤ *Click the Run button to run the query.*

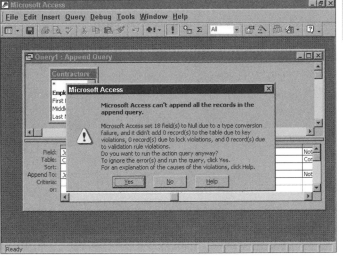

■ *If you run an action query that violates data type, Access displays this error message.*

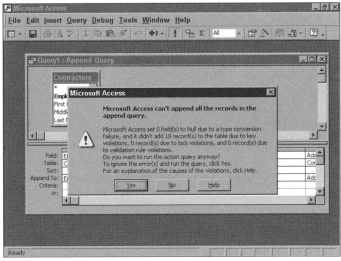

■ *If you create an action query that creates duplicate primary keys, Access displays this error message.*

Creating Queries with Totals and Groups

You can also use queries to produce summary data on a table, such as the average value in a field. You can produce summary data for the entire table or for groups. For example, you can find the average wage for all your employees, or you can find the average wage for employees in each job category.

To create a query with totals, create the query as usual, and then click the Totals button to add an extra Total row to the design grid. Add the fields needed for the query to the design grid, and use the drop-down list in the Total cell to indicate each field's function in the query. The Group By option means that this field is used as the basis of grouping. "Where" means that this field is used only to hold criteria that determine which records are included in the query. "Expression" lets you enter an expression instead of a field name in the Field cell.

The other options let you add summary values, based on the data in the field. "Sum" displays the total of all the values in the field. "Avg" displays the average of all the values in the field. "Min" displays the minimum value in the field. "Max" displays the maximum value in the field. "Count" displays the total number of records that have a value in the field. "StDev" displays the statistical standard deviation of values in the field. "Var" displays the statistical variance of values in the field. "First" displays the value in the field in the first record. "Last" displays the value in the field in the last record. Apart from the Total row, use a summary query as you do ordinary select queries.

The upper-right figure shows a sample query that displays the average hourly pay for employees in each job category, and its result is shown in the lower left figure.

TAKE NOTE

GROUPING ON MULTIPLE FIELDS

You can base totals on groups that are made up of multiple fields. Simply include these fields in the design grid and select Group By for all of them. Access produces a separate summary calculation for each set of records that has the same values in all the fields you group by. For example, the lower right figure shows the design of a query to display the average hourly pay for each job category in each state. The result will have a row for every combination of job category and state where data is actually entered in the table; for example, it will have the average wage for all the writers in New York, California, and so on. It won't show results for combinations that have no data in the table. Rather than grouping on multiple fields, it is usually better to display this sort of data using a crosstab query, described next.

CROSS-REFERENCE

See Chapter 10 for information on creating Reports with similar groups and totals.

SHORTCUT

Rather than using the drop-down in cells in the Totals row, you can simply enter the first letter of one of its options.

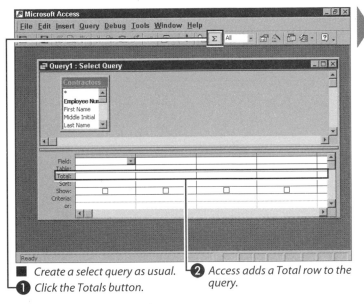

■ Create a select query as usual.

❶ Click the Totals button.

❷ Access adds a Total row to the query.

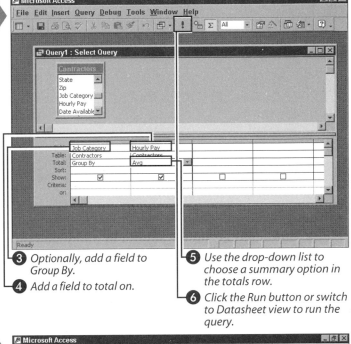

❸ Optionally, add a field to Group By.

❹ Add a field to total on.

❺ Use the drop-down list to choose a summary option in the totals row.

❻ Click the Run button or switch to Datasheet view to run the query.

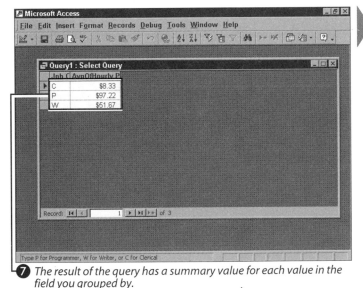

❼ The result of the query has a summary value for each value in the field you grouped by.

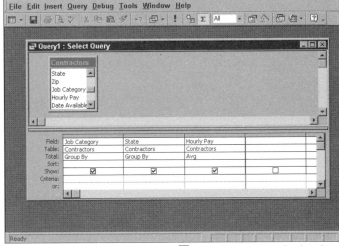

■ A query grouped on multiple fields (Job Category and State) with Average Wage as the summary value.

■ Run this query to display the average wage of in each job category for each state.

Creating Crosstab Queries

If you want to summarize data grouped on multiple fields, you can use a *crosstab query* to arrange the summary data in rows and columns based on values in the fields. For example, you might want to create a crosstab query that displays average hourly pay grouped by job category and state. The result would look like a table with columns for each job category and row for each state; each cell contains the average pay for workers in that job category in that state (see the lower-right figure).

The crosstab query uses one field as the basis of the row heading and one field as the basis of the column heading, and fills in the cells of the result table with summary information about all the records that fall under both headings. It is usually much easier to read than an ordinary columnar summary query, described in the previous section.

The values in the result of a crosstab query are all read-only. It would not make sense to edit these values, because they are all based on values in multiple records.

Using the Crosstab Query Wizard

Though you can also create them in Design view, the Crosstab Query Wizard gives you a much easier, graphic method of creating crosstab queries by illustrating the result of the query as you make your selections.

To use the Wizard, display the Query tab of the Database window, and click the New button. Then, in the New Query dialog box, select Crosstab Query

Wizard and click OK. As with all other queries, you must first determine which of the tables or queries your query will be based on. Because a crosstab query combines fields in columns and rows, you must select the fields that will be used for row headings (as shown in the upper-left figure) and column headings (as shown in the upper-right figure). When you determine the headings, you must choose the field(s) on which the value will be based and the type of summary calculation used. You can also display a summary for the entire row by selecting the check-box, as shown in the lower-left figure. The final step lets you name and create the query.

The result of a sample crosstab query is shown in the lower-right figure. It displays the average pay of contractors in each job category by state. It also has a summary line for each row, with the average pay overall for each job category.

Continued

TAKE NOTE

▶ CHOOSING ROWS AND COLUMNS

Notice that you can only include summaries for the rows. Bear this in mind when choosing which fields to use as the row and column headings.

▶ CHANGING THE COLUMN ORDER

You can set the query's Column Headings property to specify which column headings are displayed and the order in which you want them to appear.

CROSS-REFERENCE

See the previous section for information on queries grouped on multiple fields.

SHORTCUT

Remember that you cannot create this query by double-clicking Create query using wizard, as this displays the Simple Query Wizard.

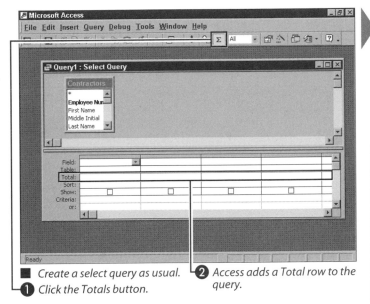

■ *Create a select query as usual.*

❶ *Click the Totals button.*

❷ *Access adds a Total row to the query.*

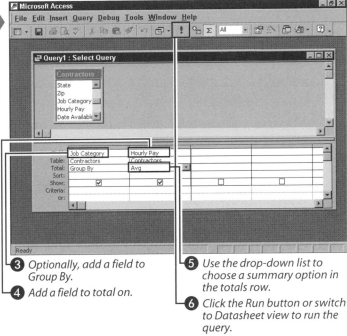

❸ *Optionally, add a field to Group By.*

❹ *Add a field to total on.*

❺ *Use the drop-down list to choose a summary option in the totals row.*

❻ *Click the Run button or switch to Datasheet view to run the query.*

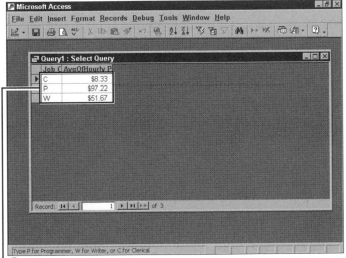

❼ *The result of the query has a summary value for each value in the field you grouped by.*

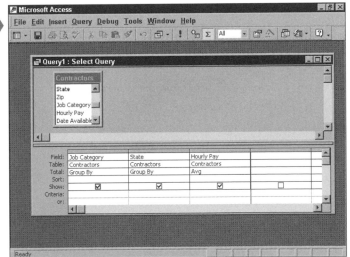

■ *A query grouped on multiple fields (Job Category and State) with Average Wage as the summary value.*

■ *Run this query to display the average wage of in each job category for each state.*

Creating Crosstab Queries
Continued

Using Design View

It is best to create crosstab queries using the Wizard. Design view, however, can be useful if you want to modify a query, because it can be quicker than going through all the steps of the Wizard again.

To create a crosstab query in Design view, create a new query in the usual way. Then choose Query ⇨ Crosstab to open the Crosstab Query window.

As you can see in the upper-left figure, a crosstab query has two extra rows in the design grid:

▶ Total is used just like the Total row in Summary queries. Choose Group By to indicate that you want to group on the field; choose Avg, Sum, or another option that specifies which summary calculation you want to perform on the field; or choose Where to specify that the field is used for a criterion.

▶ Crosstab specifies how the field functions in the crosstab that is the result of the query. If you group on a field, you may select Row Heading or Column Heading in this row. If you use it for a calculation, you must choose Value in this row, to indicate that the number that is the result of the calculation is displayed. You may also choose Not Shown in this cell to hide the field because the crosstab query design grid does not have Show boxes.

In a crosstab query, you must specify exactly one field to use as the column heading, with Column Heading in its Crosstab cell and Group By in its Total cell.

You must specify at least one field to be used as a row heading, with Row Heading in its Crosstab cell and Group By in its Total cell. You may use more than one field as row headings to create more complex groupings. This is just like grouping on multiple fields in a summary query, as described previously.

You must specify exactly one field from which the summary values are taken. Select Value in its Crosstab cell and specify the value as you do in a summary query, by selecting a summary function in the Total cell, or by selecting Expression in the Total cell and entering an expression in the Field cell.

TAKE NOTE

▶ COMPARING CROSSTAB AND SUMMARY QUERIES

You can get similar results with a select query that includes totals and groups as you do with a crosstab query, but you will see a difference in the way the results are displayed. A select query grouped on both job category and state is shown in the lower-left figure. Notice that it has exactly the same information in the Total row as the crosstab query, though it does not have a Crosstab row. In the lower-right figure, you can see that result of this query contains the same information as the crosstab query, but it is more difficult to read.

CROSS-REFERENCE

See the section "Creating Queries with Totals and Groups" earlier in this chapter for more details on the options in the Total row.

SHORTCUT

Instead of choosing Query ⇨ Crosstab, you can choose Crosstab Query from the Query Type drop-down list.

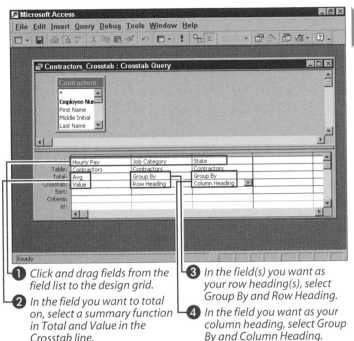

① Click and drag fields from the field list to the design grid.

② In the field you want to total on, select a summary function in Total and Value in the Crosstab line.

③ In the field(s) you want as your row heading(s), select Group By and Row Heading.

④ In the field you want as your column heading, select Group By and Column Heading.

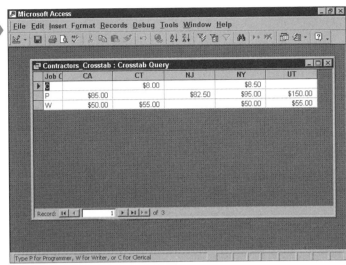

■ The result of the crosstab query.

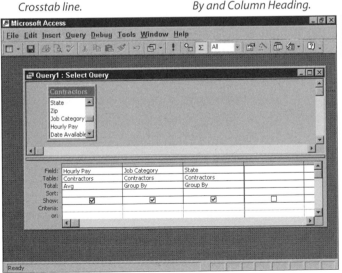

■ A select query in Design view with similar totals and groups.

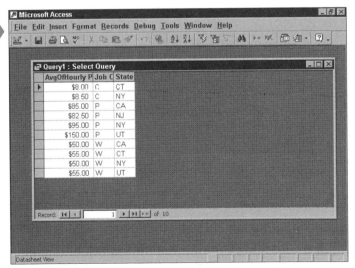

■ The result of the select query.

Using Properties in Queries

When you are working with queries, it is sometimes useful to control Field Properties and Query Properties. Properties allow you greater control over the data in the query. For example, you can tell Access you want to see only the top 25 percent of the records in the table by setting Top Values property to 25%. A few properties are particularly useful.

Creating Unique Value Queries

Sometimes you want to hide repetitive records to summarize data in a table. Select Yes for the Unique Records property to hide repetitive records. If a record has the same data in all of its fields as another record, it is not displayed in the result. Also, if you have a huge database, one quick way to determine if you have any duplicate records is to run a query with no criteria and Unique Records set to yes. If the number of records in the query is not the same as the number of records in the table, then you know your table has duplicates.

Select Yes for the Unique Values property to hide records with repetitive data in any field. For a record to be displayed, the data in all of its fields must be unique. You may use only one of these two properties at a time. If you select Yes for one, Access automatically selects No for the other.

Unique Records and Unique Values properties are useful for summarizing data in the table. For example, to list all the states in which your customers live, create a query that includes just the State field, and set the Unique Values property to Yes. The result would include each of the states in the table just once.

Outputting All Fields

If you want to create a form or report that is based on a query and includes fields not in that query, select Yes for the Output All Fields property. All the fields in the table or tables underlying the query will be displayed in the result, rather than just the fields that have a Show box selected in the design grid.

TAKE NOTE

▶ **CHANGING COLUMN HEADINGS**

By default, the field or expression in a column is displayed as the column heading in the result. If this heading is inappropriate, you can change it in two ways. In the Field Property sheet of the field or expression, enter the heading you want as its Caption property. Or enter a new name followed by a colon before the field name or expression in the design grid. Only the name before the colon is used as the column heading. If you use an expression in the Field cell of a query, Access automatically adds an arbitrary name, followed by a colon, before the expression. You must delete this arbitrary name and replace it with the name you want to use as the column heading.

CROSS-REFERENCE

For general information on property sheets, see Chapter 9. For information on Field properties, see Chapter 13.

FIND IT ONLINE

For a discussion of action queries, see http://www.fmsinc.com/tpapers/queries/index.html #Action Queries.

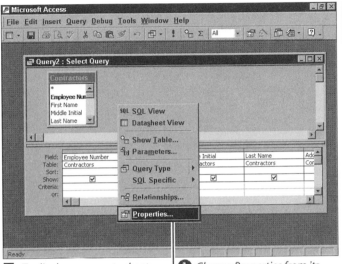

■ *To display a property sheet, right-click a query in Design view.*

❶ *Choose Properties from its shortcut menu.*

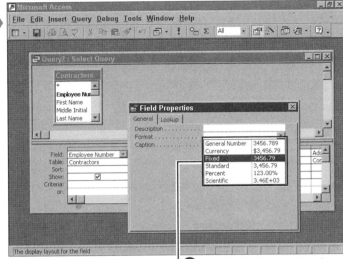

■ *Then, to display a Field Properties sheet, click in a column of the design grid that has a field in it.*

❷ *Use the Field Properties sheet to change the field properties of the field; for example, its format.*

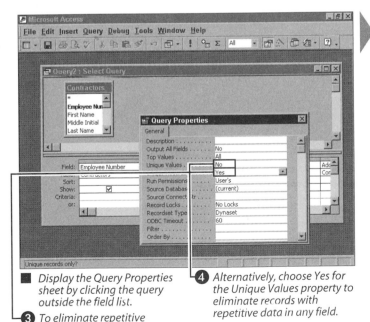

■ *Display the Query Properties sheet by clicking the query outside the field list.*

❸ *To eliminate repetitive records, choose Yes for the Unique Records property.*

❹ *Alternatively, choose Yes for the Unique Values property to eliminate records with repetitive data in any field.*

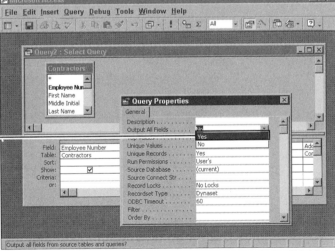

❺ *Choose Yes for the Output All Fields property to include all fields in the result.*

Personal Workbook

Q&A

1 How do you create a *parameter query*?

_____

_____

2 What are the four types of *action query*?

_____

_____

_____

3 What is the easiest way to create a new table that holds only your employees from California and to remove these employees from your old Employees table?

_____

_____

_____

4 You run an action query, and Access displays an error message saying it did not add two records due to lock violations. What should you do to correct this error?

_____

_____

_____

5 You run an action query, and Access displays an error message saying it did not add 156 records due to key violations. What should you do to correct this error?

_____

_____

_____

6 What are two ways to display the total hours worked by employees in each job category in each state? Which is preferable?

_____

_____

_____

7 What are two ways to change the heading at the top of a field in the result of a query?

_____

_____

_____

8 How can you create a query that lists all the cities in your mailing list where people live, with the state listed after each city?

_____

_____

_____

ANSWERS: PAGE 352

EXTRA PRACTICE

1. Create a parameter query that lets you display records from any state.

2. Create an update query that enters the same value in some field in every record from a table.

3. Create a make-table query that creates a new table with the records in an existing table that come from one state.

4. Create a delete query that deletes all the records that with a date field that is more than a year old.

5. Use the Crosstab Query Wizard to create a crosstab query.

6. Create a grouped query that displays the same data as the crosstab query you just created.

REAL-WORLD APPLICATIONS

✔ You want to remove customers from your mailing list if they have not placed orders in the last five years. You use a make-table query to put the records for these customers in a backup table. Then you use a delete query to purge them from your mailing list.

✔ You want to compare the total sales made by each of your salespeople in the past month, so you create a query with totals.

✔ You run a mail-order business that has tens of thousands of customers. You create crosstab queries that show you at a glance the average order by the cutomers from each state and the total number of cutomers you have from each state. You use this information to decide in which states you should focus your marketing efforts.

Visual Quiz

The figure on the right shows an update query with complex criteria. What will this query do?

_____

_____

_____

_____

_____

_____

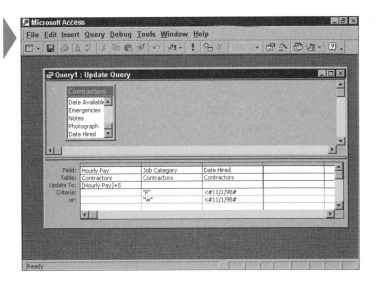

CHAPTER **12**

MASTER THESE SKILLS

▶ Creating Macros

▶ Running Macros

▶ Creating Macro Groups

▶ Using Conditional Actions in Macros

▶ Debugging Macros

▶ Creating Applications

Saving Time with Macros

As you work with Access, you will probably find yourself doing certain tasks over and over again. You can save yourself time by creating macros to perform these sorts of repetitive tasks, particularly if they involve long series of actions.

A *macro* is a group of actions that are combined so that you can execute them using a single command. You "play" the macro to perform the entire series of actions.

In many applications, macros are created by recording keystrokes. You turn on the macro recorder and actually go through the actions that you want the macro to perform. Access uses an entirely different method of creating macros: You enter the actions in a list. After you have created macros in Access, you can run them in many ways. For most users, it is most common to run macros from the Database window's Macros tab by selecting the macro and clicking the Run button.

Although macros have many features that are useful primarily for developers, in this chapter you learn the basics that are useful for the average user. You also look at features that are more advanced. We begin with an overview of macros, and then we look at how to create and run them. This is all that most users need to know about macros, but this chapter also looks at some advanced macro features, such as macro groups, conditional actions, and debugging. Finally, it covers how you can use macros and other objects to create complete applications that can be used easily by people who are not familiar with Access.

Creating Macros

To create or edit a macro, you use the Macro window, which has three areas where you make entries. The Actions column has a drop-down list that you use to select the names of the actions you want the macro to execute, as shown in the upper-right figure. The Comments column has space to enter descriptions for each of the actions which do not affect how the macro runs. The Arguments panel lets you specify the action's arguments, as shown in the lower-left figure. Most actions require arguments, which control the way they are performed.

Macro Actions

You can add many types of actions to the Action list, including the following:

- ▶ **ApplyFilter** applies a filter or query to a form.
- ▶ **Beep** makes the computer beep to alert the user.
- ▶ **Close** closes an object.
- ▶ **FindRecord** finds a record that matches a criterion that you specify.
- ▶ **GoToRecord** makes the first, previous, next, last or new record the current record.
- ▶ **Maximize** maximizes the current window.
- ▶ **OpenForm, OpenQuery, OpenReport,** and **OpenTable** each open the object specified.
- ▶ **PrintOut** prints the object that is currently selected.

This list is by no means complete. Many more actions are available in Access.

Action Arguments

Most actions in macros require arguments. For example, if you use the OpenTable action, the argument must specify which table is opened. When you highlight an action in the Action list, its arguments appear in the bottom half of the screen. The arguments differ for different actions.

The lower-left figure shows the arguments of the OpenTable action. You obviously must specify the name of the table to be opened. You also can specify the view to open the table in (Datasheet, Design, or Print Preview).

Continued

TAKE NOTE

▶ **GETTING HELP ON MACRO ACTIONS**

This book does not list all the actions and arguments available in Access macros, but it is easy to get help on them. Select an action or any of its arguments and press F1 to display context-sensitive help on that action and on all of the arguments that can be used for it. The lower-right figure shows the Help topic for the OpenTable action.

CROSS-REFERENCE

For information on using the help system, see Chapter 18.

SHORTCUT

Rather than using the drop-down list to choose an action or argument, enter its initial letters.

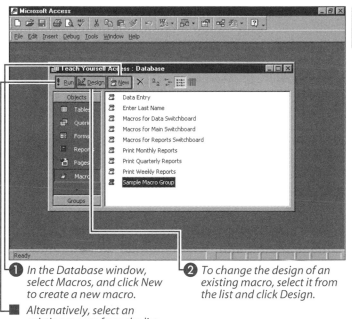

① In the Database window, select Macros, and click New to create a new macro.

■ Alternatively, select an existing macro from the list and click Run to play it.

② To change the design of an existing macro, select it from the list and click Design.

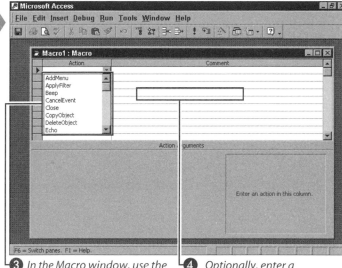

③ In the Macro window, use the drop-down list to select an action.

④ Optionally, enter a description next to the action in the Comment column to make understanding the macro easier.

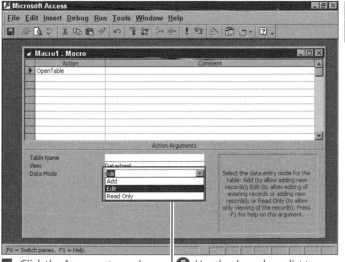

■ Click the Argument panel or press F6 to go to the Argument panel.

⑤ Use the drop-down list to select arguments for the action.

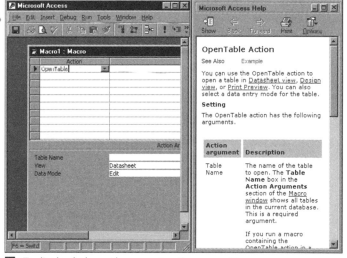

■ To display help on the current action, press F1.

Creating Macros

Continued

Using Drag and Drop

You usually add actions to macros by using the drop-down list that appears in each action cell. However, if you want the macro to include an action that opens an object, you can add the action using drag and drop. Display the Database window and the Macro window so you can see both, and then drag an object from the Database window to one of the cells in the Macro window's action list. The appropriate action for that object is added to that cell, and the object's name is used automatically as the first argument, as shown in the upper-left and upper-right figures.

Editing Macros

You can edit macros in the same way that you do tables and other Access objects in Design view, using the usual Windows editing methods.

In addition, you can click the selection box at the left edge to select the row. Then do the following:

▶ Click or drag the row to change the order in which actions are executed.

▶ Press Delete, choose Edit ⇨ Delete Row, or click the Delete Row button to delete the row and eliminate that action.

▶ Choose Edit ⇨ Copy or Edit ⇨ Cut. Later, choose Edit ⇨ Paste to place the row somewhere else.

To insert an additional action into a macro, double-click anywhere in an action to select (high-light) it. Then choose Edit ⇨ Insert Row, press the Insert key, or click the Insert Row button to add a new blank row above the selected row.

TAKE NOTE

▶ COMBINING A QUERY WITH A REPORT OR FORM

One useful feature of macros is that they let you combine a query with a form or report. If you use the OpenForm or OpenReport action, you see that one of its arguments is Filter Name, as shown in the lower-left figure. You can enter the name of a select query here to specify which records are included in the form or report and the order in which they are sorted. If the query does not include all the fields included in the form or report, display it in Design view, display its property sheet, and set its Output All Fields property to Yes.

▶ LIMITING THE RECORDS DISPLAYED BY A FORM OR REPORT

You can also limit the number of records included in a form or report by using the Where Condition argument of the OpenForm or OpenReport action to add an SQL Where clause or an Access Expression to determine which records are displayed. SQL is not covered in this book, but simple Access expressions such as [State] = "NY" are all you need to filter forms or reports in most cases. When you put the cursor in this argument, the Build button, which you can use to display the Expression Builder and create the expression, is displayed to its right.

CROSS-REFERENCE

For complete information on expressions and the Expression Builder, see Chapter 14.

SHORTCUT

You can select rows in a macro and copy them by pressing Ctrl+C. Then paste them later by pressing Ctrl+V.

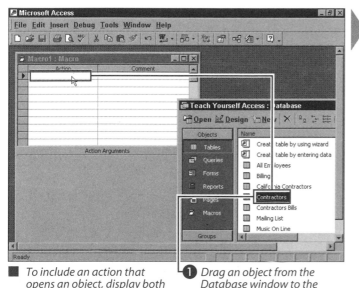

■ To include an action that opens an object, display both the Macro and Database windows.

❶ Drag an object from the Database window to the Action cell.

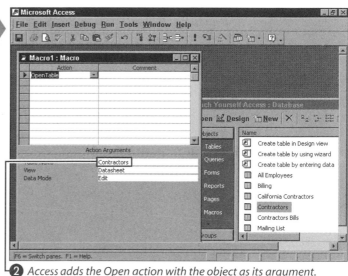

❷ Access adds the Open action with the object as its argument.

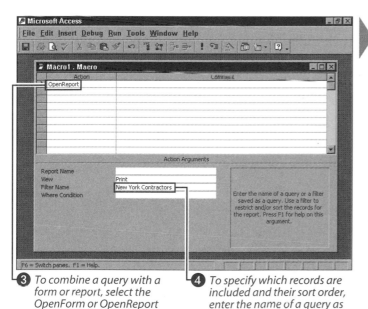

❸ To combine a query with a form or report, select the OpenForm or OpenReport actions from the drop-down list.

❹ To specify which records are included and their sort order, enter the name of a query as the Filter Name argument.

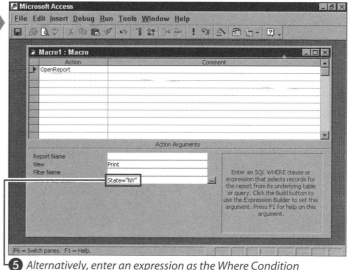

❺ Alternatively, enter an expression as the Where Condition property.

Running Macros

You can run a macro from the Database window simply by double-clicking it or by selecting it and clicking the Run button. Most users only need to run macros in these ways, but there are other methods of running macros that you may sometimes find convenient.

You can run a macro from the menu by choosing Tools ➪ Macro ➪ Run Macro, selecting a macro in the Run Macro dialog box, and clicking OK. This can be convenient if you are working in another window and do not want to bring the Database window forward.

When you are designing a macro in the Macro window, a Run button is added to the toolbar. Click it or choose Macro ➪ Run to quickly test the macro you are designing.

You can also run a macro as an Event property of an object in a report or form. For example, you can select a macro such as the On Open or On Close property, and that macro is executed automatically whenever the report is opened or closed. Reports have only a few Event properties because you cannot edit their data.

Many controls on forms also have Event properties because they are meant to be manipulated by the user. For example, for a text box that is used to enter or edit data in a field, you can select a macro as the On Enter or On Exit property, and it will be executed whenever the user moves the highlight into or out of the field.

In addition to attaching an existing macro to a given event, you can select the Build button on the right side of an Event properties cell to display the Macro window and create a new macro to associate with that Event property.

In general, only programmers would assign Event properties to controls in forms, but control buttons are an exception. Users may find it convenient to add buttons to forms that let them execute macros in this way.

You can assign a macro to a command button that has already been created by displaying its property sheet and using its On Click property. If you are creating a command button, the Command Button Wizard allows you to assign a macro to it by choosing Run Macro from the Miscellaneous category of action, as shown in the lower-left and lower-right figures.

TAKE NOTE

▶ RUNNING MACROS AUTOMATICALLY

Access lets you automate your work even further by creating a macro that executes automatically when you open a given database. Just create a macro and give it the name AutoExec, and it will run automatically when you open the database it is in. For example, if you always add data to the same table as soon as you open this database, you can create a macro that opens the table and moves the cursor to the new record at its end.

CROSS-REFERENCE

For more information on event properties and on adding control buttons to forms, see Chapter 9.

SHORTCUT

You can bypass an AutoExec macro by holding down the Shift key when you open the database.

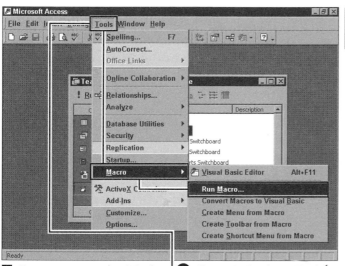

■ *To run a macro, select it in the Database window and click Run.*

■ *Alternatively, double-click it.*

❶ *Alternatively, choose Tools Í Macro Í Run Macro to display the Run Macro dialog box.*

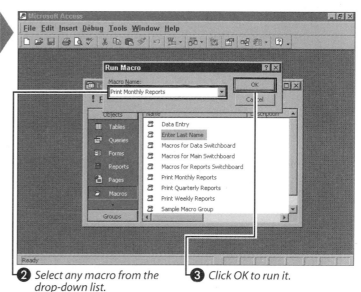

❷ *Select any macro from the drop-down list.*

❸ *Click OK to run it.*

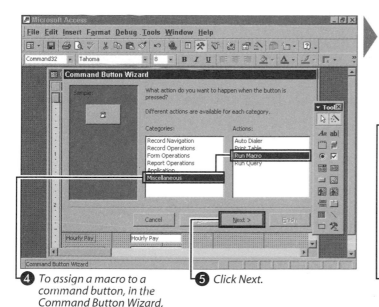

❹ *To assign a macro to a command button, in the Command Button Wizard, choose Miscellaneous and Run Macro.*

❺ *Click Next.*

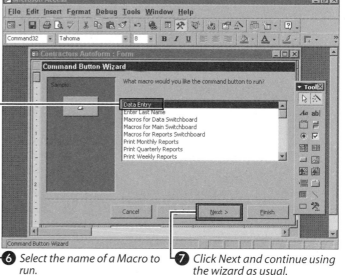

❻ *Select the name of a Macro to run.*

❼ *Click Next and continue using the wizard as usual.*

Creating Macro Groups

If you are creating a large number of macros that you do not plan to run from the Database window — for example, macros that will be attached to command buttons — the Database window's Macros list can become so cluttered that it is inconvenient to scroll through it to find the macros you actually want. To avoid this clutter, Access lets you create groups of macros in a single Macro window, so that only the group name is added to the list. Application developers use grouped macros to hold groups of macros associated with different forms.

If you click the Macro Names button, Access adds a Macro Name column to the Macro window. Use this column to name macros in a macro group.

To create a group of macros, simply enter a name for each macro in the Macro Name column to the left of its first action. Each name applies to the action to its right and all the actions that follow until the next macro name. The upper-left figure shows a macro group that includes a two macros.

When you create a macro group, you save and name the Macro window as usual, and its name is used as the group name. Only this name is displayed in the Database window. If you select this name in the Database window and run it, only the first macro in the group will be run. Other macros in the group must be run by attaching them to a Command button or other control or by making them an Event property of an object.

To run a macro that has been saved within a macro group in these other ways, you refer to it by using the group name, followed by the dot operator, followed by the macro name. In the illustration, for example, you can see in the title bar that the group is named Sample Macro Group, so that the first macro in it would be called [Sample Macro Group].[Open Contractors Table]. (You must include the brackets in the name.) You can run it by using this name as the On Click property of a command button, as shown on the lower left, though you cannot attach a Macro in a group to a command button using the Command Button Wizard.

TAKE NOTE

PREVENTING USERS FROM RUNNING MACRO GROUPS

If you are developing macros in a group and you do not want anyone to run the first one from the Database window by mistake, you can create a dummy macro in the first row, with nothing in the Action column, as shown in the lower-right figure. You can begin the first macro that you really need in the second row. The name of the group is still displayed in the Database window, but double-clicking it will run the first macro, which does nothing.

CROSS-REFERENCE

For more information on Event properties, see Chapter 9.

FIND IT ONLINE

For information on creating Macros, see http://www.istis.unomaha.edu/isqa/wolcott/isqa3310/accmacro.htm.

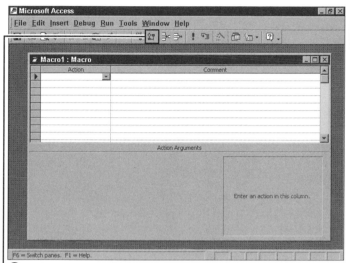

1 In the Macro window, click the Macro Names button to add a column.

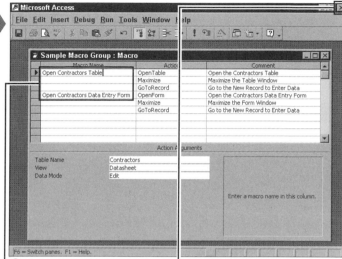

2 Use the Macro Name column to name macros in a macro group. Enter actions, comments, and arguments as usual.

3 Click the Macro window's close button, and when Access asks if you want to save the changes, click Yes.

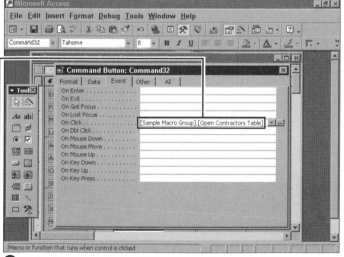

4 Make the macro the On Click property of a command button, picture, or other control to run it. The user will be able to click that control to run the macro.

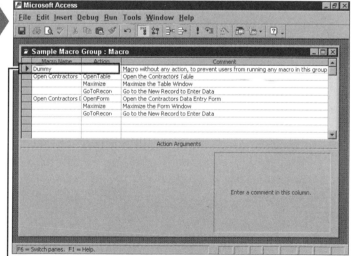

5 To prevent users from accidentally running the first macro in a group, use a macro with a name but no action as the first macro.

■ If a user double-clicks the macro name in the Database window, nothing will happen.

Using Conditional Actions in Macros

You might want to create macros that run only under certain conditions. For example, if the user makes an error, this macro will run to make it easier to correct the error.

If you click the Conditions button, shown in the upper-left figure, Access adds a Conditions column to the Macro window. If an expression is entered in this column, the action to its right will run only if the expression evaluates to true.

When you place the insertion point in a Condition cell, the Build button of the toolbar (at the top of the screen) is activated, and you can select it to use the Expression Builder to generate the expression to be entered in the cell.

If you want a series of actions to run only if a condition is true, enter the expression in the Condition cell for the first action, and enter an ellipsis (. . .) in the Condition cells for the actions that follow.

The upper-right figure shows a simple example of a conditional macro requiring the user to make an entry in the form's Last Name field. The macro is the On Exit property of the text box where the Last Name field is entered in the form, so that the macro is executed whenever the user is done making an entry in the field and leaves it.

The condition for the first action is [Last Name] Is Null, which evaluates as true if there is no entry in the Last Name field. The action on the first row is MsgBox, which displays a message in a dialog box.

The Message argument determines what this message is — in this case, the message is "Please Enter a Last Name." Because of the condition, this message is displayed only if there is no entry in the Last Name field.

The second row has an ellipsis in the Condition column, so its action also is executed only if the condition is true. The action is CancelEvent, which undoes the event that called this macro. Since this macro is used as the On Exit property of a field, as shown in the lower-left figure, CancelEvent cancels the Exit event and places the cursor back in the field. Thus, the macro not only displays an error message if there is no entry in the field, it also refuses to let the user leave the field until there is an entry in it.

This example is a simple one, and you could validate data in the same way by using a validation rule and validation text when you design the table. Programmers sometimes use macros that are much more complex and use the On Exit Property in order to validate data.

TAKE NOTE

USING LOGICAL EXPRESSIONS

You must use *logical expressions* in the Conditions column. A logical expression is one that evaluates to true or false, such as [Hourly Wage]>100 or Name=Smith.

CROSS-REFERENCE
For complete information on expressions, see Chapter 14.

SHORTCUT
Once you are accustomed to using expressions, it is usually easier to type them in the Conditions cell, rather than using the Expression Builder.

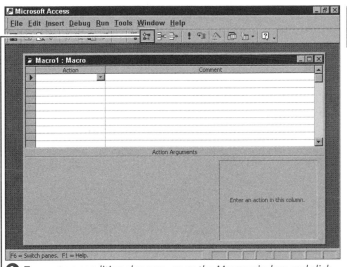

1 To create a conditional macro, open the Macro window and click the Conditions button on the toolbar.

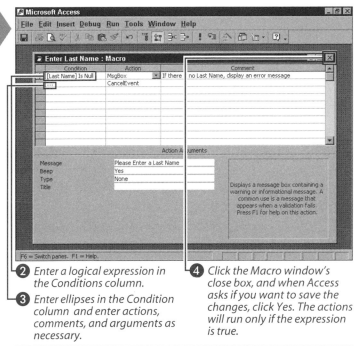

2 Enter a logical expression in the Conditions column.

3 Enter ellipses in the Condition column and enter actions, comments, and arguments as necessary.

4 Click the Macro window's close box, and when Access asks if you want to save the changes, click Yes. The actions will run only if the expression is true.

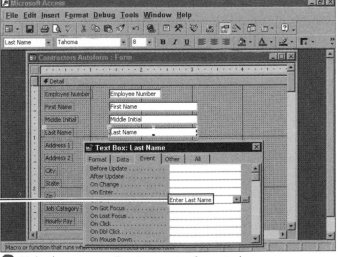

5 Make the macro an Event property of a control.

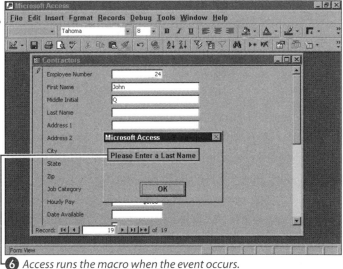

6 Access runs the macro when the event occurs.

Debugging Macros

If you experience errors when running a macro, Access displays an error message like the one shown in the upper-left figure. Sometimes, you can diagnose the problem simply by noting the error message and looking through the macro carefully to see where it applies.

When you are debugging a longer macro, however, it is often helpful to run the macro one step at a time to make it easier to find the error. To do this, display the macro in Design view and click the Single Step button or choose Run ⇨ Single Step. As long as this option remains selected, Access runs the macro one row at a time and displays the Macro Single Step dialog box, as shown in the lower-left figure.

This dialog box lists the Macro Name of the macro you are running, the Action Name of the action in the current row, and the Arguments of the action. The Condition line informs you whether the condition in the current row is True or False. (If an action has no condition attached to it, it is True, which means that the action will be performed.)

Click Step to perform the action of the macro that is displayed. The Macro Single Step dialog box is displayed again before the next action is performed. Click this button to continue running the macro one step at a time.

Click Halt to cancel the rest of the macro. No further actions are performed after using this button, but all the actions that had been performed by the macro to this point are not undone.

Click Continue to perform the rest of the macro in the usual way instead of one step at a time. If you select this button, future macros also are not performed one step at a time, unless you select the Single Step option again.

If you have trouble understanding the error message of a macro, run it one step at a time until you find out which action caused the message to appear. Then try to correct the error in that action, and run the macro again to see if it works as corrected.

TAKE NOTE

CORRECTING THE MOST COMMON ERROR

The most common reason users get error messages is because they run the macro from the wrong place in Access. For example, the error message shown on the upper left was produced by the macro that validates data entry in the Last Name field. If you run it from the Database window, Access does not know what Last Name refers to in the macro so it displays this error message. When it is run as an Event property of the Last Name field, there is no error message because it is only run when the cursor is in the Last Name field. You can prevent users from making this error by making the macro part of a macro group.

CROSS-REFERENCE

For information on using macro groups to avoid errors, see the section "Creating Macro Groups" earlier in this chapter.

SHORTCUT

If macros are running in Single Step mode, you can click the Single Step button again to deselect this option.

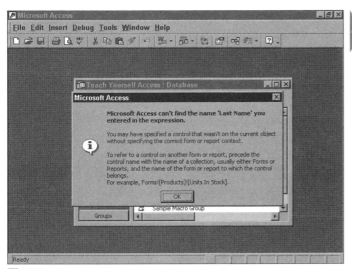

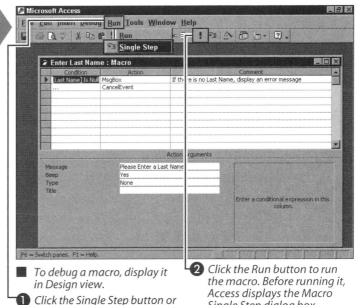

■ If there is an error in a macro, Access displays an error message
when you run it.

■ To debug a macro, display it
in Design view.

❶ Click the Single Step button or
choose Run ➪ Single Step.

❷ Click the Run button to run
the macro. Before running it,
Access displays the Macro
Single Step dialog box.

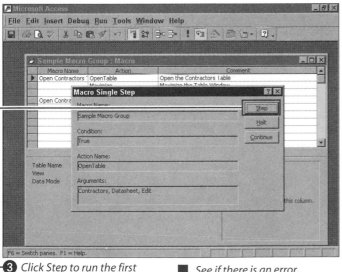

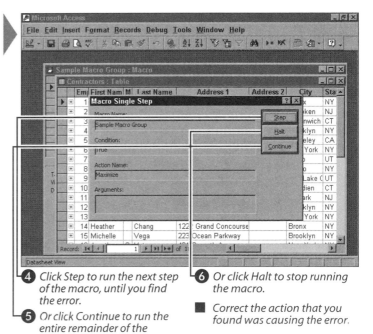

❸ Click Step to run the first
action of the macro.

■ See if there is an error.

❹ Click Step to run the next step
of the macro, until you find
the error.

❺ Or click Continue to run the
entire remainder of the
macro.

❻ Or click Halt to stop running
the macro.

■ Correct the action that you
found was causing the error.

Creating Applications

If you have read all the chapters up to this point, you have already learned enough to begin setting up applications for beginners who know nothing about Access.

A common way to help beginners use Access is to create a switchboard, which is a group of command buttons used to perform common tasks. The lower-left figure shows the switchboard for the sample application that is distributed with Access. (If this sample application is not on your hard drive, you can find it on the CD you used to install Office 2000, in the directory \Pfiles\Msoffice\Office\Samples.)

Before creating a switchboard, you must design all the tables, forms, reports, and other objects needed in an application. Then, to create the switchboard, create a form with no fields in it. Add a command button to this form for each of the tasks the user must perform, using the Command Button Wizard's built-in functions or using macros.

For example, if you wanted to create a switchboard to allow users to select from different types of mailing labels, you could design reports that hold all the different types of mailing labels you need. Then you could create macros to print all these mailing labels and attach each macro to a command button on a switchboard. After you have designed the necessary objects, it is easy to create command buttons to perform routine tasks.

For a complex application, you could create a main switchboard with buttons that open other, more specialized switchboards. For example, one switchboard lets users use any of the application's forms, another lets them print any of the application's reports, and another lets them print any of its mailing labels.

Finally, you could create an AutoExec macro in the database to open the Main Switchboard form automatically whenever this database is opened, so a user who knows nothing about Access would see it immediately.

This book is meant to teach you to use Access on your own. Designing and developing applications is a study in itself. However, you have reached the point where you know enough about using Access that you can also use it to create simple applications. To learn more, follow the instructions on the facing page to see how the sample application is designed.

TAKE NOTE

DESIGNING THE APPLICATION

Access makes it easy for you to develop simple applications for beginners without programming. If you do this, however, you must remember that designing the application can be harder than creating the objects needed to implement it. You have to analyze the application carefully to make sure the application you create performs all the necessary tasks. And you have to design the switchboards to make them easy for a beginner to understand. After seeing the main switchboard, the user should know what to do intuitively.

CROSS-REFERENCE
For information on adding command buttons to forms, see Chapter 9.

FIND IT ONLINE
For information on creating an application, see http://www.unibo.it/stse/serinf/bldapps/chapters/ba01_1.htm.

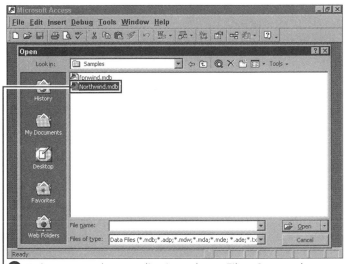

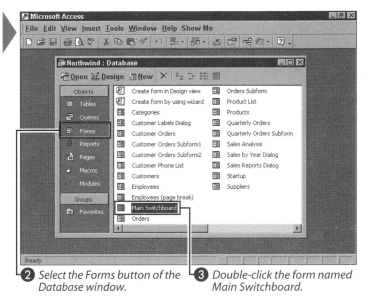

1 To learn more about applications, choose File ➪ Open and open the Sample database named Northwind.mdb.

2 Select the Forms button of the Database window.

3 Double-click the form named Main Switchboard.

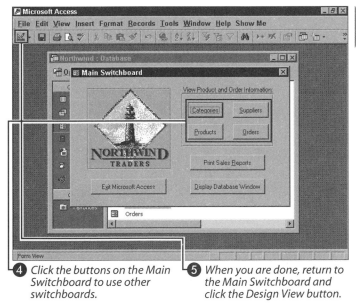

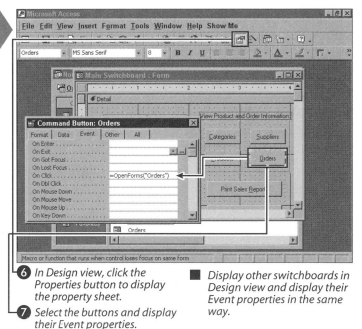

4 Click the buttons on the Main Switchboard to use other switchboards.

■ Try using the other switchboards to work with the application.

5 When you are done, return to the Main Switchboard and click the Design View button.

6 In Design view, click the Properties button to display the property sheet.

7 Select the buttons and display their Event properties.

■ Display other switchboards in Design view and display their Event properties in the same way.

Personal Workbook

Q&A

1 What are the three areas of the Macro window that you fill out to create simple macros, and what do you enter in each?

_____

_____

_____

2 What additional areas may be displayed when you create more advanced macros, and what do you enter in each?

_____

_____

_____

3 What are two ways of adding an OpenTable action to a macro?

_____

_____

_____

4 How do you add conditional actions to a macro?

_____

_____

5 What is the most common cause of macro errors and how can you avoid it?

_____

_____

_____

6 How can you prevent users from running any macros in a macro group?

_____

_____

_____

7 How do you run a macro one step at a time?

_____

_____

_____

8 How do you create a switchboard?

_____

_____

_____

ANSWERS: PAGE 353

① Create a macro that opens a table in Datasheet view and then moves the cursor to the new record, so the user can enter data. Try running this macro.

② Modify the macro you just created so that it also maximizes the table, to make data entry easier. Run it again to test it.

③ Create a switchboard to let a user work with all the tables, queries, and forms you have created while reading this book, opening them so that the user can only view the data and not edit it. Create a second switchboard that lets the user enter and edit data in these tables, queries, and forms. Create a third switchboard to print all the reports and mailing labels you have created. Finally, create a main switchboard that lets the user work with these three switchboards.

✔ At the end of each quarter, you have to print out fourteen reports. Instead of opening and printing each one individually, you create a macro that prints them all.

✔ You find that people often use the wrong label forms when they are printing mailing labels, so you create a form with command buttons labeled Print Customer Labels, Print Marketing Labels, and Print Employee Labels.

✔ Your sales are so good that you must hire temporary workers to enter new names in your database and produce reports and mailing labels, but the agencies do not have enough people who know Access. You create a simple switchboard, which makes it easy for people who do not know Access to perform these three tasks.

Visual Quiz

Users double-clicked macro groups with initial dummy macros, and when nothing happened, they complained that something was wrong, so the developer changed the initial dummy macro as shown on the right. What happens now if a user tries to run the macro group by double-clicking it in the Database window?

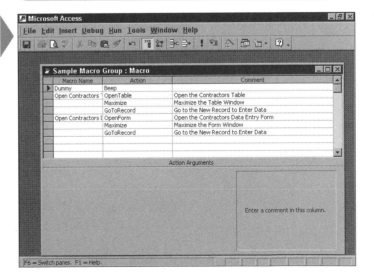

_____

_____

_____

_____

PART

III

Utilities and Advanced Topics

In Part I, you learn all the basic techniques that you need to start using Access, and in Part II, you learn some techniques that let you use Access on an advanced level. However, these parts passed over some detailed technical topics and special features of Access.

Part III covers the special topics that Parts I and II omitted. It begins with a detailed discussion of table design, including data type properties and an explanation of Access expressions and the Expression Builder. (Although you use both of these in earlier chapters, you don't cover them comprehensively until now.) Then, it discusses how to work with Web pages and OLE objects, two advanced topics that deserve special treatment because they are complex and add extra power to your work. Finally, it covers utilities and the help system, which can make it easier for you to work with Access.

Parts I and II of this book are meant to be read through from beginning to end, but Part III is primarily a reference. You can explore individual topics as the need arises.

CHAPTER **13**

MASTER
THESE
SKILLS

▶ **Understanding Text Field Properties**

▶ **Understanding Number and Currency Field Properties**

▶ **Understanding Properties of Other Data Types**

▶ **Understanding Common Properties**

▶ **Understanding Input Masks**

▶ **Creating Lookup Fields**

Defining a Table — Advanced Techniques

The Table window has some advanced features in Design view that are not necessary when you are first learning Access, but they can be helpful now that you are an intermediate user.

The most important of these is *field properties.* You learned in Chapter 2 that when you specify a field's data type, Access displays a panel with the properties you can use; for example, the length of a Text field, which controls how many characters you can enter. You can move between the properties panel and the main panel by pressing F6 or clicking the destination panel with the mouse.

Most properties work similarly when they are used with different data types, but there are a few important exceptions:

► Field Size applies only to Text, Number, and AutoNumber fields, and works differently for each.

► Decimal Places applies only to Number and Currency fields.

► Format also works differently for different types of fields, since the formats used to display text, numbers, and dates are obviously different.

In this chapter, you first look at these and other properties for each data type, and then at the general properties common to many data types. It is essential to set some field properties, such as the size of number fields. Others such as Caption, which lets you specify the label to use for a field in a form, are optional, but can be convenient even for beginners. Chapter 2 covered only essential field properties. This chapter covers them all.

An important property of Text, Number, Date/time, and Currency fields is the *Input Mask,* which controls what can be entered in the field. Although this is an advanced topic, it is a useful way of reducing errors in data entry, and it is covered in detail in this chapter. All these features are included in the General tab of the Field Properties panel. This panel also has a Lookup tab that lets you create a drop-down list that the user can use to enter values in the field. The Lookup Wizard and the Lookup properties of fields are covered at the end of this chapter.

Understanding Text Field Properties

A Text field can accept any type of data: letters, numbers, and special characters. Although most of the Text field properties (shown in the upper-right figure) are also properties of other data types, the following two properties are used differently for Text fields.

Field Size

The size of a Text field is the maximum number of characters it can hold. Text fields can contain from 1 to 255 characters. (Use a Memo field to hold text that is longer than 255 characters.) By default, Access makes Text fields large enough to hold 50 characters. You might at times also want to make Text fields smaller, to control the data entered in them. For example, if you want to make sure that users enter just a middle initial in a field, not a complete middle name, give the field the size of 1.

Format

You can specify the Format property of Text fields by using the symbols in the following table.

SYMBOLS FOR FORMATTING TEXT FIELDS

Symbol	Meaning
@	Character is required.
&	Character is not required.

Symbol	Meaning
<	Convert letters to lowercase.
>	Convert letters to uppercase.
!	Left align the text.
*	Fill all available space with the next character.
[color]	Enter Black, Blue, Green, Cyan, Red, Magenta, Yellow, White and the text is displayed in that color.
\	Use the next character literally.
"	Use all characters between quotation marks literally.
All Others	Use them literally.

TAKE NOTE

SPECIFYING MEMO FIELD PROPERTIES

Memo fields hold text, and their only difference from Text fields is that they do not have a Field Size property, as you can see in the lower-right figure. They can hold up to 65,535 bytes of data, but Access only uses as much disk space as it needs to hold what is entered. Memo fields can be formatted in the same way as Text fields, using the symbols listed in the table. It is less common to format memo fields than Text fields, however, because they are usually intended to hold freeform annotations.

CROSS-REFERENCE
The Indexed property is covered in Chapter 17.

SHORTCUT
Press F6 to move between the Field List and the Properties panel.

Using Characters Literally

Apart from the symbols in the table, other characters are used literally and inserted in the data. For example, if you have Social Security numbers stored in a Text field, and the numbers have been entered without the hyphens, you can display them with hyphens in the appropriate places by using the format @@@-@@-@@@@. The @ symbol represents any character, and the hyphens are inserted literally.

If you want to use a formatting characters literally, precede it with a backslash or put it in quotation marks: for example to display the @ character, use \@ or "@". All other characters are automatically used literally.

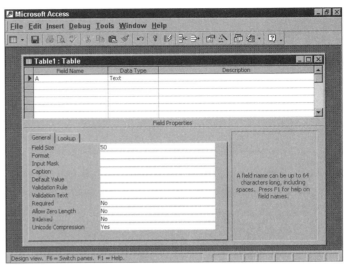

■ *Text field properties.*

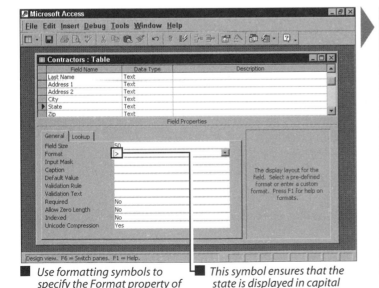

■ *Use formatting symbols to specify the Format property of text.*

■ *This symbol ensures that the state is displayed in capital letters.*

■ *The Memo field does not contain a Field Size property.*

Understanding Number and Currency Field Properties

Number formats control how a number field is displayed; for instance, how many decimal places are displayed, and whether a dollar sign is used. The Currency data type is automatically formatted with a dollar sign and two decimal places, but you can also change its format. The real difference between the Currency and Number data types is that Currency fields perform decimal calculations more quickly than Number fields, but the results will not have more than four decimal places. You can format Currency fields the same ways you do Number fields. Number field properties are shown in the upper-right figure and Currency properties in the lower right. Although most of these are also properties of other data types, size, format, and decimal places are used differently for Number fields.

Use the Field Size drop-down list to select any of the sizes described on the facing page. Use the Format property list of Number or Currency fields to give them any of the standard formats shown in the following table. In the Decimal Places property list, choose Auto to displays the number of decimal places defined by the Format property, or select the number of decimal places to display.

FORMATS FOR NUMBER FIELDS

Format	Description
General Number	The default for Number fields. The number is displayed as entered.
Currency	The default for Currency fields. It includes a dollar sign (or another currency symbol) two decimal places, and a comma to separate every three digits. It displays negative numbers in parentheses.
Fixed	Displays a fixed number of digits and two decimal places.
Standard	Uses a comma to separate every three digits, and two decimal places.
Percent	Displays the value as a percentage. For example, 1 is displayed as 100% and .5 is displayed as 50%.
Scientific	Displays the value in scientific notation, as a number multiplied by a power of 10.

TAKE NOTE

CHANGING THE SEPARATOR

Commas are used as separators in the United States, but other countries use other characters. Change the separator by double-clicking My Computer on the desktop, double-clicking Control Panel, and then double-clicking Regional Settings.

CROSS-REFERENCE

See Chapter 2 for a basic discussion of Number field sizes.

SHORTCUT

If in doubt, give a Number field the size Double, which accommodates all numbers; do not leave the default Long Integer, which does not hold fractions.

Choosing the Size of Number Fields

The size of a Number field determines what sort of number it can hold.

Byte holds numbers between 0 and 255 with no fractions or decimals.

Integer holds numbers between approximately –32,000 and 32,000 with no fractions or decimals.

Long Integer holds numbers between approximately –2 billion and 2 billion with no fractions or decimals.

Single holds numbers between approximately (-3.4×10^{38}) and (3.4×10^{38}). Calculations are accurate to six decimal places.

Double holds numbers between approximately (-1.7×10^{308}) and (1.7×10^{308}). Calculations are accurate to ten decimal places.

Replication ID creates a globally unique identifier number, an advanced data type used by programmers.

To optimize performance, choose the size of a Number field depending on what you want to do with it. For example, calculations are much faster on Integer and Long Integer than on Single or Double, but the field and the results of calculations will not include any decimals. You do not specify the size of a Currency field. It can hold up to 15 digits to the left of the decimal point and is accurate to four digits to the right of the decimal point.

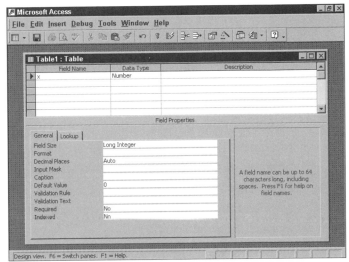

■ Number field properties.

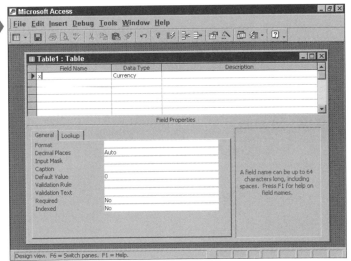

■ The Currency field has field properties similar to the Number field, but you cannot specify a Field Size.

Understanding Properties of Other Data Types

You can use the following standard formats to display the date or time for Date/Time fields by selecting them from the Format properties list box:

▶ **General Date** displays the date or time depending on your entry. If you entered only a date, the time is not displayed. If you entered only a time, the date is not displayed.

▶ **Long Date** displays the date with the day of the week and the month written out, for example, Tuesday, September 6, 1994.

▶ **Medium Date** displays the date with the name of the month abbreviated and placed between the day and the year, for example, 06-Sep-94.

▶ **Short Date** displays the date as numbers separated by slashes, for example, 9/6/94.

▶ **Long Time** displays the time as hours, minutes, and seconds separated by colons and followed by AM or PM, for example, 2:45:26 PM.

▶ **Medium Time** displays the time in hour and minutes, separated by a colon and followed by AM or PM, for example, 2:45 PM.

▶ **Short Time** displays hours and minutes as a 24 hour clock, for example, 14:45.

AutoNumber Properties

AutoNumbers are integers that are automatically entered when you add records. They are most commonly used for the Primary Key field, such as Employee Number, which has a different value for each record. AutoNumber properties control what value is automatically entered in the field.

By default, the AutoNumbers Field Size property is Long Integer. If you select this Field Size, the default New Values property is Increment, which enters new values in sequence. You can also select Random as the New Values property, to enter random numbers in this field.

You can give AutoNumber fields the same formats as Number fields, covered in the previous section.

Yes/No Properties

Yes/No fields can have three formats: Yes and No, True and False, On and Off.

Yes/No properties control how the field is displayed only if you display the field as text rather than as a checkbox.

TAKE NOTE

USING HYPERLINK PROPERTIES

Hyperlink fields are entered as text, and they have the same properties as Text fields, described earlier in this chapter.

USING OLE OBJECT PROPERTIES

OLE objects only have the properties Caption and Required, which are covered in the section on common properties, later in this chapter.

CROSS-REFERENCE
Hyperlink fields are covered in Chapter 15 and OLE objects are covered in Chapter 16.

SHORTCUT
Press the Tab key to move through the property list, so you can select values by entering their first letter.

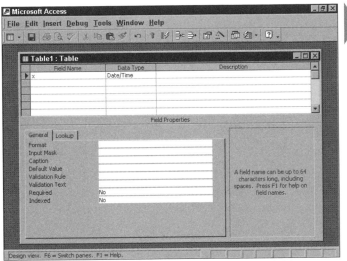

■ *Date/Time field properties: Format controls how the field is displayed.*

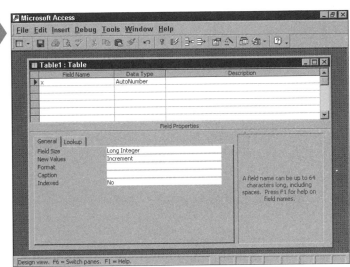

■ *AutoNumber field properties: New Values controls what number is entered automatically.*

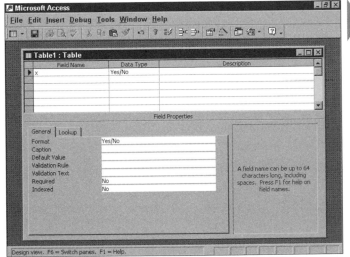

■ *Yes/No field properties: Format controls how the field is displayed.*

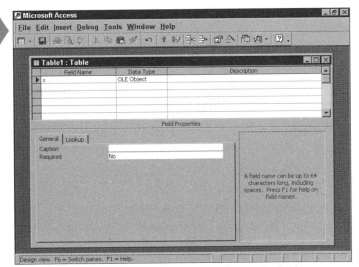

■ *Hyperlink field properties: Format controls how the field is displayed.*

Understanding Common Properties

Now that you have looked at the specific properties of individual data types, you can look at properties that apply to all the data types. These common properties vary from the simple Caption property, which changes the displayed field heading, to the powerful Validation property, which controls what data input is acceptable.

All fields have a Caption property. The caption is used as the heading of that field's column in the Datasheet view. The caption can be any text up to 255 characters. If you do not specify a caption, the field name is used as the heading instead. In most cases this is what you want, so it is not usually necessary to specify a caption.

Fields of all data types, except AutoNumber and OLE Object, have a Default Value property. The value you enter is displayed as the default value of this field each time a new record is added. For example, if most of your employees live in New York, you can enter **NY** as the Default Value property of the State field, and NY is automatically displayed each time you add a new record, as shown in the upper-left figure. Access allows you to edit this field if you need to enter a different value: simply type over the highlighted default value.

All fields have Validation Rule and Validation Text properties, which let you test the data entered. The validation rule is an expression that is evaluated whenever data is entered or edited in the field. The validation text is displayed if the entry does not conform to the validation rule. Validation Rule and Validation Text properties are discussed in detail in Chapter 14, which covers expressions.

The Required property lets you specify that data is required in a field. If Required is set to Yes, the user will not be allowed to leave the field blank during data entry, as shown on the lower-right figure.

The Allow Zero Length property lets you enter an empty string to specify that there no appropriate value for the field, so you can distinguish between these fields and ones which have not yet been filled.

The Indexed property lets you create an index based on a field. Indexes can speed up access to data but are not necessary in Access; they are covered in Chapter 17.

TAKE NOTE

USING EMPTY STRINGS

To enter an zero-length string (or empty string) in a field, type "" (two quotation marks with nothing between them). For example, if you have a field where you list the special interests of people in your mailing list, you can enter a zero length string for those who have said that they have no special interests. By contrast, a blank entry would mean that you do not know whether a person has a special interest.

CROSS-REFERENCE

Advanced users can also use an expression as a field's default value. Chapter 14 discusses expressions in detail.

SHORTCUT

If you enter a default value, Access automatically adds the delimiters needed by a value of that data type.

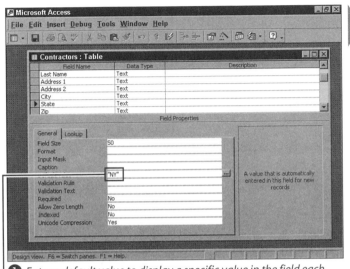

1 Enter a default value to display a specific value in the field each time a new record is added.

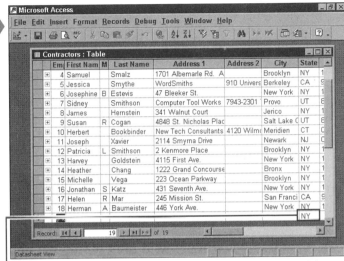

2 For example, NY is automatically entered in new records of this table.

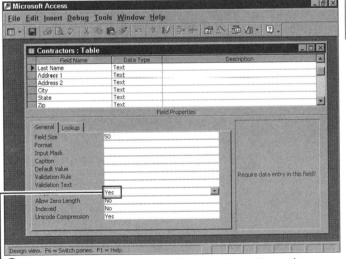

3 To ensure that certain fields are filled out, choose Yes as the Required property.

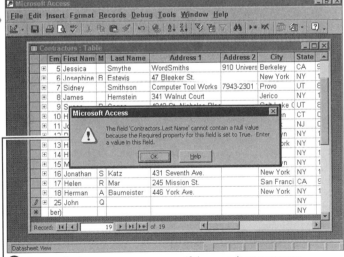

4 Access displays an error message if the user does not enter anything.

Understanding Input Masks

Text, Number, Date/Time, and Currency fields can have an Input Mask property that specifies how data must be entered. For example, if you have a six-character Text field, an *input mask* can specify that the user must enter numbers as the first three characters and letters as the last three characters. An input mask can also include literal characters, such as the hyphens of a Social Security number, that are displayed in the field when the user enters data and that cannot be edited. To create an input masks, type the symbols shown in the following table, into the Input Mask property box, as shown in the upper-right figure.

INPUT MASK SYMBOLS

Symbol	Meaning
0	Number required.
9	Number or space can be entered but is not required.
#	Number, plus or minus sign, or space can be entered but is not required.
L	Letter required.
?	Letter can be entered but is not required.
A	Letter or number required.
a	Letter or number can be entered but is not required.
&	Any character or a space required.

Symbol	Meaning
C	Any character or a space can be entered but is not required.
<	Characters that follow converted to lowercase.
>	Characters that follow converted to uppercase.
!	Characters fill from right to left rather than from left to right. Can be used when characters on the left are optional, and can be included anywhere in the mask.
\	Following character is displayed literally rather than read as a code.

Apart from the characters in this table, any other characters can be used literally in an input mask; Access automatically enters the backslash character (\) before these literals. For example, if you For example, type the mask **000-00-0000** for a Social Security number, Access inserts the literal symbol (\) before the hyphens automatically, as shown in the upper right figure. When you enter data in the table or in forms or queries based on it, the hyphens are displayed in the places you indicated, and there are spaces for the entry of the numbers, as shown in the lower left figure. If you do not enter the required characters before going on to another record, Access displays the error message shown in the lower right.

Continued

CROSS-REFERENCE

See Chapter 2 for basic information on defining fields with these data types.

FIND IT ONLINE

For a list of input masks that are often useful, see http://www.business.mankato.msus.edu/keptin/access/inputmasks.html.

TAKE NOTE

STORING INSERTED CHARACTERS

By default, Access does not store inserted characters, such as the hyphens of the Social Security number, but it is almost always best to store these characters. If you do not store them, you must use the Format property to display them in reports. Remember that, when you define the length of a field, you must take into account whether you are going to store these inserted characters. For example, the field must hold at least 11 characters to store the Social Security number with hyphens, and only 9 characters without hyphens.

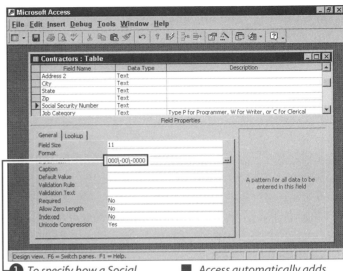

① To specify how a Social Security number should be entered, add an input mask that includes the hyphens.

■ Access automatically adds literal symbols (\) so the hyphen is displayed.

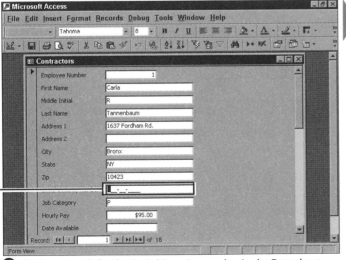

② The input mask for the Social Security number in the Datasheet and Form views displays spaces for data entry.

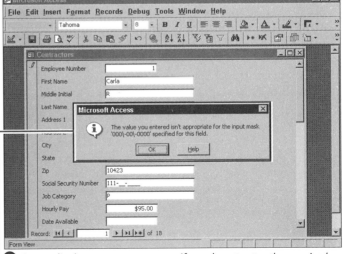

③ Access displays an error message if you do not enter the required characters.

Understanding Input Masks
Continued

Storing Inserted Characters

You can also add a semicolon followed by a 0 after the input mask to specify that the inserted characters from the input mask should be stored in the table.

Displaying Spaces

You can also enter a third part to the input mask that specifies how blank spaces are displayed. Add an additional semicolon followed by any character. By default, the underscore (_) character is used to denote blank spaces, so that our Social Security number input mask is displayed as ___-__-____ before any data is entered into it, but you may want to use a different character.

The Input Mask Wizard

You can also use the Input Mask Wizard to generate input masks for you. The Wizard creates input masks for a number of common uses, such as Social Security number and telephone number, and allows you to store literals and fill characters. To use this wizard, click the Input Mask property to display a Build button (. . .) to its right and then click this button to display the Input Mask Wizard.

The Wizard lets you choose among a number of standard input masks, as you can see in the upper left figure. You can click the Try It box to enter data and display the mask as it is currently defined. Make sure to use the Try It so you know exactly how to enter the field data. If you use Try It when you set up a Social Security number input mask, you will know that you only have to type in the numbers and not the dashes.

You can also click the Edit List button in the wizard's first step to change the list of standard options. The Wizard displays a dialog box that works exactly like an Access Data Entry Form, which you can use to edit existing options or add new ones to the list.

The remaining steps let you edit the chosen mask, choose a different placeholder instead of the standard underline character, and choose whether to store the literal characters in the mask. Access creates the input mask you defined, as shown on the lower right.

TAKE NOTE

▶ **USING INPUT MASKS AND FORMATS**
Though they look similar, you should not confuse an input mask with a format, covered earlier in this chapter. A format specifies how data is displayed. An input mask controls how data is entered.

CROSS-REFERENCE
For more information on Format symbols, see the sections on Text field data properties, earlier in this chapter.

SHORTCUT
To access the Wizard, you also can right-click anywhere on the Input Mask property and choose Build from its Shortcut menu.

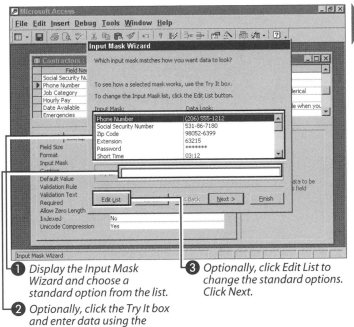

① Display the Input Mask Wizard and choose a standard option from the list.

② Optionally, click the Try It box and enter data using the mask.

③ Optionally, click Edit List to change the standard options. Click Next.

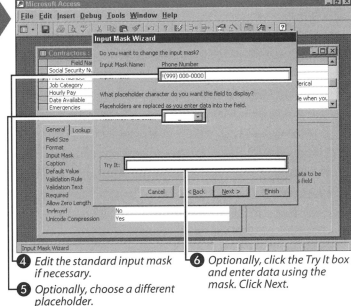

④ Edit the standard input mask if necessary.

⑤ Optionally, choose a different placeholder.

⑥ Optionally, click the Try It box and enter data using the mask. Click Next.

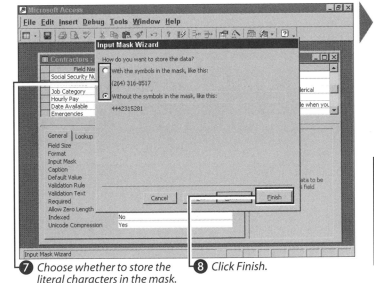

⑦ Choose whether to store the literal characters in the mask.

⑧ Click Finish.

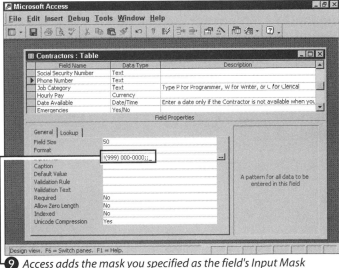

⑨ Access adds the mask you specified as the field's Input Mask property.

Creating Lookup Fields

You learned in Chapter 9 to add a combo box to a form. A lookup field is even more powerful, because it also lets the user select a value for the field from a drop-down list in tables and queries.

The easiest way to create a lookup field is by using the Lookup Wizard. Select Lookup Wizard as the data type of the field for which you want to create a drop-down list. This will not actually change the field's data type; once you have finished using the Wizard, the original data type is restored.

The Wizard's first step, shown on the upper left, lets you specify whether you want to get the values from an existing table or from a list you type in. The steps in the rest of the Wizard depend on which of these you choose.

Typing In a List

If you choose to type in a list, the second step, shown in the upper-right figure, lets you specify how many columns to display and type the values in those columns. A table with the number of columns that you enter is displayed, and you can enter values in it and resize its columns, just as you do in an ordinary Access table.

You might want to use multiple columns if the values that you want to add to the table are not clear. For example, if you are using a Lookup list to enter data in a Job Category field that allows the entries P,

W, and C, it would be confusing for the data-entry person. It is better to display two columns, one with the words the letters stand for, as shown on the upper right.

If you use multiple columns, the next step, shown on the lower left, lets you specify which column supplies the values that are actually stored in the table; this step is omitted if you include only one column.

The final step simply lets you enter the label that will be used to describe the drop-down list that this Wizard will generate. The name of the field is used by default and is generally the best label.

Once you have run the Lookup Wizard, the lookup properties you specified are entered in the Lookup tab for the field.

Continued

TAKE NOTE

CHOOSING A COMBO BOX OR LIST BOX

By default, the Wizard creates a combo box, which lets the user select a value from the drop-down list, or enter a value directly in the text box. However, you can also create a list box that only lets the user select values from the list. To do this, click the field in Design view, and click the Lookup tab. The first lookup property is Display Control. Choose List Box rather than the default Combo Box. You can also choose Text Box as the Display Control to have the user enter data directly in the field in the usual way.

CROSS-REFERENCE

For information on adding combo boxes to forms, see Chapter 9.

SHORTCUT

Data entry is quicker if you use a combo box with Yes in its Limit to List Property, as described on the next page, rather than a list box.

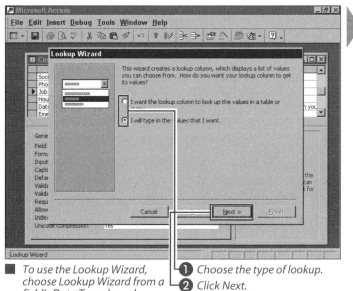

■ *To use the Lookup Wizard, choose Lookup Wizard from a field's Data Type drop-down list.*

1 *Choose the type of lookup.*

2 *Click Next.*

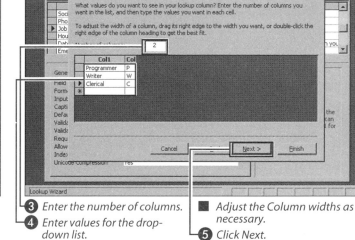

3 *Enter the number of columns.*

4 *Enter values for the drop-down list.*

■ *Adjust the Column widths as necessary.*

5 *Click Next.*

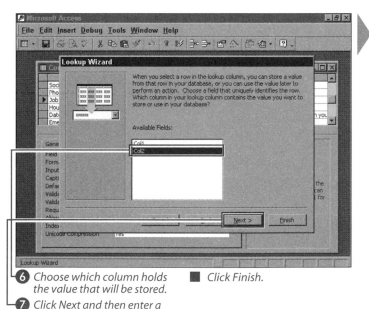

6 *Choose which column holds the value that will be stored.*

7 *Click Next and then enter a name for the column in the next step.*

■ *Click Finish.*

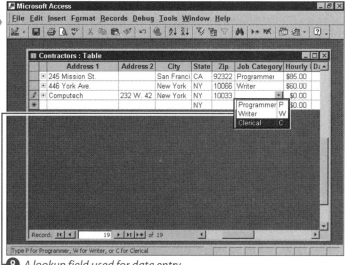

8 *A lookup field used for data entry.*

Creating Lookup Fields

Continued

Using Values from a Table

A lookup field that uses the values from a table is particularly useful for entering the foreign key field of the "many" table of a relational database. You can enter data in the foreign key field using a drop-down list that displays the values of the primary key field of the one table, so that you cannot enter invalid data.

To do this, display the "many" table in Design view, and select Lookup Wizard as the data type of its foreign key field. Using the example from Chapter 7, you would display the Billing table in Design view, and select Lookup Wizard as the Data Type of its Employee Number field. Later, when you do data entry, you could add the Employee Number to the Billing Table by selecting from a drop-down list of all contractors' names, as shown on the lower right.

You can see that the lookup field makes it easy and foolproof to add an employee number. The user simply selects the employee's name and does not even have to know that the employee number exists. You can type a name into this combo box rather than choosing from the list, but Access will not accept a name that does not have an Employee Number to enter into the table, if you choose Limit to List.

In the first step of the Wizard, choose I want the lookup column to look up the values in a table or query. The second step of the Wizard lets you choose a table or query. Choose the "one" table (the Contractors table in the example in Chapter 7).

The next step lets you select which fields to include on the drop-down list. Choose fields that identify the record in the many table, as well as its primary key field, as shown on the upper left.

The fourth step lets you set the width of the columns, as shown on the upper right. You should select the checkbox to keep the key field hidden. Click Next.

The fifth step lets you enter a name for the lookup column and click Finish to run the wizard. When the Lookup Wizard displays a dialog box that prompts you to save changes in the table, click Yes.

TAKE NOTE

USING THE LIMIT TO LIST PROPERTY

In most cases, you will want to select Yes as the Limit to List property for a combo box. Then the user will be able to type in a value rather than using the drop-down list, but only a value that is in the list. A combo box with entries limited to the list is a bit easier for the user to work with than a List Box, which requires the user to use the drop-down list.

CROSS-REFERENCE

For more information on relational databases, see Chapter 7.

FIND IT ONLINE

For more on creating tables, see **http://www. business.mankato.msus.edu/keptin/access/ buildtable.html**.

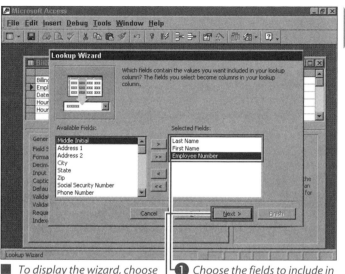

■ *To display the wizard, choose Lookup Wizard from a field's Data Type drop-down list.*

■ *Choose the table or query to look up the value in and click Next.*

① *Choose the fields to include in the list.*

② *Click Next.*

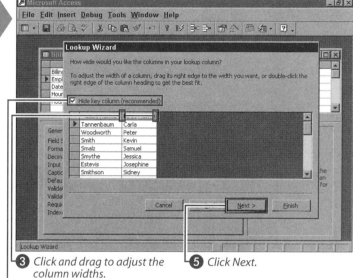

③ *Click and drag to adjust the column widths.*

④ *Select the checkbox to hide the key field.*

⑤ *Click Next.*

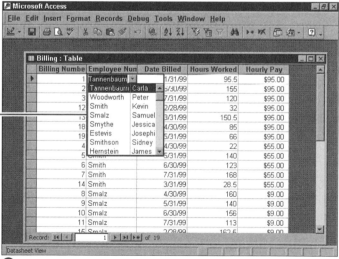

⑥ *Enter a name for the lookup column.*

⑦ *Click Finish.*

⑧ *Once you have created a lookup field, the user can select a name from the drop-down list to enter the Employee Number.*

Personal Workbook

Q&A

1 What are two reasons for giving a Text field a size that is different from the default 50?

_____

_____

2 You are creating a table with a Number field, and you do not know what sort of data it will hold. What size should you give it?

_____

_____

_____

3 What is the difference between a Currency field and a Number field? When should you use the Currency data type?

_____

_____

_____

4 Why is the Caption property used?

_____

_____

_____

5 Which properties do you use to validate data?

_____

_____

_____

6 How do you enter a zero-length string, and why would you use it?

_____

_____

_____

7 Should you store the inserted characters that an input mask displays in a field?

_____

_____

8 You have used the Lookup Wizard to create a lookup field. What are two ways that you can prevent a user from entering values that are not in the drop-down list, and which way is usually better?

_____

_____

ANSWERS: PAGE 354

EXTRA PRACTICE

1 Format a Text field so its content is always displayed in upper case.

2 Convert a Number field to a Currency field or convert a Currency field to a Number field. Change the field's Format (and if necessary its Size) so it is displayed correctly and performs calculations correctly.

3 Create a default value for a field; for example, you might use the state you live in as the default value for the State field. Try entering data using the default value.

4 Create an input mask for a field that holds telephone number, and add some sample data to it.

REAL-WORLD APPLICATIONS

✔ The temp you hired to do data entry decided to enter all state names in small letters. You change the Format of the field so they are displayed as capital letters.

✔ Some of your data entry people leave out the area codes for telephone numbers. You create an Input Mask that requires them to enter the area code, and also saves them time by automatically inserting parentheses around the area code and a hyphen within the phone number.

✔ As you enter more and more data that you have gathered for your research project, calculations start slowing. You convert the Number fields to Currency fields so calculations are performed more quickly, and you change the format so they are displayed properly.

Visual Quiz

In the figure, there is an input mask for a complicated Billing Code field. What is entered in this field?

_____

_____

_____

_____

_____

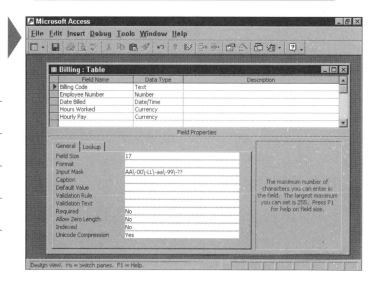

CHAPTER **14**

MASTER
THESE
SKILLS

▶ **Using the Expression Builder**

▶ **Understanding Identifiers**

▶ **Understanding Operators**

▶ **Understanding Functions**

▶ **Understanding Literals, Constants, and Common Expressions**

▶ **Using Expressions in Table Design**

▶ **Using Expressions in Queries**

▶ **Using Expressions in Forms and Reports**

Working with Expressions

An Access *expression* is a special kind of calculation. Just as you perform a calculation in arithmetic and come up with a result, Access evaluates an expression and comes up with a result.

When you use expressions, Access displays the result rather than the expression. For example, to create a calculated field that displays Total Pay, you would use the expression = `[Hours Worked] * [Hourly Pay]`. The calculated field based on this expression would display the result of this calculation, rather than displaying the expression itself.

Access expressions can include many different types of elements that are not used in arithmetic.

Identifiers identify objects from the Access database, such as tables, forms, and reports, so you can refer to fields or other objects in them. The symbol ! is used between the identifier and field name; for example, the First Name field of the Contractors table can be referred to as `[Contractors]![First Name]`.

Functions are special calculations that give expressions more power. For example, there are functions that perform financial calculations such as Present Value and Future Value, and functions that return the current date and time.

Constants are constant values defined by Access, such as Null, which refers to an empty field.

Operators are symbols that tell the expression what operations to perform on other values. For example, the + operator means that the values on either side of it are added.

Literals are values used as they appear in the expression. For example, if you multiply the value in some field by 5, the field name is used to refer to the value in the field, and the number 5 is used literally.

Unlike calculations in arithmetic, Access expressions can evaluate to true or false, to dates, or to text, as well as to numbers.

You begin this chapter by looking at the Expression Builder, which makes it easier to create expressions. Then you look in detail at all the elements of expressions. Finally, you look at practical uses of expressions in forms, queries, reports, and table definitions.

Using the Expression Builder

Before you go on, you should display the Expression Builder so you can try its features as you read about them. The Expression Builder is displayed in a complete version when you use it to enter the Control Source property of a field in a form. You can do this by following the steps on the facing page.

You can type expressions in text boxes or enter them by clicking the Build button (with three dots) to their right to display the Expression Builder. You may type elements of the expression in the Expression Builder's text box, or you may enter them there by clicking buttons representing commonly used operators. You can also add elements to the expression by selecting them from the lists of Access objects, functions, constants, operators, and common expressions.

To copy elements of the expression from these lists, first click one of the folders in the left scrolling column to display the type of element you want, such as operators or constants.

Some of these folders have a + sign on them to indicate that they have child folders, which you can display by double-clicking the + sign. When you do so, the + becomes a –, and you can click it to close the child folders. Folders with + or – on them are used only to display child folders. When you click any other folder, a list of elements that you may use in the expression is displayed to its right.

Sometimes the center column includes elements you can add to the expression, but it is usually used to limit the list on the right. For example, if you select the Operators folder, all operators are displayed by default. You can use the center column to display all the operators or only certain types of operators, such as the arithmetic operators shown in the lower-right figure.

To add an element from a list to the Expression text box, double-click it, or select it and then click the Paste button. To add commonly used operators, such as + (plus) and – (minus), simply click one of the operator buttons above this list.

Often, Access adds a word enclosed in angle brackets to the expression to tell you that an element is missing. For example, if you add two fields to the expression text box one after another, Access adds <<Expr> between them, to show that you need an expression between them.

TAKE NOTE

EDITING EXPRESSIONS

You can edit the expression in the Expression text box using the usual Windows editing techniques. After you select text in this text box, it can be replaced by a new element that you add as well as by text that you type. For example, if Access adds <<Expr> between two fields, you can click that word to select it, and then click an operator button to replace it.

CROSS-REFERENCE

For more information on the Control Source property, see Chapter 9.

SHORTCUT

You do not have to double-click words such as <<Expr> that Access adds to the text box to select them. Simply click them.

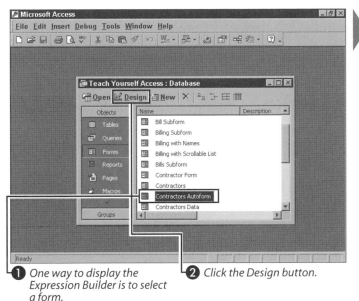

1 One way to display the Expression Builder is to select a form.

2 Click the Design button.

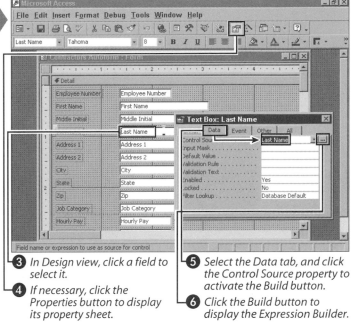

3 In Design view, click a field to select it.

4 If necessary, click the Properties button to display its property sheet.

5 Select the Data tab, and click the Control Source property to activate the Build button.

6 Click the Build button to display the Expression Builder.

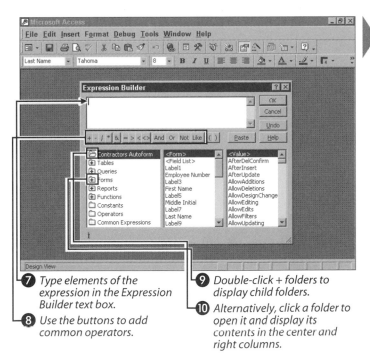

7 Type elements of the expression in the Expression Builder text box.

8 Use the buttons to add common operators.

9 Double-click + folders to display child folders.

10 Alternatively, click a folder to open it and display its contents in the center and right columns.

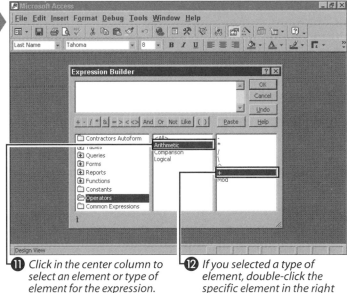

11 Click in the center column to select an element or type of element for the expression.

12 If you selected a type of element, double-click the specific element in the right column to add it.

Understanding Identifiers

The first five folders in the Expression Builder's left scrolling column are all used to select *identifiers,* Access objects that you include in an expression. They can be the name of any field or control in the table, query, form, or report to which you are adding the expression; the name of any control in any object in the database; the name of a table or query; or the name of the property of an object.

As a nonprogrammer, you will use identifiers almost exclusively to refer to fields in the table, query, form, or report that you are adding the expression to, and you can simply use their names. The upper-left figure shows how to add these in the Expression Builder. You can also add identifiers that refer to control properties the current object, as shown in the upper-right figure. Finally, you can add identifiers that refer to controls in other objects and to their properties.

You should learn how identifiers are named so you can read full names when you come across them. When you write it out in full length, an identifier may consist of an object type (such as forms or reports), the name of an object of that type, the name of a control in the object, the name of a property, and the symbol summarized in the following table.

For example, to refer to the OnClick property of the First Name field of the Billing Autoform, you would use the identifier: `Forms![Billing: Autoform]![First Name].OnClick`.

When you use the Expression Builder to create identifiers, it uses the shortest form possible. Most of the identifiers that you generate in the Expression Builder are simply field names enclosed in square brackets.

TAKE NOTE

USING THE SQUARE BRACKETS

The figures show how identifiers use square brackets to enclose object names that are more than one word long. These brackets may be omitted for objects with single-word names. However, it is generally best, as a matter of style, to include them so the object name is obvious when you look at the expression in which this identifier is used. The square brackets are the only symbols that nonprogrammers need to use in most identifiers.

CROSS-REFERENCE

For information on the properties of objects in forms, see Chapter 9.

SHORTCUT

You can add an element to the expression box by double-clicking it, rather than selecting it and clicking Paste.

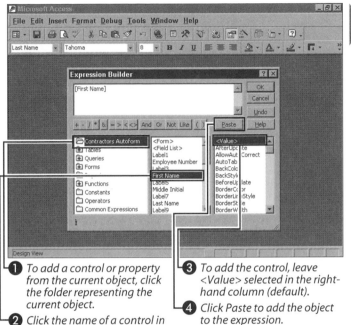

1 To add a control or property from the current object, click the folder representing the current object.

2 Click the name of a control in the center column.

3 To add the control, leave <Value> selected in the right-hand column (default).

4 Click Paste to add the object to the expression.

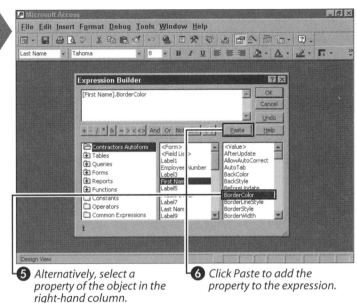

5 Alternatively, select a property of the object in the right-hand column.

6 Click Paste to add the property to the expression.

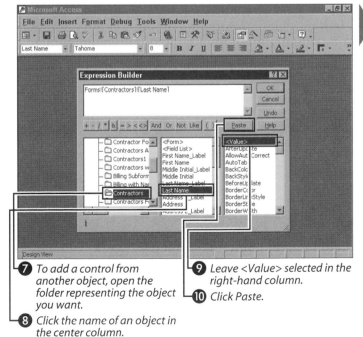

7 To add a control from another object, open the folder representing the object you want.

8 Click the name of an object in the center column.

9 Leave <Value> selected in the right-hand column.

10 Click Paste.

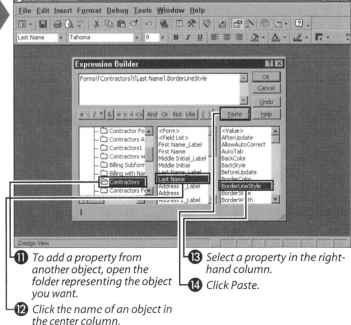

11 To add a property from another object, open the folder representing the object you want.

12 Click the name of an object in the center column.

13 Select a property in the right-hand column.

14 Click Paste.

Understanding Operators

Operators tell expressions what operations to perform on other values. You can use five different types of operators in your expressions: *arithmetic, like, comparison, logical,* and *assignment.*

Arithmetic Operators

Arithmetic operators are used for ordinary mathematical calculations, and they are summarized in the following table.

ARITHMETIC OPERATORS	
Operator	**Meaning**
+	Addition
–	Subtraction (or negation of a single number)
*	Multiplication
/	Division
^	Exponentiation (raising a number to a power)
\	Division with an integer result (decimal places are truncated)
Mod	Modulo division (returns only the remainder)

To display arithmetic operators, in the Expression Builder, click the Operators folder, and click arithmetic in the center column. The operators appear in the right column.

For example, [Date Available] – 30 subtracts 30 days from the value in the Date Available field, but – [Hours Worked] simply returns the value in the Hours Worked field as a negative number.

Arithmetic operators can be used with numbers, dates, or text. Used with numbers, the size of the result is generally the same as size of the most precise operand. For example, if you multiple an integer by a *Double* (the most precise decimal value), the result is a Double.

The only arithmetic operators that can be used with dates are addition and subtraction. You can add or subtract a number of days to a date, or you can subtract one date from another to see how many days are between them.

The only arithmetic operator that can be used with text is the addition operator, which combines, or *concatenates*, two pieces of text (called *strings*, because text is a string of characters) in an expression. Access provides a special operator for this, &, whose sole function is to combine two text strings. Though you can use +, in Access, it is clearer to use & with text.

CROSS-REFERENCE

For information on the sizes of Number fields, see Chapter 13.

SHORTCUT

To use the Like operator, click the Expression Builder's Like button. It is not in the list of operators.

COMPARING QUERY AND EXPRESSION OPERATORS

You may be confused by the difference between operators in queries and in expressions unless you remember that queries use abbreviated expressions. In queries, you leave out the identifier and enter the rest of the expression in a column under a field name. The field name is assumed as the identifier before the rest of the expression. For example, if you enter >=#1/1/94# under the Date Available field in the QBE grid, that is equivalent to using the expression [Date Available] >=#1/1/94#.

Order of Precedence

In arithmetic calculations, multiplication and division are performed before addition and subtraction. However, you can change this default order of precedence by using parentheses, just as you do in ordinary mathematics.

For example, let's say that you give a contractor a $100 bonus for a month. You could use the expression [Hours Worked] * [Hourly Pay] + 100 to calculate the total earned for a month. Because there are no parentheses, this expression uses the default order of precedence. First it multiplies hours worked by hourly pay to get the total earned for that month. Then it adds the $100 bonus to the total.

You could include parentheses and write the expression as ([Hours Worked] * [Hourly Pay]) + 100, but it would make no difference in the result.

On the other hand, let's say that you give an employee a $1 per hour bonus for a month. You would use the expression [Hours Worked] * ([Hourly Pay] + 1) to calculate the total earned. Here, you must use the parentheses to make Access add 1 to the hourly pay before multiplying it by hours worked. This is not the same as the default order of precedence, so the result would be different if you left out the parentheses.

For example, if someone worked 10 hours and earned $50 per hour, then [Hours Worked] * ([Hourly Pay] + 1) would have the result 510 — first add 50 + 1, and then multiply the result by 10. On the other hand, [Hours Worked] * [Hourly Pay] + 1 would have the result 501 — first multiply 50 by 10, and then add 1 to the result.

Even when it makes no difference to the result, it is usually best to include parentheses in complex calculations to make them easier to read.

Like Operator

The Like operator lets you create expressions with literals that use the wildcard characters * (represents any group of characters) and ? (represents any single character).

For example, the expression [Last Name] Like "A*" is true for any record with a value in the Last Name field that begins with A, and [Last Name] Like "Sm?th" is true if the value in the Last Name field is Smith, Smath, Smeth, and so on. Notice that you must include quotation marks around these literals.

Continued

Understanding Operators

Continued

Comparison Operators

Expressions based on comparison operators return a value of true or false. The comparison operators are shown in the upper right figure and summarized in the following table.

COMPARISON OPERATORS	
Operator	**Meaning**
=	Equal to
>	Greater than
>=	Greater than or equal to
<	Less than
<=	Less than or equal to
<>	Not equal to
Between ... And	Within the range indicated

These operators can be used with numbers, text, and dates, but both operands must be the same data type. For example, it makes sense to use the expression `[Date Available] >=#1/1/99#` or the expression `[Last Name] < "M"`, but it obviously does not make sense to use the expression `[Last Name] < #12/1/99#`.

The Between ... And operator lets you find a range of values. For example, the expression `[Date Available] Between #1/1/99# And #12/31/99#` is true for all records with a 1999 date in the Date Available field. The range includes the two values you enter: In the example, it would include 1/1/99 and 12/31/99. Another example would be `[Amount Owed] Between 10000 And 20000` to find all the customers who owe you between $10,000 and $20,000.

Because wildcard characters like * are treated as literals, you cannot use them with the Between ... And operator.

Logical Operators

Logical operators are used to combine two expressions evaluating to true or false into a single expression, except for Not, which only has a single operand. The logical operators are shown on the lower-right figure and summarized in the following table.

LOGICAL OPERATORS	
Operator	**Meaning**
And	Both expressions must be true for the combined expression to be true.
Or	Either expression may be true for the combined expression to be true.
Xor	One of the expressions, but not both, must be true for the combined expression to be true.
Not	The following expression must be false to evaluate as true or true to evaluate as false.
Eqv	Equivalence is a bitwise operation, an advanced feature used in programming.
Imp	Implication is a bitwise operation, an advanced feature used in programming.

CROSS-REFERENCE

For information on entering operators in queries, see Chapter 4.

SHORTCUT

To create complex logical expressions, create a simple expression and then enclose it in parentheses and combine it with other logical expressions.

TAKE NOTE

THE ASSIGNMENT OPERATOR

The = operator assigns a value to a control. For example, if you want a text box to display the last name, you use the expression =[Last Name] as its Control Source Property. Access supplies the assignment operator for you when you are using the Expression Builder. If you use the Expression Builder to select a field name as the control source of a control, Access will supply the = before it when you place the expression. Do not confuse this assignment operator with the = comparison operator. The comparison operator compares two existing values, and the assignment operator gives an object a new value.

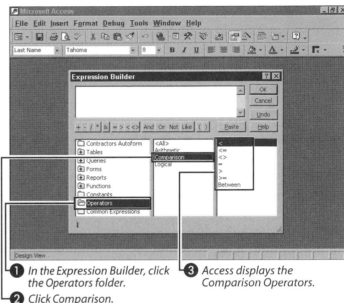

① In the Expression Builder, click the Operators folder.

② Click Comparison.

③ Access displays the Comparison Operators.

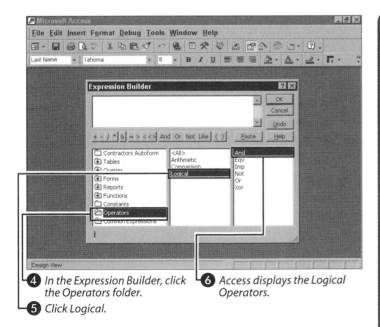

④ In the Expression Builder, click the Operators folder.

⑤ Click Logical.

⑥ Access displays the Logical Operators.

Using Parentheses

When you create complex logical expressions, you can use parentheses for grouping. Suppose that you want to find people in these categories who earn $80 per hour or more. Use:

```
( [Job Category] = "P" Or [Job
Category] = "W" ) And Hourly Pay
>= 80
```

The expression above gives you a different result from:

```
[Job Category] = "P" Or ( [Job
Category] = "W" And Hourly Pay
>= 80 )
```

If someone in Job Category P earned less than $80 per hour, the first expression would evaluate as false, but the second would be true.

Understanding Functions

A *function* is a specialized calculation that is built into Access. Most functions are useful primarily for developers, but intermediate users will find some functions handy. For example, if you want to display the current date and time on a form, you can use the functions `Date()` and `Time()`.

All functions return a value and all include the open and close parentheses after them. In most functions, these parentheses contain arguments that the function acts on. Even if a function does not take an argument, you must include the parentheses after it.

If a function has multiple arguments, they are all included in the parentheses, separated by commas. For example, the function `Left(stringexpr, n)` returns the initial letters of a text string. The first argument is the string expression, and the second argument is the number of letters to return. Thus, the function `Left([Last Name],2)` returns the first two letters of the Last Name in the current record.

Access also enables developers to create user-defined functions, but beginners should always use the Built-In Functions folder under the Functions folder.

Access has a complete set of math functions that perform more advanced mathematical operations than the math operators; for example, `Sqr()` returns the square root of a number. The upper-left figure shows some math functions in the Expression Builder.

Access also includes a complete set of functions used in financial analysis, such as `PV()`, which returns Present Value, as shown in the upper-right figure.

There is also a complete set of functions for working with text, such as `Left()`, which returns the initial characters of a text string, as shown in the lower-left figure.

The SQL aggregate functions, such as `Avg()` are based on Structured Query Language, and they are useful for creating controls that display summary calculations. They are shown in the lower-right figure.

Access also includes equivalents for virtually any other functions you might know from using other database or spreadsheet programs. One useful function is `IIF()`, the Immediate If, which takes three arguments, and returns the second argument if the first evaluates to true, or returns the third argument if the first evaluates to false.

TAKE NOTE

LEARNING MORE ABOUT FUNCTIONS

If you want to become a more advanced user, browse the Expression Builder and the Help system to learn more functions. When you highlight a function, the function and the types of argument it takes appear in the Expression Builder's lower-left corner. For detailed information on any functions, select it in the right-hand column and click the Help button.

CROSS-REFERENCE

For more information on SQL summary functions, see Chapter 6, which describes how to use the Reports Wizard to create grouped reports.

FIND IT ONLINE

For a discussion of possible errors in mathematical calculations done by Access, see http://www.fmsinc.com/tpapers/math/index.html.

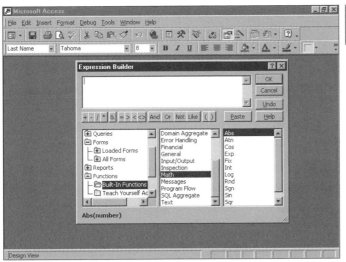

■ Math functions let you calculate absolute value, cosine, logarithm, and many other values.

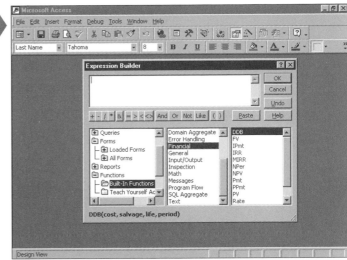

■ Financial functions let you calculate depreciation, present value, internal rate of return, and many other values.

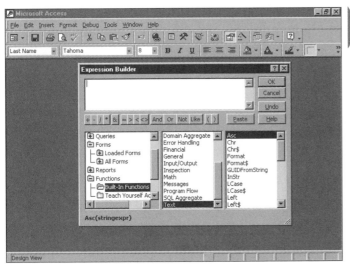

■ Text functions let you change capitalization, isolate certain letters, and manipulate text strings in many other ways.

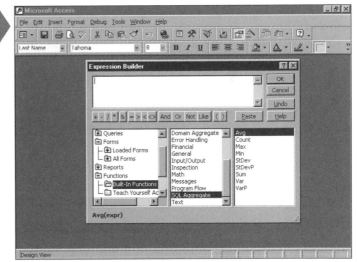

■ SQL Aggregate functions let you calculate the average, sum and other values based on a series of records.

Literals, Constants, and Common Expressions

Literals are parts of the expression used with their literal meaning. For example, in the expression [State] = "NY", State stands for the value in a field, but NY is used literally. In the example [Revenue] < 300000, Revenue stands for the value in the field, but 300000 is used literally. You simply type literals into the Expression Builder text box. As in queries, literals in expressions must have delimiters that depend on the data type:

▶ Text literals must be surrounded by " delimiters; for example, "NY".

▶ Date literals must be surrounded by # delimiters; for example, #1/31/99#.

▶ Number literals need no delimiters, but they must not include separators, such as commas to indicate thousands; for example, 1000.

Access expressions also let you use *constants*, which are like literals, as they do not change depending on the content of the table.

Common Expressions

The Common Expressions folder includes useful expressions, such as the one used to add a page number and the current date and time.

If you open the Common Expressions folder, Expression Builder shows the meaning of commonly used expressions in the center column, as shown in the lower-right figure. If you select one, the expression itself is in the right column, and you can double-click it to add it to your expression. These common expressions are useful in printed reports.

CONSTANTS

Constant	Meaning
""	Matches a text expression with the empty string in it.
Null	Matches any expression with nothing in it.
False	Matches a logical expression that evaluates to false.
True	Matches a logical expression that evaluates to true.

TAKE NOTE

▶ USING THE IS AND IS NOT OPERATORS

The *Is* and *Is Not* operators are used only in comparisons that use the constant Null. For example, the expression [First Name] Is Null would evluate as true for recoreds that have no entry in the First Name field. These operators are not available in the Expression Builder, but you can type them in. For example, if you double-click the field First Name and then the constant Null, Access displays [First Name] <<expr> Null in the text box. You can click <<expr> and type **Is Not** to replace it.

CROSS-REFERENCE

For information on using literals and constants in queries, see Chapter 4.

SHORTCUT

Use Now ( ) to display Date and Time when designing a report. Change it to Date ( ) in the final report.

Common Expressions in the Expression Builder

Sometimes the center column does not make it completely clear what the common expressions are used for.

Page Number uses the expression `"Page " & Page` to specify the specific page of a form or report on which it appears. For example, it might display `Page 2` and the like.

Total Pages uses the expression `Pages` to specify the total number of pages in a form or report.

Page N of M uses the expression `"Page " & Page & " of " & Pages` to specify the specific page of a form or report and the total number of pages in the report. For example, it might display `Page 4 of 12.`

Current Date uses the `Date()` function to display the current date.

Current Date/Time uses the `Now()` function to display the current date and time.

Current User uses the `CurrentUser()` function to display the name of the current user.

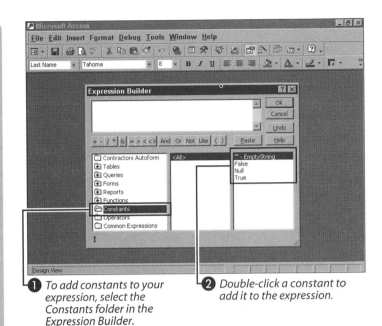

1 To add constants to your expression, select the Constants folder in the Expression Builder.

2 Double-click a constant to add it to the expression.

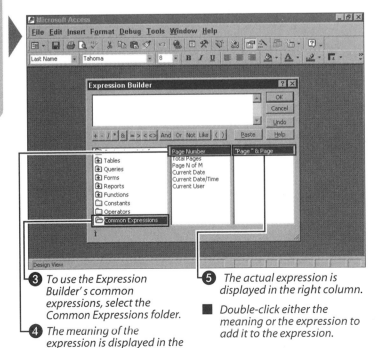

3 To use the Expression Builder's common expressions, select the Common Expressions folder.

4 The meaning of the expression is displayed in the center column.

5 The actual expression is displayed in the right column.

■ Double-click either the meaning or the expression to add it to the expression.

Using Expressions in Table Design

Acommon use of expressions is validation of data. You have learned that fields have Validation Rule and Validation Text properties, which let you test the data that is entered. For example, let's say your table has a Job Category field that allows three entries: *P* for programmer, *W* for writer, or *C* for clerical. You can validate it by entering the Validation Rule **="P" Or ="W" Or ="C"** and the Validation Text **You must enter a P, W, or C in this field**, as shown in the upper-left figure. If the user enters an incorrect value, Access displays an error message, as shown in the upper-right figure, and returns the cursor to the field when the user clicks OK.

The validation rule is an expression that is evaluated whenever data is entered or edited in the field. This expression must evaluate to true or false, and the validation text is displayed if it is false.

When you enter a validation rule, however, you do not use the entire expression. The name of the field that you are validating is assumed as the identifier. In most cases, you would have to use an expression such as `[Job Category] ="P" Or = [Job Category] "W" Or [Job Category] ="C"`. Each logical expression that is combined using `Or` must be able to stand on its own. In a validation rule, where the identifier is assumed, you can use expressions such as `="P" Or ="W" Or ="C"`.

Assigning Default Values

Use the = (assignment) operator to assign a value to a text box or to assign a default value to a field. In some cases, the = can be omitted when you assign a value, but it is best to use it to make clear that you are assigning a value.

For example, let's say that you realize that most of the people you do business with are from the state of New York and you want this to be displayed in the State field. Enter **="NY"** as the field's Default Value property, as shown in the lower-left figure, and this value is automatically included in new records, as shown in the lower-right figure. You can edit this value if a contractor is from another state, and you can save time by using it for contractors from New York.

TAKE NOTE

USING THE IN() FUNCTION

The `In()` function is useful for validating data. Its argument is a list of values, separated by commas, and it is true if the field has any value in the list. Thus, instead of using an expression with `Or`, you could use the Validation Rule `In("P", "W", "C")` in the example on the upper left. This is much easier than using `Or` if there is a long list of valid values.

CROSS-REFERENCE

For more information on table design, see Chapters 2 and 13.

SHORTCUT

If you use the Expression Builder to assign a value, Access supplies the = operator if it is needed.

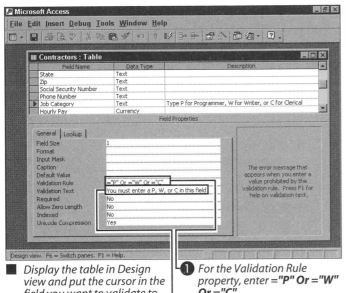

■ *Display the table in Design view and put the cursor in the field you want to validate to display its properties.*

① *For the Validation Rule property, enter ="P" Or ="W" Or ="C".*

② *Enter You must enter a P, W, or C in this field.*

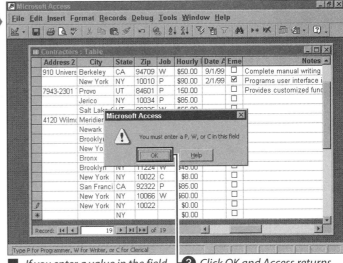

■ *If you enter a value in the field that does not match the validation rule, Access displays an error message.*

③ *Click OK and Access returns the cursor to the field so you can correct the error.*

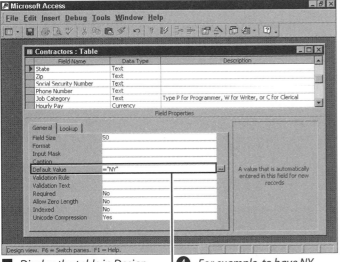

■ *Display the table in Design view and put the cursor in the field you want to validate to display its properties.*

④ *For example, to have NY appear in the State field by default, enter ="NY" as its Default Value property.*

⑤ *Later, when you add data, this value is automatically included in new records.*

Using Expressions in Queries

Expressions are flexible, and therefore are useful for queries. When you are designing a query, you can click the Build button of the toolbar to display the Expression Builder, and use it to enter expressions. This button is enabled only when you are in a cell that can hold an expression.

Using the Date() Function

The `Date()` function, which represents the current date, is invaluable in queries to identify records with time limits that have passed.

For example, if you want to identify contractors who are available, you can use a query with the criterion `<Date()` in the Date Available field. This is much easier than re-entering the current date each time you run the query.

You can also do calculations using the `Date()` function. For example, to find all contractors who are not yet available but will become available in the next 30 days, you can use the criterion `> Date And < Date() + 30`, as shown in the upper-right figure.

Using Expressions for Updates and Summaries

Expressions are also invaluable in update queries, to replace the values in a field with a calculated value. For example, if you want to give all of your employees in job category P a 10 percent raise, you could use the update query with P as the criterion in the Job Category field and `[Hourly Pay] * 1.1` as the Update value in the Hourly Pay field (by multiplying the current value by 1.1, you increase it by 10 percent).

It is also common to use expressions in queries with groups and summaries. You can use it as the basis of a grouping to group on some value that is not the value of a field. For example, if you wanted a report that showed how much you paid your contractors each month, you could use the expression `Month( [Date Billed] )` in the Field cell of a column and select Group By in its Total cell. Rather than having a separate group for each date, you have a group for each month.

To create complex summary calculations that are not available in the Total drop-down list, enter an expression that uses functions, operators, and the field names to specify the calculation in the Field cell. Select Expression in the Total cell.

TAKE NOTE

CREATING QUERIES WITH TWO CRITERIA IN THE SAME FIELD

You learned in Chapter 4 that you can create queries with two criteria in an And relation, by entering the criteria in two cells on the same line. But if the two criteria are based on the same field, you must enter them in one cell using the And operator, as shown in the upper-right figure. You can also use the Or operator in a criterion, rather than entering criteria on multiple lines, as you learned in Chapter 4.

CROSS-REFERENCE
For more information on queries, see Chapters 4 and 11.

SHORTCUT
You can type expressions directly in the query's design grid, rather than using the Expression Builder.

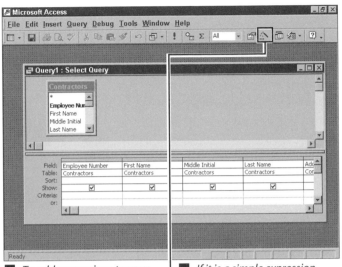

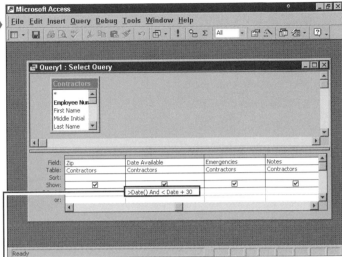

■ To add expressions to your query in Design view, place the cursor in the cell where you want to add the expression.

■ If it is a simple expression, simply type it in the cell.

① Alternatively, if you find it difficult to type the expression you need, click Build to display the Expression Builder.

② Use an expression with the Date() function, so you do not have to re-enter a criterion based on the current date when you rerun the query.

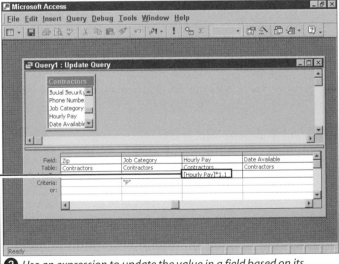

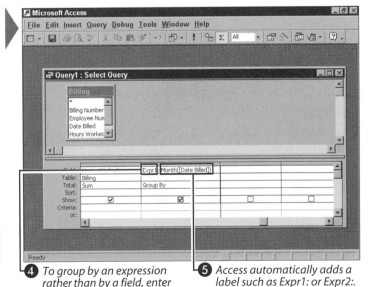

③ Use an expression to update the value in a field based on its current value.

④ To group by an expression rather than by a field, enter the Expression in the Field cell.

⑤ Access automatically adds a label such as Expr1: or Expr2:.

Using Expressions in Forms and Reports

Use expressions to create calculated fields in forms and reports. For example, if you have a form displaying fields for Hourly Pay and Hours Worked, you can display the total by creating a text box with the Expression =[Hourly Pay] * [Hours Worked] as its Control Source Property, as shown in the upper-left figure.

Often, you must format the calculated field to display the results properly; for example, you must format Total Pay as Currency, as shown in the upper-right figure. Although you cannot edit the amount in this calculated field, it changes automatically if you edit one of the fields on which the calculation is based.

Editing Summary Text Boxes

You may also want to include text in calculated fields. For example, if you generate a grouped report using the Report Wizard, it includes an inadequate summary description . You can delete unnecessary descriptions and give the summary field a better description. In the example shown on the lower right, you can edit =Sum([Hours Worked]) so that it reads ="This contractor worked " & Sum([Hours Worked]) & " hours." This is a simple expression. It just concatenates two text strings with the summary function.

Displaying a Name

In a report, you might want to create a single expression that displays the entire name. Displaying the

first and last name is easy. Access automatically trims trailing blanks, so if you used the expression [First Name] & [Last Name], Access would display something like JohnSmith. To create a calculated field that displays the name, you have to use the expression [First Name] & " " & [Last Name], with a blank space literal (a space enclosed by quotation marks) between the two fields to display John Smith.

But it is harder to add a Middle Initial to the name. You might try the expression:
[First Name] & " " & [Middle Initial] & ". " & [Last Name] which uses both a period and a space as the text literal after the middle initial, to display names in the form John Q. Smith. The problem is that some people do not have a middle initial entered in the table, and this expression would also include the extra space and period after the first name for them.

Continued

Continued

TAKE NOTE

USING A LONGER IDENTIFIER

For the expression that displays the full name to work, you have to include the Middle Initial field in the report when you define it. If you do not, you must use a longer identifier in the expression, such as [Contractors]![Middle Initial].

CROSS-REFERENCE
For more information on adding text boxes to forms, see Chapter 9.

SHORTCUT
If you use the Expression Builder to generate the expression used as Control Source property, Access automatically adds the = (assignment) operator.

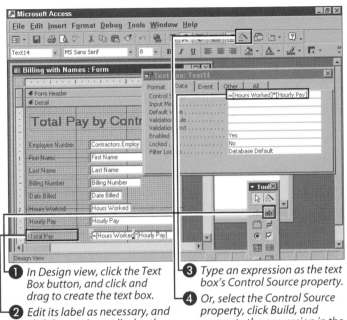

1 In Design view, click the Text Box button, and click and drag to create the text box.

2 Edit its label as necessary, and click Properties to display the property sheet if necessary.

3 Type an expression as the text box's Control Source property.

4 Or, select the Control Source property, click Build, and generate the expression in the Expression Builder.

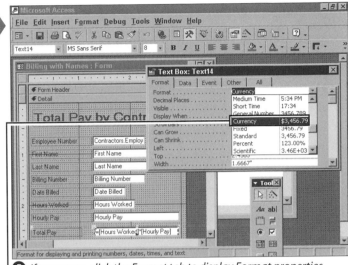

5 If necessary, click the Format tab to display Format properties and choose a format for the calculated field.

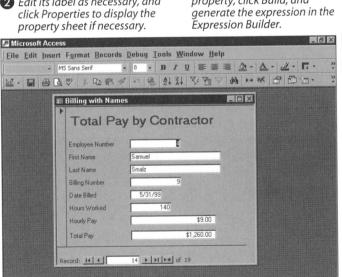

■ Display the form in Form view to see the result of the calculation.

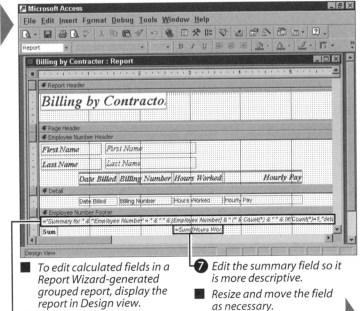

■ To edit calculated fields in a Report Wizard-generated grouped report, display the report in Design view.

6 Delete unnecessary descriptions in the summary field.

7 Edit the summary field so it is more descriptive.

■ Resize and move the field as necessary.

Using the IIf() Function to Display a Name

To display the name with the middle initial, you need an expression that uses the `IIf()` function to display nothing if there is no entry in the Middle Initial field:

```
IIf( [Middle Initial] Is Null, "" ,
[Middle Initial] & ". " )
```

If the first argument is true, `IIf()` returns the second argument, and if the first argument is false, it returns the third. That is, if the Middle Initial field is blank, it returns an empty string, and if the Middle Initial field has an entry, it returns this entry followed by a period and a space. To display the entire name, you must concatenate this `IIf()` function with the First Name and Last Name fields, as shown in the upper-left figure, in the expression:

```
[First Name] & " " & IIf( [Middle
Initial] Is Null, "", [Middle
Initial] & ". " ) & [Last Name]
```

There is always a space following the first name, included as a literal right after the First Name field. If the Middle Initial field is blank, the last name comes right after this space. If the Middle Initial is not blank, it displays followed by a period and another space.

Using Now() Properties to Display Date and Time

The `Now()` function returns the current date and time and is a useful expression to help keep track of multiple drafts of a report. When you generate a

report using the Report Wizard, the Print Preview has the date in the report title band, which it creates by using the expression `=Now()`. Though this function returns both the current date and time, it is formatted to display only the date, as shown in the upper-right figure.

Including both the date and time in a report is useful, because you may print many sample copies as you work on the report design. To do this, change its format temporarily, and change it back when you have finished the report. Display the report in Design view again. Select the text box containing the expression `=Now()`. If necessary, click the Property Sheet button, and display the Format tab. The first property on this tab is Format, and it is currently Long Date. Display this cell's drop-down list, scroll up this list, and select General Date. When you display the report in Print Preview, it displays the date and time. When you are finished designing the report, change the format of Now() back to Long Date, so it displays just the date again.

TAKE NOTE

▶ **OTHER USEFUL EXPRESSIONS**

It is often useful to include both the date and the time in a report, because you may print many sample copies while working on the report design. To do this, follow the steps on the facing page. When you are ready to print the final report, change the format to `New()` back to Long Date, so just the date displays again.

CROSS-REFERENCE

For more information on displaying page number or current user, see the section on literals, constants, and common expressions, earlier in this Chapter.

SHORTCUT

You can use the `Date()` function to display the current date, rather than changing the properties of `Now()`.

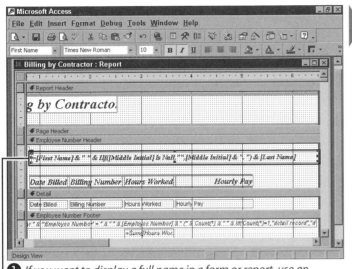

1 If you want to display a full name in a form or report, use an expression instead of separate name fields.

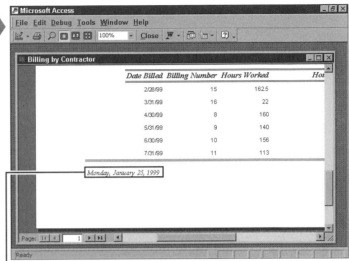

2 A report generated by the Report Wizard includes the current date in the footer.

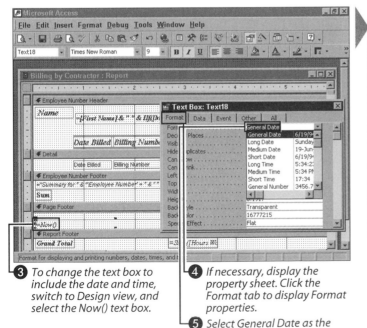

3 To change the text box to include the date and time, switch to Design view, and select the Now() text box.

4 If necessary, display the property sheet. Click the Format tab to display Format properties.

5 Select General Date as the Format.

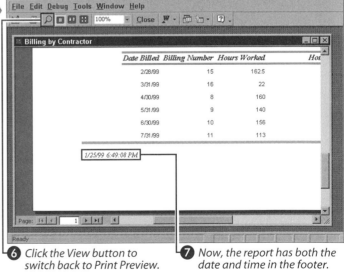

6 Click the View button to switch back to Print Preview.

7 Now, the report has both the date and time in the footer.

Personal Workbook

Q&A

1 What is a *literal*, and how do you enter one in the Expression Builder?

_____

_____

_____

2 What is *string concatenation*, and what are two operators that perform it?

_____

_____

_____

3 What are two functions you can use to display the current date?

_____

_____

_____

4 What is the result of the expression #1/1/00# − #1/1/99#?

_____

_____

_____

5 How do you validate data entered in a field?

_____

_____

_____

6 How do you create a default value for a field?

_____

_____

_____

7 How do you create a query that only displays records whose Date field is either today or some future date?

_____

_____

_____

8 How do you add page numbers to a report?

_____

_____

_____

ANSWERS: PAGE 355

EXTRA PRACTICE

1. Use an expression to create a validation rule for one of the fields of the sample table you have been working with.

2. Use an expression to create a default value for one of the fields of the sample table you have been working with.

3. Use the Form Wizard to generate a form that includes a numeric field. Display the form in Design view, and add a calculated field that displays a mathematical calculation based on the numeric field.

4. Create a grouped report with summaries using the Report Wizard. Display it in Design view, and edit fields to add text that explains the summary functions. Include text both before and after the summary function that the wizard generates.

REAL-WORLD APPLICATIONS

✔ You want to do a mailing once a week to send a birthday card to each of your customers who has a birthday that week. You create a query with the expression `Between Date() And Date() + 6` as the criterion in the Birthday field.

✔ You want to give a bonus equal to nine hours of pay to all your employees who have worked for you for more than a year. You create a query with a criterion in the Date Hired field to identify employees who were hired more than a year ago, and with a calculated field that displays the amount of the bonus.

✔ You are creating a report that shows your company's total sales in each state to show to investors. You begin by using the Wizard to generate the summary report, and to improve the report's appearance, you edit some of the expressions that the Wizard creates.

Visual Quiz

The expression in the figure includes the most common error that users make when they are concatenating text strings. What is the error, and how can you change the expression to correct it?

_____

_____

_____

_____

_____

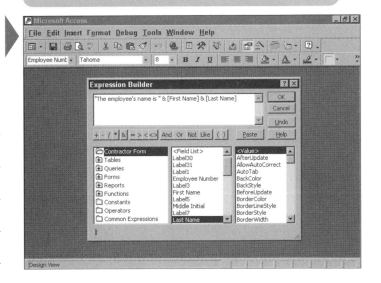

CHAPTER **15**

MASTER
THESE
SKILLS

▶ **Working with Data Access Pages**

▶ **Creating and Using Data Access Pages**

▶ **Creating a Data Access Page in Design View**

▶ **Using Hyperlink Fields**

▶ **Adding Hyperlinks to a Form or Report**

Working with Web Pages

One of the most important new features of Access 2000 is the data access page, a new Access object that is displayed in the Database window like tables, queries, forms, and reports. Data access pages can be used like forms to enter or edit data, but they are HTML (Hypertext Markup Language) documents that either can be used directly in Access, or posted on the World Wide Web and used by anyone with a compatible Web browser (even if they do not have Access).

Web browsers are programs that read HTML and display the text in the proper format. When HTML was first invented, it was a simple set of tags you could add to text to do simple formatting. Recently, the HTML standard has expanded dramatically. The two most popular browsers, Netscape Navigator and Microsoft Internet Explorer, have competed by adding new extensions to the HTML language. As a result, Web pages designed for the latest version of one of these browsers often cannot be read by the latest version of the other.

Currently, you need to have at least Microsoft Internet Explorer 5.0 in order to view data access pages without Access. Within a year or two, most browsers will support the extensions of HTML that data access pages use, but today, the vast majority of users cannot use their Web browsers to work with data access pages.

So for now, you can use data access pages internally if your business has settled on Internet Explorer 5.0 as its browser. In a year or two, you should be able to put pages on the World Wide Web for others to use.

Another way in which Access lets you work with the World Wide Web is by including links (called *Hyperlink fields*) to Web pages in your tables, queries, forms or reports. When you click a hyperlink in one of these Access objects, it displays the Web page that you linked to it. You learned how to include Hyperlink fields in Access tables in Chapters 2, 3, and 9. Hyperlink fields are covered in detail in this chapter.

Working with Data Access Pages

If you have Internet Explorer 5.0 or later installed on your computer, you can work with data access pages within Access as you do with other objects. Click the Pages button of the Database window (see upper-left figure) to display the Data Access Pages tab, and then:

► Select a page in the list and click Open to display it with data.

► Select a page and click Design to display it in Design view.

► Click New to display the New Page dialog box, shown in the upper-right figure, which gives you several options for creating new pages.

You can also create an AutoPage as you create an AutoForm or AutoReport: Select a table or query, and choose Insert ⇨ AutoPage or choose AutoPage from the New Object drop-down list, or choose Columnar AutoPage in the New Data Access Page dialog box. Like AutoForms, AutoPages simply display fields in columnar form.

Unlike other Access objects, data access pages are not part of the Database file. They must be stored in a separate file, with the extension HTM or HTML, so you can put them on the World Wide Web, and people can read them using their Web browsers.

Because they are separate HTML files, data access pages are saved and deleted differently than other Access objects.

When you save a page, rather than just entering a name as you do with other objects, you enter the name and specify the folder, using the Save As Data Access Page dialog box (see the lower-left figure). This dialog box works like the dialog box you use to save a New Database File and new files in other Microsoft Office applications.

When you delete a data access page, Access displays a dialog box asking if you want to delete the page from its current location. You have the option of choosing Yes to delete the link and the page or No to delete just the link. Because the data access page is in a separate HTML file, the Database window just includes a link to that file, and you can delete this link without deleting the page itself.

TAKE NOTE

BASING A PAGE ON AN HTML FILE

Because they are based on HTML files, Access also gives you the option of creating data access pages based on existing Web pages. One of the options in the New Data Access Page dialog box is Existing Web Page, and you can also double-click Edit Web Page that already exists in the Database Window to base a data access page on a Web page. Access displays the Locate Web Page dialog box, which works just like the Open dialog box and lets you find and open a Web page. It includes this Web page in the list of data access pages in the Database window, enabling you to open any Web page as an Access object.

FIND IT ONLINE
To download Internet Explorer 5.0, go to http://www.microsoft.com/msdownload/.

SHORTCUT
To create a new page, double-click Create data access page in Design view or Create data access page by using Wizard.

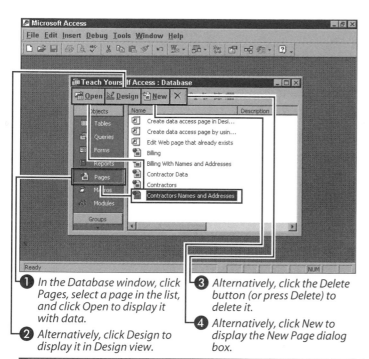

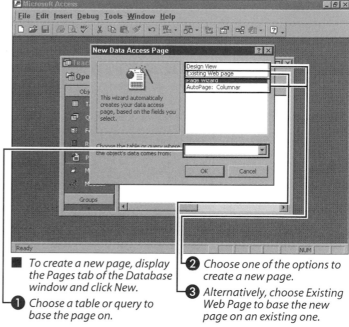

① In the Database window, click Pages, select a page in the list, and click Open to display it with data.

② Alternatively, click Design to display it in Design view.

③ Alternatively, click the Delete button (or press Delete) to delete it.

④ Alternatively, click New to display the New Page dialog box.

■ To create a new page, display the Pages tab of the Database window and click New.

① Choose a table or query to base the page on.

② Choose one of the options to create a new page.

③ Alternatively, choose Existing Web Page to base the new page on an existing one.

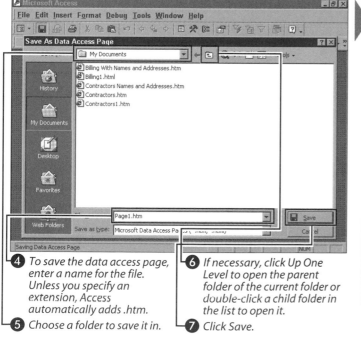

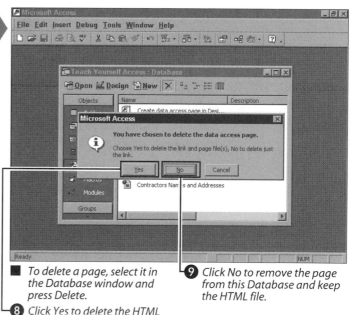

④ To save the data access page, enter a name for the file. Unless you specify an extension, Access automatically adds .htm.

⑤ Choose a folder to save it in.

⑥ If necessary, click Up One Level to open the parent folder of the current folder or double-click a child folder in the list to open it.

⑦ Click Save.

■ To delete a page, select it in the Database window and press Delete.

⑧ Click Yes to delete the HTML file completely.

⑨ Click No to remove the page from this Database and keep the HTML file.

Creating and Using Data Access Pages

A typical data access page looks like an Access form, except that it has a navigation bar at the bottom, so people who do not have Access can work with the table on the Web as an HTML document (see upper-left figure).

You enter, edit, and display data as you do in a form. From left to right, the buttons on this navigation bar let you do the following (just as with a table or form):

- ▶ Go to the first record
- ▶ Go to the previous record
- ▶ Go to the next record
- ▶ Go to the last record
- ▶ Add a new record
- ▶ Delete the current record
- ▶ Save the change
- ▶ Undo the change
- ▶ Sort Ascending
- ▶ Sort Descending
- ▶ Filter by selection
- ▶ Apply/Remove Filter

Using the Page Wizard

The Page Wizard lets you convert an Access table or query into a data access page. The Page Wizard combines elements of other Wizards that you learned about in earlier chapters.

The first step lets you choose the table or query and the fields that the page will include. It works like the field picker in the Table Wizard, which is described in Chapter 2. If you are working with a relational database, you can add fields from multiple tables, as described in Chapter 7.

The second step lets you choose fields to group on. It works like the step of the Report Wizard that you use to create grouped reports, which is covered in Chapter 6. As you learned in that chapter, the Grouping Options button lets you group on a range of values.

The next step, shown on the lower right, lets you choose the sort order. It is exactly like the step that lets you choose the sort order in the Report Wizard.

The next step is similar to the final step of other Wizards. It lets you name the page, and choose to display it with data or display it in Design view, so you can modify its design. It also includes a checkbox that you can select to apply a theme to the page: Themes are covered in the next section.

TAKE NOTE

USING SAVE AS TO CREATE A PAGE

The easiest way to convert a table, query, or form to a data access page is to select it in the Database window and then choose File ➪ Save As. In the Save As dialog box, choose Data Access Page and click OK. Access displays the New Data Access Page dialog box, so you can choose the folder for the HTML file.

CROSS-REFERENCE

The buttons on the page's navigation bar are like those used in forms, covered in Chapter 3, with the exception of filters, covered in Chapter 5.

SHORTCUT

The fastest way to use the Page Wizard is to double-click Create data access page using wizard in the Database window.

■ A simple data access page.

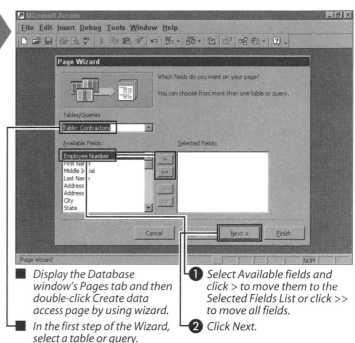

■ Display the Database window's Pages tab and then double-click Create data access page by using wizard.

■ In the first step of the Wizard, select a table or query.

1 Select Available fields and click > to move them to the Selected Fields List or click >> to move all fields.

2 Click Next.

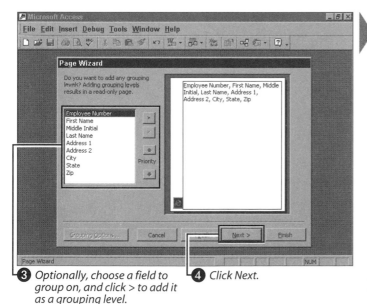

3 Optionally, choose a field to group on, and click > to add it as a grouping level.

■ Optionally, add more grouping levels in the same way.

4 Click Next.

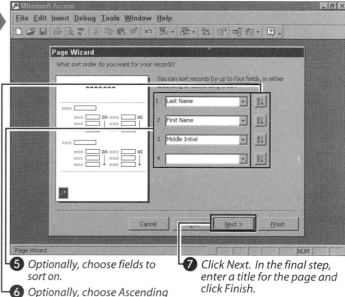

5 Optionally, choose fields to sort on.

6 Optionally, choose Ascending or Descending Sort.

7 Click Next. In the final step, enter a title for the page and click Finish.

Creating a Data Access Page in Design View

It is generally best to begin creating a page using the Wizard and then customize it in Design view, if necessary. However, you can also create a page from scratch in Design view, which will help you understand how pages work.

In Design view, you work with objects in data access pages much as you do when you work with forms.

When you create a new page in Design view, Access displays the prototype page, shown in the upper-left figure, which contains heading text, body text, and an Unbound Section to hold records (this section is called Unbound because it is not yet tied to a table). When you click the heading or body text, it is replaced by a cursor and you can type in a heading for the page or explanatory text that appears under the heading, or press Delete to get rid of it.

To display the data of a table or query in the Unbound Section, you must first assign the Section a table or query as its Record Source Property; Access adds a navigation bar at the bottom of the Section that lets you move through the table or query's records.

Then you must use the field list to assign fields to the section. As you can see in the upper-right figure, the field list for pages lets you choose fields from any table or query in the database. Like forms and reports, pages are always based on an existing Access table or query. Click the + sign next to the folders to display a list of all tables or queries, and click the + sign next to a table or query name to display a list of all its fields. Select the name of a table or query or of a field, and click Add to Page to include it in the Section. Access displays a dialog box asking if you want to include a table or query in Banded (columnar) or Grid (datasheet) form.

Access adds the fields and labels to the Section, which you can manipulate much as you do in a form. Click a label or field to select it, and then click and drag its edge to move it, or click and drag one of its resize boxes to resize it. After selecting a label, you can click it again to place an insertion point in it and edit the text.

TAKE NOTE

USING THEMES

The easiest way to design the style of a page is by using themes. While the page is displayed in Design view, choose Format ⇨ Theme to display the Theme dialog box, shown on the lower right. Click one of the styles in the list on the left to see it on the right. Each style has its own way of displaying headings, bullets, text, hyperlinks, command buttons, field labels and text boxes, and its own background, which may include graphics.

CROSS-REFERENCE

For information on working on forms in Design view, see Chapters 8 and 9.

SHORTCUT

Click the Set Default button of the Themes dialog box to use a style automatically in all new pages.

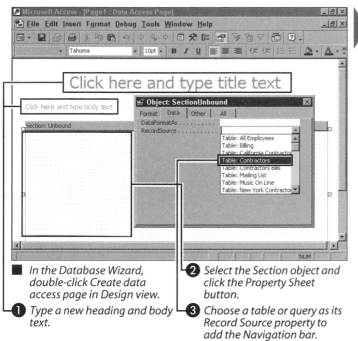

In the Database Wizard, double-click Create data access page in Design view.

➊ Type a new heading and body text.

➋ Select the Section object and click the Property Sheet button.

➌ Choose a table or query as its Record Source property to add the Navigation bar.

➍ If necessary, click the Field List button to display the field list.

➎ Select a table, query, or their fields, or another page.

➏ Click Add to Page to add the fields to this page.

■ Access displays a dialog box that lets you add them in a column or grid.

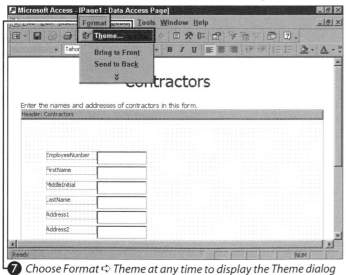

➐ Choose Format ➪ Theme at any time to display the Theme dialog box.

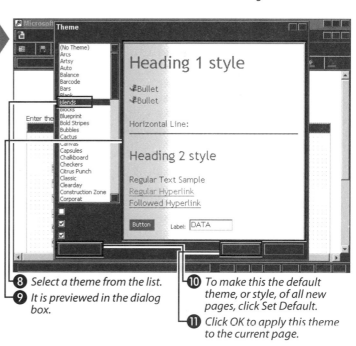

➑ Select a theme from the list.

➒ It is previewed in the dialog box.

➓ To make this the default theme, or style, of all new pages, click Set Default.

⑪ Click OK to apply this theme to the current page.

Using Hyperlink Fields

Use a Hyperlink field to include links to Web pages or to other documents in an Access table. To display the Web page or document, simply click this field in the table, or in a query, form, or report based on the table.

You create a Hyperlink field in the same way that you create a field of any other data type. With the Table window in Design view, enter its name in the Field Name column and use the drop-down list to select Hyperlink in the Data Type column.

To enter a hyperlink when you enter data in the table, simply type the address of an object, document, or Web page in the Hyperlink field.

For example, the upper-right figure shows the design of a table with a Hyperlink field to hold the names and addresses of search engines. The lower-left figure shows the table in Datasheet view: You can click the address of a search engine to go to the Web site of that search engine.

You can use Hyperlink fields to link to other documents besides Web pages. For example, if you create a table to keep track of Microsoft Word documents that you have written, you can include a Hyperlink field which you can click to display each Word document. You can enter several types of addresses in Hyperlink fields.

The entries in this field are displayed in blue and are underlined, like hyperlinks on the Web or in Windows help systems. When the pointer is placed on one of these fields, it is displayed as a hand with the index finger extended, as it usually is on hyperlinks, to indicate that you can click the field to jump to the address.

Editing Hyperlink Fields

Because the pointer becomes a finger on a Hyperlink field, you cannot click it to place an insertion point in it when you want to edit it. Instead, you should Tab to the field and press F2 to place an insertion point in. When you do this, a # sign is added at either side of the address, to indicate that it can be edited: While the # sign is there, the pointer is displayed as an insertion bar, and you can use the mouse and keyboard to edit the field entry in the usual ways. When you move the cursor to another field, the # sign is automatically removed.

Continued

TAKE NOTE

DISPLAYING AND HIDING THE WEB TOOLBAR

When you click a Hyperlink field, Access automatically adds the Web Toolbar, which you can see below the usual toolbars in the lower-left figure. To add or remove this toolbar at any time, right-click the Toolbar to display its Pop-up menu, and choose Web.

CROSS-REFERENCE

For more information on designing a table, see Chapter 2.

SHORTCUT

You can omit *http://* from the beginning of addresses that you enter in Hyperlink fields.

Entering Data in Hyperlink Fields

▶ **Internet addresses.** Type the URL (Uniform Resource Locator) of the Web page you want to display. For example, http://www.microsoft.com/pagename.html.

▶ **Files on your network.** Enter the UNC (Universal Naming Convention). For example, //servername/pathname/filename.doc

▶ **Files on your computer.** Enter the full path name of the file. For example, C:\My Documents\filename.doc

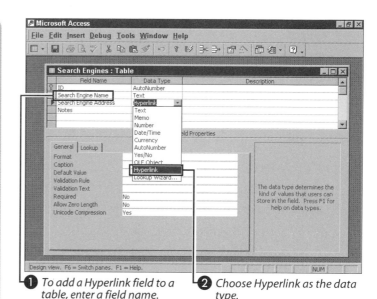

1 To add a Hyperlink field to a table, enter a field name.

2 Choose Hyperlink as the data type.

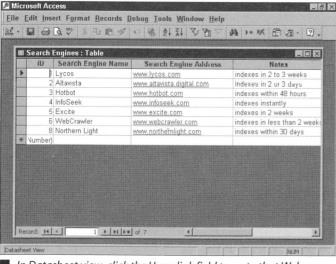

■ In Datasheet view, click the Hyperlink field to go to that Web page or document.

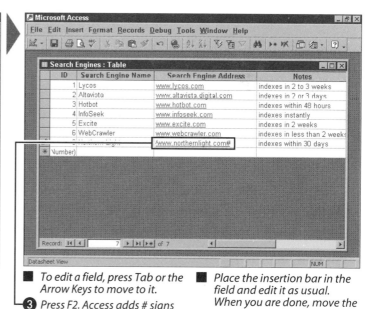

■ To edit a field, press Tab or the Arrow Keys to move to it.

3 Press F2. Access adds # signs to show you can edit the field.

■ Place the insertion bar in the field and edit it as usual. When you are done, move the cursor to another field.

Using Hyperlink Fields
Continued

Properties of Hyperlink Fields

Hyperlink fields do not have any special properties of their own, but they do have the following common properties, shared by many data types:

▶ **Caption** Used as the heading of that field's column in Datasheet View.

▶ **Default Value** Displayed as the default value when you enter new data. This is not normally useful for Hyperlink fields.

▶ **Validation Rule and Validation Text** Lets you test data. The validation rule is a logical expression. When data is entered, if it evaluates as False, Access displays an error message with the validation text. For example, for a table of Web sites of nonprofit organizations, you could allow only entries that end with .org.

▶ **Required** Lets you require data entry in a field.

▶ **Allow Zero Length** Lets you enter a zero-length string in the field, to specify that there is not a value for the field. You could use this to specify that some records do not have a Web site, while blank fields mean that you have not yet found the Web site.

Using the Web Toolbar

When you use a Hyperlink field, Access displays the Web toolbar, shown in the upper-right figure. Its buttons are similar to those found on most Web browsers.

The most frequently used buttons when you are navigating the Web are Back, to go back one page; Forward, to return to the page displayed before you clicked back; Start, to go back to your start/first page; and Stop, to stop a download that is taking too long.

Other useful buttons are the Favorite button, which displays a list of Web pages where you have added "bookmarks" to let you return to them instantly, and the Address area, which displays the address of the current Web page. Finally, use the Search button, which displays the Microsoft Network Search page, to search for specific information on the Web.

You can choose which buttons are displayed by clicking the arrow to the right of the toolbar and clicking Add or Remove buttons to display a drop-down list of buttons, as shown in the upper-right figure. Just click a button to remove or add a button. Click Reset Toolbar to go back to the original settings.

TAKE NOTE

▶ **INSERTING A HYPERLINK COLUMN**

The fastest way of adding a Hyperlink field to an existing table is to choose Insert ➪ Hyperlink Column when the table is displayed in Datasheet View. Access adds a new field with the Hyperlink data type and gives it a name such as Field1. Then you can rename the field by double-clicking the column's heading to display it as editable text, and typing a new name.

CROSS-REFERENCE

For more information on all these properties, see Chapter 13.

FIND IT ONLINE

For technical information on adding links to html files, see http://www.unibo.it/stse/serinf/bldapps/chapters/ba18_7.htm.

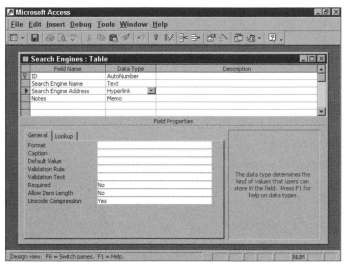

■ *The general properties of a Hyperlink field.*

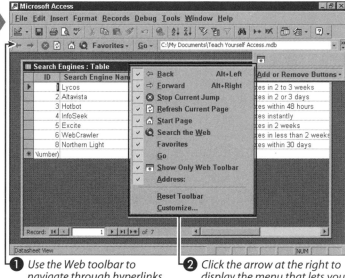

❶ *Use the Web toolbar to navigate through hyperlinks that you have displayed.*

❷ *Click the arrow at the right to display the menu that lets you customize the Web toolbar.*

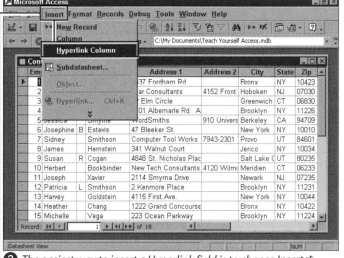

❸ *The easiest way to insert a Hyperlink field is to choose Insert ➪ Hyperlink Column in Datasheet View.*

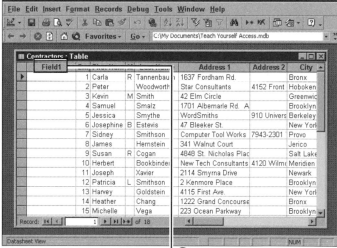

■ *Access adds a Hyperlink field.*

❹ *Double-click the column title to edit its name.*

Adding Hyperlinks to a Form or Report

You may want to add two types of hyperlinks to an Access form or report. A *bound* hyperlink changes when the record changes. For example, if you create a form to display information on different universities, you would want each form to include a link to that university's World Wide Web home page. An *unbound* hyperlink remains the same as records change. For example, you might want all the forms with information on universities to include a link to a Web page that has general information on all the universities in the country.

Adding a Bound Hyperlink

To include a bound hyperlink in a form or report, simply add a Hyperlink field to the table it is based on, as described in the previous section, and include this Hyperlink field in the form or report. Access adds a textbox that you can click to jump to the hyperlink address for the current record.

Adding an Unbound Hyperlink

To add an unbound hyperlink to a document, choose Insert ⇨ Hyperlink, click the Insert Hyperlink button, or press Ctrl+K. (Notice that this button is part of the toolbar, not the toolbox.) Access displays the Insert Hyperlink dialog box. In the Insert Hyperlink

dialog box, you must enter the text of the Hyperlink, which will be displayed in the document, and the address to go to when the user clicks the hyperlink. You can also click the Screen Tip button and enter text that Access displays as help when you move the pointer over the link.

Rather than typing the address, you can click the buttons to the left of the list to display recently opened files, browsed pages, or inserted links, and choose one of them to enter it in the address box. Or click the buttons on the right to browse all files, Web pages, or bookmarks in Office documents. Or, you can add a link to an object in the current database or an e-mail address. You can also click the Create New Document button to display a panel that lets you create a new document to link to.

TAKE NOTE

ADDING HYPERLINKS TO PICTURES OR BUTTONS

If you use Insert ⇨ Hyperlink, Access adds text that users click to access the hyperlink. You may also want to add a picture or command button that takes users to a hyperlink. To do this, first add the picture or command button as usual. Then display its property sheet, and enter an address as the Hyperlink Address property in the Format tab. You can also click Build to add the address with the Insert Hyperlink dialog box.

CROSS-REFERENCE

For more information on adding pictures and command buttons, and on property sheets, see Chapter 9.

SHORTCUT

You can insert a hyperlink quickly by copying its address, returning to the Access object, and choosing Edit ⇨ Paste as Hyperlink.

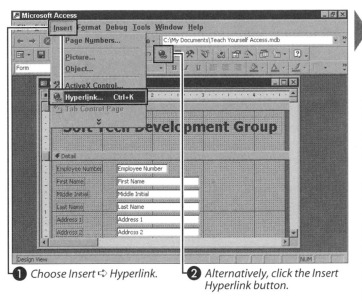

❶ *Choose Insert ➪ Hyperlink.*

❷ *Alternatively, click the Insert Hyperlink button.*

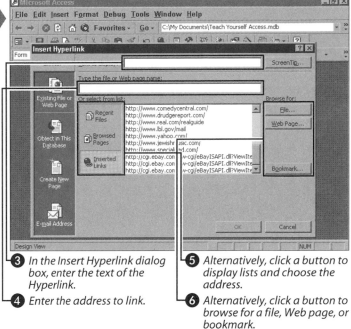

❸ *In the Insert Hyperlink dialog box, enter the text of the Hyperlink.*

❹ *Enter the address to link.*

❺ *Alternatively, click a button to display lists and choose the address.*

❻ *Alternatively, click a button to browse for a file, Web page, or bookmark.*

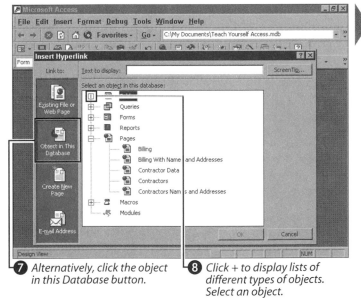

❼ *Alternatively, click the object in this Database button.*

❽ *Click + to display lists of different types of objects. Select an object.*

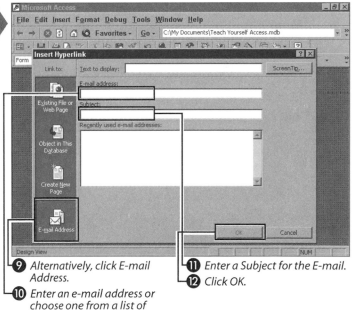

❾ *Alternatively, click E-mail Address.*

❿ *Enter an e-mail address or choose one from a list of addresses.*

⓫ *Enter a Subject for the E-mail.*

⓬ *Click OK.*

Personal Workbook

Q&A

1 What is the fastest way to convert a table, query, or form into a data access page?

_____

_____

_____

2 What extensions can be used in the filenames of data access pages, and what do they stand for?

_____

_____

_____

3 What is the easiest way to give all your data access pages a distinctive style?

_____

_____

_____

4 How do you edit a Hyperlink field? Why can't you edit it like other fields?

_____

_____

_____

5 What is the fastest way to add a Hyperlink field to an existing table?

_____

_____

_____

6 What are the two types of hyperlinks that you can add to a form or report?

_____

_____

_____

7 How do you add a hyperlink to a picture or command button?

_____

_____

8 You have closed a table that has a Hyperlink field, but the Web toolbar is still displayed. How do you get rid of it?

_____

_____

_____

ANSWERS: PAGE 356

EXTRA PRACTICE

1. Open a form in Design view and add an unbound hyperlink to it, pointing to your favorite Web site.

2. Use the Page Wizard to convert this form to a data access page. Display the data access page in Design view. Customize it by resizing the text boxes to make them the right size to hold the data.

3. Open the same form and use Save As to convert it to a data access page.

4. Create a table with Hyperlink fields pointing to some of your favorite Web sites and a description of each.

5. Display this table in Datasheet view and edit one of the entries in the Hyperlink field.

6. Use the Wizard to convert this table to a data access page.

REAL-WORLD APPLICATIONS

✔ You want everyone in your company to be able to look up customers in your database. Rather than buying copies of Access 2000 for everyone, you create data access pages, which they can view using free copies of Microsoft Internet Explorer 5.0.

✔ You are a realtor and you create a Web page for each house you have listed. You create a table with basic information on the houses and a hyperlink to Web pages that provide a virtual tour of each house, which you show to customers when they come to your office. Access lets you display only houses in the location and price range a customer is interested in, and jump directly to their Web pages.

✔ You include an unbound hyperlink to your company's home page in the header of all your data-entry forms.

Visual Quiz

The form in the figure includes an unbound hyperlink in its header. How do you add this hyperlink?

_____

_____

_____

_____

_____

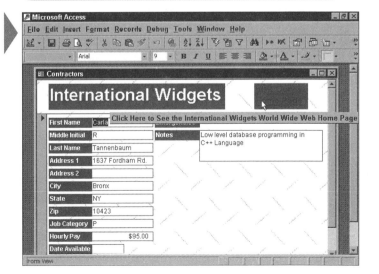

CHAPTER **16**

MASTER
THESE
SKILLS

▶ **Using OLE Objects in Tables and Queries**

▶ **Adding OLE Objects to Forms and Reports**

▶ **Formatting OLE Objects in Forms and Reports**

Working with OLE Objects

Object Linking and Embedding (OLE) is a feature of many Windows applications that allows objects from one application to be used in another. The most common use of OLE objects in databases is to hold pictures. For example, you can scan photographs of your employees and include a picture in an OLE field in each employee's record.

Or you could use a spreadsheet application to record the hours that each of your employees worked, and you could include either an entire spreadsheet file or certain cells from the spreadsheet in each record as an OLE object. You could also use the spreadsheet application to graph the hours worked, and then you could create a form that displays the graph of the hours each contractor worked whenever it displays that contractor's name and address.

In any case, you must have another Windows application that supports OLE to create the picture, graph, or other OLE object before you can use it in Access.

As the name implies, OLE objects can be included in Access in two ways:

▶ **Linking.** If the object is linked, it retains its connection with the application where it was created. Access displays the object, but it is still stored in its original file. Any changes made to it in the original application will also be incorporated in Access. You can also double-click the object in Access to open the application and change the OLE object.

▶ **Embedding.** If the object is embedded, a copy of the original object is made and actually stored in your database. If you use the application where it was created and change the object, the changes are not reflected in the embedded OLE object. You must double-click the OLE object in Access to open the application and change the OLE object.

It is generally best to use embedded objects, because they are portable. Because linked objects are stored in separate files, they are not included if you copy a database to a floppy disk and give it to someone else. Embedded objects are included with the database. Of course, this also means that they require more disk space.

Using OLE Objects in Tables and Queries

Y ou create an OLE Object field like any other field: Enter the field name and then select OLE Object as the data type. OLE Objects have only two properties: Caption and Required. If you do not enter a column heading in Caption, the field name is used. You may also choose Yes for Required to require data entry in the field.

Adding Objects to an OLE Field

Access does a great job storing data, but you would not do your budget or write a memo with it. Sometimes it is better to add data from other programs to Access.

For example, if you use a large number of Excel spreadsheets to analyze your business operations, you could create a table to store information on these spreadsheets, such as who prepared them, when they were prepared, and which department they analyze. The table could also have an OLE Object field, where you store the spreadsheets themselves (or documents or images from another application).

In a simpler example, if you manage many employees, you could use an OLE Object field to store pictures of your employees, along with other data about them. If you ran a query or searched for an employee's record, you could easily associate the name with the face.

After you have created an OLE Object field, you can add objects to it in several ways. The most common is to select an OLE Object field where you want

the object to be embedded, and choose Insert ⇨ Object. Doing this displays the Insert Object dialog box, which lets you create a new object or insert one you have already created and stored in a file. The options in the Object Type list depend on the applications you have available that support OLE.

By default, the object is embedded, but you can select the Link checkbox of this dialog box to link it instead.

When you are entering data in a table or query, the OLE Object field displays text instead of the actual object. For example, the field might have the words "Bitmap Image" or "Excel Chart" in it, to let you know what kind of object it contains. You can double-click this text to display the object in the source application.

Continued

TAKE NOTE

► USING DRAG AND DROP

If you are working with Access and another Microsoft Office application, you can embed an existing object in Access by using drag and drop. Size the two application windows so you can see them both. Select the data you want in the source application. Hold down the Ctrl button and click and drag the selected data from the source application to the OLE Object field in Access. Release the mouse button to place it in the field.

CROSS-REFERENCE
For more information on creating a field, see Chapter 2.

SHORTCUT
Rather than using the drop-down list to choose the data type of a new field, simply type **O** to make it an OLE Object field.

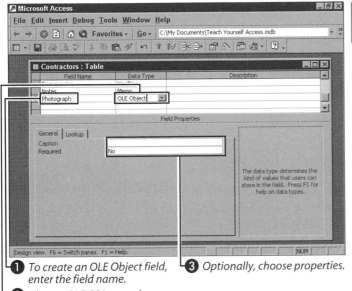

1 To create an OLE Object field, enter the field name.

2 Choose OLE Object as the data type.

3 Optionally, choose properties.

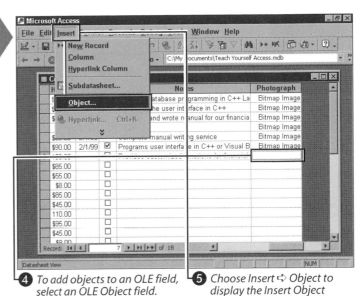

4 To add objects to an OLE field, select an OLE Object field.

5 Choose Insert ➪ Object to display the Insert Object dialog box.

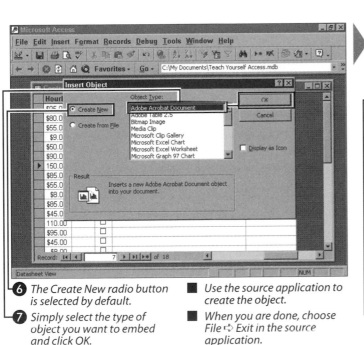

6 The Create New radio button is selected by default.

7 Simply select the type of object you want to embed and click OK.

■ Use the source application to create the object.

■ When you are done, choose File ➪ Exit in the source application.

8 Alternatively, select the Create From File radio button.

9 Enter a filename, or click Browse to choose the file in a Browse dialog box.

10 Optionally, select Link to link the file rather than embed it.

When you enter data in a form, the actual OLE object is displayed by default. If you like, you can display an icon instead, so the user clicks to view the object. You can do this by selecting the Display as Icon checkbox. In most cases, people prefer to display the object (such as a picture), however, you might want to display just an icon to save space, if the form is filled with other data.

Copying and Pasting OLE Objects

You can copy and paste objects from most source applications into an OLE Object field. You must first create the object in the source application. Then you can select and copy or cut it in the source application, select an OLE Object field in Access, and paste it in order to embed the object in the field.

To link rather than embed the object, use the Paste Special dialog box, shown in the lower right figure. Select the Paste Link radio button to add it as a linked OLE object, so any changes made in the source file are automatically reflected in the Access file. You can ensure accuracy and save time by linking, because you don't have to copy the data into Access.

The Paste Special dialog box also lets you embed an object in a different format. Select the Paste radio button and Access displays the formats that you can use for the object in the As list of this dialog box. These formats may reduce the amount of space that the object occupies in the database, and they let you change its size in forms and reports. However, you usually can no longer use the original application to edit the object after changing its format.

Editing and Deleting OLE Objects

To edit an OLE object from within Access, double-click it or choose Edit ⇨ Object ⇨ Edit. (The ellipsis is included before the word "Object," because this option changes depending on the type of object that is selected.) Access opens the application with the object displayed in it. You can edit linked OLE objects directly in the source application, but not embedded ones. To delete an OLE object from a table or query, simply select its field and choose Edit ⇨ Delete or press Delete. This does not affect the object in the source application.

TAKE NOTE

ADDING OBJECTS THAT DO NOT SUPPORT OLE

You can use Copy and Paste to add objects from Windows applications that do not support OLE to Access databases. You will, however, be unable to open the source application from Access, and the object in Access will not reflect changes in the object made in the source application. The only way to change the object is to change it in the source application, and once again use Copy and Paste to add the new version to Access.

CROSS-REFERENCE

For information on how to use the File Open dialog box, see Chapter 2.

SHORTCUT

Virtually all Windows applications let you use Ctrl+X, Ctrl+C, and Ctrl+V instead of Edit ⇨ Cut, Copy, and Paste.

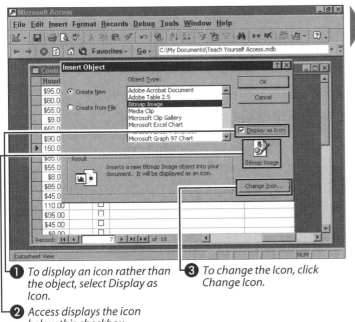

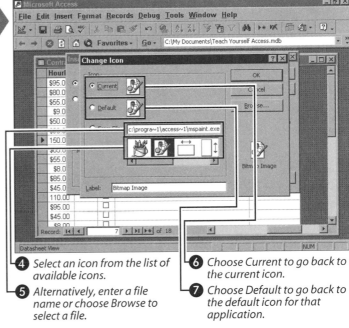

1 To display an icon rather than the object, select Display as Icon.

2 Access displays the icon below this checkbox.

3 To change the Icon, click Change Icon.

4 Select an icon from the list of available icons.

5 Alternatively, enter a file name or choose Browse to select a file.

6 Choose Current to go back to the current icon.

7 Choose Default to go back to the default icon for that application.

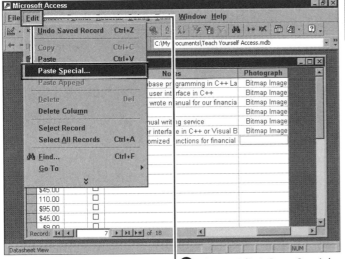

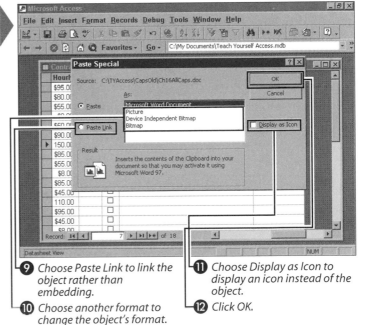

■ Cut or copy the object in another application then return to Access.

8 Choose Edit ➪ Paste Special.

9 Choose Paste Link to link the object rather than embedding.

10 Choose another format to change the object's format.

11 Choose Display as Icon to display an icon instead of the object.

12 Click OK.

Adding OLE Objects to Forms and Reports

You will often want to include OLE Object fields in forms and reports. For example, you may want a picture of each employee in his or her record. However, in addition to objects in OLE Object fields, you can add individual OLE objects to forms and reports, such as a company logo at the top of each form or report.

Like other controls, OLE object controls can be bound or unbound.

Bound OLE object controls display the objects in a field, and they change when you change records. For example, you would use a bound OLE object control to display people's photographs, stored in a table with their names and addresses.

Unbound OLE object controls display objects not stored in the table. For example, you would use an unbound OLE object control to display a company logo in a form's header. The logo remains the same as the records change.

Bound OLE Objects

You can add a bound OLE object to a form or report just as you add ordinary fields. The easiest way is to display the field list and click and drag the name of an OLE Object field to the form or report design.

You can also use the Bound Object Frame tool of the toolbox and click and drag to the form or report design to display the frame. Then use its Control Source property to indicate the field to which it is bound.

You work with bound OLE objects in forms and reports in the same way you work with OLE Object fields in tables and queries as described in the previous section.

Unbound OLE Objects

To add an unbound OLE object to a form or report, click the Object Frame button on the toolbox and click and drag to place the frame. When you release the mouse button, Access displays the Insert Object dialog box. The previous section described how to use this dialog box to add OLE objects to fields. You use an unbound object the same way to either open an application and create an object, or to specify a file that holds the object.

You can also use Copy and Paste to add an object to the frame, as described in the previous section. This is particularly useful to embed part of an existing object or to embed an object from an application that does not support OLE.

TAKE NOTE

LETTING THE USER RUN AN OLE OBJECT

You can double-click an unbound OLE object in Design view to open the source application and edit it, but you usually do not want users to edit the object in Form view. For example, you do not want others redesigning the company logo. For this reason, an unbound OLE object's Enabled property is set to No by default.

CROSS-REFERENCE
For information on using the Control Source property, see Chapter 9.

SHORTCUT
You can use drag and drop to add a bound or unbound object from another Office application, as described in the previous section.

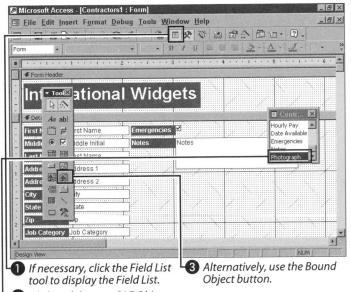

1 *If necessary, click the Field List tool to display the Field List.*

2 *Click and drag an OLE Object field to add it to the form.*

3 *Alternatively, use the Bound Object button.*

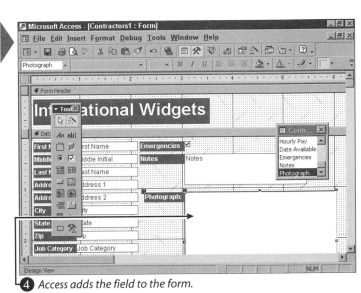

4 *Access adds the field to the form.*

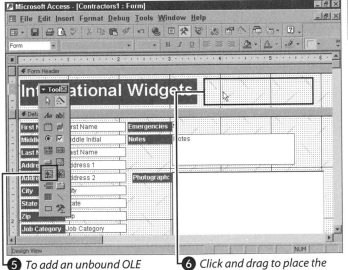

5 *To add an unbound OLE object, click the Unbound Object button.*

6 *Click and drag to place the object frame.*

■ *Use the Insert Object dialog box to add the object to the frame.*

313

Formatting OLE Objects in Forms and Reports

You can select, move, and resize bound or unbound OLE objects as you do other objects in form and report designs. Doing so can enhance the appearance of the form or report dramatically.

You can move or resize an object by selecting it and clicking and dragging its Move or Resize handles. You can also format the object to change its appearance. For example, you can use the Fill Color tool to change the background color of OLE objects, and the Line/Border Color, Line/Border Width, and Special Effects tools to format the border around the object.

When you add a bound OLE object, Access automatically adds a label. You can use the Move handle to move the object or label without moving the other, or you can click and drag its edge to move both the object and the label, as you do with other fields.

Scaling an OLE Object

Bound and unbound OLE objects are different from other controls, because the object may not be the same shape or size as the frame you create for it. When you size it so it fits correctly in the frame, you are scaling the object.

You can use the object frame's Size Mode property to specify how Access should deal with objects that do not fit in their frames properly. This property has three settings to choose from:

▶ Clip displays only a part of the object that can fit into the frame without changing its size or

shape if the object is too large. Clip is the default setting.

▶ Stretch makes the object larger or smaller to fill the frame, even if this means distorting its shape. For example, if the frame is square and the object is taller than it is wide, this property compresses the height of the object more than it compresses its width, so that it fills the frame completely.

▶ Zoom makes the object larger or smaller to fit the frame without distorting its shape. For example, if the frame is square and the object is taller than it is wide, the zoom property compresses the height of the object to fit into the frame, and compresses the width of the object proportionately. The shape of the object is not distorted, but there is empty space in the frame.

Rather than changing the size of the object to fit the frame, you can choose Format ➪ Size ➪ To Fit to expand or shrink the frame to fit the object, as you can with other types of controls.

TAKE NOTE

▶ RESTRICTING ENTRIES

The OLE Type Allowed property on the Data tab lets you restrict what can be entered in a bound or unbound frame. By default, it is Either, but you can choose Embedded or Linked to limit the user to entering that type of object.

CROSS-REFERENCE
See Chapters 8 and 9 for more information on working with objects in forms.

SHORTCUT
To move an object a small distance, hold down Ctrl and press an arrow key.

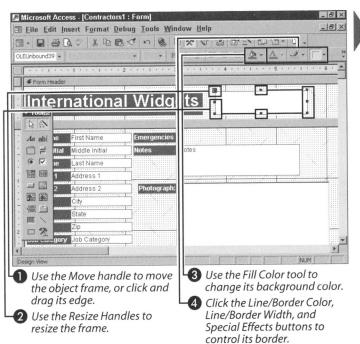

① Use the Move handle to move the object frame, or click and drag its edge.

② Use the Resize Handles to resize the frame.

③ Use the Fill Color tool to change its background color.

④ Click the Line/Border Color, Line/Border Width, and Special Effects buttons to control its border.

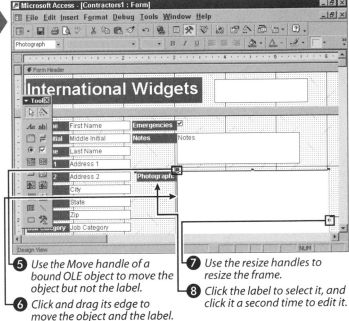

⑤ Use the Move handle of a bound OLE object to move the object but not the label.

⑥ Click and drag its edge to move the object and the label.

⑦ Use the resize handles to resize the frame.

⑧ Click the label to select it, and click it a second time to edit it.

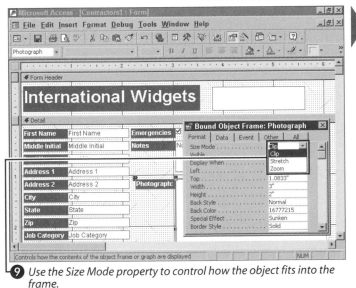

⑨ Use the Size Mode property to control how the object fits into the frame.

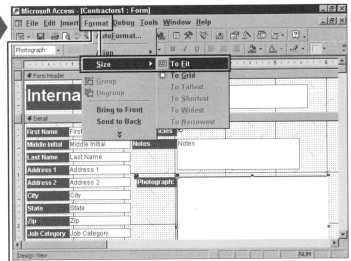

⑩ Alternatively, choose Format ⇨ Size ⇨ To Fit to make the frame the right size for the object.

Personal Workbook

Q&A

1 What is the difference between *linked* and *embedded* objects?

_____

_____

_____

2 What are the two most common ways to add an OLE object to a field?

_____

_____

_____

3 How do you edit an OLE object?

_____

_____

_____

4 What are the two types of OLE objects you can add to forms or reports?

_____

_____

_____

5 How do you delete an OLE object that you have entered in a Table?

_____

_____

_____

6 What is the difference between a *bound* and *unbound* OLE object in a form or report?

_____

_____

_____

7 How can you add and edit an OLE object from a source application that does not support OLE?

_____

_____

_____

8 How do you scale an OLE object, and what are the three options for scaling?

_____

_____

_____

ANSWERS: PAGE 357

EXTRA PRACTICE

1. Add an OLE Object field to your sample table, and add objects from existing files to the field in one or two records. You can use almost any file as an OLE object — for example, a Microsoft Word file — or you can choose Start ⇨ Programs ⇨ Accessories ⇨ Paint from the Windows Taskbar and use Microsoft Paint to create sample graphic objects.

2. Add objects to the field in one or two other records by creating new objects while entering data.

3. Add the OLE Object field to a form that you created for the sample table.

4. Move the field's label so it is under the field instead of next to it, and give the OLE object a thicker border.

REAL-WORLD APPLICATIONS

✔ To improve security at your business, you might get photographs of all your employees, scan them into your computer system, and include a photograph of each employee in your database. You create a form with the employee's name, address, and photograph, and then give employees a printout of their record to use as identification.

✔ You hire a graphic designer to create a new logo for your business, and you add this logo to the header of all your reports as an OLE object.

✔ You run a music store, and you use Access to maintain a table of all the recordings you have in stock. You get an application that digitizes music, so it can be played on your computer. Then, along with the data on each recording, you include an OLE Object field that customers can double-click to play a sample of its music.

Visual Quiz

The data entry form in the figure has two OLE objects: a logo in its header to the right of the words "Music On Line," and a field with sounds that you can double-click to play a sample. Explain how both of these OLE objects are added.

_____

_____

_____

_____

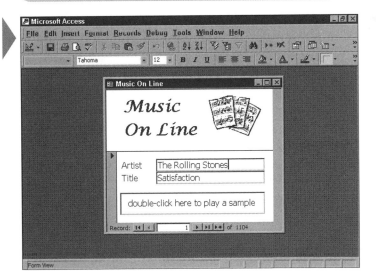

CHAPTER **17**

MASTER
THESE
SKILLS

▶ **Using Utilities to Manage Access Objects**

▶ **Creating Indexes**

▶ **Using Access Options**

▶ **Customizing Toolbars and Menus**

Using Access Utilities

I n this chapter, I cover a number of *utilities*, or capabilities, that are not necessary for you to know in order to use Access, but that can make your work easier or faster.

I begin with utilities that you use to manage objects in the Database window, including basic functions such as renaming, copying, and pasting objects, and using groups to organize objects so you can more conveniently work with them. Copy and paste is particularly useful, because it is the quickest way to back up an existing table before you modify it in a way that could cause you to lose data.

I go on to discuss indexes, which you can use to speed up finds and sorts. You may find yourself waiting for these processes if you are working with a large database, and indexes can eliminate this wait time. However, Access can begin to work more slowly if you have too many indexes, so you must know when to create indexes and when not to.

The Options dialog box lets you control Access's behavior in many ways. For example, you can change the default folder where new databases are stored, you can create templates for forms and reports, and if you are uncomfortable with Access's default keyboard behavior, you can change so it behaves like other Windows applications. This chapter covers the most useful options. You can easily get help on the others.

Finally, this chapter covers the Customize dialog box, which lets you customize the Access toolbars and menus and create custom menus. You can often speed up your work by creating a custom toolbar with just the tools you need to use, and Access makes it easy to do this simply by clicking and dragging tools onto it.

Using Utilities to Manage Access Objects

The Access Edit menu includes useful utilities for managing the database objects. One of the most important utilities is *copy and paste,* which is the easiest way to back up a table, as shown on the facing page. If you are modifying a table in a way that can cause you to lose data—for example, if you are creating a delete query or an update query—it is best to back it up first, so that you still have the original data if the query causes unexpected changes.

You can cut or copy and paste either within a single database or between two databases.

After you paste into a new object, as shown in the upper-left figure, Access displays a dialog box that lets you rename the copied or pasted object. For most objects, you just enter a name. If you are pasting a table, the Paste Table As dialog box also gives you these options:

▶ **Structure Only.** The table will have only the structure of the table you are pasting, but no data.

▶ **Structure and Data.** The table will have both the structure and the data of the table you are pasting.

▶ **Append Data to Existing Table.** You must enter the name of an existing table, and the data in the table you are pasting will be added to it.

Using Groups

Groups in the Database window, such as Tables, Reports, and Favorites, let you organize your objects. You can click and drag objects from any panel to a group's button: The object remains in the original panel, but a shortcut to open it or design it is added to the group. To delete a shortcut from a group, select it and press the Del (or Delete) key; doing this does not delete the object itself. You can also create your own groups. For example, you can have objects for your Northwest territory clients in a group named Northwest. Simply right-click an existing group, select New Group from its pop-up menu, and enter a name for the group in the New Group dialog box. You can also use a group's pop-up menu to delete or rename it. Click either the Object or the Group button to display or hide the buttons for objects and groups.

TAKE NOTE

▶ **RENAMING AND DELETING OBJECTS**

You can rename or delete a database object by clicking the object and selecting either option from the Edit menu. You can undo a table or query delete, but you cannot undo the deletion of other types of database objects.

CROSS-REFERENCE

See Chapter 2 for a description of valid names for Access objects.

SHORTCUT

Often, the quickest way to create a new table is to copy and paste a table with a similar structure from another database.

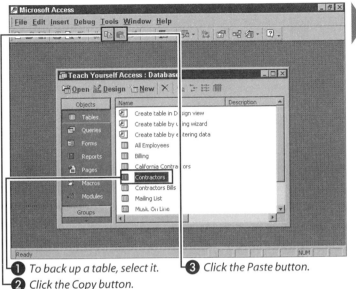

① To back up a table, select it.

② Click the Copy button.

③ Click the Paste button.

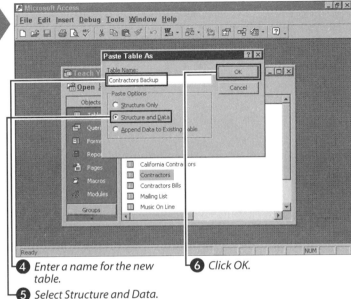

④ Enter a name for the new table.

⑤ Select Structure and Data.

⑥ Click OK.

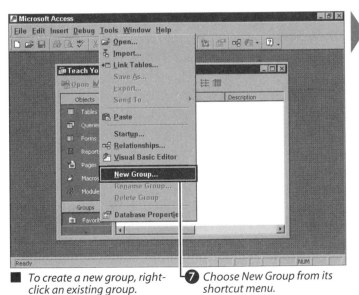

■ To create a new group, right-click an existing group.

⑦ Choose New Group from its shortcut menu.

⑧ Enter a group name in the New Group dialog box.

⑨ Click OK.

Creating Indexes

Indexes are great for speeding up queries and sorts, particularly if you are working with a large table. A table's index works like a book's. In a book, looking up the topic in the index and then going to the page is quicker than reading the entire book until you find the topic. Likewise, Access can look up a value in an index and go to the record much more quickly than it can search a file to find a value.

Indexing a Single Field

To create or remove an index based on a single field, open the table in Design view and select an option for the Indexed property:

▶ **No** means there is no index based on the field (default).
▶ **Yes (Duplicates OK)** creates an index based on the field, and it accepts the same value in any number of records in the field.
▶ **Yes (No Duplicates)** creates an index based on the field and does not accept a value in the field if that value has already been entered in another record.

You cannot create indexes for Memo, Hyperlink, or OLE Object fields. Yes (No Duplicates) is used for the primary key. You should select Yes (Duplicates OK) if you are using the index to speed up searches and sorts based on a field.

Indexing on Multiple Fields

You need to index on multiple fields to speed up sorts based on multiple fields, such as sorts based on the Last and First Name. To create an index based on multiple fields, display the table in Design view and click the Indexes button to display the Indexes window. Then enter a name for the index in the Index Name column, and select field names and sort orders. Field names and sort orders without an index name are used as part of the index having a name above them. The extra rows are used as tie-breakers.

In the upper-right figure, for example, there is a primary key, an index named Names, and an index named Zip. Names is based on the Last Name, First Name, and Middle Initial fields.

TAKE NOTE

▶ **SETTING THE INDEX PROPERTIES**

Set these properties in the Index window:
▶ **Primary.** The index is the primary key. Only one index can have this property.
▶ **Unique.** Unique values must be entered in the field. This property is equivalent to selecting Yes (No Duplicates) when creating the index.
▶ **Ignore Nulls.** Any records with no entry for the index expression is excluded from this index.

CROSS-REFERENCE
For more information on table properties, see Chapter 13.

SHORTCUT
If you tab to the Indexed property and press Y, it displays Yes (Duplicates OK), the most common index.

Advantages and Disadvantages of Indexing

Why doesn't Access just create indexes automatically when you do a find or query, so they are ready to reuse when you do the find or query again?

There is a disadvantage to creating too many indexes. When you enter or edit data, Access automatically updates indexes, and it takes a tiny amount of time to update each. If you have a few indexes, you do not notice the time it takes to update them. If you have a large number of indexes in a table with many records, however, the time it takes to update them can slow Access enough to make you wait as you do data entry.

For this reason, you should create indexes for only those fields that are the basis of frequently used finds, queries, and sorts.

If you are always looking up people by last name, for example, you should index on the Last Name field to speed up the find. If you often print mailing labels in zip code order and reports in alphabetical order by name, you could create an index on the Zip field and another on the Last Name and First Name fields.

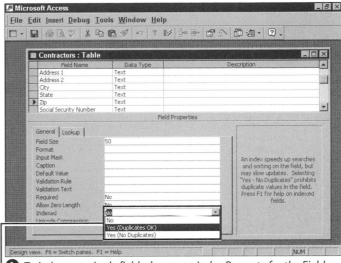

1 To index on a single field, choose an Index Property for the Field.

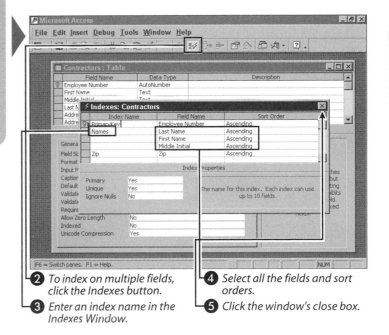

2 To index on multiple fields, click the Indexes button.

3 Enter an index name in the Indexes Window.

4 Select all the fields and sort orders.

5 Click the window's close box.

Using Access Options

You can customize Access's behavior in many ways by using the Options dialog box. Choose different tabs to display options for controlling different features of Access.

Here, we look at some of the most useful options in each tab to give you a general idea of what this dialog box can do. For complete details, display the dialog box using the steps on the facing page, select any control, and press F1 to display context-sensitive help on it.

The View tab lets you choose what is shown on the desktop and in the Macro window; the Macro options duplicate the tools that let you display the names and conditions column. You may find it useful to select the click option Single-click open, so you can open objects more easily from the Database window. Some people use the Status bar, but other people would rather have the extra screen space. Deselect Status bar if you want to see a little more onscreen.

The General tab is used to change the default margins for printing and to change the Default Database folder, if you want to keep an application in some folder other than My Documents. If you use a large number of databases, it is very useful to set the recently used file list to some number that is larger than 4, so you can open more databases directly from the list at the bottom of the File menu. The New Database sort order lets you choose how objects are sorted in the Database window: The options let you sort alphabetically for different languages.

You can also click the Web Options button of the General tab to display the Web Options dialog box, which lets you specify the appearance of hyperlinks and other options.

The Edit/Find tab is useful to control the default find behavior. The options are similar to choices in the Find dialog box; if you usually choose to find records if the beginning of the field matches the search criterion, for example, you can choose Start of field search as the default. The Filter By Form defaults can also be useful, if your filters are slow: The more options chosen here, the longer it takes to apply the filter, so you can speed up performance by deselecting options you do not need.

Continued

TAKE NOTE

BE CAREFUL WITH CONFIRM

The Confirm radio buttons of the Edit/Find tab can be useful on occasion. For example, if you have to delete a large number of objects in the Database window, you can save time by deselecting Document Deletions, so Access does not ask for confirmation each time you delete an object. However, it is dangerous to leave these off permanently: Select them again as soon as you are done with the work that you turned them off for, so you do not accidentally change or lose data.

CROSS-REFERENCE
For information on finds, see Chapter 3. For information on filters, see Chapter 5.

SHORTCUT
Rather than clicking the tabs, you can press Ctrl+Tab to move to the next tab, and Shift+Ctrl+Tab to move to the previous one.

1 Choose Tools ➪ Options.

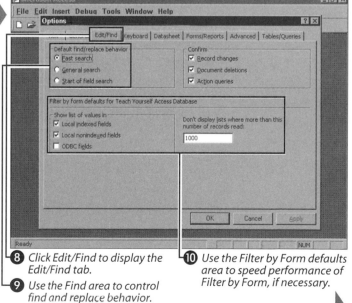

2 Click View to display the View tab.

3 Use the Show area to control what is displayed on the desktop.

4 Use the Show in macro area to control what is displayed in the Macro window.

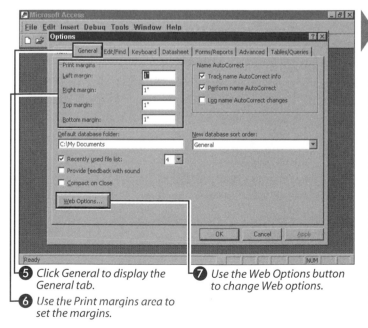

5 Click General to display the General tab.

6 Use the Print margins area to set the margins.

7 Use the Web Options button to change Web options.

8 Click Edit/Find to display the Edit/Find tab.

9 Use the Find area to control find and replace behavior.

10 Use the Filter by Form defaults area to speed performance of Filter by Form, if necessary.

Using Access Options

Continued

The Keyboard tab is useful if you are not comfortable with Access's special keyboard behavior, which is meant to make it easier to move among fields and records. Select Next Character (rather than Next Field) as Arrow key behavior, and select Go to start of field (rather than Select entire field) as Behavior entering field, and Access will feel more like other Windows applications.

The Datasheet tab lets you choose default features of datasheets, such as their colors, fonts, and cell special effects, which you use the toolbar to control for individual datasheets. You may find changing the default column width useful, if you are working with data that does not fit well in Access's 1-inch default column.

The Forms/Reports tab's options may help speed up design of forms and reports. The Selection behavior radio buttons let you choose which controls are selected when you click and drag around a group of controls. By default, controls are selected if any part of them is within the area you drag around, but you can select Fully enclosed to select them only if they are completely within the area. You may save time by entering the name of an existing form or report in the Form template or Report template box to use them as the template for new forms and reports that you create in Design view: New forms will have the same section and control properties as the templates you specify here, but this does not apply to forms or reports created using the wizards.

The Advanced tab has options used by system administrators. These options control how records are locked in a multiuser environment, and similar technical issues.

The Tables/Queries tab lets you change the default field size and data type for table design. The AutoIndex box lets you specify which fields are automatically indexed when you create a new table or import data. Fields beginning or ending with the characters in this box's list are automatically indexed. Since ID, key, code, and num are in the list by default, fields with names like EmpID, CustCode, and CustNum are automatically indexed.

TAKE NOTE

CHANGING THE DEFAULT FIELD SIZE

You may want to change the default field size for numbers in the Tables/Queries tab, if inexperienced users are defining tables. Long Integer is the default field size for Number fields, but it is not useful for most purposes, because it can only be used for values that have no decimal places. The most versatile size for Number fields is Double, because it can hold decimals as well as integers and can be used for the most accurate calculations. Though it requires a bit of extra disk space to store and slows calculations a bit, the difference will not be noticed in most cases.

CROSS-REFERENCE

Chapters 2 and 4 contain more information on table and query design. Chapters 8 through 10 explain form and report design.

SHORTCUT

You can also press Tab and Shift+Tab to move among the controls, and press the Spacebar to select and deselect checkboxes.

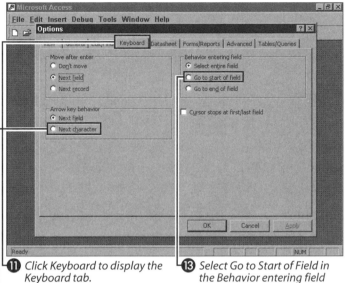

11 Click Keyboard to display the Keyboard tab.

12 Select Next character to make Access behave more conventionally when you press the Arrow key.

13 Select Go to Start of Field in the Behavior entering field area to make Access behave more conventionally when you move among fields.

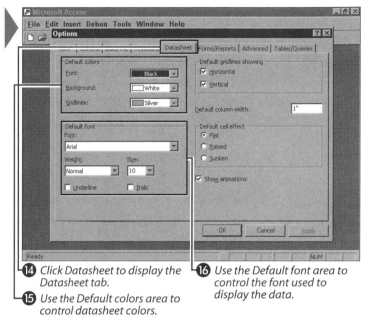

14 Click Datasheet to display the Datasheet tab.

15 Use the Default colors area to control datasheet colors.

16 Use the Default font area to control the font used to display the data.

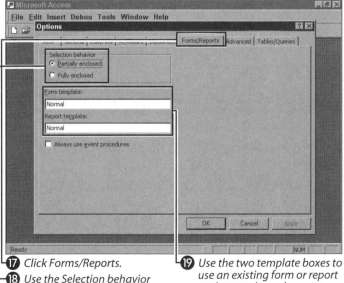

17 Click Forms/Reports.

18 Use the Selection behavior area to choose which controls are selected when you click and drag around a group of controls.

19 Use the two template boxes to use an existing form or report as the template when you create new forms or reports.

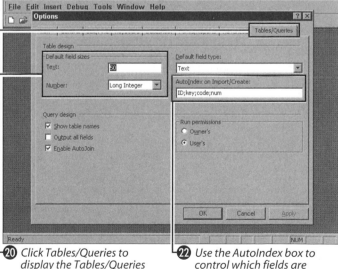

20 Click Tables/Queries to display the Tables/Queries tab.

21 Use the Default field sizes area to control the default size of text and number fields.

22 Use the AutoIndex box to control which fields are automatically indexed.

327

Customizing Toolbars and Menus

There are times when you can speed up your work by creating custom toolbars or menus that only include tasks that you must perform frequently. Access menus and toolbars are customized in the same way.

You can reposition a toolbar so that it is more convenient for you to use. Any toolbar or menu can either be *docked* (attached to any edge of the Access window) or *floating* (contained in its own window). To move a docked toolbar, click and drag its move handle, the double line on its left, or top edge. To move a floating toolbar, click and drag its title bar. For example, in the upper-left figure, the main menu bar has been changed to a floating toolbar. You can click and drag its title bar to move it back to its normal location.

To customize toolbars, choose Tools ➪ Customize to display the Customize dialog box, shown on the upper right, which you can use to control which toolbars are displayed, or to create a new toolbar or rename a toolbar, or to reset a toolbar so it has its default buttons.

Click its Properties button to display the Toolbar Properties dialog box, which controls what sort of docking is allowed. The checkboxes let you allow or prevent the user from customizing, resizing, moving, and hiding this toolbar. The Restore Defaults button restores all the original settings of the toolbar and its buttons, including property settings; this restores the original toolbar completely, while the Reset button only restores the original buttons.

The Commands panel of the Customize dialog box, shown in the lower-right figure, lets you add buttons to toolbars. Just click a category on the left to display a list of buttons and commands, and click and drag a command from this list to any toolbar to add that button to the toolbar.

While the Customize dialog box is open, you can also remove any button from any toolbar simply by clicking and dragging it off the toolbar and dropping it onto the desktop.

TAKE NOTE

▶ CREATING A CUSTOM TOOLBAR

Imagine that you want to create a toolbar containing only the Cut, Copy, Paste, and Undo buttons, so you can use it for editing without other buttons getting in the way. Creating this custom toolbar is easy. Simply choose Tools ➪ Customize, click New in the Toolbars panel of the Customize dialog box, enter a name such as **Quick Edit** in the New Toolbar dialog box, and then click OK. Access creates a toolbar with this name, but with no buttons in it. Then click the Commands tab in the Customize dialog box, click Edit to display a list of editing buttons, and click and drag the Cut, Copy, Paste, and Undo buttons from this list to the new Quick Edit toolbar.

CROSS-REFERENCE

For more information on customization, search for customizing toolbars in the Index panel of the Access help system.

SHORTCUT

Right-click a toolbar and use its pop-up menu to hide and unhide some toolbars, or choose Customize to display the Customize dialog box.

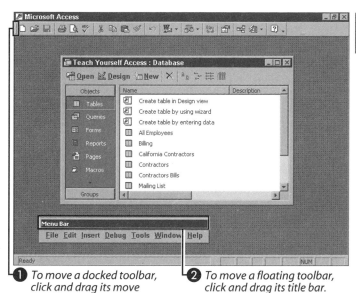

❶ To move a docked toolbar, click and drag its move handle.

❷ To move a floating toolbar, click and drag its title bar.

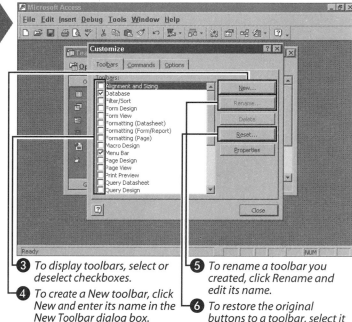

❸ To display toolbars, select or deselect checkboxes.

❹ To create a New toolbar, click New and enter its name in the New Toolbar dialog box.

❺ To rename a toolbar you created, click Rename and edit its name.

❻ To restore the original buttons to a toolbar, select it and click Reset.

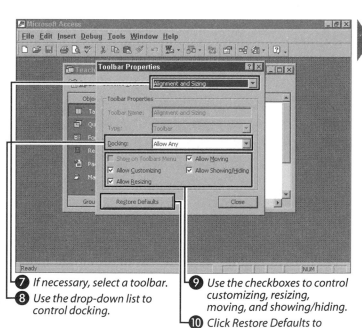

❼ If necessary, select a toolbar.

❽ Use the drop-down list to control docking.

❾ Use the checkboxes to control customizing, resizing, moving, and showing/hiding.

❿ Click Restore Defaults to restore all the original settings of the toolbar and its buttons.

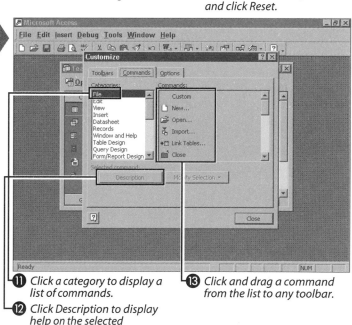

⓫ Click a category to display a list of commands.

⓬ Click Description to display help on the selected command.

⓭ Click and drag a command from the list to any toolbar.

Personal Workbook

Q&A

1 What are two ways to rename a database object?

_____

_____

_____

2 What is the easiest way to back up a database table?

_____

_____

_____

3 How do you create a new group in the Database window?

_____

_____

_____

4 How do you add objects to a group and remove objects from a group?

_____

_____

_____

5 What is the easiest way to index on a single field?

_____

_____

_____

6 How do you index on multiple fields?

_____

_____

_____

7 When you use the arrow keys to move through a table, you want Access to place the cursor at the beginning of the field, rather than highlighting the entry in the field. How do you do this?

_____

_____

8 How do you convert Access's main toolbar into a floating toolbar? How do you convert the Toolbox displayed when you design forms into a toolbar at the top of the screen?

_____

_____

_____

ANSWERS: PAGE 358

EXTRA PRACTICE

① Create a backup of your sample table.

② Create an index for your sample table to speed up sorts based on the zip code.

③ Create an index for your sample table to speed up sorts based on the entire name.

④ Change Access options so it stores new database files by default in some other folder, rather than in My Documents.

⑤ Change the Access Main Menu into a floating menu, and move the main Toolbar to the bottom of the screen.

⑥ Add a button that you can click to display the Database window to your main toolbar. (Hint: Look in the Window and Help category in the Customize dialog box.)

REAL-WORLD APPLICATIONS

✔ You have to work with the same tables, queries, and reports at the end of each month to create your monthly report. To save time, you might create a Monthly Report group with shortcuts to these objects.

✔ You are working with a very large database, and you often must sort it by Name. To save time, you could create an index based on the Name fields.

✔ You have hired temporary workers to do data entry, and they are confused by Access. You could change the main menu and toolbar, so they only have the options the temps need.

Visual Quiz

Someone who does not use most of the tools in the Toolbox for Form and Report design created the Quick Toolbox shown on the right. What steps are needed to create this Quick Toolbox?

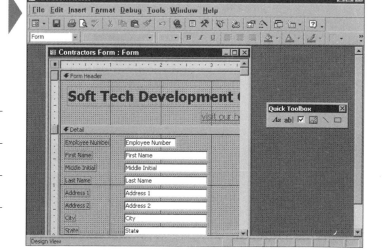

CHAPTER **18**

MASTER
THESE
SKILLS

▶ **Using Quick Help and the Assistant**

▶ **Using the Help System**

▶ **Customizing the Assistant**

Using the Help System

This book has given you a general overview of all the major features of Access that you need as a user. In the future, you can continue learning more about Access by using its help system.

Access has the same sort of help system used by other Office applications. Its most prominent feature is the Assistant, which lets you type in questions in plain English and displays a list of topics that might give you answers. You can customize the Assistant in a number of ways; for example, by choosing which figure is displayed and by controlling its behavior and the information it gives you. When you are working with Access and want quick help to let you finish the task you are working on, it is usually easiest to use the Assistant. Type in your question, and you should be able to find the topic you want without much delay.

You can also use the tabs of the Help window to search for help, either by bypassing the Assistant completely or in combination with the Assistant. The Help window gives you three different ways of searching for help. The Contents tab displays a relatively short list of general topics, which you can browse to find the subject you want, and then displays more specific topics on that subject. Use this tab if you want to learn about some topic in depth. The Index tab presents a long list of key words in alphabetical order, and let you display a list of topics for each key word. The Answer Wizard tab works like the Assistant, by letting you enter questions in plain English and displaying a list of related topics.

In some cases, it is easiest to display the feature of Access that you want to learn about and to use context-sensitive help. For example, to learn more about properties, display the property sheet, put the cursor in a property that you want to learn more about, and press F1 to display help on it.

However you display Help, its topics will have links to other topics. Your online help is integrated with help topics on the World Wide Web, so you can use a very extensive help system, which is updated regularly.

Using Quick Help and the Assistant

In addition to the usual help system, Access gives you a couple of quick methods of getting help. Help on toolbar buttons is available if you move the mouse pointer to any of them. After you keep the pointer on the button for a moment, Access displays its name in a box next to the pointer.

What's This? help lets you get more extensive context-sensitive help on menus, toolbars, windows, and other features of the Access interface. After you choose Help ➪ What's This?, the mouse pointer is displayed with a question mark next to it. You can then click any feature of the Access interface or choose any menu item to display the Access help system with help on that feature.

After you use interface help once, the pointer is restored to its normal appearance, and you can continue using Access as usual. To restore the pointer to its normal appearance and continue using Access without using interface help, choose What's This? from the Help menu a second time.

The Office Assistant

The Office Assistant is the primary form of help available in Access and other Office applications. It is an animated cartoon figure that lets you enter questions in ordinary English, and in response, it displays lists of related topics. You can choose among a variety of Assistants, which behave a bit differently from one another: Many automatically pop up and ask you if you want help on tasks that you are performing. All of them provide an extremely easy way of getting help.

When you press F1 to display the Assistant, a Help balloon is also displayed. To use the Office Assistant, just enter a question in the text box and click Search. It displays a list of topics related to your question, and you can click a topic to display help on it. If you choose Show the Office Assistant from the Help menu, the Assistant simply pops on screen and waits around for you to use it. When you need to use the Assistant, click it to display the Help balloon and then type in your question.

When you are done using help, you can click the Help window's Close (X) box to close it. You can leave the Office Assistant on your desktop if you want to, but it is usually easier to get it out of the way by choosing Help ➪ Hide the Office Assistant.

TAKE NOTE

CONTEXT-SENSITIVE HELP

Context-sensitive help for some features of the interface is available by pressing F1. For example, if you are using a property sheet, pressing F1 will display help on the property where the cursor is located. (You can display the same help by using What's This? help and clicking the property.) If you press F1 and you are not using a feature that has context-sensitive help, Access displays the Assistant, if it is not already displayed.

CROSS-REFERENCE
The Assistant may give you unnecessary tips. For information on dealing with this problem, see the section on customizing the Assistant later in this chapter.

FIND IT ONLINE
If none of the Assistant's topics is what you want, click the option "None of the above, look for more help on the Web" to go to **http://www.microsoft.com** for help.

1 To get context-sensitive help on features of the Access interface, choose Help ➪ What's This?

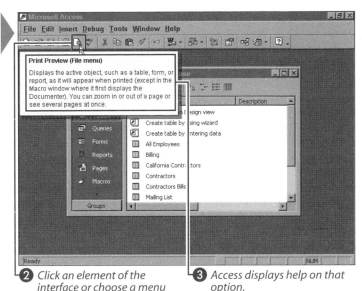

2 Click an element of the interface or choose a menu option.

3 Access displays help on that option.

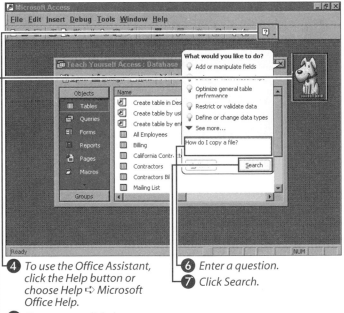

4 To use the Office Assistant, click the Help button or choose Help ➪ Microsoft Office Help.

5 If necessary, click the Assistant for Help.

6 Enter a question.

7 Click Search.

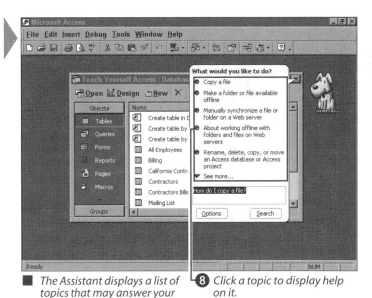

■ The Assistant displays a list of topics that may answer your question.

8 Click a topic to display help on it.

335

Using the Help System

ccess makes it easy for you to navigate through its help system. The help topic links that you click to display related topics are displayed in blue and underlined. As you click links and move from one topic to another, Access remembers the history of topics you viewed. You can click Back to display previous topics in the history or use the Back and Forward buttons to move through a topic you have already seen.

If the problem you are getting help on is complex, you may want to either print the current topic or print all the topics under the current heading.

The Options button drop-down list has two extra choices that are useful when you are working with help on the Web. Stop prevents the current page from downloading, and it is often useful if a page is taking too long to load. Refresh redraws the current page, and it is useful if you are working with pages that are updated frequently, such as pages with news reports, or if you are developing and testing your own Web pages.

Using the Contents Tab

The Contents tab displays a relatively small number of general topics, which you can scroll through to find the one you want. It is organized as general topics (folder icons) and as topics that have their own help pages (page icons). Look through the general topics until you find one you want, click the + to display its pages, and then click a page to display help on that subject.

Clicking a folder may display a list of folders that hold subtopics. Keep opening the folders, until you finally display a list of pages, which you can click to display help.

Using the Index Tab

The Index tab lets you type in a key word or phrase and search for related topics. As you type, key words beginning with those letters are displayed below it in a list. After you find a key word you want to learn more about, you can display a list related topics. You must display help on a topic, not on a key word.

Using the Answer Wizard Tab

The Answer Wizard tab works like the Assistant. Type a question in English, and the Answer Wizard displays a list of related topics. Then click a topic to display help on it.

TAKE NOTE

BYPASSING THE ASSISTANT

If you prefer working with the Contents and Index tab, you can display them without the Assistant. Right-click the Assistant and choose Options from its pop-up menu. Deselect the Use the Office Assistant checkbox. The Assistant will be disabled for the rest of your current Access session, and the help system will be displayed when you click the Help button or choose Help ⇨ Microsoft Office Help. To use the Assistant again during the same session, choose Help ⇨ Show the Assistant.

CROSS-REFERENCE
The links in the help system are similar to hyperlinks, covered in Chapter 15.

SHORTCUT
When the tabs are displayed, the Show button changes to a Hide button. Click this to hide the tabs.

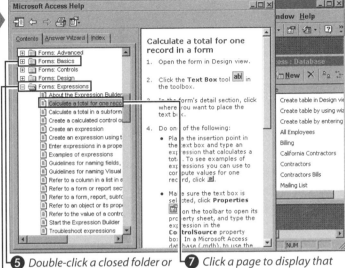

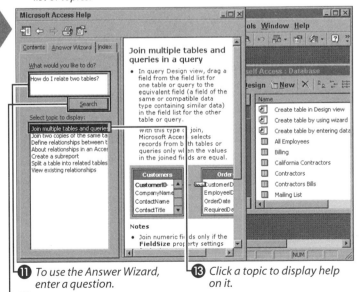

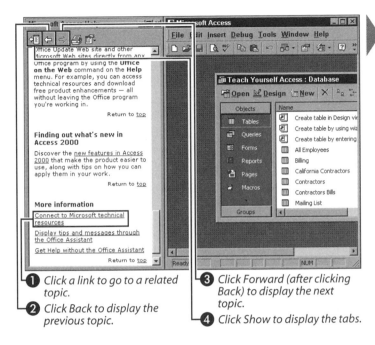

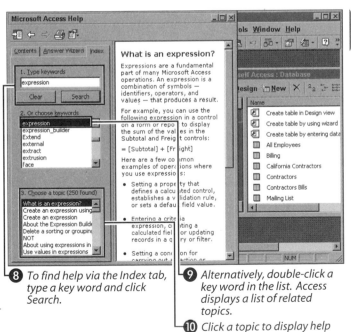

1 Click a link to go to a related topic.

2 Click Back to display the previous topic.

3 Click Forward (after clicking Back) to display the next topic.

4 Click Show to display the tabs.

5 Double-click a closed folder or click the + to its left to display a list of topics.

6 Double-click an open folder or click the – to its left to hide the list of topics.

7 Click a page to display that topic.

8 To find help via the Index tab, type a key word and click Search.

9 Alternatively, double-click a key word in the list. Access displays a list of related topics.

10 Click a topic to display help on it.

11 To use the Answer Wizard, enter a question.

12 Click Search to display a list of related topics.

13 Click a topic to display help on it.

Customizing the Assistant

Some Assistants pop up and offer you advice while you are working. While some people appreciate this extra help, others who are already comfortable working with Access do not need it. To deal with this problem, you can customize the Assistant and choose a less active one.

The Assistant is used for all Office applications, and any changes you make here will be reflected in other applications.

Choosing the Assistant

If you select the Assistant from the pop-up menu, it displays the Gallery tab, which you can scroll through to check out the other Office Assistants. Click the Back and Next buttons to see the Dot, the Genius, the Office Logo, Rocky the dog, and others. Because these Assistants behave differently, you might want to try a few to see which you like best. The Office Logo is the least intrusive of the Assistants.

Choosing Options

If you find the Assistant distracting and would prefer to use the Contents or Index tabs of the help system, you can deselect the Use the Office Assistant checkbox to turn off the Assistant for the rest of the session.

You can also use the checkboxes in the Options panel to control what assistance it gives — whether it is activated by the F1 key, gives help with the Wizards, displays Alerts, and displays application help while programming — and to control its behavior —

whether it moves to get out of the way of what you are doing, tries to guess what help you want, and makes sounds.

You can use the Options panel to control a few other help features, such as what features it displays help for when you click the Tip button, and whether it shows the tip of the day when you start Access. If you click Reset Tips, it ignores the history of tips it has displayed, and may repeat tips you have seen.

TAKE NOTE

MANAGING THE ASSISTANT

If you find the Assistant distracting:
- Click and drag the Assistant to move it out of the way.
- Change the Assistant. Some are much less active than others. The Office Logo is the least active, and it does not offer help unless you ask.
- In the Options tab, deselect Make sounds and Move when in the way if you find the sound and motion distracting. Deselect Guess help topics if you find it distracting that the Assistant offers help when you do not ask.
- You can rerun the Setup program to remove the Assistant permanently. Insert installation disk 1 or the installation CD-ROM in your computer, choose Start ➪ Run from the Windows taskbar, and enter the drive letter followed by **setup**. In Setup, click the Add/Remove button, and use the Options list to remove the Assistant.

CROSS-REFERENCE

For information on using the Assistant, see the first section of this chapter.

FIND IT ONLINE

You can get other versions of the Assistant at the Microsoft Web site by choosing Help ➪ Microsoft on the Web ➪ Microsoft Office Home Page.

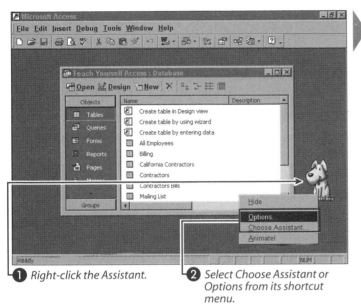

❶ Right-click the Assistant.

❷ Select Choose Assistant or Options from its shortcut menu.

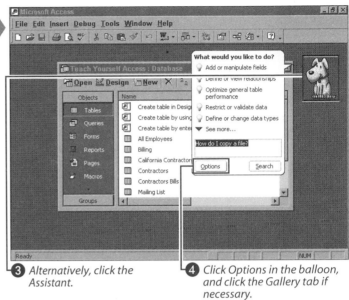

❸ Alternatively, click the Assistant.

❹ Click Options in the balloon, and click the Gallery tab if necessary.

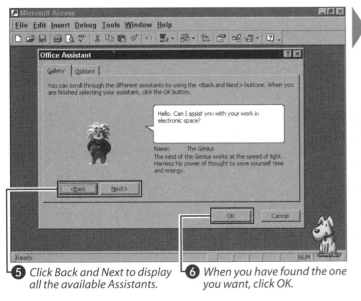

❺ Click Back and Next to display all the available Assistants.

❻ When you have found the one you want, click OK.

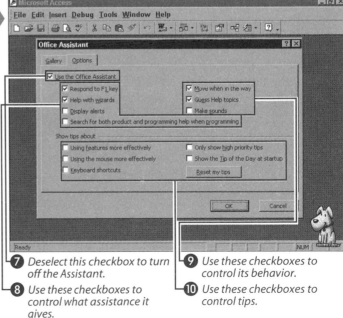

❼ Deselect this checkbox to turn off the Assistant.

❽ Use these checkboxes to control what assistance it gives.

❾ Use these checkboxes to control its behavior.

❿ Use these checkboxes to control tips.

Personal Workbook

Q&A

1 What are two easy ways to get help about a button on the toolbar?

_____

_____

_____

2 What are two easy ways to get help about a property of a field or other object?

_____

_____

_____

3 What are two easy ways to get help about a tool on the toolbar?

_____

_____

_____

4 How do you use the Assistant to get help?

_____

_____

_____

5 How do you use a different Assistant?

_____

_____

_____

6 How do you use the Contents tab of the Help system?

_____

_____

_____

7 How do you use the Index tab of the help system?

_____

_____

_____

8 The Assistant is driving you crazy. What should you do?

_____

_____

_____

_____

ANSWERS: PAGE 359

EXTRA PRACTICE

1 Use What's This? help to display help on a tool of the toolbar.

2 Display a form in Design view, display the property sheet, and get context-sensitive help on one of the properties.

3 Display the Assistant, enter a question in it, and display one of the help topics it lists.

4 Display the tabs of the help system and use the Contents tab to search for help.

5 Now, use the Index tab to search for help. See whether you find the Contents or Index tab easier to use.

6 Display the Gallery and choose a different Assistant.

REAL-WORLD APPLICATIONS

✔ When you are designing a report, you might not understand one of the properties of a text box you have added. You put the cursor in that property and press F1.

✔ You forget which button to use to display the Relationships window, so you move the pointer over a few buttons until you display the name Relationships under one.

✔ You need to create new mailing labels, and you have forgotten how. You could display the Assistant and enter, "How do I create mailing labels?"

Visual Quiz

The figure shows help on using wildcard characters in a find. What steps did the user go through to display this help?

_____

_____

_____

_____

_____

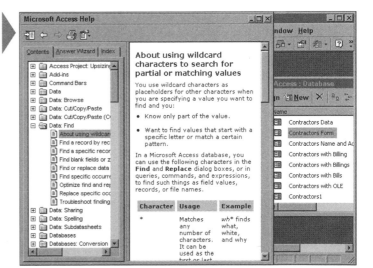

Personal Workbook
Answers

Chapter 1

see page 5

① **What is the definition of a database in Access, and how is it different in other database applications?**

A: In Access, a database is made of all the objects you use to work with an application. In other database applications, the word *database* usually just refers to the tables that hold the data.

② **What are *records* and *fields?* What else are they called?**

A: A *record* holds all the data on one entity in a table; for example, in a name and address table, a record would hold the name and address of one person. A *field* holds one piece of data within a record; for example, in a name and address table, a field might hold the last name. Because of they way they are displayed in tables, records are also called *rows*, and fields are also called *columns*.

③ **What are the four most important objects in Access databases, and what are they used for?**

A: The four most important objects in Access databases are *tables*, which are used for holding data; *queries*, which are used to display selected records and fields from tables; *forms*, which are used for entering data on screen; and *reports*, which are used for printing data.

④ **What object would you use to let people work with data through the World Wide Web?**

A: To let people work with data through the World Wide Web, use a *data access page.*

⑤ **What is the fastest way of creating a form, report, or data access page?**

A: The fastest way of creating a form, report, or data access page is to select the table or query you want it to be based on in the Database window. Then select the AutoForm, AutoReport, or AutoPage button.

⑥ **If you are looking at the data in an object and you realize that you have to change its design, what should you do?**

A: If you are viewing data in an object and want to change its design, click the View button to display it in Design view.

⑦ **What should you look for to decide whether to keep data in one table or to break it up into multiple tables?**

A: To decide whether to keep data in one table, you should look for a one-to-one relationship between the record and each field. For example, in a name and address list, each person has one name, one home address, one zip code, one Social Security number, and so on.

Personal Workbook Answers

8 **If you break up data into multiple tables, what field must you include to relate them?**

A: If you break up data into multiple tables, you must include some key field, such as the Employee Number, to relate them.

Visual Quiz

Q: How would you open the C:\Business\Personnel\ Employees.mdb database using the Open dialog box displayed on the right?

A: To open the database C:\Business\Personnel\ Employees.mdb, double-click My Computer to display your local disk drives. Double-click **C:** to display the folders on the C: drive. Double-click the Business folder to open it. Double-click the Personnel folder to open it. Double-click the Employees.mdb file to open it.

Chapter 2

see page 19

1 **Which data type should you use for an Employee Number field, and why?**

A: For an Employee Number field, use the AutoNumber Data Type, because it automatically enters a unique value in each record that cannot be changed.

2 **Which data type should you use for a field that holds general notes on each record?**

A: Use the Memo data type for a field with general notes.

3 **Which data type should you use for a field that holds zip codes?**

A: Use Text as the data type of a field that holds zip codes, because you do not have to do calculations on it.

4 **What are two reasons why you would you want to change the field size of a text field?**

A: You would want to change the size of a Text field to let the user enter more text in the field than the default 50 characters, or to reduce data-entry errors in fields that have a fixed number of characters, such as a Middle Initial field.

5 **What field size should you use for a number field where you must perform calculations that are accurate to many decimal places?**

A: Use Double as the field size of a Number field where you must perform very accurate calculations.

6 **Should you ever use the Currency data type for fields that do not hold amounts of money?**

A: You can use the Currency data type for any fields that require calculations with no more than four decimal places of accuracy.

7 **Can you lose data if you add a new field to an existing table?**

A: No, you cannot lose data if you add a new field to an existing table.

8 **What sort of data loss is possible if you change the size of a field in an existing table?**

A: If you change the size of a field in an existing table, you will lose any characters at the end of Text fields that do not fit into the new field size, and you may lose accuracy when numbers are rounded to fit into the new field size.

Visual Quiz

Q: Why is Long Integer the wrong size for the Hourly Pay field?

A: The Hourly Pay field will hold amounts of money. If its size is Long Integer it can only hold values that are integers without decimals. It can only hold dollars, not cents, and it will not give accurate results in many calculations.

Personal Workbook Answers

Chapter 3

see page 39

① **What are two ways to enter data in a Yes/No field?**

A: To enter data in a Yes/No field, either click the checkbox to add or remove the checkmark, or move the cursor to it and press the Spacebar to add or remove the check mark.

② **What data can you enter in a Hyperlink field?**

A: In a Hyperlink field, you can enter a URL (Uniform Resource Locator), the location of a file on your network, or the location of a file on your own computer.

③ **How do you edit a Hyperlink field?**

A: To edit a Hyperlink field, use Tab (or other cursor movement keys) to move the cursor to the field. Then Press F2 to place an insertion point in it and edit it. It has the # sign around it when it can be edited. Move the cursor to another field when you are done.

④ **How do you save your data entries? How often should you do this?**

A: In general, you do not have to save your entries, because the data entered in a record is saved automatically when you go to a new record. You can save your data while working on a record by pressing Shift+Enter.

⑤ **What is the fastest way to enter a record that is almost identical to an existing record?**

A: The fastest way to enter a record that is almost identical to an existing record is to select the existing record, press Ctrl+C to copy it, choose Edit ⇨ Paste Append to add a new record identical to the existing record, and then edit the new record as necessary.

⑥ **How do you move a column to make it the first column displayed in the datasheet?**

A: To make a column the first column displayed in the datasheet, click its title to select it, then click and drag its title to the left.

⑦ **What is the fastest way to sort records alphabetically by Last Name?**

A: The fastest way to sort records alphabetically by Last Name is to put the cursor in the Last Name field and click Sort Ascending.

⑧ **What should you do if you want to print a table, but it is a bit too wide to fit on a standard page?**

A: If you want to print a table, but it is a bit too wide to fit on a standard page, choose File ⇨ Page Setup, display the Page tab of the Page Setup dialog box, and choose Landscape orientation.

Visual Quiz

Q: The figure shows a Mailing List table with the data display altered. What steps are necessary to display the data in this way?

A: Hide all the columns except the names, city, and state. Put the cursor in the State column and click the Sort Ascending button. Click the title of the State column and click and drag to move it to the far left. Click the title of the City column and click and drag to move it left. Choose Format ⇨ Font, choose Times New Roman as the Font and 12 points as the size. Widen the columns as necessary to display all the data.

Personal Workbook Answers

Chapter 4

see page 67

❶ What are four ways to add a field to the query's design grid?

A: The four ways to add a field to a query's design grid are (1) click and drag the field from the field list to a field cell of the design grid; (2) double-click the field in the field list to place it in the next available column; (3) use the drop-down list in a field cell to choose the field; or (4) type the name of the field in the field cell.

❷ What is the easiest way to select all fields in the field list?

A: To select all fields, double-click the title bar of the field list.

❸ What are two ways to include all fields in the result of the query, and how do they differ?

A: To include all fields in the result of the query, individually add all the fields to the design grid or add the asterisk. They differ in that the asterisk allows the query to be automatically updated if you modify the parent table to add extra fields.

❹ Why would you want to hide a field?

A: You would want to hide a field if you add it to the query to use for a criterion or a Sort but do not want it displayed in the result.

❺ What does it mean if there are several criteria on one line?

A: If there are several criteria on one line, records are included in the result if they match all the criteria.

❻ What does it mean if there are several criteria, one above another, on different lines?

A: If there are several criteria, one above another, records are included in the result if they match any of the criteria.

❼ What are three ways to run a query?

A: You can run a query by choosing Query ⇨ Run, clicking the Run button, or switching to Datasheet view.

Visual Quiz

Q: What do you think the user is trying to do with this query? Is there anything wrong with the query's design?

A: The user is trying to create a query that uses the asterisk to include all the fields of the record, sorts the result alphabetically by name, and includes records just from New York state. The sort order will not be correct, because the query will sort by First Name first (its field is to the left of Last Name). Also, the First Name, Last Name and State fields will be included twice in the result, because their Show checkboxes are not deselected.

Chapter 5

see page 85

❶ What are the four ways of creating a filter?

A: The four ways of creating a filter are *Filter By Selection, Filter For, Filter By Form,* and *Advanced Filter/sort.*

❷ How do you create a Filter By Selection?

A: To create a Filter By Selection, select the value you want to find in the table and choose Records ⇨ Filter ⇨ Filter By Selection, or click the Filter By Selection button.

Personal Workbook Answers

③ How do you create a Filter By Selection or Filter Excluding Selection with multiple criteria?

A: To create a Filter By Selection or Filter Excluding Selection with multiple criteria, simply create a Filter By or Filter Excluding Selection more than once. The new criteria are added to the existing ones in a logical AND relationship.

④ How do you create a Filter For?

A: To create a Filter For, right-click a column and enter the criterion in the Filter For line of its pop-up menu.

⑤ How do you create a Filter By Form?

A: To create a Filter By Form, choose Records ⇨ Filter By Form and enter the criteria in a form that looks like one record of the table.

⑥ How do you create an Advanced Filter/Sort?

A: To create an Advanced Filter/Sort, choose Records ⇨ Advanced Filter/Sort and fill out the Filter window like you fill out a Query window.

⑦ What are three ways to display all records except those from California?

A: To display all records except those from California, you can (1) select CA in the State field and create a Filter Excluding Selection; (2) create a Filter By Form with <>CA as the criterion in the State field; or (3) create an Advanced Filter/Sort with <>CA as the criterion in the State field.

⑧ How do you modify a filter?

A: To modify a filter, display the Filter By Form window or the Advanced Filter/Sort window. It will include the design of the current filter, which you can modify, as you do when you create a new Filter By Form or Advanced Filter/Sort.

Visual Quiz

Q: Here is a filter used with a table that lists employees, with a one-letter code for their job category. What does this filter do?

A: The filter displays all employees who live in New York or New Jersey or Connecticut, and who are in Job Category P, sorted alphabetically by name.

Chapter 6

see page 95

① What is the fastest way to create a form and a report?

A: The fastest way to create a form and a report is to select a table or query in the Database window and then select the AutoForm or AutoReport button.

② What is the one field that should usually be left out of data-entry forms? Why should it be left out?

A: The primary key field should usually be left out of data entry forms, because its value is entered automatically, and if a user edits it by mistake, you can lose data in a relational database.

③ Describe the three views in which you can display a form.

A: The three views you can display a form in are *Design view,* which lets you customize its design, *Form view,* which displays the data in the form, and *Datasheet view,* which displays the form's data in a datasheet.

④ How do you add a filter to a form or a report?

A: You can add a filter to a form by highlighting data and clicking the Filter By Selection button, by clicking the Filter By Form button and entering the data you want to match, or by selecting Records ⇨ Advanced Filter/Sort and entering criteria in the Filter window. You cannot add a filter to a report.

Personal Workbook Answers

5 **Describe the two views in which you can display a report.**

A: The two views you can display a report in are Design view, which lets you customize its design, and Print Preview, which shows you the report as it will be printed.

6 **Describe the three basic report layouts for nongrouped reports.**

A: The three basic report layouts for nongrouped reports are *Columnar,* with fields one above another and the name of each field to its left; *Tabular,* with fields one next to another and the name of each field at the top of each page; and *Justified,* with field width adjusted so the lines are the same length.

7 **On which ranges of values can you group reports?**

A: If the report grouping is based on a Date/Time field, you can group it by year, quarter, month, week, day, hour, and minute. If the report grouping is based on a Text field, you can group it by first letter, first two letters, first three letters, etc. If the report grouping is based on a Numeric field, you can group it by increments of 10, 50, 100, 500, 1000, 5000, and 10000.

8 **What are the summary options for grouped reports?**

A: If Numeric fields are included in a grouped report, you can include their Sum, Average, Minimum value or Maximum value in the summary line for each group and for the report.

Visual Quiz

Q: What is wrong with the prototype label shown on the right, and how can you correct it?

A: The user designed the label incorrectly by just adding fields to it, and forgetting about spaces and punctuation. To add punctuation or spaces on the Prototype Label, place the cursor at the appropriate place and type in the change.

Chapter 7

see page 117

1 **What relationship should each field have to the record it is in?**

A: Each field should have a one-to-one relationship to the record it is in. For example, you have a mailing list with a person listed in each record, you can include the person's name, home address, and Social Security number, because each person has only one of these.

2 **Give an example of a one-to-many relationship.**

A: One possible example of a one-to-many relationship is a list of employees and the number of hours they have worked each week. Each employee works many weeks.

3 **Give an example of a many-to-many relationship**

A: One possible example of a many-to-many relationship is classes and students. Each class has many students in it, and each student is in many classes.

4 **How do you normalize a one-to-many relationship?**

A: To normalize a one-to-many relationship, put the data that can have multiple values in a separate table, and assign it a foreign key that is the same as the primary key in the one table.

5 **How do you normalize a many-to-many relationship?**

A: To normalize a many-to-many relationship between two tables, create a third table that is in a one-to-many relationship with both tables. The third table should include two foreign keys that are the same as the primary keys in the two tables.

Personal Workbook Answers

6 When is a primary key valid, and how can you be sure that only valid values are entered?

A: For a primary key to be valid, it must have an entry that is unique in each record. To make sure it has valid values, use an AutoNumber field as the primary key.

7 When is a foreign key valid, and how can you be sure only valid values are entered?

A: For a foreign key to be valid, it must have an entry that is the same as the value of the primary key in the related table. To make sure it has valid values, select the Enforce Referential Integrity checkbox in the Join Properties dialog box.

8 What data type should you use for a foreign key?

A: If you use an AutoNumber field with default properties as the primary key, you should use a Number field with Long Integer as its Size property as the foreign key in the related table.

Visual Quiz

Q: The picture here shows a data-entry form for two tables in a many-to-one relationship, which does not use a subform. How was this form created?

A: To create this data-entry form without a subform for two tables in a many-to-one relationship, first create a query that joins the two tables. Then use the Form Wizard to create a form based on the query.

Chapter 8

see page 141

1 What are the three types of controls in Access forms?

A: The three types of controls in Access forms are *bound controls,* which are associated with data in the table; *unbound controls,* which are independent of the data in the table; and *calculated controls,* which are created using expressions.

2 What are three features of the Form window that you display or hide by clicking buttons on the toolbar? What is their purpose?

A: The three features of the Form window that you display or hide by clicking buttons on the toolbar are the *field list,* which you can use to add fields to the form; the *toolbox,* which you can use to add controls to the form; and the *property sheet,* which you use to specify properties of the form or its objects.

3 What are three ways of selecting an entire form?

A: Three ways of selecting an entire form are to choose Edit ⇨ Select Form, choose Form in the Select Object drop-down list, or click the Form Selector box in the upper-left corner of the form.

4 What are three ways of selecting multiple controls in a form?

A: To select multiple objects in a form, hold down the Shift key when you click objects, or click and drag a dotted rectangle to enclose group of objects, or choose Edit ⇨ Select All.

5 How can you move a field and move its label at the same time?

A: To move a field with its label, select it and click and drag its edge.

6 How can you move a field without moving its label?

A: To move a field without moving its label, select it and click and drag its Move box.

7 What is *tab order* and how do you change it?

A: Tab order is the order of the fields that the cursor moves to when the user presses the Tab key. To change it, choose Tab Order from the pop-up menu to display the Tab Order dialog box. Then click the Auto Order button to set the tab order so the user tabs through from top to bottom and from left to right, or click and drag the rows in the Custom Order list to set the order manually.

8 **What are the three elements of an object whose color you can change?**

A: The three elements of an object whose color you can change are Fill/Background Color, Font/Foreground Color, and Line/Border Color.

Visual Quiz

Q: **This form was created by modifying an AutoForm, using techniques covered in this chapter. How do you change an AutoForm to produce this Form?**

A: After you create the AutoForm, display it in Design view. Select and delete the key field and other unneeded fields and their labels. Delete the labels of the Middle Initial and Last Name field, of the second Address field, and of the State and Zip fields. Resize the form to make it wider, if necessary. Drag the Middle Initial field to the right of the First Name field, and resize it, so it is just large enough to display one letter. Drag the Last Name field to the right of the Middle Initial field. Drag the second address field so it is to the right of the first address field. Drag the State and Zip field to the right of the City field and resize them, so they are large enough to display a two-letter state name and a zip code. Edit the label of the First Name field so it just reads "Name." Edit the label of the Address 1 field so it just reads "Address." Edit the label of the City field so it reads City/State/Zip. Select all the labels, and then click the size drop-down list to make them 10 point and the Bold button to make them boldface. Choose Format ➪ Size ➪ To Fit to make the label boxes fit the new size. Select the Address and City/State/Zip line and click and drag them upward, so they are not too far from the Name line. Click and drag the edge of the form to resize it, so it fits around these fields.

Chapter 9

see page 161

1 **How do you add a field to a form?**

A: To add a field to a form, click the Field List button, and then click and drag a field from the field list to the form.

2 **What are two ways to add text to a form?**

A: To add text to a form, click the Toolbox button to display it, and click the Label button. Then either (1) click and drag on the form to define a label box and enter the text in it, or (2) just click on the form and type, and the label box will automatically fit the text you enter.

3 **You want to add an option group enabling the user to choose from three values for a field. You also want to add a control enabling the user to choose a value for a Yes/No field. What is the best control to use for each?**

A: Use Radio Buttons for the Option Group, and use a Checkbox for the Yes/No field, unless you have some special reason for using another control. These are the controls that people expect to use to choose among several values and to choose Yes or No.

4 **How do you add a drop-down list to a form to let the user choose from three possible entries for a field?**

A: To add a drop-down list to a form, display the toolbox, click the Combo Box button, and follow the instructions in the Wizard to add the control. Then, to restrict the user to the three options, display the Combo Box's property sheet and select Yes as its Limit To List property.

5 **How do you add a colored rectangle behind a group of four fields on your form, to highlight those fields?**

A: To add a colored rectangle behind a group of four fields on your form, display the toolbox, click the

Rectangle button, and click and drag on the form to place the rectangle. Then, with the rectangle selected, click the Fill Color button to choose its color. Finally, choose Format ⇨ Send to Back, so the rectangle does not hide the fields.

6 How do you make a form print out with basic information (such as name and address) on one page, and the other information for the record on a second page?

A: To make a form print out with basic information (such as name and address) on one page, and the other information for the record on a second page, click the Page Break button. Then click in the form below the basic information, to add a page break there.

7 You want your fields to be grouped on two tabs, so users can click a tab to display only the fields they need to see. How do you do this?

A: To group your fields on two tabs, first, display the toolbox, click the Tab control, and click and drag to place the tabs. Then click the Field List button to display the field list, click Tabs of the Tab Control to bring them to the front as necessary, and click and drag the fields onto each tab.

8 How do you control the fineness of the grid that is used to align controls on the form?

A: To control the fineness of the grid that is used to align controls, click the Properties button to display the Property Sheet, if necessary. Click the form's selection box to select it and display its properties. Click the Format tab of the Property Sheet, if necessary. Enter integers as the Grid X and Grid Y property to control the fineness of the grid. For example, if you enter 4, gridlines will be one-quarter inch apart.

Visual Quiz

Q: The figure shows a form that lets you enter the employee number in the Billing table by choosing from a scrolling list that includes the employee number and name from the Contractor table. How do you create this form?

A: Create an AutoForm for the Billing table. Display it in Design view. Delete the Employee Number field. Display the toolbox. Click the List Box button, and click and drag to locate the List Box. In the first step of the Wizard, select I want the list box to look up the values in a table or query. In the second step, choose Contractors as the table to find the value in. In the next step, choose Employee Number, First Name and Last Name as the fields to include in the List Box. In the next step, select the checkbox to display the key field; adjust the column width. In the next step, select Employee Number as the value to store in the table. In the next step, click the Store the value in this field radio button, and select Employee Number as the field to store it in. In the final step, give the list box the label "Choose the Employee" and click Finish. Move the label so it is under the list. Resize and move the objects on the form as necessary.

Chapter 10

see page 189

1 What is the difference between *sorting* and *grouping*?

A: To group records, you must sort them and add a group header or footer to separate the groups. The only difference between sorted records and grouped records is the presence of a group header or footer.

2 How do you create a complex sort?

A: To create a complex sort, select all the fields you want to sort on in the Sorting and Grouping window. The first field you select (for example, the Last Name) will be the basis of the sort, and the remaining fields (For example, the First Name and Middle Name) will be tie-breakers.

3 **How do you create groups with subgroups?**

A: To create groups with subgroups, create a complex sort as described above, and add group headers or footers for each field you sort on.

4 **How do you group records by month and sort them by date within each month?**

A: To group records by Month on a Date field and sort them by date within each month (based on the same Date field), create two different sorts based on the field. Keep Each Value as the Group On property of one, and do not include a group header or footer. Choose Month as the Group On property of the other, and include a group header or footer.

5 **What should you do to make sure that a group's header is not printed at the bottom of a page, with the first record in that group printed on the top of the next page?**

A: To make sure that a group's header is not printed at the bottom of a page, with the first record in that group printed on the top of the next page, choose With First Detail as the groups Keep Together property in the Sorting and Grouping window. Alternatively, choose Whole Group as the Keep Together property to begin printing the group at the top of a new page.

6 **What are two ways that you can use Page Setup to fit more fields on each line of a report?**

A: To fit more fields on each line of the report, use the Margins tab of the Page Setup dialog box to create smaller left and right margins, and use the Page Tab of Page layout to select Landscape Orientation.

7 **You use the Label Wizard to create labels sorted alphabetically by name, and you find that the names are listed across each row. How can you change the labels so the names are listed down each column instead?**

A: To change labels created by the Wizard so the names are listed down each column, choose File ➪ Page Setup. In the Columns tab of the Page Setup dialog box, select the Down, then Across radio button.

8 **How do you add a calculated field to a report?**

A: Add a calculated expression to a report in the same way you add one to a field. Use the Text Box button of the toolbox to add a new text box. Then select this text box and click the Properties button if necessary to display its Property Sheet. Display the Data tab. Enter an expression as its Control Source property, or click the Build button to the right of this property and use the Expression Builder to generate the expression.

Visual Quiz

Q: **You let someone else work on your computer, and when you came back, you found that your mailing labels looked like the figure. What can you do to correct them?**

A: The labels do not have enough room to display all the data on one line. To correct them, use the Margins tab of the Page Setup dialog box to make the margins smaller. You may also have to use the Columns tab to change the Column Spacing and Width. To see if this is necessary, print out a sample page, and compare it with the size and spacing of the labels you use.

Personal Workbook Answers

Chapter 11

see page 205

1 **How do you create a *parameter query*?**

A: To create a parameter query, create a select query. In the Criteria line of the design grid, enter a Parameter enclosed in square brackets instead of a criterion. Then choose Query ⇨ Parameters to display the Query Parameters dialog box, and enter the same Parameter and its data type.

2 **What are the four types of *action query*?**

A: The four types of action query are *make-table queries, update queries, append queries,* and *delete queries.*

3 **What is the easiest way to create a new table that holds only your employees from California and to remove these employees from your old Employees table?**

A: To create a new table that holds only your employees from California, use a make-table query with CA as the Criteria for the State field. Then, to remove these records from your old Employee table, choose Query ⇨ Delete to convert this query into a delete query, and run it.

4 **You run an action query, and Access displays an error message saying it did not add two records due to lock violations. What should you do to correct this error?**

A: If you run an action query and Access displays an error message saying it did not add records due to lock violations, it means that those records could not be modified, because other people on the network were using them. Cancel the query, and run it again when other people are less likely to be using the table.

5 **You run an action query, and Access displays an error message saying it did not add 156 records due to key violations. What should you do to correct this error?**

A: If you run an action query and Access displays an error message saying it did not add records due to key violations, that means that records you are adding to the table have the same primary key as records already in the table. Assuming that the primary key is an AutoNumber field, you should correct this error by not including this field in the action query. Then Access will automatically add consecutively numbered primary keys to the records that the action query adds to the table.

6 **What are two ways to display the total hours worked by employees in each job category in each state? Which is preferable?**

A: You can display the total hours worked by employees in each job category in each state by using a query with groups and totals or by using a crosstab query. It is preferable to use a crosstab query, because the result is easier to understand, and because it is easier to create the query using the Crosstab Query Wizard.

7 **What are two ways to change the heading at the top of a field in the result of a query?**

A: There are two ways to change the heading displayed at the top of the column in the result of the query. In the Field property sheet of the field or expression, enter the heading you want as its Caption property. Or enter a new name followed by a colon before the field name or expression in the design grid. Only the name before the colon is used as the column heading.

8 **How can you create a query that lists all the cities in your mailing list where people live, with the state listed after each city?**

A: To list all the cities where people in your mailing list live, with the state listed after each city, create a query that includes just the City and State field, and set the Unique Records property to Yes. The result would include each combination of cities and states in the table just once.

Visual Quiz

Q: The figure on the right shows an update query with complex criteria. What will this query do?

A: This update query will increase the value in the Hourly Pay field by $5 for employees who are in job category P or W and who also were hired before January 1, 1998.

Chapter 12

see page 227

❶ What are the three areas of the Macro window that you fill out to create simple macros, and what do you enter in each?

A: Three areas of the Macro window that you fill out to create simple macros are the Action column, where you specify each action that the macro performs, the Comment column, where you enter a description of the Action for your own use, and the Arguments panel, where you enter arguments that control how actions are performed.

❷ What additional areas may be displayed when you create more advanced macros, and what do you enter in each?

A: When you create more advanced macros, Access may display a Macro Name column, where you enter the name of Macro Groups, and a Conditions column, where you enter conditions that determine whether an action will be performed.

❸ What are two ways of adding an OpenTable action to a macro?

A: You can add an OpenTable action to a Macro by selecting OpenTable in the Action column and selecting a table name as its argument, or by clicking and dragging the table from the Database window to the Macro window.

❹ How do you add conditional actions to a macro?

A: To add conditional Actions to a Macro, click the Conditions button to add a Conditions column to the Macro window, and enter a logical expression in this column (or place the cursor in this column, click the Build button of the toolbar, and use the Expression Builder to generate a logical expression); the action to its right will run only if the expression evaluates to true. To add a series of conditional Actions, type an ellipsis (three dots) in cells under the logical expression; the Actions to their right also will run only if the expression evaluates to true.

❺ What is the most common cause of macro errors and how can you avoid it?

A: The most common cause of Macro errors is running the macro from the wrong place: for example, if the user double-clicks the macro in the Database window, but it was meant to be run from a data-entry form. You can avoid this problem by including the macro in a group, so it cannot be run from the Database window.

❻ How can you prevent users from running any macros in a macro group?

A: To prevent users from running any macros in a macro group, include an initial "dummy" macro that does not have any Action. If users try to run the macro group from the Database window, nothing will happen.

7 How do you run a macro one step at a time?

A: To run a macro one step at a time, display the macro in Design view and click the Single Step button or choose Run ⇨ Single Step. Then, when you run the Macro, Access will display the Macro Single Step dialog box, and run one action of the macro each time you click the Step button.

8 How do you create a switchboard?

A: To create a switchboard, create a form with no fields. Add Command Buttons that the user can click to use different features of an application.

Visual Quiz

Q: Users double-clicked macro groups with initial dummy macros, and when nothing happened, they complained that something was wrong, so the developer changed the initial dummy macro as shown on the right. What happens now if a user tries to run the macro group by double-clicking it in the Database window?

A: If users try to run this Macro Group by double-clicking it in the Database Window, it beeps to let them know they are making an error.

Chapter 13

see page 247

1 What are two reasons for giving a Text field a size that is different from the default 50?

A: You may want to give a Text field a size that is different from the default 50 so it can hold more data (up to 255 characters) or to reduce errors in data entry (for example, by giving a Middle Initial field the size of 1 character).

2 You are creating a table with a Number field, and you do not know what sort of data it will hold. What size should you give it?

A: If you want a Number field to hold any possible numeric data, give it the size Double.

3 What is the difference between a Currency field and a Number field? When should you use the Currency data type?

A: Currency fields use fixed point calculations, and Number fields use floating-point calculations, which are slower. Use the Currency data type for any field that requires extensive calculations that do not have to be accurate to more than four decimal places.

4 How is the Caption property used?

A: The text you enter as a field's Caption property is used as the heading of that field's column in the Datasheet view. By default, the field name is used as the heading, and you can enter a caption if you want to replace the field name.

5 Which properties do you use to validate data?

A: To validate data, use the Validation Rule and Validation Text properties, which let you test the data entered. As the validation rule, enter a logical expression. This expression is evaluated whenever data is entered or edited in the field, and the validation text is displayed if it evaluates as false.

6 How do you enter a zero-length string, and why would you use it?

A: To enter a zero-length string in a field, type "" (two quotation marks with nothing between them). You use it to distinguish between fields that you know have no appropriate value (where you enter a zero-length string) and fields that have not yet been filled in (which are blank).

7 Should you store the inserted characters that an input mask displays in a field?

A: Unless there is some special reason not to, you should always store the inserted characters that an input mask displays in a field. It requires a very small additional amount of disk space, which usually is not noticeable, and it makes it easier to create reports.

8 You have used the wizard to create a lookup field. What are two ways that you can prevent a user from entering values that are not in the drop-down list, and which way is usually better?

A: Two ways that you can prevent a user from entering values that are not in the drop-down list of a lookup field are (1) choose List Box as its Display Control property or (2) choose Yes as its Limit to List property. It is generally better to choose Yes as the Limit to List property, because the user can still type entries in the box rather than choosing them with the drop-down list, which is sometimes more convenient.

Visual Quiz

Q: In the figure, there is an input mask for a complicated Billing Code field. What is entered in this field?

A: The initial > converts all characters entered to upper-case. The billing code must have any two characters (letters or numbers), followed by any two numbers, followed by any two letters. Then it optionally can have any two characters (letters or numbers) followed by any two numbers, followed by any two letters. All these groups of two are automatically separated by hyphens.

Chapter 14

see page 267

1 What is a *literal*, and how do you enter one in the Expression Builder?

A: A literal is part of an expression that is used as it is entered in the expression, rather than standing for some other value. You must enter literals in the text box of the Expression Builder, with the # delimiter around date literals and the " delimiter around text literals.

2 What is *string concatenation*, and what are two operators that perform it?

A: String concatenation means combining two pieces of text in an expression. You can perform it using the operator & or +.

3 What are two functions you can use to display the current date?

A: You can display the current date using the function Date( ) or the function Now( ) with the Long Date format.

4 What is the result of the expression #1/1/00# − #1/1/99#?

A: The result of the expression #1/1/00# − #1/1/99# is 365 (the number of days between Jan. 1, 1999 and Jan. 1, 2000).

5 How do you validate data entered in a field?

A: To validate data entered in a field, display the table in Design view, and put the cursor in the field. For the field's Validation Rule property, enter an expression that evaluates as true or false. For the field's Validation Text property, enter an error message that will be displayed when the Validation Rule expression evaluates as false.

6 **How do you create a default value for a field?**

A: To create a default value for a field, display the table in Design view, and put the cursor in the field. As its Default Value property, enter = followed by the value you want, with delimiters if necessary. For example, to make NY the default value, enter **="NY"** as its Default Value property.

7 **How do you create a query that only displays records whose Date field is either today or some future date?**

A: To create a query that only displays records whose Date field is either today or some future date, as the criterion for the Date field, enter the expression **>=Date()**.

8 **How do you add page numbers to a report?**

A: To add page numbers to a report, add a text box to the report. As its Control Source Property, use one of the Common Expressions in the Expression Builder that displays page numbers.

Visual Quiz

Q: The expression in the figure includes the most common error that users make when they are concatenating text strings. What is the error, and how can you change the expression to correct it?

A: The expression does not include spaces. As a result, it would read something like `The employee's name is JohnSmith.` To correct the error, add a space at the end of the text literal, and add another text literal that just contains a space between the first and last name, so the expression reads `="The employee's name is " & [First Name] & " " & [Last Name].`

Chapter 15

see page 291

1 **Apart from Access, what software do you need to use data access pages?**

A: To use data access pages, you must have Microsoft Internet Explorer 5.0 or later installed on your computer.

2 **What extensions can be used in the filenames of data access pages, and what do they stand for?**

A: Data access pages can have the extensions .htm or .html. HTML stands for Hypertext Markup Language, the code used for Web pages.

3 **What is the easiest way to give all your data access pages a distinctive style?**

A: To give all your data access pages a distinctive style, choose Format ➪ Theme. Select a style in the Theme dialog box, and if you like, click Set Default to make it the default style of all new pages.

4 **How do you edit a Hyperlink field? Why can't you edit it like other fields?**

A: You cannot edit a Hyperlink field like other fields, because clicking it will jump to the hyperlink, rather than put the cursor in it. To edit a Hyperlink field, press Tab or the arrow keys to move the cursor to it. Then press F2 to put the cursor in it and add signs around it to show that is can be edited. Move the cursor to another field when you are done.

5 **What is the fastest way to add a Hyperlink field to an existing table?**

A: The fastest way to add a Hyperlink field to an existing table is to choose Insert ➪ Hyperlink Column. Then double-click the title of the column and edit the text to rename it.

6 **What are the two types of hyperlinks that you can add to a form or report?**

A: The two types of hyperlinks that you can add to a form or report are a *bound hyperlink,* which changes when the record changes, or an *unbound hyperlink,* which does not change when the record changes.

7 **How do you add a hyperlink to a picture or command button?**

A: To add a hyperlink to a picture or command button, create it as usual. Then enter an address as the Hyperlink Address property, in the Format tab of its property sheet.

8 **You have closed a table that has a Hyperlink field, but the Web toolbar is still displayed. How do you get rid of it?**

A: To get rid of the Web toolbar, right-click it and then click Web in its pop-up menu.

Visual Quiz

Q: The form in the figure includes an unbound hyperlink in its header. How do you add this hyperlink?

A: To add this unbound hyperlink, display the form in Design view, select its header, and choose Insert ➪ Hyperlink. In the Insert Hyperlink dialog box, as the Text to display, enter **Visit Our Company's Home Page.** As the File or Web Page Name, type the address of your Home Page. Click the Screen Tip button and in the Hyperlink Screen Tip dialog box type in **Click Here to See the International Widgets World Wide Web Home Page.** Click OK to return to the Insert Hyperlink Dialog Box and click OK again to insert the Hyperlink. Select the Hyperlink, and change its Font Size. Click and drag to resize it and place it as necessary.

Chapter 16

see page 307

1 **What is the difference between *linked* and *embedded* objects?**

A: Linked objects are stored in the source application, and Access contains a link to them. If they are changed in the source application, they will also change in Access. Embedded applications are in Access; if they change in the source application, they will not change in Access.

2 **What are the two most common ways to add an OLE object to a field?**

A: To add an OLE object to a field, choose Insert ➪ Object and use the Insert Object dialog box to open a source application and create the object or to select it in an existing file. Alternatively, display the object in the source application, choose Edit ➪ Copy, return to the Access field, and choose Edit ➪ Paste or Edit Paste Special.

3 **How do you edit an OLE object?**

A: To edit an OLE object, double-click it in Access to open the source application, which you use to edit it. If the object is linked, you can also edit it directly in the source application.

4 **What are the two types of OLE objects you can add to forms or reports?**

A: The two types of OLE objects you can add to forms or reports are *bound OLE objects,* which are based on an OLE Object field and change when the record changes, or *unbound OLE objects,* which are not based on a field and do not change.

Personal Workbook Answers

⑤ How do you delete an OLE object that you have entered in a table?

A: To delete an OLE object from a table, simply select its field and choose Edit ⇨ Delete or press Delete.

⑥ What is the difference between a *bound* and *unbound* OLE object in a form or report?

A: A *bound* OLE object displays the data in an OLE Object field in the table or query that the form or report is based on, so it is different for different records. An *unbound* OLE object does not depend on data in the table or query, and it remains the same regardless of the record.

⑦ How can you add and edit an OLE object from a source application that does not support OLE?

A: To add an OLE object from a source application that does not support OLE, use Copy and Paste. To edit it, you must edit it within the source application and use Copy and Paste to add it again. (You cannot edit it by double-clicking it in Access.)

⑧ How do you scale an OLE object, and what are the three options for scaling?

A: To scale an OLE object, use the object frame's Size Mode property in the Format tab of its Property Sheet. The three options for scaling are Clip, which displays only part of the object that can fit into the frame; Stretch, which makes the object larger or smaller to fill the frame exactly, even if this means distorting its shape; and Zoom, which makes the object larger or smaller to fit the frame without distorting its shape, even if it does not fill the frame completely.

Visual Quiz

Q: The data-entry form in the figure has two OLE objects: a logo in its header to the right of the words "Music On Line," and a field with sounds that you can double-click to play a sample. Explain how both of these OLE objects are added.

A: The logo in its header to the right of the words "Music On Line" is an unbound OLE object: it does not change as the records change. To add it, click the Unbound OLE Object button, click and drag to add the object frame, and use the Insert Object dialog box to choose the file that it is contained in. Alternatively, copy it in another application and paste it into the Access form. The music sample is a bound OLE object: It is different for each record. To add it, include an OLE Object field in the table that this form is based on, and add that field to the form as you add any other field; for example, by clicking and dragging it from the field list to the form. The words "Double-click here to play a sample" are a text object placed on top of the bound OLE object. You add the text object by clicking the Label button of the toolbox, typing the text, and changing its font and size, then you click and drag it to move it above the bound OLE object.

Chapter 17

see page 319

① What are two ways to rename a database object?

A: Two ways to rename a database object are to select it in the Database window, then either choose Edit ⇨ Rename or click the name again to change the name to editable text. Then edit the name to rename it.

② What is the easiest way to back up a database table?

A: Select the database in the Database Window, press Ctrl+C to copy it, and press Ctrl+V to paste it. In the

Paste Table As dialog box, enter a new name for the file, be sure Structure and Data are selected, and click OK.

③ How do you create a new group in the Database window?

A: Right-click the button for an existing group and choose New Group from its pop-up menu. Enter its name in the New Group dialog box.

④ How do you add objects to a group and remove objects from a group?

A: Display that object's panel in the Database window, and click and drag the object from that panel to the group's to button. To remove objects from a group, display the group's panel in the Database window, select the object, and click the Delete button or press Delete.

⑤ What is the easiest way to index on a single field?

A: Display the table in Design view, place the cursor in the row of that field, and choose Yes (Duplicates Allowed) as its Index property.

⑥ How do you index on multiple fields?

A: Display the table in Design view, and click the Indexes button to display the Indexes window. Enter a name for the index in the Index Name column, and select field names and sort orders to its right and in the rows below it.

⑦ When you use the arrow keys to move through a table, you want Access to place the cursor at the beginning of the field, rather than highlight the entry in the field. How do you do this?

A: Choose Tools ⇨ Options to display the Options dialog box. Click Keyboard to display the Keyboard tab. In the Behavior entering field box, choose the Go to start of field radio button.

⑧ How do you convert the main Access toolbar into a floating toolbar? How do you convert the Toolbox displayed when you design forms into a toolbar at the top of the screen?

A: To convert Access's main toolbar into a floating toolbar, click and drag the double-line at its left edge to move it to the middle of the screen. To convert the toolbox displayed when you design forms into a toolbar, click and drag its title bar to the top of the screen.

Visual Quiz

Q: Someone who does not use most of the tools in the toolbox for form and report design created the Quick Toolbox shown on the right. What steps are needed to create this Quick Toolbox?

A: To create the Quick Toolbox, choose Tools ⇨ Customize. In the Customize dialog box, click Toolbars to display the Toolbars tab, if necessary. Click New. In the New Toolbar dialog box, enter the name Quick Toolbox, and click OK. Then, click Commands to display the Commands tab. Click Toolbox in the Categories list. Click and drag the Label button, the Textbox button, the Checkbox button, the Image button, the Line button and the Rectangle button from the Commands list to the Quick Toolbox window.

Chapter 18

see page 333

① What are two easy ways to get help about a property of a field or other object?

A: Put the cursor in the property (in the Property Sheet or property panel of the Table window in Design view) and press F1, or choose Help ⇨ What's This and then click the property.

Personal Workbook Answers

② What are two easy ways to get help about a toolbar button?

A: Put the cursor on it to display its name, or choose Help ⇨ What's This? and click it to display a longer explanation.

③ How do you use the Assistant to get help?

A: Click the Help toolbar button or choose Help ⇨ Microsoft Access Help to display the Assistant, if necessary. Or click the Assistant to display its balloon, if necessary. Enter a question in the balloon and click Search. When Access displays a list of topics, click one to display help about it.

④ How do you use a different Assistant?

A: Right-click the Assistant and select Choose Assistant from its pop-up menu. Access displays the Gallery tab of the Office Assistant dialog box. Click the Back and Next buttons to display the available Assistants, and click OK when you have found the one you want.

⑤ How do you use the Contents tab of the help system?

A: Click the Show button to display the tabs, and click Contents, if necessary. Browse through the list of books until you find the general topic you want. Double-click that topic, or click the + sign to its left to display a list of pages. (If Access displays subtopics instead of pages, double-click subtopics until you reach a list of pages.) Click a page to display help about that topic.

⑥ How do you use the Index tab of the help system?

A: Click the Show button to display the tabs, and click Index, if necessary. Enter the initial letters of the key word you want to search for. When Access displays the subject you want in the key words list, double-click it to display a list of related topics. Then click a topic to display help about it.

⑦ The Assistant is driving you crazy. What should you do?

A: Replace it with the Office Logo, which is the least Active Assistant. Right-click the Assistant and select Choose Assistant from its pop-up menu. Then click the Back and Next buttons in the Gallery until you find the Office Logo, and click OK. Or, change the Assistant's behavior by clicking it and clicking Options in its balloon, and then using the checkboxes in the Options panel to change the behavior that bothers you.

Visual Quiz

Q: The figure shows help on using wildcard characters in a find. What steps did the user go through to display this help?

A: The user displayed the help system by using the Assistant for a search. Then the user clicked the Show button to show the tabs, clicked Contents, browsed through the folders, clicked the folder labeled Data: Find to display its pages, and clicked the page labeled About using wildcard characters to display that help topic.

Glossary

A

action query A query that changes the data in a table. The types of action query are make-table queries, update queries, append queries, and delete queries.

advanced filter/sort A filter where you specify the records are displayed and their order by using the Advanced Filter/Sort Window, which is like the Query window.

Answer Wizard (help system) A tab of the help system that lets you enter questions in ordinary English and displays lists of related topics, like the Assistant.

append query A query that appends data from one table to another existing table, without affecting the data already in that table.

Assistant (help system) The primary form of help available in Access and other Office applications, an animated figure that lets you enter questions in ordinary English and displays lists of related topics.

AutoForm A form that is created automatically, based on a table or query.

AutoFormats Predefined formats that you can apply to forms and reports, with distinctive styles for their background and controls.

AutoNumber data type A field type that holds numbers that Access automatically enters. You cannot change the numbers that Access enters in this field.

AutoPage A data access page that is created automatically, based on a table or query.

AutoReport A report that is created automatically, based on a table or query.

B

bound hyperlink A hyperlink that is bound to a field, so it changes when the record changes.

bound OLE object An OLE object that is bound to a field, so it changes when the record changes.

Build button A button with three dots on it to the right of many properties. You can click the Build button to display a dialog box that lets you choose the property.

C

checkbox A box that the user clicks to add or remove a check mark, to enter the value in a Yes/No field. You can also create an Option Group with checkboxes, to let the user choose among several values.

column Because of the way they are arranged in the table, fields are also called *columns*. See field.

combo box A control in a form that let you choose a field's entries from a drop-down list or enter it in a text box.

GLOSSARY

command button A control in a form that the user clicks to execute some action, like the OK and Cancel buttons of most dialog boxes.

constant An element of an expression that contains a constant value defined by Access, such as Null, which refers to an empty field.

Contents tab (help system) A tab of the Help System that displays a relatively small number of general topics, which you can click to display subtopics and specific help pages.

control Any element that you add to an Access form or report, such as a field, a label, a line, a hyperlink or an OLE object.

crosstab query A query that displays the summary data in rows and columns based on values in the fields, using one field as the basis of the row heading, one field as the basis of the column heading, and filling in the cells of the result table with summary information about all the records that fall under both the row and the column heading.

Currency data type A field type that holds numbers used as amounts of money, or any numbers used in calculations with up to four decimal places of accuracy.

data access page A database object that lets users view or edit data, which is in a HTML file and can be used on the World Wide Web.

database In Access, all the tables, queries, forms, reports, pages, and programs that are used to manage the data for an application. (In other database management systems, *database* just refers to the tables that hold the data.)

Datasheet view A view of a table or form that displays its data with a record in each row and a field in each column.

Date/Time data type A field type that holds dates and times. Whether you can enter a date or a time depends on the format you give to the field.

default relationship A relationship among tables in a relational database which you define in the Relationships window and which is used by default when you create an object that includes those tables.

delete query A type of action query that delete records that meet some criterion.

Design view A view of a database object that lets you change its design.

E

expression A special kind of calculation, a bit like a calculation in arithmetic, but it can include identifiers, functions, constants, operators, and literals, and it can evaluate to true or false, to dates, or to text, as well as to numbers.

field A piece of data that appears in each record. For example, if you have a list of names and addresses, the first name might be one field, the last name might be the second field, and the street address might be the third field.

field list A box displayed in Design view that includes all the fields in the table or query that the query, form, report, or page is based on. You can add field to the design by clicking and dragging it from the field list.

filter An element of a table or form that determines which records are displayed and their order, like a query except that is not an independent object.

Filter By Form A way of creating a filter that specifies which records are displayed by filling out a form that is similar to the table in Datasheet view.

Filter By Selection A way of creating a filter that specifies which records are displayed by highlighting a value in the table in Datasheet view that you want the records to match.

Filter Excluding Selection A way of creating a filter that specifies which records are displayed by highlighting a value in the table in Datasheet view that you want the records not to match.

Filter For A way of creating a filter that specifies which records are displayed by entering a criterion directly in the shortcut menu.

Find Lets you look up a record with the value you specify in fields that hold text or numbers. For example, you can use a Find to look up someone by name.

foreign key A field that is not the primary key field of the table it is in, which is used to link the table to another table by matching the primary key field of that table.

form A database object used to enter and edit data, which displays one record at a time.

function An element of an expression that is a special calculation built into Access. For example, there are functions that perform financial calculations such as Present Value and Future Value, and functions that return the current date and time.

groups Tabs in the Database window let you organize your objects conveniently, by holding shortcuts to objects of different types that you work with at the same time.

HTML *See* Hypertext Markup Language.

hyperlink Text or a graphic that you click to jump to a document on the World Wide Web or on your own computer or network.

Hyperlink data type The field type that holds the address of a Web page or other document, which you can display by clicking the field.

Hypertext Markup Language (HTML) A set of tags that add to text to indicate how it should be displayed in a Web browser, such as Netscape Navigator or Microsoft Internet Explorer. Simple tags indicate that a line is a heading and should be displayed in larger type, that a paragraph begins, or that a graphic should be inserted.

I

identifier An element of an expression that identifies objects from the Access database, such as tables, forms, and reports, and to fields or other objects in them. For example, the First Name field of the Contractors table can be referred to as `[Contractors]![First Name]`.

index An ordered list of values in one or more fields of a table, with pointers to the records that hold these values. A table's index works like a book's. For example, looking up a topic in a book's index and then going to the page is faster than reading the entire book until you find the topic. It is faster for Access to look up a value (such as a name) in an index and go to the record than it is to read through the entire table until it finds the name.

Glossary

Index tab (help system) A tab of the help system that lets you search through al long list of key words and display the Help topics related to a key word.

input mask A property of text, number, date/time, and currency fields that specifies how data must be entered. For example, if you have a six character text field, an input mask can specify that the user must enter numbers as the first three characters and letters as the last three characters; it can also include literal characters, such as the hyphens of a Social Security Number, that are displayed in the field when the user enters data and that cannot be edited.

L

Label tool A tool that you use to add new text to a form, report, or data access page.

list box A control that lets the user choose a field's entries from a scrollable list of values.

literal An element of an expression that is used literally as it appears in the expression. For example, if you multiply the value in some field by 5, the field name is used to refer to the value in the field, and the number 5 is used literally.

lookup field A type of field whose value the user can select from a drop-down list.

M

macro A series of actions that are combined, so you can execute them all using a single command.

make-table query A type of action query that creates a new table that holds the result of the query, or that replaces all the data in an existing table with the result of the query.

many-to-many relationship A relationship among tables in a relational database, where each entity in the first table is related to many entities in the second, and each entity in the second is related to many entities in the first. For example, in a database for a school, the Students and Classes table are in a many-to-many relationship, because each student can take many classes, and each class has many students enrolled.

many-to-one relationship A relationship among tables in a relational database, where each entity in the first table is related to many entities in the second, and each entity in the second is related to only one entity in the first. For example, in a database holding records of employee's paychecks, the Paycheck and Employee tables are in a many-to-one relationship, because each employee gets many paychecks, but each paycheck goes to only one employee.

Memo data type A field type that holds text of up to 65,000 characters. Unlike text fields, memo fields are variable length: You do not specify a maximum size for them.

N

normalization The process of breaking up the data in a relational database into multiple tables.

Number data type A field type used to holds numbers actually used in calculations. The type of number it can hold and accuracy of calculations depends on the size you give to the number field. Some number fields hold only integers and others can hold numbers with many decimal places.

O

Object Linking and Embedding (OLE) A feature of many Windows applications that allows objects from one application to be used in another.

OLE *See* Object Linking and Embedding.

OLE Object data type A field type that holds data from other Window applications that support Object Linking and Embedding (OLE). This field can be used to attach pictures, sound files, or any other type of data available from other Windows applications.

operator An element of an expression that tell the expression what operations to perform on other values. For example, the + operator means that the values on either side of it (the operator) are added.

option button A radio button that the user clicks to enter the value in a Yes/No field. You can also create an option group with option buttons, to let the user choose among several values.

option group A group of controls that work together to let the user enter data in a field that has only a few possible entries. It is usually made up of radio buttons (option buttons), you can also create an option group made up of checkboxes or toggle buttons. In any case, if the user selects one of the options, the others are automatically deselected.

orphan record In a relational database, a record in the many table whose foreign key does not refer to any record in the one table.

P

page *See* data access page.

Page Break tool A tool used to add a page break that breaks a form into pages, which the user moves among by pressing the PgDn and PgUp keys, so you can control exactly which parts of the form the user sees at one same time. Page breaks also control how the form is printed.

parameter query A query whose criterion you enter in a dialog box that Access displays each time you run it. For example, you could use one query to find records from any state, by entering the state in the dialog box when you run the query.

primary key A field or a combination of fields that uniquely identifies each record in a table. The most common primary key is a sequentially numbered field, such as Employee Number or Customer Number, which is given a unique value for each record in the table.

Print Preview A window that displays an object exactly as it will look when it is printed, and that lets you zoom in and out to see the page in different sizes.

property sheet A list of many features of an object. For example, a property sheet for a field includes its size, its background, foreground and border colors, the source of its data, validation rules, and many other properties.

Q

QBE *See* Query By Example.

query An object that lets you select records and fields of a table or another query and to specify their sort order. Select queries control what data is displayed, and action queries change data.

Query By Example (QBE) The method of designing queries used in Access, based on entering examples of the data you want in the result of the query.

R

record All the data about one entity. For example, if you have a list of names and addresses, each record includes the name and address of one person.

GLOSSARY

referential integrity In a relational database, the Foreign Key field in the many table of a one-to-many relationship must correspond to the primary key of a record in the one table. This is called *referential integrity,* because each record in the many table must refer to a record in the one table.

relational database A database where the data is stored in multiple tables that are related to each other using common key fields. For example, you might have a table that lists your employees, with an Employee number in each record, and a second table that lists how many hours each employee worked each week, also with an Employee Number in each record. The Employee Number is the is the primary key of the table that lists employees and the foreign key of the table that lists hours worked each week.

report An object that is meant primarily to be printed. In Access, mailing labels are a type of report.

row Because of the way they are arranged in the table, records are also called *rows. See* record.

S

search *See* Find.

select query A query that specify which fields and records of a table are displayed and their sort order. A select query can also be used join several tables in a relational database.

subform In a relational database, when you create a form that displays records from a one table of a one-to-many relationship, you can include a subform that displays the related records from the many table under each record from the one table.

T

tab control An object that lets you create multipage forms, where each page is displayed in one tab of the form. Instead of scrolling through the form, the user clicks a page's tab to display the page, as you do in many dialog boxes of Windows applications.

tab order The order in which the cursor moves through the controls of a form when the user presses Tab and Shift+Tab.

table A list of repetitive data, such as names and addresses.

Text data type A field type that holds up to 255 characters, including letters, numbers, and special characters.

toggle button A button that the user clicks to enter the value in a Yes/No field; it appear to be depressed when it is selected. You can also create an Option Group with Toggle Buttons, to let the user choose among several values.

toolbox A box displayed in Design view that holds tools you use to add controls to a form, report, or data access page.

U

unbound hyperlink A hyperlink that is not bound to a field, so it remains the same as records change.

unbound OLE object An OLE Object that is not bound to a field, so it remains the same as records change.

update query A query that change the values in some or all of the records of a table.

W

wildcards Characters used in a Find or a query to stand for any character. The wildcard characters are * (which represents any group of characters) and ? (which represents any single character).

wizard A series of steps that lets you create an object (such as a database, table, query, form, report, or page) by making selections following instructions in simple English.

Y

Yes/No data type A field type that holds only two values, defined as Yes/No, True/False, or On/Off, depending on the format you give it in the Field Properties panel.

Index

INDEX

INDEX

text boxes, 162, 164-165, 184
bind to field or expression, 184, 185
changing size, 144
date and time, 287
expressions, 268
summary, editing, 284-287
text color
controls, 150
Text data type, 8
Text fields, 30, 34, 46, 58, 343, 354
grouping by range, 196, 197
text literals, 355
themes, 294, 296, 356
title bar, 329, 345
toggle buttons, 166, 168-169
option groups, 166
toggle keys, 42
toggling, between views, 80
toolbars, 236, 282, 359
customizing, 328
formatting, 142, 144, 148
Help, 334
Insert Hyperlink button, 180
Properties button, 182
queries, 205
Web, 298, 300-301
toolbox, 143, 348
Bound Object Frame, 312
display, 192
hiding, 142
Object Frame button, 312
page breaks, 196
Tools menu
Customize, 328
Macro, 232, 233
Option command, 41
Options, 359
Relationships, 126, 127
Total Pages, 279
Total row, 220
transparency
background or borders, 156
True and False format, 252
Type conversion failure, 214
typing errors, programming to reduce, 170

U

unbound controls, 142, 143, 348
unbound hyperlinks, 180, 302, 356
unbound OLE objects, 312, 314, 357
Unbound Section, 296
Underline, 143, 193
underlined. *See also* hyperlinks
character, 258
text, 46
Unique, 322
Unique Records property, 222
Unique Values property, 222
update queries, 80, 210, 320, 352
Update To row, 210
updates
expressions, 282
indexes, 323
URL, 344
utilities
indexes, 322-323
introduction, 319
menu customization, 328
object management, 320-321
Options, 324-325, 326-327
toolbar customization, 328

V

validating
data, 354, 355
validation rule, 254, 280, 300, 354, 355
validation rule violations, 214
Validation Text, 254, 280, 281, 300, 354
values
constants, 267
default, assigning, 280
extracting from table or query, 172
finding range, 274
group reports, 347
literals, 267
table, in lookup field, 262-263
typing, 170

Var option, 216
vertical scroll bars, 41
videos, 46
view, specifying, 228
View menu, 190
Properties, 182
views
form, 346
reports, 190, 347
Visual Basic (Microsoft), 10
Visual Basic code, 142

W

Web, 6
browsers, 291, 292
data access pages, 291-305
data manipulation, 342
Stop and Refresh buttons, 336
using data access pages on, 10
Web pages, 356
hyperlinks, 180
Where option, 216, 220
wildcard characters, 78, 274, 360
within the range, 274
wizards. *See also* Label Wizard; Report Wizard; Form Wizard
adding controls to forms, 162
adding lists of possible entries, 170
adding option groups, 166
adding subforms, 176
assigning macros to command buttons, 232, 233, 234
command buttons, creating, 174-175
convert tables or queries into data access pages, 294
creating command button switchboard, 240
creating objects with, 12
creating queries with, 68-69
Crosstab Query Wizard, 218, 352
description of, 12
enabling/disabling, 162

extracting values from table or query, 172, 173
forms, 136
help, 336, 338
input masks, 258-259
label, 351
Lookup fields, 260, 355
margin settings, 200
modifying form of, 148-149, 150-151
reports, 134, 192, 284, 285, 286
using, 12
World Wide Web. *See* Web

X

Xor, 274

Y

Yes or No answers, 355
customizing forms to allow forms , 168-169
Yes/No properties, 252-253
Yes/No fields, 46, 344, 349

Z

zero-length string, 254, 354
zip codes, 343
Zoom, 314, 358
Zoom tool, 62

my2cents.idgbooks.com

Register This Book — And Win!

Visit **http://my2cents.idgbooks.com** to register this book and we'll automatically enter you in our fantastic monthly prize giveaway. It's also your opportunity to give us feedback: let us know what you thought of this book and how you would like to see other topics covered.

Discover IDG Books Online!

The IDG Books Online Web site is your online resource for tackling technology — at home and at the office. Frequently updated, the IDG Books Online Web site features exclusive software, insider information, online books, and live events!

10 Productive & Career-Enhancing Things You Can Do at www.idgbooks.com

- Nab source code for your own programming projects.

- Download software.

- Read Web exclusives: special articles and book excerpts by IDG Books Worldwide authors.

- Take advantage of resources to help you advance your career as a Novell or Microsoft professional.

- Buy IDG Books Worldwide titles or find a convenient bookstore that carries them.

- Register your book and win a prize.

- Chat live online with authors.

- Sign up for regular e-mail updates about our latest books.

- Suggest a book you'd like to read or write.

- Give us your 2¢ about our books and about our Web site.

You say you're not on the Web yet? It's easy to get started with IDG Books' *Discover the Internet*, available at local retailers everywhere.